PETER JACKSON
From prince of splatter to lord of the rings

PETER JACKSON
From prince of splatter to lord of the rings

IAN PRYOR

RANDOM HOUSE
NEW ZEALAND

This book is dedicated to all those New Zealand filmmakers
who crawl up clifftops in the face of logic.

Disclaimer: The opinions expressed in this book are those of the author or
of other persons and are not those of the publisher: the publisher has no
reasonable cause to believe that the opinions set out in the book are not the
genuine opinions of the author or of those other persons.

A catalogue record for this book is available from the
National Library of New Zealand

A RANDOM HOUSE BOOK
published by
Random House New Zealand
18 Poland Road, Glenfield, Auckland, New Zealand
www.randomhouse.co.nz

First published 2003

© 2003 Ian Pryor

The moral rights of the author have been asserted

ISBN 1 86941 555 8

Grateful thanks is given for permission to use the following quotations:
p.23 from *The Wishing Well* by the late E Eynon Evans, published by Samuel French
Ltd; p.181 from *Money into Light* by Jon Boorman, and p.226 from *John Boorman*
by Michel Ciment, both published by Faber & Faber Ltd; p.235 from *The Hollywood
Reporter* article 'How Peter takes Lord of the Rings to the screen' by Martin A
Grove, published by VNU Business Publications; p.289 from *Entertainment Weekly*
article 'The Power of Towers' by Gillian Flynn, © Entertainment Weekly Inc.

Text design: Kate Greenaway
Cover design: Dexter Fry
Cover photo: Mark Coote, *The Dominion Post*
Back cover photo: Simon Haxton
Printed by Publishing Press Ltd, Auckland

CONTENTS

Prologue: In a house by the sea 6

1. The lunatics are taking over the field 9

2. Beginnings 18

3. The movie that grew: *Bad Taste* 36

4. Not your everyday average creatures: *Meet the Feebles* 59

5. Beating the curse of the zombies: *Braindead* 87

6. The undead on set 99

7. A different kind of murder: *Heavenly Creatures* 123

8. Putting it on film 139

9. Empire-building: *Forgotten Silver* and the birth of Weta 163

10. Finding Hollywood without really looking: *The Frighteners* 181

11. The political animal 201

12. Finding the Ring 219

13. Roll camera 239

14. Spies in Middle-earth 260

15. Unveiling the Ring 271

16. Past and future 296

Epilogue: In a house by the sea 313

Author's note 315

Acknowledgements 317

Appendix 1: Timeline 319

Appendix 2: Filmography 322

Appendix 3: Inspirations and influences 332

Appendix 4: Movies as yet unmade 336

Bibliography 341

IN A HOUSE BY THE SEA

If this book were really a motion picture — a motion picture made by a director named Peter Jackson — it might go in all number of ways. Most likely though, it would go something like this.

Scene one. An only child named Peter stands outside his peaceful New Zealand home, perched high above the ocean. One day the boy borrows his parents' home-movie camera and begins sprinting through the garden with it, pretending he is an aeroplane. Bored with the back garden, Peter wanders into the dusty basement of a neighbour's house, where he discovers an old tea chest. A rusting collection of metal boxes and wiring lies under the lid, encased in felt.

Peter carries the boxes back to his father's workroom beneath the house, and sets to fixing them. As he works, he notices some words stamped onto the corroded metal of one of the boxes: *Mark 4 — Geraldine June 1916*. From its basket at the end of the workbench, the family cat Lionel watches proceedings with curiosity. Peter plugs the machinery into the mains, at which point one of the boxes erupts into a beam of white-hot light. Peter turns, realising with a start that Lionel has been reduced to a liquid green puddle, which quickly begins to run onto the concrete.

Peter will not be put off. Using the end of an old hacksaw, he sets about reversing the polarity of the current. Then he grabs the neighbour's cat Butterbur and plops it down onto the workbench, directly in front of the machinery. When Peter switches on the power, the air fills with another blinding beam of light, and one cat has become five. The five Butterburs — curiously enough, all the same colour and size — yawn for a moment, then begin to miaow.

Cut to Peter's face, jaw hanging wide open. A smile begins to creep slowly across his features. It looks as though he won't need the bucket and sponge again after all. Peter grabs a length of four-by-two from the corner and clambers onto the bench. By stretching out with the piece of timber, he can just reach the power switch without moving from his position in front of the box. A slice of pure white light empties the room of all shadows.

By the end of the day, Peter and his assembled army of Secondary Peters have drawn up their ten-year plan to take over the world, using the secret weapon of cinema. But they will start small. The original Peter goes off to get a job that will raise no suspicions, at a newspaper in the city. After he comes home and drops off to sleep, the first clone emerges silently from the row of Peters in the cupboard to start the eight-hour graveyard shift: creating fake body parts for Peter's first motion picture.

As the years go by, the use of a small troupe of specialised Peters will help confound all those who try to pigeonhole the multiple skills for which New Zealanders are famed. Chainsaw Peter takes a child-like glee in concocting movies ripe with erupting blood, prima donna hippos and over-eager zombies. To him, actors are merely another prop in a joyous comedy of carnage. On occasion he even dispenses with actors entirely, and spends entire films trying to coax drama from a cast of puppets.

Another Peter is more sensitive — this Sensitive Peter makes lively and innovative films about friendship, the contradictions of human behaviour, and even of filmmaking itself. The actors rave about Peter's kindness; the movies win prizes on the Continent; the scripts are nominated for Academy Awards.

Lacking enough people to act in his first movie, Chainsaw Peter has already cloned off Actor Peter, who takes on not one but two of the funniest parts. Actor Peter enjoys the play-acting so much that he demands cameo roles in all future Jackson productions. This Peter is a natural showman with a knack for lying to the motion-picture camera — occasionally even while appearing onscreen as a film director named Peter Jackson. Stuntman Peter proves useful for more dangerous scenes, dangling off cliffs above the ocean when no one else is available.

Meanwhile another Peter appears to have been dreamed up especially to meet the demands of the press: he can be relied upon to calmly, rationally defend the concept of turning slaughter into comedy. But, interview over with, Media Peter is always courteous enough to roll his eyes when asked, and pose maniacally with chainsaw in hand for a photo.

None of these Peters likes yelling. On a film set, it is sometimes hard to work out who exactly is in charge, because he employs other people to do the yelling for him. But his mastery of celluloid is clear. In lands far from the bottom of the South Pacific Ocean, people begin to whisper about the qualities of Peter's movies, in voices tinged with wonder.

Soon Peter has a Hollywood agent. He unrolls an empire-building model with grand visions of going off to Hollywood, grabbing all its cash and flying directly back to New Zealand to make bigger and better films.

Empire-building Peter gets together with some friends to create a company that specialises in cinema magic — conjurers of ghosts, demons and old verandahs. As all these visions begin to approach reality, many of the extra Peters become surplus to requirements, and are sent to live out their remaining days in the old family home, watching horror videos while the ocean laps at the shore below. Peter can now employ others to do their work, saving him from the stresses of being needed in more than one place at the same time. But some mornings, as Peter tries to explain to twelve of his workers exactly how he wants a certain shot to look, he pines for the old days, when the only person he needed to delegate to was himself.

The friendly Media Peter has meanwhile begun to mutate — still periodically manning the telephone for rounds of interviews, but known also to have considered suing reviewers who dared to say the wrong thing about his movies.

Then something stirs down under. Its name is Tolkien. Across the globe, scores of wizards in the arts of monstermaking and digital manipulation hear the whisper, and begin to dream of other lands. Their destination is a peaceful suburb in a city named Wellington, a suburb known only as . . . Miramar. One morning, Peter stands on a hill above the city, ready to begin work on a tale whose sheer scale has already scared off some of the biggest names in Hollywood. A project that will require unlimited courage and legions of orcs, computer boffins, and accountants.

In this case at least, reality can be every bit as complicated as cloning.

This book is the story of nine movies — and how all those Peter Jacksons are one.

CHAPTER ONE

THE LUNATICS ARE TAKING OVER THE FIELD

'When you grow up in the suburbs of Sydney or Auckland, a dream like this seems vaguely ludicrous and completely unattainable. But this moment is directly connected to those childhood imaginings.'
NEW ZEALAND-BORN RUSSELL CROWE, ONSTAGE IN LOS ANGELES TO ACCEPT
THE BEST ACTOR OSCAR FOR *GLADIATOR*

'It sure beats working in an office.'
CREW MEMBER TANIA RODGER, ON THE SET OF *MEET THE FEEBLES*

It's almost the end of Saturday afternoon, and the shadows are beginning to stretch across the sports field. Peter Jackson stands on the grass in his shorts during a break in an international cricket match. Slowly, he begins to stamp his bare feet on the ground — first one foot, then the other.

In the stands all around him, thousands of sunburnt cricket fans start to follow Jackson's lead. Within moments, the metal oval of the sports stadium echoes with an unearthly sound. It is not the noise you expect from 25,000 cricket fans, but the deep and sinister march of an army on a direct route to slaughter. The smallest of smiles alights on Jackson's face, then quickly disappears again. He is concentrating on maintaining his stomping rhythm.

When he first strides out onto the field, the crowd greet this bearded, bespectacled figure with applause that is long and spontaneous. Jackson takes the mike and announces that he is here to record some sound effects for the second movie of the *Lord of the Rings* trilogy, in a scene where 'thousands and thousands of orcs attack a castle called Helm's Deep . . . We thought that you guys would be able to help us.' The Wellington crowd dutifully go wild. Soon most of them are chanting in a mythical language, beating their chests in time and following the director's every command. Not that any of the set tasks are especially difficult — this is a great opportunity to be idiotic and culturally useful at the same time, while helping New Zealand to get heard around the world.

Jackson thanks them and ambles off. Compared to the nightmares of making his second feature *Meet the Feebles* — filmed thirteen years ago in a rat-infested railway shed, literally a stone's throw from the stadium in Wellington — today has gone pretty well. In fact, Jackson's brief turn in front of a crowd of sports fans marks something of a sea change in New Zealand culture: for a moment, one branch of lunacy has been allowed to take over the field from another.

The game of cricket represents New Zealand's traditional mode of lunacy — the idea that fun is had by spending a day in the sun, waiting for those few short seconds when a batsman connects with a small round ball. But the main thing to recognise about this tradition is that the shape of that ball does not really matter: just so long as it involves some kind of sport.

The opposing mode of lunacy could easily be represented by setting up a bunch of microphones in front of a crowd, and hoping that a few minutes' work will result in some decent sound effects for your next blockbuster movie. But it could just as easily be the idea of turning a historic homestead into an alien spaceship. Or recreating the Vietnam War by using a bunch of glove puppets and a small patch of forest. Whether you are making monsters out of Plasticine or spending hours filming two lovers talking in the kitchen, the act of moviemaking is almost by definition an act of madness. Some would argue that the whole task becomes even more demented when your location is a bunch of islands at the bottom of the South Pacific Ocean.

In New Zealand, decades of infatuation with things sporting — especially rugby — mean that even today many locals still think of creativity primarily in terms of how well you can pass a ball. The country's impressive record in so many arenas of physical activity — steamrolling through most of the opposition on the rugby field, throwing up fences on a rain-lashed farm, being first up Himalayan mountains — has inadvertently helped stifle wider acceptance of other forms of talent.

Many countries get worked up about their sport: England, Italy and the US all spring quickly to mind. But ball-play aside, each of these nations has an equal knack for turning their own creative talents into the stuff of major-league public appeal — whether on television, in opera houses, or at the cinema. Unfortunately, when it comes to noticing their own talents, New Zealanders have an impressive history of looking the other way — usually across the oceans to the latest imports from the US and England.

But now Peter Jackson is standing in front of a crowd of New Zealand sports fans, and most of them are clapping as if there is no tomorrow. His public profile is currently higher than any local filmmaker or actor in the nation's history, including *Piano* director Jane Campion and *Xena* star Lucy Lawless. And no wonder: at the time of writing, Jackson's *The Two Towers* is the fifth-highest grossing movie in the history of cinema, with *The Fellowship of the Ring* not far behind. The trilogy is winning him labels like 'visionary' and 'genius', rocketing him from nowhere onto magazine lists of Hollywood's most powerful, and turning heads towards a country with a population less than half that of Los Angeles.

Jackson's place in the rollcall of international blockbusters is remarkable in more ways than just size. After Canadian-born James Cameron's chart-topping *Titanic,* the first two *Lord of the Rings* movies clock in as the second- and third-highest grossing films ever made by a non-American. But success at the international box office is no guarantee of wonderful cinema. If it were, the man at the centre of this book would arguably have another three mega-grossing movies on the list (and narratively undernourished epics like *Twister* and *Pearl Harbor* would not be found anywhere in the top 40). Nonetheless, *The Fellowship of the Ring* has taken an unusual path among recent blockbusters, swiftly joining the ranks of instant pop culture classics like *Shrek* and *The Empire Strikes Back,* movies which three normally disparate groups —film critics, the general moviegoing public and the majority of diehard fans — have all embraced.

Peter Jackson had already taken a number of steps down the road of cinematic infamy before his encounter with Middle-earth swung him back towards respectability. Along with their share of positive press, Jackson's movies have been variously labelled as sick and pornographic, and even attacked for deceiving the public. A number of international critics have declared *Braindead* one of the bloodiest movies in cinema history (some, admittedly with great enthusiasm).

Controversy is great publicity, and the salacious nature of the characters that populate many of Jackson's movies — drug-addicted frogs, repulsive orcs, murderous teenagers — have helped his rise to fame. But such images have also helped obscure the depth of Jackson's talent: how his films are in their best moments the work of a natural, trying out a colourful form of cinematic ballet. There are moments in *Braindead, Heavenly Creatures* and *The Fellowship of the Ring* — three very different movies — that leave the viewer breathless.

Over the years Jackson has turned down a number of lucrative offers to work in Hollywood, arguing that there is more sense to staying in the country where he was raised. That way he can make movies with less money, but more freedom. In choosing this path, Jackson has broken the mould that requires New Zealand filmmakers to be either semi-anonymous, or else based permanently in other countries. Along the way, he has also helped change the course of a nation's cinema: not only by making it that much bloodier and funnier, but by showing that there can be a middle way between Hollywood and home. You see New Zealand has a sad yet noble tradition of making movies which are more often admired than actually seen. Now, using Hollywood money, Jackson has pulled off a series of epics that in terms of sheer audience numbers, have comprehensively beaten Hollywood at its own game.

FROM BLOODSHED TO BILBO BAGGINS

Talent, ingenuity and a strong degree of self-belief have all played vital parts in Jackson's rise to fame, as has his refusal to bow to the expectations of either fans or the film industry. The director's do-it-yourself solutions to that common dilemma of first-time filmmakers — not having enough cash — are echoed in the work of a number of New Zealand movie pioneers. It is probably no coincidence that one of Jackson's only rivals for the title of youngest moviemaker in New Zealand's history is Rudall Hayward, who wrote, directed and produced his debut feature at the age of twenty-one (when the century was not much older). That is the age at which Jackson began directing and acting in the short film that eventually become the amiable alien-invasion tale *Bad Taste*. With the help of friends Jackson built his own camera cranes, shot much of the movie silent, and created many of the makeup effects himself.

Jackson's basic ingredients range widely, from horror and action-movie shenanigans through to lurid melodrama. But his trademark style of cooking is to pour ample servings of violence over whatever plotline he is working with, then stretch the results into the stuff of outrageous comedy. The combination in one meal of two such strong flavours could well prove a nightmare for a lesser cook. Yet the joy which Jackson gets from combining blood and laughter is so palpable and childlike onscreen that it has won him fans all the way from splatter addicts to those who normally avoid horror movies like the plague.

This trademark style was established in three titles which proved variously just how extreme one could get with a non-existent budget, a bunch of depraved puppets and a house-load of zombies. In fact, the trio of *Bad Taste*, *Meet the Feebles* and *Braindead* displayed such a naturally winning way with comedy and bodily fluids that it was something of a surprise to learn that Jackson might be capable of other types of filmmaking. Peter Jackson hardly seemed the first director you would arrange a meeting with if you were hoping to evoke the tragedy of a real-life murder. But that is exactly what he did with *Heavenly Creatures*, a movie based on the infamous Parker–Hulme tragedy in which two teenage girls together murdered one of their mothers. The film led Jackson and his creative and romantic partner Fran Walsh towards their first Academy Award nomination, and marked the breakthrough of a young British actor named Kate Winslet.

Heavenly Creatures revealed an originality of vision and mastery of character which won it keen international audiences, while simultaneously helping propel Jackson into the vague, amorphous world of the 'worthy' filmmaker. This unexpected lurch into artiness left many film critics and movie financiers, both of whom profess to desire originality while secretly finding that pigeonholing makes their job a whole lot easier, rather confused. And the two productions that followed — one whimsical and inspired, the other twisted but spectacular — hardly clarified anything, apart from the fact that talent hates being stuffed into simple boxes.

Forgotten Silver appeared one Sunday evening on New Zealand television. That now-legendary screening in late 1995 had many viewers believing that a young, unappreciated New Zealander had been responsible for history's first full-length movie, the first use of colour film and the first talkie. Once the hoax was revealed, scores of irate viewers wrote letters to their local editor, asking why a government broadcaster could have had anything to do with such lies, and the filmmakers received threats of bodily harm.

If Jackson had come to you after *Forgotten Silver* and his failed entrée into Hollywood — the Michael J Fox ghost story *The Frighteners* — with plans to make a major-scale, mass-appeal epic, you might well have wondered if he was living in some alternative reality of his own. One could easily imagine the Kiwi prince of splatter revelling in the gore of the battle scenes, and chucking in dollops of off-colour humour wherever there was a danger of any sense of grandness. But an epic fantasy with at least fifteen major characters, and a whole universe of mythical peoples to introduce? The chasms such moviemaking can throw up have sprained the ankles of people with far more expensive footwear than Peter Jackson. Yet somehow, Jackson's feet have survived the journey unscathed.

A COMPLICATED KIND OF CELEBRITY

Peter Jackson's path to mainstream celebrity began long before hobbits or orcs entered the picture. On his home turf, Jackson has been photographed by the media more often than any other local filmmaker: sometimes grinning, with chainsaw in hand, sometimes standing alongside his latest menagerie of cinematic creatures. Obvious PR skills, perhaps, but important ones, especially in a country where worthy local movies often drown in the sea of advertising that helps Hollywood product to rule the waves.

As the years have gone by, the images captured by the media have gradually changed, though on few occasions could you argue that Jackson has ever been a victim of fashion. From the boyish, curly-haired figure of the early photos, he has begun more and more to resemble the American cliché of the movie-brat director — the messy beard, the spectacles, the T-shirt. The later image certainly tells us part of the story: Jackson's feet grounded in New Zealand earth, while his head is up in the clouds, dreaming up new cinematic visions. Yet this picture helps downplay Jackson's ability to be a master of public relations one minute, and a fearsome adversary the next.

The young filmmaker who burst from a small seaside town near Wellington onto the cult movie scene, proved to be a journalist's dream — unpretentious, intelligent and able to make cinematic slaughter sound like the healthiest thing in the world. But as he has become more powerful, so has the contrast between Jackson's low-key, quietly-spoken exterior and his expressions of annoyance at those who don't share his particular vision.

Much of this annoyance has been directed at the New Zealand Film Commission, the body which enabled Jackson's first three films to be made. Over the years the director's relationship with the Commission, the government-appointed body that funds the majority of local films, has taken as much of a rollercoaster ride as any Jackson movie, as Chapter Eleven will show. At one point in the late 1990s Jackson seemed to be putting himself forward as the Film Commission's Mr Fix-It, telling US entertainment magazine *Variety*, 'I have a choice: either try to do something about the NZFC's problems, or leave the country.' But his attempts to make the Commission more filmmaker-friendly have often taken the form of full-frontal attacks, and succeeded mostly in getting a lot of backs up. When *The Two Towers* had its splash Wellington premiere in the final days of 2002, the Jackson–NZFC relationship reached perhaps its lowest ebb. Thanks partly to his anger at the Commission for refusing to pay him out on bills owed by a local film company that had gone belly-up, Jackson publicly revoked invitations for two of the Commission's senior staff to come to the premiere party.

FANTASTIC VISIONS

Jackson's dreams — and those of some vital collaborators, not least writers Fran Walsh and Stephen Sinclair — have helped reinvigorate film genres from which much of the magic has been bled dry. These days fantasy, horror and science-fiction movies often rush us directly to other worlds in order to open our eyes to some new creature, spectacle or chase. But many of these films give the fantasty genres a bad name, because all that eye-candy arrives without the backup of a satisfying narrative.

That Jackson's movies have never fallen into this trap is perhaps surprising, especially when you consider his long fascination with the nuts and bolts of special effects — a fascination which would later see him co-owning one of the biggest effects factories on the planet — and the fact that his debut movie lacked even a script. The easy thrill of spectacular effects is surely a big part of how modern fantasy cinema gets by with such uninspired scriptwriting. And something of the show-off — the magician who wants to stun us, just because he can — still lurks in most of Peter Jackson's films.

This is the same person who as a child lapped up the monsters of Ray Harryhausen fantasies like *Jason and the Argonauts* and the puppet rescue missions of television's *Thunderbirds*. Both Harryhausen and *Thunderbirds* creator Gerry Anderson built careers from enthralling audiences with fantastic battles and death-defying visions, most of it created with models and puppets. Jackson's own style of showing off can be even more colourful: the first feature he unleashed on the world has only been running for a few minutes before we witness the results of someone getting their head blown off. Yet despite this love of shocking the audience with over-the-top images, there is a naivety in Jackson's work which perversely elevates it. He likes nudging his audience, reminding them how silly all of this is, yet somehow his work rarely seems insincere. A *Monty Python* fan from an early age, Jackson in his early films almost always ensures a touch of the ridiculous to undercut the spectacular or disgusting moment.

The *Rings* epics reflect Jackson's growing maturity as a moviemaker. *The Fellowship of the Ring* contains more special effects and manipulations of reality than anything he had worked on to that date, yet it has all been put at the service of creating a universe we can believe in. It is a universe of such breadth and complexity that many fans of Tolkien thought it could never be satisfactorily recreated onscreen. Jackson's habit of nudging the audience has no place in *Fellowship*, and thankfully he knows it: instead, the movie presents us with a persuasive vision of a lyrical rural world, along with a palpable sense of danger and evil.

Even before his cinematic encounter with the work of JRR Tolkien, Jackson's place in fantasy cinema had been assured. *Meet the Feebles*'s unusual mixture of puppetry and bodily fluids is extreme enough that one US guide to all that is truly tacky and B-grade in cinema warns that 'most viewers will find this a bit much'. Unfortunately, most audiences did: *Feebles* is a rare case of Jackson's magic touch deserting him. But *Bad Taste* remains one of the fastest-selling films in New Zealand history, and on video and DVD it continues to win fans around the world. *Braindead* sent critics in France and the US into shock and ecstasy, yet despite its cult status it was a failure upon its US release, doing much better in Europe. In

England it rose as high as number four on the video rental charts. Leaving aside the mass Internet phenomenon that is the *Rings* trilogy, the sheer number of websites devoted to Jackson's career indicates that most of his films have spawned a cult of their own.

CINEMA DOWN UNDER

New Zealand has never been the kind of place where the words 'movie' and 'celebrity' are much used in the same sentence, at least not when describing a local. The country has produced an impressive number of movies since early in the century, yet the careers of our filmmaking pioneers remain unknown to many. New Zealand's small population — in 1931, only one and a half million — hardly provided ideal conditions for investment in the arguably loony business of combining celluloid and sound. The country's economic backbone reflected a more practical, conservative nature: the meat and butter which farmers sent back to Mother England helped fuel the economy for much of the century.

After an initial burst of filmmaking during the silent movie era, the period from 1940 to 1970 saw only three local feature films appear — hardly the exposure needed to create the indigenous local movie stars that help attract moviegoers into cinemas. But in the late 1970s, a second wave of local talent began making their presence felt. For a golden period in the early '80s it looked as if this second wave would prove unstoppable — each year saw keen audiences arriving for the latest cinematic sensation; overseas, film festivals of all varieties opened their arms to New Zealand cinema, from horror movies like *Death Warmed Up* to arthouse fare like the moody *Vigil*. Yet despite all the global acclaim, the country's list of international moneymakers remains small compared to that of Australia. Local film 'stars' have proven equally slow to rise above the waterline.

Faced with a limited pool of local funding, many moviemakers have relocated to Hollywood, a temptation Peter Jackson has resisted on multiple occasions. The American output of that second wave of local directors has varied all the way from dross like *Freejack* to films as strong as *13 Days*, as entertaining as *Young Guns II*, and as unusual as *What Dreams May Come*. Others, like gifted jack-of-all-trades Ian Mune, have remained in New Zealand, managing impressive work on much lower budgets.

Hollywood continues to operate as a magnet for filmmakers worldwide. Many directors harbour dreams of using their newly-won clout in Los Angeles to nip back home occasionally and use corporate money to make cherished movies of their own. But Hollywood financiers, who naturally prefer American characters in the centre of their movies, can be hard to persuade. Talented foreigners have managed strong work within such confines. Other directors have fallen victim to Hollywood's peculiar blend of opportunity and conservatism — abandoning their best ideas for easier challenges, which can mean doing formulaic work on exorbitant paypackets.

American moviemakers have occasionally ventured to New Zealand themselves, attracted mainly by its unspoilt locations and low rate of exchange. But in terms of being shot entirely here, *Rings* is definitely something out of the ordinary. Only rarely has a Hollywood studio bankrolled a local director to take charge of a movie made in New Zealand, let alone one of the largest projects in the history of cinema.

New Line's faith in Peter Jackson's abilities has certainly paid off. But if the past is anything to go by, such faith is often sorely lacking in Jackson's own country. New Zealanders continue to show an amazing ability to under-rate and undermine their own talents. They have been known to boo their own rugby team off the field, even after victory. There have been (admittedly rare) occasions where local musical talents have caught on at home only after managing to score top-five hits in the US charts. And the mantra that New Zealand is no good at comedy continues to be endlessly regurgitated, despite evidence to the contrary from stage, screen and television set. So often lacking the confidence to publicly admire our own creativity, New Zealanders' powers of passion and analysis are often diverted to events on the sports field.

These traditions are under major attack, but they go a long way towards explaining Peter Jackson's popular appeal. He is the perfect 'arty type' for a country that has never been comfortable with the challenges presented by artiness. In his shorts, Swanndri, and John Lennon-style glasses, he looks like some kind of intellectual farmer. He is polite and quietly spoken. Yet clearly Jackson has balls. Underneath the unthreatening exterior lurks the kind of self-belief that is willing to take on major icons of fantasy like *King Kong* and Tolkien. And icons aside, Jackson's films are for the most part effortlessly Kiwi. Sure, the type of stories which he likes to tell — full of bloodshed and bizarre creatures — won't be to everyone's taste. But his dislike of artistic pretension remains gold to many a New Zealand heart.

As the coming pages will attempt to demonstrate, a no-nonsense, can-do attitude prevails in the New Zealand character, a mindset which has a major part to play in Peter Jackson's journey from splatter-movie maestro to major force in world cinema. The story that follows is one of zombies and dreamers, of bloodshed and hobbits. Most of all, though, it is about how a talented bunch of moviemakers got on with it, in spite of the obstacles lying in their way: counting pennies, creating monsters and breathing life into the dead, armed only with ingenuity and the ability to laugh oneself silly.

CHAPTER TWO

BEGINNINGS

'I just remember him as the pure human he was.'
CHILDHOOD FRIEND ANNE MORRIS

'He's got his dad's disposition, and his mum's determination.'
FAMILY FRIEND JEAN WATSON

If you were able to jump on the back of a giant eagle at London's Houses of Parliament and then fly northwest for twenty-five kilometres, you would eventually pass over a small pond. The pond — dark, roughly triangular, home to a half-submerged tree and a couple of ducks — edges onto the main street of a village known as Shenley. Between the pond and the nearby pub is Shenley's most famous building, a tiny jail shaped strangely like a beehive.

In 1974, a local English newspaper published a photograph of a twelve-year-old boy standing next to this pond with his parents. The article on the same page was far from the most thrilling to hit the world's news-stands that day: it told how the family of three were visiting Shenley and other old haunts, on a vacation around England.

The boy in the photo is named Peter. This boy will eventually grow a beard, and change the face of a nation's movie history. But as the lens of the photographer's camera snaps open that day in 1974, probably the most important thing in his head is getting to the next aircraft museum on the itinerary. The giant eagle is a character in a fantasy novel he is yet to read.

The village of Shenley is the perfect place for Peter Jackson's story to begin. Not unlike many a rural town down in New Zealand, Shenley impresses more for how far it stretches along the main road than for the size of its population: locals sometimes talk wistfully about the days when the village had twelve shops. It is not a place that speaks of glamour or grandeur, although the fields around Shenley were once littered with grand estates, where the rich came to escape from London.

For a cinema fan, all riches lie directly south. Five kilometres away as that Tolkienesque eagle flies, the town of Borehamwood is home to one of the most famous moviemaking centres in Europe. In Borehamwood, often known as Elstree, classics like *The Dambusters, The Shining* and *Star Wars* have all gone before the cameras. For decades people in Shenley have been encountering actors filming on the roadsides, sometimes even in the village itself.

Peter Jackson's mother Joan was born in a town close to Shenley on May 5, 1920, into a world where the eight-kilometre journey from Shenley to the movie studios in Borehamwood might as well have been a boat trip to the bottom of the globe. She would soon become 'the jam between the bread' — the only girl in a family that contained two elder brothers, and two younger. Such an environment appears to have encouraged young Joan Ruck to a certain robustness and directness of expression.

It's a man-made world I was brought up in. Can I say little things as they cross my mind? Being brought up with brothers I had to play boys' games, and that meant cricket with a hard ball. So when I came out to New Zealand, I joined the Ladies Cricket Club. I was chosen as wicketkeeper and opening bat because I was the only one of them gathered for practice who wasn't afraid of the hard ball. I put that down to my childhood.
What it was like growing up with only brothers?
Oh very good. My mother and I were very close. Great friends. She and I used to stand our ground with four boys and a father.

Mrs Ruck's husband Fred worked in the Shenley area as a gardener, and was known around the village as a friendly old chap with a hunchback and flat cap. 'Oh he was a case,' says Shenley resident Beryl McKay. 'When we had a horticultural show up on the playing field, he slept up there overnight so that nobody got in and mucked things up. I can always remember Rucky sleeping up there in the tent.'

When Joan was around nine, the owner of a nearby estate sold his property to the local county council, who had plans to build a mental hospital on it. The first section of the hospital opened in 1934, and the hospital's 2000 patients would later come to outnumber the rest of the village. Mrs Ruck told her daughter not to go alone in the streets after dark, in case she met a patient. That same year, aged fourteen, Joan left school and began a full-time job in Borehamwood. But her entry into the workforce was a world away from the movies being shot in the studios all around her. She was learning the art of invisible mending — fixing stockings by hand at a hosiery manufacturer.

When World War II erupted, the Hertfordshire area witnessed a takeover. Along with many of the film studios in Borehamwood, the army commandeered Shenley village hall and many of the nearby estates. The croquet lawns and ordered gardens of one estate were destroyed by searchlight and gun emplacements. A house in Shenley became the secret home of a group tied to the Enigma codebreakers; at Salisbury Hall, the oldest stately home in the area, a team of designers from de Havilland Aircraft Company worked in secret on the prototype of a radical new aeroplane, the Mosquito.

As the war continued, Joan and a number of her female workmates were sent from the stocking factory to an enormous hangar to work on the miraculous new bomber. Once there, Joan found herself in an unusual position: she would be shown how to do someone's job, and then the person would be called off to war. Soon she was doing the work of four. 'I would say the men didn't work very hard. As I took on another man's work, it was all streamlined into one.'

At times, the contents of the Ruck family garden marked the difference between a meal and no food at all. At the factory, seven-day working weeks were the norm, with just a Saturday afternoon off every month. Joan's job involved ensuring a constant supply of thousands of aircraft parts, many of which were made in wood at workshops and furniture-makers around the district.

Following the end of the war, Joan went back to work at the hosiery factory in Borehamwood. More than once she donned a costume and appeared on the floats which run through Shenley each August to mark the village fete. Sometimes the fun and games were officially opened by a film star from the Borehamwood studios.

Joan regularly won prizes in the monthly competitions run by the local Women's Institute. 'She could turn her hand to anything and do it well,' recalls Shenley resident Joyce Herbert. 'Friendly. She was very much a country girl.' Life wasn't only needlework and baking. Each winter, a locally-produced play would pack crowds into the local village hall. Joan appeared in a number of them, sometimes directing as well. She took on both tasks for one play called *The Wishing Well*, after the original director had to withdraw. The play was so successful that they performed it in a number of nearby towns. Nelly Taylor, who acted in the play, remembers Joan as a 'very bossy' director:

> She wouldn't stand any nonsense from us. We sort of had to do as we were told.
> Was she a good actor?
> Oh yes.

The Wishing Well has stayed in the minds of many in Shenley for longer than any other play from this period. Written by the late Welsh playwright

E Enyon Evans, *The Wishing Well* is about a group of people, many emotionally wounded by World War II, who come to stay in a Welsh inn. Each of them has arrived there after hearing about a place where they can find their wishes coming true.

A LONG JOURNEY

William Jackson grew up in the South London suburb of Brixton. Like Joan Ruck's, his childhood was surrounded by brothers. And like millions born during that period, he would find his life overtaken by war.

Brixton, known for street markets dating back as far as the 1870s, was by Bill's birth in early 1920 a popular dormitory suburb for people commuting to work in central London. For the Jackson family, conditions were cramped: their often bedridden grandfather lived upstairs with an aunt and uncle, while Bill, his parents and four younger brothers took the bottom floor. Bill's mother found herself increasingly balancing the needs of five children with caring for the sick members of the family.

William Jackson senior had fought in Turkey and France during the First World War. Recalled Bill Jackson:

> *My father was decorated with a DCM at Gallipoli. He was wounded in France at the battle of the Somme. Anyway he came back and found he had arthritis in the toe, so they put him down a grade or two and he was granted a small pension — fifteen percent or something. That was enough, after ten or twelve years, for the arthritis to cripple him totally. He was granted a hundred percent pension and we depended on that. He wasn't working and we were all at school. My mother had to look after us. He died in 1940. The Blitz was on. He was fifty-one.*

In the period before Bill's father died, the family moved twice. Though Bill had passed an examination to go to a higher-grade school, he was unable to take up the opportunity as the family had just secured a space on a housing estate in Sutton, a little south of London. Bill often played soccer and cricket with his brothers on the gigantic sports field just up the road. And his father, for all his sickness, had a habit for laughter. In later years, the laugh of a son named Peter would remind Bill of his own father, a man who could be the life and soul of the party.

In 1940, the year his father passed away, Bill was called up into the army. Three years in Malta followed. The island marked a stopping point on Britain's supply route to North Africa, and both the Allies and the Axis felt it was of vital strategic importance. As a result, Malta endured sustained attacks from the skies.

It wasn't all that good. It was the time of the bombing and the siege. Fresh vegetables and fruit and meat — nothing like that — it was all tinned stuff. I had jaundice twice. That's the only time I was in hospital. I never got hit by a bomb or anything like that.

Later, on a troop ship taking him from the Middle East to Italy, Bill had one of his first encounters with New Zealanders. The boat was dominated by them and South Africans: 'They had a great big tug of war, and the old ship rocked as they pulled their ropes.' The young soldier liked the New Zealand attitude, and noted the friendliness of the soldiers.

While Bill was in Italy, the war finally ended. After leaving the army he worked in a number of jobs, before joining the stock and payments division at the London headquarters of Thomas Cook. But travel agencies can be dangerous places: they provide constant reminders of all the other places in the world you can be.

I met up with this girl who had a bit of trouble with a married man. She wanted to leave England and possibly emigrate. I had at my fingertips all about New Zealand, I knew a little about places in the world, so I suggested 'Why don't you go to New Zealand?' So she was quite happy and then as an afterthought, I said, 'I'll come with you.' Of course I'd forgotten the fact I was going to leave my mum and four brothers at home, but that's what happened anyway. We both boarded the Atlantis *and went into the sunset. We went through the Med, stopped and looked at Cairo, sightseeing for a few hours, then through the Suez Canal, went on from there to Colombo in Ceylon, and over the Indian Ocean to Fremantle. It took us six weeks to get to Wellington. I landed at Wellington and I reported to the Post Office. I found that the hills I'd seen from the water were going to be mine.*

I lost the girl on the boat. She found a chap who knew all about composers, operas and all that. They used to talk about music for hours on end and I just pulled away and left them to it, and that was that. She played a part in me leaving in a way, the fact that I thought she was the right one, but it wasn't to be and I never regretted the move. It got me out here and I met Joan and her brothers, and her family in time, and other good people.

Bill Jackson began his new job delivering mail up the hillside streets of Mount Victoria and Kelburn, which overlooked the harbour he had recently sailed into. 'Six years in the army doesn't do anything for your claustrophobia,' he later said. 'I was glad to be out in the fresh air.' He also had a postal round in Karori, where he shared the work with a young poet named James K Baxter. 'He was a queer type. He used to stop and mow people's lawns. It was ages before he finished his rounds.'

Keen to find new members for the soccer club he was now involved in, Bill heard about two brothers recently arrived from England. The brothers were called Frank and Bob Ruck, and their sister Joan would often come to watch the team play.

Following in the path of her brothers, Joan had travelled with her mother out to New Zealand in 1951, after the death of her father. The two planned to stay only six months; but the shipboard menu on the way over offered a glimpse of a better life. After the trials of post-war rationing in England, there was now a different menu to choose from every day, with morning tea to follow the three-course breakfast. Joan and her mother were sailing towards a land heading into an economic boom that would keep New Zealand's standard of living in the world's top dozen countries for another two decades. Arriving in Wellington, Joan found the city a refreshing change from the generally flat environs around Shenley. She wondered how all the houses were able to stay up on the hills.

Joan returned, somewhat reluctantly, to the trade of invisible mending, then rarely practised in New Zealand. She began working for Bonds in a factory at one end of Tasman Street, close to Wellington's main hospital. For years to come she would train up new staff, and deal with mountains of faulty pantyhose.

Something sparked between Joan Ruck and the thirty-one-year-old postie from the far side of London. Two years after meeting, they married in Wellington, in November 1953.

'All those wonderful hills, and the little houses stuck on the side of them.
They look like toppling over into the valley.'
THE WISHING WELL, BY E EYNON EVANS

PUKERUA BAY

Stop for a breather on the road leading down to the beach at Pukerua Bay, and there is so much ocean in front of you, it is easy to imagine you can make out the curvature of the earth. Nature and human design have done much to make a mess of this town, but the surroundings have more than enough beauty to withstand the attack.

The main road from Wellington snakes noisily right through the middle of Pukerua Bay township. The highway then falls away to the ocean, hugging the coastline a while as it heads north. Adding to the feeling of a place perched between paradise and disaster, a steep overgrown valley slices much of the town in two on its way down to the beach.

Between the beach road and the horizon is the bush-covered outline of Kapiti Island, a major stronghold for Maori chief Te Rauparaha in the nineteenth century. 'Pukerua' is Maori for Two Hills. Originally the site of a Maori settlement, the land was gradually bought by European farmers from around 1875, who began to subdivide it. Trains began passing through Pukerua Bay the following decade. For years after that, the town's population was limited mainly to some railway cottages and baches close to the beach, the latter usually inhabited only on the weekends. But by 1950 towns on the Kapiti Coast were growing rapidly, and many young couples moved to Pukerua Bay, attracted partly by lower house prices. Over the years, the cheap housing and sea views have attracted many artists and writers to the Kapiti area.

Cut to 1953. Some friends of the newly married Jackson couple mention that Pukerua Bay might be worth taking a look at. When the Jacksons arrive, they discover that the man at the local store is a real-estate agent, and he mentions a little place just up the road, overlooking the ocean. Life-changing events can spin upon such moments. Like many houses in Pukerua Bay, the building in question is a bach, 'a little two-bedroom, small lounge place'. The couple decide to buy it on the spot. According to Bill:

> We were only in the house a year or more and I decided to build three rooms myself. I had never built rooms on houses before but the chap next door — we had an architect there — said he could make up some plans for me so we could get a permit and build. I got the permit, and I took one glance at the plans and then went ahead and built these rooms.

In 1954 Bill got a job as a clerk with the Wellington City Council, the organisation that would continue to pay his wages until retirement. Eventually, he worked his way up to the position of paymaster. He rarely took days off work — according to Joan he was a stickler for tidy ledgers, and hated to see the mess others made of them. Every Wednesday and Thursday afternoon Bill set out to pay council staff spread across the city.

Both Joan and Bill were active in the close-knit Pukerua Bay community. Bill was treasurer of the local RSA for more than a decade; Joan joined the local Women's Institute, continued to act in amateur plays, and would often help look after her many nieces and nephews. She and her friend Jean Watson performed comical sketches during the dances held regularly at Pukerua Bay hall — back in the days when the only way to get a beer was to sneak outside.

Leone Downes remembers Joan as the natural storyteller of the two. 'Most of the stories she told were true. She'd have us in stitches. She was very droll, very matter-of-fact.' Bill was quiet and gentle. Few ever saw him angry — one of those who knew him in Pukerua Bay for many years recalled that on those very rare occasions when Bill grew annoyed, he would stutter instead.

The 1960s saw major changes in the Jacksons' methods of getting around. After years of commuting to work by train, Bill and Joan could finally afford a car of their own. And not just a new car: by late 1961, a pram was also in order. Shortly before sunset on October 31, Joan Jackson gave birth to her first child at Wellington Hospital. It must have been a worrying time to become a parent. The day before, the Soviet Union had detonated a fifty-megaton hydrogen bomb, bigger than anything before it in history. The USSR and the US were boasting about who had the biggest arsenal of bombs, just months away from a missile crisis in Cuba that almost resulted in nuclear war.

Thankfully, despite all indications to the contrary, it was not to be the end of the world. The local cinemas were playing American musicals, and the Embassy had a scandalous new Fellini movie called *La Dolce Vita*. The sole television channel in Wellington was just a day away from a major expansion — to four hours of programming a night. Peter Jackson's press material has made a habit of mentioning his birthdate as being on Halloween, but his later fascination with the history of the date was not shared by the general New Zealand populace — Halloween was rarely celebrated in New Zealand during this decade, or the one that followed.

Doctors advised Joan that due to complications resulting from a serious bout of tuberculosis in her past, having a second child would be risky. For Peter's parents, this only made their baby more special. According to his parents, he had a habit as a young child of vomiting while travelling in other people's cars. When his parents took him for his first drive in their own car, they prepared blankets and a bowl for him in case things went wrong again. Peter promised that since it was their own car, they would no longer be needed. They weren't.

Peter loved stories from an early age. When a neighbour tried to save some reading time by missing out a few pages of the story, he insisted they go back and read it all. One day he asked his mother to read him 'a story without words'. She happily obliged. 'I had loads of stories I could tell. Give me a subject and I can spin a tale around it.'

Peter Jackson later said of his upbringing:

> *Being an only child does make you more imaginative, I think, because you have to create your own games by yourself, with whatever props come to hand — Matchbox toys and building blocks and that sort of carry-on. You don't have anybody else to bounce off, so you're creating it in your own head. I think it certainly helps exercise the mind. It trains you to be imaginative.*

Jackson was not always alone. Often he would be playing with the tomboyish Anne Morris, who lived next door. 'He didn't have any brothers, and my brother is fifteen years older than me,' says Morris. 'Peter just made me laugh to pieces.'

Just a few minutes' walk from Peter's house, a wide gully dropped away into bush on its way down to the ocean. The gully could double as a battleground, a prehistoric world or home to Tarzan, depending on one's mood. 'Pukerua Bay was a wonderful place for somebody to grow up, because it's all cliffs, gullies, bush and beach,' says Morris. 'We'd go down into the bush, leaping through Cape Cod ivy, hurling toitoi spears at each other. We had forts all over the place.' Sometimes, Anne and Peter would sneak outside at night-time and run round the streets trying to scare each other. 'Horror was always fun. Down in the bush, it was very elemental. Looking back now I can see why he's a director. He was directing games as a little boy. He always had a theme in his mind, something that he wanted to do. So he's always been a director — it's not even that he made the choice.'

STARTING OFF

When Peter was aged eight or nine, a close friend of the Jackson family decided to do him a favour. Jean Watson worked at the Kodak company in Porirua. When the company introduced its latest 8mm movie camera, they offered the old demonstration model to staff at a discount. Watson noted how Peter enjoyed taking photos. 'I bought it because I thought it would come in handy for Peter,' she says. 'He was only a little fella then.' Watson planned to save the camera until Peter was older, but when his parents heard about the idea, they 'had to have it there and then'. According to Joan, 'As soon as it came into the house, that started Peter off.'

As Peter quickly discovered, even the 'off' button of a movie camera can be a valuable aid in creating cinema magic. Point your camera at someone walking on a road, stop the camera, put a watermelon on the spot where they were last walking (making sure not to move the camera) then start the camera again. When you run the film back — hey presto! You have turned someone into a watermelon. As Joan put it:

> The first special effect he ever made with that little camera was the cat around the corner with a saucer of milk. When the film was developed, well, there was the cat drinking the milk and then there was a puff of smoke, and there was no cat. And he got very excited about this, so what he did was to take his camera to school the next day, get his teacher to come out of the door, look at rain and put his umbrella up. And when it was developed the teacher came out and looked at the rain and started to put his umbrella up, and then he was gone.

The earliest of Jackson's cinematic dabblings to have been seen publicly is a thirty-second sequence from a film known as *The Dwarf Patrol*, shot in the family backyard around 1971, when Peter was nine. We witness some underaged soldiers, one (Peter) with a cigarette dangling from his lips, fighting one another in a makeshift trench and shooting a machine-gun. Peter, who would have known nothing of New Zealand film legend Len Lye at this point, created the flash of the machine-gun by physically making holes in the film for the light of the projector to shine through (Lye had earlier constructed entire films in similar fashion, by painting directly onto the film stock). Peter and his friends Peter O'Herne and Ian Middleton staged mock attacks on passing trains for the camera, and wandered the hills above Pukerua Bay dressed in khaki outfits, pretending they were in war-torn Europe.

According to Ian Middleton, these early films were extensions of the games the boys were playing around Pukerua Bay. 'That's what we used to do, go bush and play war on the weekends, run around and shoot each other. He was always the director — it was his camera. He came up with the storylines, with what he wanted to shoot, and where we were supposed to be.' Another childhood friend, Steven Valentine, recalls borrowing barbed wire from a local farm in order to add the right touch of war-movie authenticity.

Around the time Peter was first discovering his new toy, he saw the movie that helped lock him on course to becoming a filmmaker. A giant ape stomped through jungles, fighting off dinosaurs, falling in love with a beautiful woman and battling aeroplanes from the top of the Empire State Building. Watching *King Kong* for the first time on television, Peter was entranced. He had been taken out of himself, taken somewhere else. Peter was no less excited on learning that many scenes had been created using a model gorilla, only forty-five centimetres high. The camera's ability to cheat time by turning a cat into a puff of smoke could be used in another way — to transform an inanimate object into a living creature.

In the case of *King Kong*, the process involved shooting a frame of film of the model ape, then moving the ape forward just a fraction of an inch. By repeating the process again and again, and then playing the completed footage back, the illusion was given of a creature moving under its own power.

The stop-motion techniques utilised by American effects wizards like Willis O'Brien and Ray Harryhausen could be tried by anyone with patience, a camera and a tabletop to shoot on. Peter began building his first creature, 'a crazy hunchback rat', and retired to his room for long periods to bring these new monsters to life. There was only one problem: the camera he was using was unable to shoot individual frames of film, so Peter had to make do with pressing the camera's 'on' button for a split second, grabbing a few frames each time he was ready to record the next shot. He recalled later:

> When I was young all I wanted to be was a special-effects man. For a long time
> I wanted to be a stop-motion animator, like Ray Harryhausen . . . You know,
> the Sinbad movies with all those monsters? He was one of my childhood heroes.
> Then I got interested in other prosthetics and special effects.

Cult television show *Monty Python's Flying Circus* is another childhood influence often cited by Jackson. 'We used to beg and plead with our parents so we'd be allowed to stay up and watch it,' recalls Anne Morris. The two took turns tuning in to the show on Sunday evenings at one another's houses, and sometimes other children were allowed to come along. In the relatively conservative climate of New Zealand in the 1970s, Morris argues, the new series was 'pretty outrageous'.

Anne and Peter cut photos out of magazines, and attempted to make animated films in the absurdist style made famous by Python member Terry Gilliam. In their last year at Pukerua Bay School, Peter and a group of classmates were given permission to go a step closer to Python: by making a film to raise funds for a class trip down south. Jackson directed, and classmates brought props. 'It was very Pythonesque,' says Morris. 'We blew up Trevor Shoesmith, the teacher, and threw people off cliffs.' Some of the scenes were direct copies of Python sketches. The finished film was later played to students in the school assembly hall. Jackson has said that at ten cents per student, the box office take was just enough to cover the $12 budget.

Jackson later argued that the full-frontal, bloodsoaked humour of his early movies owed most to *Monty Python*, a connection that has not always been clear to viewers. The Python team sometimes milked humour from extreme acts of violence, though they only rarely showed it onscreen. But one unusually bloody *Monty Python* sketch provides a vital link to Jackson's later work.

> The humour I do comes from a skit I saw on TV when I was nine or ten. It was
> called 'Salad Days'. It was a parody of a picnic scene Sam Peckinpah had
> directed in one of his films. This Monty Python picnic goes horribly wrong.
> People try to play tennis and get their arms chopped off by tennis rackets, and
> someone's playing the piano and the lid drops and chops off his fingers
> and there's blood spurting everywhere. I thought that was so funny. I don't set
> out to disgust people. I just have a very childish, immature sense of humour.

Jackson appears to have been lucky in finding himself at a close-knit school where individual teachers encouraged creative activities. Trevor Shoesmith not only allowed his pupils to make a Monty Python movie, but allowed himself to be killed by them onscreen. A few years earlier, Pukerua Bay teacher Prue Ursell had got in trouble with the headmaster for regularly reading aloud to her classes and inviting poet Sam Hunt along to talk. 'She read us the entire *Narnia* trilogy,' recalls Anne Morris. 'Peter was right into that.'

GETTING A REACTION

Much of Jackson's early Super 8mm footage was directly inspired by the films and television shows which excited him at the time — the monsters of *King Kong* and the Ray Harryhausen fantasies, or the puppet rescue missions of *Thunderbirds* on television.

King Kong, The Seventh Voyage of Sinbad and *Thunderbirds* all have one thing in common — they exist to present sights and visions which will make an audience go 'Wow'. Ultimately, what these tales might lack in terms of multi-layered narrative, they make up for with the thrill of spectacle: tiny humans facing off against gigantic monsters, or exploding bridges. As for Monty Python and the horror films that were now increasingly winning Peter's attention, they mined strong responses as well — that of laughter and, in the case of horror movies, terror or disgust.

Many of these early films were abandoned before completion, demanding special effects that were beyond the capability of Peter or his equipment. Other times he experimented — cycling down the hill to the beach with the camera recording the journey, or condensing a long family road trip down to a few minutes of film, through time-lapse techniques. His parents began buying him books and magazines about Ray Harryhausen. Later Peter became a regular reader of a host of magazines devoted to fantasy film, among them *Fangoria, Starburst* and *Famous Monsters of Filmland*, the latter a touchstone to a generation of American moviemakers.

Peter was lucky. He grew up in an environment where instead of being frowned upon as a waste of time, his imagination was nurtured through storytelling and another roll of film stock. Though Joan and Bill worried at times about his interest in horror movies and war, they did little to discourage it. Having grown up in environments with little money and more competition for their parents' attention, they lavished all the attention they could on their own son and let him follow his interests where they might lead.

Jackson's interest in film rather than sports made him something of a loner. 'He was extroverted in the things he did, in the way that he thought,' says Jan Spencer, who lived for many years in Pukerua Bay. 'But as far as communicating with adults, he was quite shy. If he knew you, you were okay.'

Spencer goes further in speculating that Jackson's famed distaste for fashionable clothing goes back to childhood. 'He was always a scruffy little boy. He just didn't care. "Why do I have to go back and put shoes on my feet when I could go out with nothing on my feet?"'

Anne Morris remembers the range of Peter's interests, all the way from the Bayeaux tapestry to the American Civil War. 'He was a very gentle person. In a sense he was reclusive, but he wasn't an anti-social kid at all. He was just very involved in what he had in his mind — which helped keep him out of trouble, or in trouble, whichever way you want to put it.'

HIGH SCHOOL

Kapiti College sits north of Pukerua Bay, just a few minutes' walk from the beach. By 1975, the year Peter Jackson arrived at Kapiti to start his third-form year, the college roll had grown to around 1200. School magazines from this period paint a picture of Kapiti College as a hive of activity — strong on sports and clubs (as well as discipline). The college was running out of classrooms. When it became clear how close the school's outdated plumbing system was to complete collapse, the Minister of Education fast-tracked the opening of Paraparaumu College in 1977, and after that the Kapiti roll began to fall.

Academically Peter was a good student — stories of his mythically unbeatable score in School Certificate maths still float around Kapiti College — but he has not stuck in the minds of many of those who taught him. Barry Johnston, Peter's form teacher in the third and sixth form, used to show movies to him and other students at lunchtimes. 'He was a good student,' says Barry. 'But he wasn't the kind of guy who shone out above anybody else. He just wasn't interested in sport. He was always mad on films.'

One report from his high-school years notes that he was imaginative in his writing, but shy about standing up and presenting it. By now, many of the students from Pukerua Bay were starting to break off into new groups. 'It was like separating a family,' recalls Anne Morris. 'We all knew each other, we'd played together for years. Peter went into himself a bit. He got a little more withdrawn.' As Jackson later told one journalist, he was never a particularly confident child or young adult.

Joan Jackson once went along to a 'meet the teachers' evening at Kapiti College, and was asked if she was having any problems with her son.

I said, 'Well it concerns me a little bit about Peter, he's so interested in guns, he just lives guns, cuts guns out and makes guns.' So he [the teacher] said, 'Mrs Jackson, be thankful that he's interested in something. There's lots of parents here who have got children who are interested in nothing. He'll change,

you mark my words, he'll change.' When I look at all the blood and gore on his
films I wonder if that teacher ever associates our interview with Peter Jackson
[laughter]. He's better off just with the guns.

Sports-mad Kapiti College student Andrew Neal, whose parents also hailed from England, got to know Peter in the third form. He remembers Peter for wearing a black duffle coat with 'a dedication verging on the religious'.

Dark curly hair. Introvert. I mean you tend to superimpose these images on
him, but as I sit here now I think of him keeping himself to himself. But if
people showed an interest, if you were interested in being in his films, then
you had a friend for life almost.
. . . in that situation he became more lively?
Absolutely. Because it was his passion. He was a changed person on the weekend
with his filming. He was in control . . . and doing what he wanted to do. It was
almost as if five days of college were getting in his way.

The following year at Kapiti College, Peter Jackson discovered someone else in the world who read *Famous Monsters of Filmland*. Movie-mad Ken Hammon had grown up in a railways cottage in Paekakariki, the first town up the coast from Pukerua Bay. Kapiti College was not his favourite place. Thanks to some discipline problems with two of his brothers, Ken recalls being called into the principal's office on arrival and being warned to toe the line. Yet he later came to realise that, being 'a short kid with a big mouth', the school's emphasis on discipline probably helped this self-confessedly morose student escape a major beating from other students.

The two teenagers bonded over a love of movies — they both had their own Super 8mm projectors. 'He built a screen and a projection booth with speakers,' says Hammon. 'He was very good at that kind of stuff.' In the days before video, movie fans could hire and purchase 8mm prints of their favourite movies. Between them, Jackson and Hammon had a fairly impressive collection: Lon Chaney's original *Phantom of the Opera*, *King Kong*, Buster Keaton's *The General*. But *The Texas Chainsaw Massacre* proved a little harder to find. A substantially shortened version of Tobe Hooper's highly charged horror movie had recently been banned by the New Zealand censor; but Hammon, Jackson and Andrew Neal managed to find a man in the Hutt Valley willing to hire a copy to them on 8mm. Back at Peter's place, after watching the first twenty-minute reel, Hammon and Neal were not sure if they were up to watching the rest. 'It really freaked us out. Pete loved it.'

Chainsaw massacres aside, most of Jackson and Hammon's 8mm films came from overseas. Government import controls meant that each time Hammon wanted to buy one, he would have to get someone different to sign the bank draft. 'That was when dinosaurs ruled the earth,' says Hammon. 'It was a different place. Back before the days of video, if you wanted to watch an older movie, the only other way you could see it was at these double features. Wellington was dead on a Sunday, like *The Quiet Earth* [in which Bruno Lawrence's character wonders if he is the last man alive]. You could walk through Lambton Quay and not see a single shop open, not a single person. I used to like those Sunday double features.'

That sixth-form year, Peter decided to enter a film competition being run by *Spot On*, a popular children's programme that played each weekend. He asked the others if they wanted to get involved. Neal says the plan was for each of them to try to come up with a possible story idea, but when they met up to share their stories, it became clear that Ken and Peter had cooked up something of their own. Andrew canned his idea about aliens and spaceships without even mentioning it.

The plotline Ken and Peter had hatched involved a bunch of gold prospectors who fell into a gully which had 'somehow ducked out of the normal evolutionary process'. Says Hammon:

> The prospectors fall into this time/space continuum, and emerge from that and get attacked by these two different strange creatures — the Trochoid, which was kind of like a Ray Harryhausen harpy, and later by a Cyclops. The Trochoid kills one of them, and at the end it's me and Andrew Neal. Andrew kills the Cyclops, and then they build a raft. They are floating along on the raft and they see the Beehive. So the punch-line is they didn't go back in time to a primeval age. They actually went forward to some kind of post-apocalyptic time when humanity is dead, and the world is overrun by monsters.

The plotline was designed to allow lots of opportunities for Jackson's stop-motion effects, while the 'God-awful ending' was inspired by the surprise finale of *Planet of the Apes*. The Trochoid itself got its name from a term heard in a technical drawing class. Andrew Neal made some prop Martini Henry rifles out of wood on his father's lathe, and Peter added finishing touches. *The Valley* was shot over five or six weekends, largely in the gully through Pukerua Bay that Peter had been playing in for years. Says Hammon:

> We started out with four of us, me, Pete, Andrew Neal and a kid named Ian Middleton. But after a while it became clear Ian Middleton couldn't act to save himself. We were all terrible, but he could not keep a straight face. Any time anyone pointed a camera at him he would start to grin, so he just died. He

was killed by the Trochoid. The Troch comes flapping down, grabs him and flies off. Which is interesting because the film is silent. Ian is being carried away by this weird flapping creature in silence.

Peter was the dominant one. We always used to say, 'Pete is the director, because he owns the camera.'

Was there any script?

No. Never. Just figured it out. We'd go for a bit and we would discover that Ian couldn't act, so it was like, 'We've got to kill Ian next week.' We just worked from there. The next thing we did was we killed Pete off. His character basically fell off a cliff. So that left Pete free to actually operate the camera, and shoot the thing. It ended up with me and Andrew as the two guys who survived.

How did you do the Beehive?

We just cut a photo of the Beehive out and slapped it on a board. We messed around with it a little so it looked sort of worn out and decayed. It seemed to take forever to actually build the damn thing [the real Beehive], and this crane was next to it for what seemed like years, so Peter left the crane in.

One weekend while filming around Pukerua Bay, the crew were simulating an earthquake by throwing some tree branches down a bank. At one point they ripped a small tree from the ground and sent it sailing down the hill. Says Neal, 'I think it upset one of the locals and he was ranting and raving at us and was going to call the police, so we decided to pack up for the day.'

According to Hammon and Neal, Jackson's only real concern about the credits was that his name be listed next to the special effects (at the time of writing, Jackson appears to be the only person in the world with a copy of *The Valley*). Hammon recalls that the 'directed by' credit was split between Jackson, himself and Andrew Neal. 'It was more of a hoot for me, to just get out and do stuff,' says Neal. 'I wasn't anywhere near as keen or fanatical as Ken and Pete were. They might be talking films, and I'd be on the back field playing baseball or softball.'

The time came to see if *The Valley* had won or lost. In its prizegiving episode, *Spot On* screened sections of *The Valley* alongside a small number of other films. But in the end the group had to settle for a consolation prize. As filmmaker Sam Pillsbury, who was one of the judges, says: 'We all thought it was a really impressive piece of work, but the storyline was almost non-existent. I think he was more interested in technique.' The competition was limited to movies of around five minutes' duration; *The Valley* came in at around eighteen. But the next day at school, the foursome had become minor celebrities. Students went up to Ken to check whether his character really had silently mouthed the word 'fuck' when

Ian got dragged off into the sky by the monster. Ken could proudly say 'Yes'.

The glory of having been involved in *The Valley* spread further when the film won a special scholarship — and a cash prize — sponsored by the local newspaper, the *Kapiti Observer*. Jackson's appreciation of the power of the media may well have sprung to life at this moment. Ian Middleton recalls that when the editor of the *Kapiti Observer* turned up at the school to judge the film, Jackson laid on some music from *King Kong* to play over the screening.

When the $100 was given out to Peter, Ken and Andrew at the school prizegiving, Ken gained further notoriety by not being present. Andrew Neal remembers sitting in the audience, thinking, 'How very Oscar'. Ken could not be bothered taking the bus back to school, partly because he felt the film's moments of bloodshed would count it out of contention.

Later the school principal called Peter and Ken into his office for a meeting. He wondered if they might want to make a film about Kapiti College to show to parent groups. 'It was going to have shots of happy children running around the place,' says Hammon. 'To me it was like making a pro-doco about Dachau. Peter thought the idea was terrible as well. But he didn't hate Kapiti as much as I did.'

Having been accredited his University Entrance, Peter Jackson now faced a big decision. Film was his major passion. Now a film he had played a big part in creating had won cash, and been seen on television by thousands. But success on 8mm and a job in the New Zealand film industry were like two separate islands.

The day before Peter went up onstage to receive his prize for *The Valley*, the New Zealand Film Commission opened its doors in Wellington. Its stated function was to encourage, participate and assist in 'the making, promotion, distribution and exhibition of [New Zealand] film'. The country's filmmakers were like a line of horses who had been waiting hours at the starting gate, ready to run themselves crazy now that the pistol was finally about to be fired. But Jackson did not have the connections or the professional experience to get into the race. His parents wanted to be encouraging, but they knew nobody in the local film industry. Instead they began to mention words like architecture and design, and leave leaflets from the polytechnic around the house.

Peter wanted to be a special-effects man. Over the years he had stayed in contact with a relative in England, who worked in the film industry. If there was nothing in New Zealand, he had long harboured a dream of going to England to find movie work over there.

Peter's parents ferried him and some of his models to the National Film Unit in Lower Hutt, home to the government body that produced mainly documentaries and promotional films. It was one of the only film possibilities that any of them could think of.

The legend that has been heard countless times is that the National Film Unit had no place for Peter Jackson, with the unspoken implication that they somehow erred in failing to recognise the youngster's talents. This account is certainly open to debate. His parents' recollection was that though staff at the Film Unit were impressed by his models, the Unit had little in the way of special effects to offer. Instead, they said, the Unit offered him a job in the film laboratory. In New Zealand, like anywhere else, getting your head in the door is always half the battle. But Bill Jackson sided with Peter:

It sounded to me and him that it was just a 'make do' job. When he came home he was sort of flattened. He didn't want to go back to school. He wanted to make special effects.

Said Joan:

He was really one-eyed about that. I opened the Evening Post *and among all the jobs, the* Evening Post *wanted a photo-engraver. We had no idea what a photo-engraver was, so Peter said, 'Well I'll go for it, but it will only be temporary.' He kept saying that. He ended up getting a three-year apprenticeship.*

SHENLEY

Due partly to its proximity to Borehamwood studios, the village in England where Joan Jackson spent three decades still pops up from time to time in television and movies. Shenley Hill, one of the area's grand estates, was seen in the '60s fantasy series *The Avengers*, and later in English thriller *The Hole*.

BRIXTON

The house where Bill Jackson spent his early years in the London suburb of Brixton has been destroyed. The housing estate in Sutton where he spent some of his puberty still exists, as do the nearby fields where he once played soccer and cricket with his brothers.

CHAPTER THREE

THE MOVIE THAT GREW:
BAD TASTE

'It's a very Kiwi film with a very Kiwi feel — basically a Kiwi film about Kiwi jokers.'
PETER JACKSON, DESCRIBING *BAD TASTE*

'I just liked the renegade sense of it, that here from nowhere was someone who had put his money where his mouth was.'
PRODUCER TONY HILES, DESCRIBING PETER JACKSON

Peter Jackson's new job at the *Evening Post* involved taking photographs of images needed for the newspaper. And in his second life as a filmmaker, he was developing increasingly grand visions of his own.

Jackson had long been a fan of epic movies. Now he had a bright idea for a way to make his own films appear bigger and grander, without having to replace all his equipment. He sent off to England for a special lens to screw onto the front of his 8mm camera. The lens gave the images Cinemascope dimensions, so that the picture frame spread right across the wall. But the idea was like slapping a new paint-job on an old Morris Minor — while the results might look better, it didn't make the engine any more powerful than before.

The new movie would be shot around the Kapiti Coast, partly in a makeshift graveyard in his parents' back garden, and almost entirely on weekends. Jackson created swords, costumes and makeup. Again he took turns about with Ken Hammon, acting and operating the camera. Peter O'Herne, his old home-movie co-star from childhood, was the third member of the *Curse of the Gravewalker* team.

Jackson took the starring role of the heroic Captain Eumig, who roams the Carpathian mountains of eastern Europe, killing vampires with a crossbow. The vampires are shambling, zombie-like creatures, and many of their battles take place in daylight. The names of the characters make it clear that *Curse of the Gravewalker* is the work of movie addicts. Jackson's character is partly inspired by the little-seen Hammer horror movie *Captain*

Kronos, Vampire Hunter. Count Murnau, the mystical, all-powerful vampire Eumig goes up against, is named after the German director of the early vampire classic *Nosferatu* and 1924's *The Last Laugh,* two silent movies that Jackson and Hammon knew well. Even the name Eumig is an in-joke — Eumig is a brand of film projector. Hammon recalls:

> *It wasn't that gory. I can't remember us doing decapitations or anything like that. Mostly it was gravewalkers getting staked, and falling down dead. It was all quite mad really.*

By this point, partly through clever use of such household staples as toilet paper, Jackson had begun to experiment with some complex facial makeup. Hammon sometimes doubled for Pete O'Herne as Murnau, despite being around half a foot shorter than him, when O'Herne began complaining of headaches from the makeup. Preparations were now lasting as long as an hour. Hammon says of the makeup:

> *It just completely covered your face. Every week he would glue this wig to your hair so when you took it off, half your hairline came off. Once he was trimming a wig, and he cut me. 'You cut me!' 'No I didn't.' 'You cut me!' 'No I didn't.' I'd get back and take the makeup off at the end of the day, and there was all this dried blood down the side of my face. He knew I wouldn't find out until I took the damned makeup off.*

The few people spoken to who have sat through the *Gravewalker* footage generally remember it positively. Hammon recalls one impressive scene in which a gravewalker opens his coffin, and the audience sees the shot from the gravewalker's point of view as a stake rushes from a crossbow towards the movie screen.

Andrew Neal acted for a few days on *Curse of the Gravewalker* shortly before leaving New Zealand for good in the early '80s. The location was an overgrown graveyard not far from Pukerua Bay.

> *I remember the final day, when I thought my filming days were done. The makeup was getting quite involved. We were all dressed up as zombies. There were people coming in to put flowers on graves — that made me feel quite uneasy. I remember thinking, 'I'm not sure I'd like to be doing this — that's me done.'*

While occasional visits to the graveyard continued, Jackson had begun another acting career in shopping malls around Wellington. In 1981, he watched on television in Pukerua Bay as American Rick Baker won the first Academy Award for makeup. Baker had conjured up the eye-opening werewolf transformations seen in the horror comedy *An American Werewolf in London.* Following on from the gorilla masks he had made as a child, Jackson decided to construct an elaborate gorilla suit of his own.

That year, a local radio station ran a costume competition around the Wellington region. As the competition moved from mall to mall, a succession of strange characters got up onstage before the assembled children, hammed it up a little, then ran off with first prize: among them was a hairy troll and a creature who looked suspiciously like the vampire killer from *Curse of the Gravewalker,* complete with a bag of severed heads. One day Jackson couldn't make it, so he got a volunteer from the *Evening Post* photolithography department to go along and take the prize for him.

In late 1982, a few weeks after Jackson turned twenty-one, he and Hammon went on a holiday to Los Angeles. Jackson spent two days at Disneyland, but the trip was mostly about movies: a chance to go to a science-fiction convention, a horror convention, and catch *ET* and *The Texas Chainsaw Massacre* on Hollywood Boulevard. Hammon recalls that many of the stranger characters inhabiting the Boulevard seemed to be 'quite drawn' to Jackson: 'He walks really fast — we were practically jogging around Los Angeles.' On the Universal Studio Tour, they witnessed that famous old house on the hill, as preparations began to film the sequel to *Psycho.*

Perhaps it was in Hollywood that Jackson began to realise that continuing to make films on 8mm was a short route to nowhere. With an hour of *Gravewalker* footage in the can, he decided to let the vampires go free.

AMBITION ON 8MM

Peter Jackson has been a James Bond fan since childhood. Ken Hammon recalls Jackson once declaring he would like to be the first New Zealander to direct a Bond movie: Jackson would later be beaten to the achievement by Martin Campbell (*Goldeneye*) and Lee Tamahori (*Die Another Day*).

Somewhere in the five-year period between making *The Valley* and beginning work on *Bad Taste,* Jackson made his own Bond homage. Memories as to when this film was shot are contradictory, but it appears likely that it was made in 1979, the year after Jackson left high school.

Hammon, who worked with Jackson on *The Bond Thing,* is fond of mentioning that Jackson fancied a resemblance between himself and Sean Connery. Later known as *Coldfinger, The Bond Thing* consisted of two fight scenes featuring Jackson dressed in a hat and black dinner suit lent to him by his father. Jackson spent a day filming a complex fight scene on the family's back verandah before discovering that the film had been loaded incorrectly, and none of the footage was usable. The scene was later reshot with Jackson and Peter O'Herne. The other fight involved an encounter with a Peter Lorre type on the beach (played by Hammon), who attempts to strangle Bond using a fishing line. Jackson's character frees himself with a flick knife disguised as a bow tie, and according to Hammon, 'He beats the hell out of me and kills me with this fish bucket over my head.' A short section of the bow-tie scene can be seen on the documentary *Good Taste made Bad Taste*.

Another film that remains unseen from this period is an ambitious experiment filmed in one extended take. It is shot from the point of view of an intruder as he goes down a pathway, and enters a house. The shot ends on an elderly figure sitting shaking in a chair (played by Peter O'Herne in a wig). Possibly inspired by the extended Steadicam shots featured in the classic horror movie *Halloween*, the film looks to have been an early example of the highly mobile camerawork that would come to be a Peter Jackson calling card.

TRADING UP

Traditionally, feature-length movies are shot on 35mm film. (These days video is fast becoming a vital medium for low-budget moviemakers, but at the time of writing few of these movies have found mainstream success.) On film, the smaller format of 16mm has long marked the borderland between amateur and professional. Over the years a number of low-budget movies — from 1960s zombie classic *Night of the Living Dead* through to British ensemble drama *Wonderland* — have been shot on 16mm. The print is then blown up in a laboratory so the movie can be screened in cinemas on 35mm projectors.

And what of little old 8mm, the medium Jackson had been playing about with his entire filmmaking life? In those days before video, 8mm offered a cheap and effective way to learn the basics of film. Shooting silent, 8mm is a perfect training ground for exploring the basic building blocks of cinema — namely how two different shots cut together. It has never been the easiest way to get your movies seen in a cinema. One problem is sound — it is very difficult to synchronise dialogue and sound effects precisely with 8mm. On top of that, the size of the actual 8mm frame (only a quarter as large as 16mm) means that the grain of the film stands out like a hailstorm when projected on anything larger than a dining-room wall. A group of American moviemakers with hopes of making a feature film cheaply once did a test on Super 8mm, using the best professional cameraman and equipment they could find. When they blew the completed footage up to 35mm and played it in a cinema, it was 'the most horrifying experience' of the producer's life.

Jackson told his parents that the only way he was going to get any recognition was by making a film, and that it was going to cost a whole lot of money. His parents went down to the garden to think about it. 'We decided we would get behind him,' recalled Joan Jackson. A short time after that, Jackson bought a secondhand 16mm Bolex camera. This particular camera can only hold two minutes of film stock, and the camera is spring-loaded to expose only thirty seconds each time you turn it on. He was still thinking of his movies in terms of amateur filmmaking competitions. Yet despite thinking small, the decision to switch to 16mm would help leapfrog Jackson a lot closer to the concept which keeps the movie industry rolling: the possibility of profit.

Bad Taste began as a cute idea, a short film designed to test out the new camera. But the film would grow like some kind of indecisive yet unstoppable plague — claiming new victims week by week, bringing old ones back to life, and constantly changing direction as the plotline morphed into yet another new shape. By the end of the movie, the lead character had been sidelined by a bunch of gun-toting hoons, the baddies had transformed into extraterrestrials, half of the cast had met nasty onscreen deaths, and a talented amateur had discovered there can be a market for making it up as you go.

For a short period in the beginning, there existed a plotline. Ken Hammon, one of those who was there on the first day of filming, describes it thus:

> *This young guy called Giles was collecting for famine relief. He went to this town, and a family of cannibals knock him on the head. That was the set-up and the punch-line. This guy is trying to fight famine and these people eat him. Initially it was called* Roast of the Day.

Playing Giles was Craig Smith, a one-time Kapiti College student and Housing Corporation workmate of Ken's. Smith had acted in some plays around Kapiti after leaving school, but was best remembered for his musical performance as the Elvis-like Pharaoh in a college production of *Joseph and the Amazing Technicolour Dreamcoat*. Says Smith:

> *It just became a weekend thing. We thought we could knock it off in six weeks or something. We were incredibly naive, thought, 'Oh yeah, let's do it for a laugh,' and it would all be done by the end of the year.*

Roast of the Day began filming one Sunday in October 1983, outside Wellington. The police arrived within hours.

After some deliberation, Jackson had decided to set his film in a mythical town called Kaihoro — a Maori word translating roughly as 'eat greedily' ('eat entrails' was briefly considered, then rejected for possibly being culturally insensitive). That October day on the road to the seaside town of Makara, Jackson installed a fake road sign — one direction pointing to Kaihoro, the other to Castle Rock (a reference to the mythical town where many of Stephen King's novels are set). But when the drivers of a passing Telecom van saw the group taking down the fake sign after filming, they contacted the police, who arrived to tell the *Roast* crew they had been spotted vandalising road signs. Some quick talking saved the day.

Aside from the Kaihoro incident, the first day's footage consisted mainly of Craig driving around in his wife's blue Morris Minor, or walking in Makara (Morris Minors would be a recurrent theme in Jackson's movies). 'The town was supposed to be deserted — all the people had been eaten,' recalls Hammon. 'But Makara is deserted anyway, so it worked out quite well. That's what this little New Zealand town looks like on a Tuesday.'

The movie would eventually be stitched together from footage shot in three main locations around the greater Wellington region — Makara, Pukerua Bay and the grounds of a historic house in Porirua. At this stage, the story contained little in the way of onscreen violence, but an early scene provides an indication of the way things would later head. As Giles wanders the town, he comes across an eye-rolling bearded man in a blue shirt, eating a dead possum from the road. The strange man, called Robert (played by Peter Jackson), proceeds to chase Giles up the road even after he tries to escape in his car. Weekend by weekend, this chase scene got longer and longer. Eventually though, both onscreen and off, Craig/Giles made it safely to a nearby house.

Gear House is a colonial homestead in Porirua, open to the public. Jackson's parents knew the caretakers, and asked if Peter might come in and film there for one or two weekends. Once they were safely in the grounds, the *Roast of the Day* team kept coming back regularly for a number of years.

It was at around this point that *Roast of the Day* began to transform. Jackson decided that instead of dying at the hands of the cannibals, Giles would be rescued by a group of SAS/Swat team-style commandos. That way Giles could live on for the film's finale, to battle a strange alien called the Botha Beast of Trom in his flying car (models of Craig and the flying car were built, although there is little evidence they were ever used). To play the commandos, Jackson enlisted three friends who had already been helping him out, both on and offscreen. One was trusty Peter O'Herne, who now worked at the Ministry of Transport; the others were Mike Minett and Terry Potter, workmates from the photolithography department. Minett and Potter had been hearing about Jackson's filmmaking endeavours for months, and there had even been talk of filming a short spoof movie with Potter named *Terry the Barbarian* (Potter was something of a bodybuilder).

Terry and Mike began turning up after their Sunday morning soccer game to help lug gear around and occasionally act onscreen. 'I can't remember first meeting Pete O'Herne. To me they've all just always been there,' says Minett. 'We'd all meet up — we got on like a house on fire.' In the evenings after filming, the group would sometimes stay on to have a few beers and watch movies from Jackson's collection. Terry in turn would bring his mate Dean Lawrie on board the gang of blokes making *Roast of the Day*. Dean worked in the fruit and vegetable markets in the city, and was as much of a James Bond fan as Peter Jackson. Though others would help out from time to time, the core *Bad Taste* group had been established: Jackson, Ken Hammon, Peter O'Herne, Craig Smith, Mike Minett, Terry Potter, and Dean Lawrie.

Jackson later tried to describe how a short film could have grown so long. 'When you're shooting on Sundays, you get all these ideas in the week, and the next Sunday you've got a whole lot of gags you want to film. It was almost like making it up as you go along.'

By the middle of 1984, the group were making regular weekend appearances at Gear House, shooting the scenes where the Swat team rescue Giles. These involved extensive gun battles in the grounds of the homestead. Terry and Ken competed with each other to perform the most idiotic stunts as they jumped out of trees, pretending to be dead loonies. 'I remember once some Scottish country dancers on one side of the house,' says Craig Smith. 'We were creating mayhem on the other. Bizarre, surreal.'

In the bowels of Press House, the set of interconnecting buildings which housed Wellington's two daily newspapers, Jackson continued to work six-day weeks in order to be able to fund the next laboratory bill, and filming occasionally came to a stop until he could afford more film. Though he was named the country's top photo-engraving apprentice three times during this period, the job had its quiet moments. Sometimes he could be found snoozing in the darkroom, or playing table tennis with his workmates while waiting for the next photographic order. Practical jokes were the order of the day: paper bats swooping unexpectedly down from the ceiling, or a pile of bottles placed right in the middle of a darkroom. On occasion Jackson snuck a camera into the building, filming shots of loonies in the darkroom, to intercut with scenes of Craig marinating in a barrel (the barrel shots themselves were done in the Jacksons' garage).

'I almost had two jobs,' Jackson told me after the release of the film. 'One was at the paper, and one an unpaid, eight-hour stretch in the evenings.' From aluminium, wood and Fimo he built exact replicas of a number of weapons. As the film grew gradually more bloody, he began building increasingly elaborate makeup effects and two vital pieces of camera equipment. One was a homemade camera mount tied to the operator's waist — like a no-budget Steadicam — which allowed him to follow his actors up roads and hillsides without too much camera shake. The other was a primitive crane which could be pivoted up above the ground for surprisingly professional shots, many overlooking Pukerua Bay beach.

Somewhere around this point, Jackson sat down at the dinner table in his parents' home, with some borrowed editing equipment, and began cutting together all the film that had been piling up in cans beneath his bed. The footage ran to almost an hour. That year, a ferocious low-budget horror movie called *The Evil Dead* had screened at the Wellington Film Festival on its path to international cult status. Jackson loved it. He discovered that *The Evil Dead* had been shot in America on 16mm by a group of dedicated amateurs. *Evil Dead* was a triumph of devotion over resources, and the similarities to Jackson's own endeavours went beyond the film's highly mobile camerawork and gloopy special effects. *Evil Dead* continued a no-budget movie tradition of putting the cast through hell. At one point half of the actors decided they had seen enough and drove home, leaving the crew to make the best of it. (Some of the *Evil Dead* team would later make New Zealand their base for the TV shows *Xena* and *Hercules*, but that is another story.)

After seeing *Evil Dead*, Jackson decided that *Roast of the Day* had the potential to become an actual movie — and there would be a massive twist in the plotline. Once the SAS men had successfully rescued Giles from Gear House, they would take off their masks, and reveal that they had actually been members of the cannibal family all along. Under this proposed storyline the entire escape has been a ruse, and no one has died at all. But once Jackson decided he had the makings of a feature-length movie, the plot twists grew even more extreme, partly as a way to accommodate more special effects. The movie's cannibal villains, long called 'the loonies' by the crew as filming progressed, would actually be aliens. The SAS escape presented major plotting problems in light of the decision to make the loonies aliens. Says Hammon:

> We had a hell of a hard time figuring that one out. Me and Pete were trying to work out why [the escape] happens. In the end I came up with this idea that it was a form of performance art — these aliens don't just eat their food, they play with it first. The whole fight scene was supposed to be fake. I came up with this horseshit about how the aliens believe meat tastes better if it's shot full of adrenalin.

In his spare moments between being a photolithographer, a filmmaker and sleeping, Jackson set to work creating a fake, elaborate, rod-operated head for the character played by Peter O'Herne. The plan was for a head that could change shape onscreen, for the scene when the SAS man transforms into an alien. But the finished fake head only complicated further the haphazard development of the plotline. Having built it, Jackson wanted to ensure that O'Herne's character remained an alien, whatever the newest plot direction might be. That way his maskmaking efforts wouldn't have gone to waste:

> There were plenty of times I had severe doubts about what I was making, but then I was back into it again. The thing that keeps you going is that you get to the point of no return. The fact that you can't actually turn back, that you've already put too much money into it, and people have put too much time into it.

Says Mike Minett:

> We thought Pete was mad, but if that's what he wanted to do we'd help him. And then after months and months of just shooting Craig, we realised, well shit this is boring, we need something to liven it up. So they changed the script and they got me and Terry to come in. I don't know how that worked. One minute we were helping out and the next minute we were the main people. And that went on for years.
>
> We never got directions or anything — we played ourselves right from the start. Just hammed it. By no account would I call it acting, but it just seemed to work. I always refer to it like when you're a kid you play war games, and you really get into it and start talking to each other like a soldier, imagining the troops coming over the hill. It was a bit like that, being a kid again, running around with these fake guns.

Along the way, a host of scenes would be filmed and then abandoned — scenes where the actors walked at waist-height through ice-cold streams, or slid down hillsides on strange chutes, or dressed as aliens wearing suits and dinner gloves, or ran around paddocks, trying to look as if they were being chased by a rabid sheep (in reality, the sheep was too terrified to act).

The shoots for *Giles' Big Day* (as it was now called) stretched on into another year. But for a number of the team, the Sunday filming sessions were beginning to pale. Some of them were getting tired of lugging equipment around for a project that increasingly looked as if it might never end, let alone have any audience beyond themselves. On more than one occasion, Peter Jackson found himself the only person who turned up.

Craig Smith, playing the film's lead character, was the first to head for the exit. Having recently found God, he was beginning to wonder if he should be working on the movie at all.

It must have been the beginning of 1986. I was going through a bad phase of being involved in fundamental Christianity. My wife and her family were very much into it. They started giving me the guilts about being involved in something like this.

What were they saying was wrong?

Well you know . . . aliens, cannibals, blood and guts. Looking back, you're young and stupid. At the time I thought I was making some sort of moral stand. But it was just bullshit. I was doing it to keep her and her family happy. I was completely unstable, doing far too much drinking and drugs. When I left the film, that's when the whole plotline changed completely. In hindsight it was the best thing that could have happened, because it turned it into a completely different film. My part was cut down considerably. It made for a goddamned far better movie.

Bad Taste's extended birth meant that events in the real lives of the cast were overtaking the plotline. As a result, death scenes were also filmed months later for Terry Potter (spiked through the head), who was getting married and moving to Australia. With hardly any of his original cast left, Jackson made plans to hand the climactic scenes in the movie to Mike Minett, who would bazooka the alien spaceship and go crazy with a chainsaw once he got on board. But as the actors dwindled away, inspiration would be born from desperation.

On the clifftops that stretch southwards from the main beach at Pukerua Bay, Jackson began filming some of *Bad Taste's* most dangerous and idiotic scenes; scenes where Peter Jackson, playing a bearded alien named Robert, battles Peter Jackson playing a bespectacled earthling named Derek. When he wasn't aiming the camera at Peter, Ken put on a wig to play the back of Peter's head for the scenes where both Robert and Derek are in shot together. To make matters even more complicated, these were shot over a six-month gap. The hilltop in question is just a short walk up through the bush from Pukerua Bay township (a short walk, that is, when you are not carrying heavy camera equipment). Looking down from the top, there is plenty of grass, scrub and the occasional wire fence as the hillside drops away to the ocean. It is easy to imagine that a fall would not be the end of the world, but judging by the sheer length of the journey, you wouldn't want to find out. Jackson tied a rope to himself, the other end to a nearby stump, and dangled himself above the drop. The person filming him often had no rope at all.

Hammon has written a fascinating nine-page account of the making of *Bad Taste* which provides some idea of the many injuries sustained during the shoot, including the time he sailed off the top of a van after a sudden break from filming. But the closest thing to a near-death experience involved Mike Minett, back on the clifftop. His brother-in-law Michael Griggs, playing one of the aliens, was preparing to film a scene involving a sledgehammer and was practising swinging it. Minett, standing on the hilltop between Griggs and the ocean, took a cigarette break.

I looked up and he'd let go of this thing and it came straight towards me in slow motion and went past my ear. I just heard a whoosh and it went flying down the bank. If that had hit me it would have killed me.

CASH

Moviemaking has long been about two things — the art of how you go about telling a story onscreen, and the challenge of finding enough money to switch on the camera at all. If you were trying to make movies in the 1980s, the money part often meant knocking at the door of the New Zealand Film Commission.

In early 1985, Jackson wrote his first letter to the NZFC, asking for some cash. At this point, he hardly knew anything about the Commission at all — but he knew that its executive director was a man named Jim Booth. Booth became Jackson's personal bogeyman, the unknown quantity who stood between him and completing his movie.

Too nervous to do it himself, Jackson got Ken Hammon to ring up Booth to ask how one went about getting Film Commission finance. So began a relationship where Jackson periodically wrote twelve to eighteen-page letters to the Commission boss about how well *Bad Taste* was going, and how much better it could be going if the Commission got involved. Booth's replies were polite but encouraging turndowns. In October 1986, when another letter arrived proclaiming that *Bad Taste* was now seventy-five minutes long, Booth decided it was time to go take a look.

FLASHBACK TO THE 1970S

For much of the 1970s, the New Zealand film industry was like two forts, with a bunch of mercenaries running around in between, trying to get their hands on the armoury. The first fort was that of New Zealand television. Designed optimistically to be a hybrid of commerce and public-service broadcasting, it ran on one government-controlled channel, and was periodically reorganised. On rare occasions, television opened its doors to the work of independent filmmakers, but the addition of a second channel in 1975 saw that door swing quickly shut again. The second fort was the National Film Unit, the government's unofficial tourist and promotion arm, long seen by the independents as a bastion of self-interest and underused resources.

Throughout the 1970s, filmmakers struggled to survive, mainly by making commercials and industrial films. Occasionally some made efforts to persuade the government to set up an organisation fostering New Zealand feature films. Like the kiwi itself, the lesser-spotted New Zealand feature film in those days only rarely crossed from the imagination into reality. But in 1977, the filmmakers got together and began lobbying politicians and the media, campaigning for a special commission to encourage local feature films. The timing was good. For some reason three local movies had appeared out of nowhere that year — one of them, Michael Firth's *Off the Edge*, even got nominated for a best documentary Academy Award. As a result, Arts minister Alan Highet helped persuade the National government to set up the New Zealand Film Commission, which was officially established in 1978. Its stated purpose was to encourage, participate and assist in the making of, promotion, distribution and exhibition of films with a significant New Zealand content. Funded initially by grants from the Lotteries Board, and later by taxpayer money as well, the Commission provided money to develop scripts, and loans and finance to finish movies.

The industry exploded. In 1985, the year Commission executive director Jim Booth sent his first rejection letter to Peter Jackson, ten New Zealand films premiered at the Cannes Film Festival (four had some form of Commission funding). But the government's removal of tax incentives was about to lead to a massive drop in local film production, and a situation the Film Commission had never wished for — an environment where for years, many saw the underfunded Commission as the only likely source of funding to make New Zealand movies.

A genial man whose laidback demeanour hid a subversive streak of humour, Jim Booth had come to the Film Commission from a background in government funding for the arts. In the 1970s, he had played a vital part in a number of initiatives for authors, including establishing residencies for writers at Victoria and Auckland universities. After a short stint as interim director for the Film Commission in its early days, Booth returned as executive director in 1983. Booth was keen for the keepers of the public purse to keep a dialogue going with the film industry, and on Friday nights filmmakers, editors and writers would often turn up at the Commission offices for a drink and a talk.

The Film Commission has long faced accusations of not doing all it can to keep local movie talents in New Zealand. It is difficult to level this criticism in Peter Jackson's case. But certainly New Zealand film history might have been very different, had it not been for Jim Booth's next few moves.

In August 1986 Booth met Jackson for the first time in a Wellington screening room, watched his seventy-five minutes of footage, laughed a little, then left. He was impressed with Jackson's work, but knew that the film would be a tough sell to the rest of the Commission because of its low-tech, homemade qualities, and its bloodshed. Thinking that the support and guidance of someone in the film industry could help the project along, he asked Wellington filmmaker Tony Hiles to provide an assessment of the footage to date.

Hiles had heard about Peter Jackson already. A few months before, a friend of his who worked as Jim Booth's personal assistant had said to him, 'Has Jim ever talked to you about Peter Jackson? He's got these amazing letters from this guy, they're really funny.'

Hiles was in the Commission's good books, partly because his whimsical documentary *Flight of Fancy*, about a man trying to fly unaided, was selling well for them around the world. English-born, he had arrived in New Zealand in the 1960s and spent years working in television before becoming an independent producer/director. One weekend, Jackson showed Hiles his film. Only ten percent of the footage had sound, the aliens were of a different design from those seen in the final version, and many scenes went on far too long. The film came to a halt after a gun battle at Gear House, when everyone ran away. Hiles says, 'The thing that struck me when I first saw it was, where had all this talent come from? People can be dedicated and shoot a film for four years, and it can be a pile of shit. But he'd been dedicated for four years, and it was on the way somewhere.'

Jackson had already shown his movie to a couple of producers around Wellington. One encouraged him to dub the main characters with American accents, in order to make the film more marketable overseas. Hiles felt differently.

I thought they were fantastic — the casting was just so idiosyncratically delightful. I thought, you cannot plaster anybody else's voices on, they've got to do it themselves. I think Peter liked this . . . it went along with his philosophies.

In October 1986, Jackson received his first cheque from the Film Commission. The next day he quit his job at Press House to devote his time to the movie. Booth had agreed to provide the $30,000 needed to complete filming. Although Jackson did not know it at the time, his payments were being drip-fed by Booth to help ensure that the film did not have to go to the full Commission board for approval. Booth could approve money for script development in amounts of up to $5000, so

Jackson's support took the form of a series of $5000 cheques.

By now Ken Hammon, worried that the film was so violent it would be unreleasable, had come up with a new title: *Bad Taste*. 'I never particularly liked it, but it grows on you,' said Jackson at the time. 'Now I think it's a good name.'

As the new hired help, Hiles quickly learned some important news: Mike Minett and Terry Potter had grown tired of the movie and refused to do any more weekends. A meeting was arranged with the two actors. At the arranged time, Jackson was nowhere to be seen. The other three had some beers, Hiles eventually managed to persuade them of his own good intentions and that the film had a finishing date, then Jackson appeared.

Proposals to fund violent or edgy material were not unheard of at the Film Commission. In the organisation's first year in existence, David Blyth showed it stills for a proposed film called *Angel Mine* — one shot showed a naked woman sitting on a lavatory bowl, on a waveswept beach. A few years later, Blyth asked for help with *Death Warmed Up*, a horror piece involving murderous mutants and out of control brain surgery. The Commission gave funding in both cases.

At a meeting in July 1997, the Commission decided to give *Bad Taste* a further $128,000 to complete post-production. But a report written by Commission members after watching a rough cut indicates that their faith in the film's prospects was not high.

> [Bad Taste's] *weaknesses include minimal acting talent, and characters who are unsympathetic and crude. The film includes a lot of mis-judged humour, which could be enjoyed by the crassest of audiences, but very probably not, because much of the dialogue is incomprehensible, especially so for anyone outside New Zealand.*

According to the report, the still uncompleted *Bad Taste* did not have 'the style and verve' to match the overseas sales of *Death Warmed Up*, and its only potential market was video. Certainly the film embraced crassness. According to Hiles:

> *One day Peter said, 'There is one scene that I don't know whether I'd be able to get away with or not. The guys have to drink this guy's sick.' And I said, 'Look, if you don't do it now you'll never get another chance. Whack it in, let's do it.' Those were things I did not consult with the Film Commission at all. I mean, could you imagine me writing, 'Well, there's a scene in which massive amounts of vomit spends hours coming out of somebody's mouth and then everybody gets to eat it'? They'd be like, 'What?' You just don't tell anyone.*

The alien vomit was really a mixture of yoghurt, food colouring and mixed vegetables. Composer Michelle Scullion later added laidback dinner music as backing to the scene.

Jackson saw *Bad Taste* as a live-action *Tom and Jerry* cartoon.

People who see the film seem to realise in the first few minutes that it's fun, and get right into the spirit of it all. That's the whole idea of why the film was made, not so people would spew up in the aisles or to give them bad dreams for days afterwards — it's entertainment that's specifically adapted to the type of people who like splatter movies. Very few of the gore effects in Bad Taste *are realistic really — they're cartoon gore effects, very exaggerated and over-the-top.*

'I know it's medically impossible for anyone to walk along with three-quarters of their head missing,' added Hiles. 'So I'm not at all upset to see it onscreen.'

As for the film's lack of female characters (there are one or two women among the massed aliens in the vomit scene, but none elsewhere), that was unintentional. According to Jackson, 'There were no women I knew who were either good enough actors or who were available to give up Sundays for a few years on end.'

Jackson had dumped an earlier design for the heads of the aliens (which can be seen on the film's soundtrack). When he started over again, the size of his final latex mask was defined partly by the size of his mother's oven.

As *Bad Taste* headed into the home straight, Jackson heard from a young visual communications student in Christchurch. Cameron Chittock was a longtime monster fan, now experimenting with puppetry and animatronics. Chittock initially stayed at Jackson's house while he helped make the aliens in the basement. 'It was a pretty humbling experience,' he says.

I was struck about how focused he was about all the different levels of making a movie. I guess I learned about the difference between an artistic vision and the simple process of making something work on film. Everything we did was going to be used the next day, so there was no pissing around. For instance, on my first day of work he said, 'What I want you to do is make a brain and paint it inside this head.' I very carefully cut it around and then got a picture of a brain, and started to carefully paint it. He was patient for a while and then he said, 'Cameron, look. It's a beautiful job, but at the end of the day it's going to be over in a second. I just want you to paint it red and put a few pink bits on.' He basically did the job for me in about ten minutes. I was absolutely shocked. The next day I saw his decisions working.

Jackson's parents continued to help out on the film in all number of ways, whether in transportation or readying another plate of baked beans for the boys. On a number of occasions, the family oven was put out of commission while Jackson got the next alien mask ready, while at other times the kitchen table was taken over by film-editing equipment. Throughout much of this period, the Jacksons charged their son no board. 'They didn't see one frame until the film was completed,' Jackson said in one interview at the time. 'Not their cup of tea really — but they saw the humour in it.'

In May 1987, arrangements were made for one final week of shooting. With Craig Smith keen to be involved again now that he was divorced, the whole *Roast of the Day* team were able to take a paid week off work and finish the movie they had begun all those weekends before.

'It was quite a fun week because we got to do a lot more outlandish things, and blow things up,' recalls Dean Lawrie.

Tony Hiles remembers the delights of filming the scene where Gear House takes off. 'Wind machines, they're great, a VW motor with a bloody great propeller on it and handle bars so you could steer it — it made a shitload of noise and created a huge draught. Good fun.'

Hiles begged and borrowed favours from contacts in the film industry, many of whom were further persuaded after seeing the quality of Jackson's footage. In that final week relatives, amateurs and professionals worked side by side on a farmland property on the Kapiti Coast, as the modelmaking, destruction and alien slaughter came to a head. The interiors of the alien spaceship were recreated in an old hall in the middle of a paddock. Dean Lawrie spent long periods inside the latex mask of lead villain Lord Crumb, his cowboy boots tucking out of Crumb's pinstripe suit, his lips operated by cables. A number of late nights were devoted to completing a series of models of Gear House for scenes where the homestead is attacked by bazooka and transforms into an alien spaceship. 'If you looked at the big model with the naked eye you would think, my God, I can't believe he's actually going to stick that on a screen,' says Chittock, who helped make it. 'But Peter knew exactly when how much steam and smoke was going to be in front of it.' The modelmaking team finished the model and got just a few hours' sleep before driving up to Caroline Girdlestone's farm to shoot the scene.

'He was impossible to stop, the energy and the work he put in,' says Hiles of Jackson during this period. 'It wasn't, "That was a good day." It was, "I'll race home now, I've got two more masks to make and I've got to wire up these." His commitment was the largest of anybody's.'

Some of the goriest scenes were saved till the very end of the schedule. The climactic rebirth scene required some creative use of available power.

This moment involves Jackson, playing Derek, chainsawing his way through the inside of an alien before emerging out his bottom half (the Film Commission report recommended removal of the 'gratuitous' line of dialogue which is often quoted by fans to this day.) Shooting the scene late at night in a shed on the farm, the crew were unable to use more than two plugs, or else the safety switch cut in — which meant choosing between lights, a heater or the jug to make cups of coffee. Says Hiles:

> I ran an extension cord through a safety transformer because it was going across wet grass. There was just the four of us in a freezing cold shed, and it was a matter of shooting take after take. First of all, let's hang the body up and we'll do the drop into the top. There was Peter crawling his way through the mess, and all the time there was bloody offal going all over the place, landing on a big carpet. We got about two or three hours' worth of shooting, turn the lights off, let's warm up for a minute and put the jug on and have a cup of coffee. But in the end we're all covered in goo and blood, except Don [Duncan] who was shooting it, because we were picking this stuff up and putting it back in the corpse. Suddenly Matt [Noonan] didn't quite throw up but he said, 'I can't do this any more,' and I was just about at the point where I couldn't do any more. It was like being in an automaton.

SOUNDING GOOD

When filming finally came to an end, one vital element was still missing. Only a small amount of the movie had been recorded with sound, which meant that an entire soundtrack was now required. Veteran actor Peter Vere-Jones (who also provided the voice of lead villain Lord Crumb) joined as dialogue coach, helping ready the cast of non-professionals for the difficult task of synching their lines of dialogue to what was happening onscreen. Craig Smith is sure that this is the first time in the four-year making of *Bad Taste* he saw a script (although odd pieces of paper had been used to write down exchanges of dialogue during filming — at which point the boys would sometimes reject Peter's lines and ask if they could say something else instead).

Hiles felt strongly that an energetic soundtrack was important, partly to counteract the homemade feel of the visuals. The post-production team made sure there was a sound for everything that happened. 'There was no two ways,' says Hiles, 'When someone's brain hit the floor, you heard it.'

The music was another story. At one point, Jackson had hoped he might be able to put one or two Beatles songs on the soundtrack, but the idea came to nothing. Early in 1987, Hiles gave Michelle Scullion a call. She played in a variety of bands, and had composed music for theatre, dance and the occasional short film and corporate video.

Scullion first saw an early rough cut of *Bad Taste* in an editing room on Cuba Street, as Jackson and Hiles stood by to supply their own live soundtrack. What with the pair's sound effects and Scullion's laughter, people kept coming into the room to check what was going on. 'I just fell about the floor,' says Scullion. 'Within the first four minutes I was in fits.' Something about the footage — possibly its 'small-town New Zealand charm' — reminded her of Saturday afternoons as a child at the local bughouse in Stokes Valley, watching Jaffas bounce across the cinema floor.

In a country where tight budgets often mean that soundtracks and editing are overly rushed, *Bad Taste*'s schedule at least offered Scullion some time. During recording, she hired a guitarist for a few hours, but otherwise the soundtrack is entirely her playing a variety of synthesisers and samplers.

Much earlier, Jackson had proposed that Terry Potter and Mike Minett supply the soundtrack themselves. But after a tense meeting in Hiles's office, it was agreed that Potter and Minett's bands would each contribute one song, with Scullion supplying the remainder of the music. Minett has no recollection of such a meeting, but he agrees that there were growing tensions among the cast that the film was no longer 'our little Sunday club' any more.

> At the end of the day they did a bloody good job. Without Tony, Booth, Michelle, we wouldn't have got anywhere. Because it needed to go up a level, it needed to go out of our hands. You realise that years later. At the time we were excited, big-headed. We made a movie!

Scullion says that a number of the cast made a point of coming up to her at the film's Wellington premiere, and congratulating her on the music: 'Time resolved it.'

Bad Taste's title song was written in a night. Minett recalls ringing band member Dave Hamilton right after composing it. Hamilton initially refused to drive all the way from the Wairarapa at little notice to help him practise, until Minett threatened that he would not be on the song: 'Forty minutes later there's a knock at the door.'

Minett's band The Remnants normally performed with a drum machine, so for the recording session Madlight drummer John Derwin provided the drums. For Minett, recording professionally in a proper studio was a special thrill. 'The film was just a hobby. But to get my song on it, that was a big thing.'

Veteran television editor Jamie Selkirk oversaw the task of putting sound and vision together (Selkirk remains one of the only key crew members from *Bad Taste* who is still working with Jackson today).

The finished film contained a bewildering 2300 shots — more than the laboratory grading computer at the National Film Unit could then handle. By this point, around $17,000 of Peter Jackson's own wages had gone into creating them.

Needing a company name, Peter Jackson came up with the 'slightly silly' WingNut films, partly out of a desire to avoid anything that sounded pretentious. Some say the original logo was to have been of a nut with wings; the one that was finally used shows a cherub, wearing what appears to be a royal crown, flying around on an insect.

OUT INTO THE WORLD

The French Riviera can be a depressing place for a young filmmaker. The Cannes Film Festival is like a concentrated mixture of drinking party and bunfight. Each May, hundreds of films fight for the attention of buyers. A few of the more prestigious films have already been selected to go into competition, which hopefully means some media attention at least. Others are discovered in the festival marketplace. The rest drown.

The year 1988 was a big one for the Film Commission, but thanks partly to the fallout from the 1987 stock market crash, it wasn't a great year for selling movies. The Commission had seven new titles on show at Cannes, joining the 600 or so at Cannes that season. Jackson's father warned him before going not to get his hopes up. 'We were like the kids at the back of the class,' is how Hiles describes *Bad Taste*'s lack of mana. 'Vincent Ward was head prefect.'

Ward's second feature film, the artful fantasy *The Navigator*, had won a prestigious place in the festival competition, and long before its official screenings buyers began knocking on the Commission's office overlooking La Croisette. Ward and Jackson in some ways came from different worlds — Ward, the art school student whose acclaimed debut *Vigil* had been almost entirely about image and mood; Jackson, the home-movie horror fan who wanted only to entertain. But sharing some beers on the verandah at the Commission's Cannes headquarters, Ward and Jackson got on fine. The two may have recognised something in each other, beyond their shyness — perhaps a shared determination to see a movie through to its finish, in each case against fairly trying circumstances.

Hiles's recollection is that at least half of the staff of the Commission at the time thought *Bad Taste* was 'not a very nice film at all'. Certainly the publicity magazine the Commission organised for Cannes supports his theory — *Bad Taste* is the last of the seven features listed, pages behind a number of films that have since completely sunk from sight. When Jackson and Hiles learned that Commission marketing director Lindsay Shelton had begun selling rights to *Bad Taste* days before any of its official screenings, tempers flared. 'Lindsay was doing what he thought was right,' says Hiles, adding that selling a film sight-unseen is not unheard of. 'But it was just the principle. We'd had such a long bloody trip to get here, and we didn't have a chance to hold it up to be booed.'

Once the tension died down a little, Shelton reluctantly agreed to hold off further sales. Six days after its first screening, *Bad Taste* had jumped from the back of the class. Back at the Commission's office in Wellington, many of the phone calls were about the goriest film in its catalogue. In the months to follow, *Bad Taste* would go neck and neck with *The Navigator* as the fastest-selling movie in New Zealand history. More important, its tiny budget helped ensure it was one of the rare local movies to go into profit.

The French were especially keen on *Bad Taste*. The month after Cannes, Jackson watched his first feature in a theatre packed with 3000 people, at the Paris Festival of Fantasy and Science Fiction. 'They screamed and cheered and threw paper aeroplanes all around the place,' he said later. *Bad Taste* walked off with the prize for best gore film.

Bad Taste proved a perfect attention-grabber for Jackson. Two elements would form the backbone of many reviews and interviews: the film's gleeful sense of the disgusting, and the jack-of-all-trades contributions of its director. For all its truth, the latter angle downplayed the contributions of the others, who had worked on the film for so long with little hope of return. But Jackson had ensured that each now had a percentage of any future profit.

Mike Nicolaidi reviewed *Bad Taste* for international film magazine *Variety* in a cinema in Palmerston North, shortly before Cannes. He found the film 'an outstandingly awful, at times awfully brilliant, first feature' that announced the arrival of 'a new and considerable talent' in the New Zealand film industry.

Considering the eye-opening nature of some of the film's imagery, local reviewers were generally surprisingly upbeat in their reactions. *Metro* reviewer John Parker called it a 'black comedy/splatter masterpiece'. Stephen Ballantyne wrote in the *Dominion Sunday Times* that *Bad Taste* was the best kind of home movie: it operated 'entirely on enthusiasm unfettered by any sign of preachiness or moralising' in a country where films were generally 'made by liberal, middle-class minds, and generally pay their respects to the values upheld by that group'. Despite *Bad Taste*'s success at Cannes, New Zealand exhibitors were not falling over themselves to screen it. Distributor John Barnett endeavoured to create a cult audience for the film through a policy of mainly late-night sessions, a plan which proved only partially successful. The film won strong showings in the university town of Dunedin, but its overall New Zealand gross was nothing remarkable.

In England the critical response varied wildly. Many loved the movie, but a number of papers agreed with the *Daily Telegraph*, which felt that *Bad Taste* was for 'connoisseurs of the unremittingly offal only'. The *Evening Standard*'s review consisted largely of a dictionary entry for the word vomit, before arguing that the film 'offers the best reason yet for not having to visit New Zealand'. In the *Monthly Film Bulletin*, fantasy specialist Kim Newman commented upon some aspects of the film's 'hand-to-mouth budgeting', including the 'endless' central shoot-out around Gear House. But overall the review was admiring: 'While the effects are never technically as good as those in a George Romero or Sam Raimi film, they do serve well enough in their slapstick pantomime way to defuse any potential offensiveness in the horror content . . . *Bad Taste* is quite a remarkable achievement. It follows *The Quiet Earth* and *The Navigator* in establishing New Zealand as a leading source of *cinefantastique*.'

Jackson initially expected that *Bad Taste* would not be allowed to play in England at all, perhaps bearing in mind the plight of *The Evil Dead*, which had been the subject of a number of unsuccessful obscenity trials and police seizures. In the end, it was only *Bad Taste*'s poster that caused any trouble in England. In August 1989, the London Underground decided that the poster image of an alien giving a one-finger gesture was more than its customers could handle. 'I don't know what the gesture means in New Zealand, but in this country it carries a fairly clear and distinct message,' said a spokesman. Artists went off on missions around the Underground, painting over the offending fingers individually.

In Ontario, the censor banned *Bad Taste* for 'indignities to the human body'. But in Queensland, it was the censors themselves who were put out to pasture. Having been released in a shortened version thanks to Federal censors, *Bad Taste* had been playing for three weeks under an R16 rating when the Queensland Board of Review decided to ban it. The board's strong stand on censorship had seen the banning of more than 100 films already passed for exhibition by Australian censors (Queensland had been one of the only places in the Western world to ban Martin Scorsese's *The Last Temptation of Christ*). Weeks after the *Bad Taste* decision, Minister of Justice Glen Milliner announced that the Board of Review was to be permanently axed.

One of the only important film territories that had failed to bite at Cannes was the United States. 'I was screening it in the States as well,' recalls Lindsay Shelton. 'All the horror-film companies I targeted found it too extreme.' Potential distributors appeared to be worried that the film's violence would automatically earn *Bad Taste* an X certificate, or require it to be released unrated, both of which limited the film's commercial prospects. 'It's pretty clear to any distributor who's got a brain in his head that to cut *Bad Taste* would remove most of the humour from the film,' said Jackson after Cannes. Apart from a small number of film festival screenings, *Bad Taste* largely bypassed American cinemas and headed to video, despite some enthusiastic reviews.

And what about profit? Though Jackson's debut had quickly shown itself to be a clever investment, the low budget of $300,000 made it appear more of a money-spinner than it really was. Four years after first appearing at Cannes, *Bad Taste*'s net income for the Film Commission had not even reached $500,000. Yet the film would be a long stayer, continuing to draw fans on video, and seeing a new lease of life as Jackson found greater fame. In 2001, author Steven Paul Davies included it among 130 films listed in the *A–Z of Cult Films and Filmmakers*.

More than a decade since making the movie came to an end, most of the *Bad Taste* team still keep in touch. 'With the rest of us, there's still a sense of family,' says Craig Smith. 'This strange relationship we all seem to have where we talk, and backbite, and have arguments.'

Ken Hammon stayed in regular contact with Peter Jackson for a number of years and has made short appearances in two of his movies, but now talks to Jackson rarely. Craig Smith occasionally caught up with Jackson during the early '90s, while Smith was living in England. But these days, the closest the *Bad Taste* team normally get to their old filmmaking partner is being invited to one of his film premieres.

Yet talk of getting 'the boys' together to make another movie has become a Peter Jackson mantra. As recently as 2001, Jackson could still be heard mentioning the idea of a *Bad Taste* sequel in media interviews. Back in the late '80s, there were said to be plans for several — one to feature forty-foot mutant monsters rampaging through Wellington, another involving the kidnapping of the Beatles, with the *Bad Taste* gang as high-school students at Kapiti College.

The horror genre is awash with sequels and rematches, in which characters unexpectedly rise up from the dead, to engage in another round of bloodletting. Who is to say that Derek and the boys might not one day return, called in to mop up an even nastier mess than they did the first time they assaulted cinema screens.

THE BOYS

Continue to receive regular royalty payments for their work on *Bad Taste*. Ken Hammon wrote and directed the yuppie satire *Market Forces* in 1991, which was nominated for best short film at the New Zealand Film Awards the following year. His script for *The Murder*

House came to the screen under the direction of noted cinematographer 'Waka' Attewell in 1997. Hammon has written scripts for a number of as yet unmade features. Mike Minett is the only one of the original *Bad Taste* team still working for Wellington Newspapers. His band The Remnants occasionally pick up their guitars, though rarely in public. Dean Lawrie is one of the biggest James Bond fans in Wellington. Peter O'Herne got married at Gear House in 1988: Peter Jackson shot his wedding video. O'Herne continues to correspond with *Bad Taste* fans from around the world. Terry Potter works for a graphic design company in Wellington, and Madlight also occasionally jam. Craig Smith remarried in 1988, the same year a motorcycle accident put him out of action for six months. Smith left the Court of Appeal in late 2003, after working there as a registrar for six years.

DOUG WREN

Spotted by Peter Jackson in the Press House cafeteria as the perfect person to play cheerful lead alien Lord Crumb, Doug Wren retired from his job in the process department soon after. Wren had written and acted in a number of plays. He died before *Bad Taste* saw completion, so the voice of the alien leader was provided by actor Peter Vere-Jones.

CHAPTER FOUR

NOT YOUR EVERYDAY AVERAGE CREATURES: *MEET THE FEEBLES*

'If it was a puppet film that didn't have a massacre at the end,
it wouldn't be the Feebles.'
PETER JACKSON

'To me the blacker it is, the funnier it gets.'
PETER JACKSON ON *MEET THE FEEBLES*

It is April 1989, and Peter Jackson is lying on a couch. He is imagining a movie, a movie that revolves around an assortment of animal performers who sing offensive songs, snort drugs and generally poke their noses in the gutter-stuff of life. The movie does not yet exist. But the voices and groans of the puppet characters have already been recorded in preparation for the film shoot to come. Jackson listens to this aural blueprint as it spews forth from a tape recorder, in one concentrated 90-minute burst of melodrama.

The first voice, cute and shy, talks in starstruck fashion about the honour of getting to appear in the *Feebles* stage show. The second voice replies with a buzz of tiny wings, and offers the newcomer good money for any filthy stories that might come his way.

Jackson lies back on the couch with his eyes closed, calling up an image to go with each new voice — a brief shot of a wide-eyed hedgehog here, a deceased puppet there, a burst of hippopotamus crying over there. He giggles. Like a ballet suite waiting for its dancers, the entire depraved *Feebles* plotline is now safely locked down on audiotape, before the cameras start to roll. This is that dream-like point in the life of a motion picture — the moment where the final script has been printed off, but none of the compromises of transferring it onto celluloid have occurred. Yet capturing images to accompany the voices on tape will prove to be Peter Jackson's trial by fire.

COMMERCE AND COMPROMISE

Sometimes moviemakers spend the rest of their careers trying to rediscover the strange alchemy that made their first feature film so special. Shooting a picture in fits and starts as you struggle to find the cash for film stock is a frustrating process. Yet for all the drawbacks, low-budget moviemaking can also allow a certain freedom, the chance to discover the shape of a film along the way. The bloodymindedness of talented young directors inventing their own rules can translate into something unique on celluloid: David Lynch's dark and otherworldly *Eraserhead*, Sam Raimi's unstoppable *The Evil Dead*, Jane Campion's blackly comic *Sweetie*.

Out in the world of mainstream moviemaking, the rules are normally very different. In an industry as cost-intensive and insecure as that of cinema, years can be spent trying to find someone willing to supply the cash to turn on the camera. And when the cash does materialise, it often carries with it strange conditions, like having to give a certain ex-model one of the lead roles, or relocate the entire storyline to Los Angeles. Faced with such challenges, it must be tempting just to lie back on a couch and dream of the perfect film, freed from all the nightmares of real life.

Peter Jackson's second movie is a strange beast in many ways, one of them being that none of the money-people has anaesthetised its nastiness on the way to the screen. *Meet the Feebles* is a story of remarkable creative freedom born paradoxically from limitation; a movie born from crisis, and prepared in a self-created whirlwind. The period encompassing the movie's conception is characterised most by endless changes of gear. The script is thrown together in weeks, but heads towards cinemas at the pace of a very slow turtle; afterwards Jackson finds himself being wined and dined by Hollywood, only to end up in creative limbo again, struggling to get behind a camera on his own terms. But this chapter of Jackson's career is also about the forging of important creative partnerships, some of which will be on hand to help make the kind of cinematic blockbusters that conquer planets.

Meet the Feebles is a twisted melodrama which follows a troupe of theatre types as they rush to ready a variety show for its first-ever live transmission. An innocent young hedgehog arrives to find himself among a group whose insecurities include being unloved, over-sexed and just plain on their last paws. The show's star performer is an angst-ridden hippopotamus. The knife-throwing frog is a drug-addict with a bad case of the shakes. Combine the cast of animals with the real-life team who brought them to the screen, and this chapter ought to come with a censor's warning: there are almost as many walk-on parts as in the first episode of *The Lord of the Rings*. But if you can remember only two names in the pages which follow, remember those of Stephen Sinclair and Fran Walsh. One will later turn Peter Jackson on to zombies and help him tackle Tolkien; the other will become his partner.

FRAN WALSH

Frances Rosemary Walsh was born in Wellington in mid-1959, daughter of Mary Walsh and a painting contractor named Francis. She grew up in Wellington with one older brother and a great many books. Fran's mother was employed to vet children's literature for school courses, and taught her 'everything about loving books and language and literature'.

Fran enjoyed writing as a child, and 'was always praised for it'. She has also said in interviews that her mother was a better academic than a mother. Their relationship has been reported as being a rocky one, and at the age of twelve, Fran left home and moved in with an aunt.

> *I wanted to be a dress designer, but then discovered I couldn't sew. When I was about fourteen I tried to make a pair of trousers and I sewed all the wrong legs together. I just had these shredded floppy things. In the end I could only make ponchos — just a square with a hole in the middle. But they rapidly went out of fashion.*

After leaving school Walsh studied English literature at Victoria University. The degree took her five years to complete, partly because she dropped out from time to time 'to pursue the destruction of my eardrums', playing guitar in two bands. The trashy punk of the Wallsockets still has a small group of devoted fans, but the band were outlasted by Naked Spots Dance, who released a number of records. 'She was all gothy with a big black mop of teased hair, like Siouxsie Sioux [lead singer of English band Siouxsie and the Banshees],' remembers a former Victoria student who knew her during this period. 'She looked fantastic.'

Walsh later said of Naked Spots Dance, 'You didn't have to play in time. People thought we were wonderfully uncoordinated, and it was quite unintentional. It was part of the spirit of the times, really.'

Around the age of twenty-one, Walsh travelled to England and spent time working as a nanny for investigative writer David Yallop (*Beyond Reasonable Doubt*). Though not the most brilliant nanny, she says, she 'very much connected with his job'. On returning to New Zealand the following year, she decided to develop her writing skills on a government work scheme for the unemployed. The Arts Centre on Willis Street was 'a school for people who insisted wilfully on procuring some creative pursuit instead of joining the government bureaucracy. Then I started writing while doing other jobs like being a photographer for a health magazine.'

Walsh's first stint at professional writing came soon after, when producer Grahame McLean enlisted her to do some rewrites for the 1982 television movie *A Woman of Good Character*. More television scriptwork followed, including episodes of McLean's television series *Worzel Gummidge Down Under*.

I feel hugely indebted to Grahame because he employed me at a time when I really needed work experience, but I wasn't experienced enough to be employed. That kind of period for a writer can last a long time. And that was his attitude to all sorts of people in the film industry — to give people who hadn't had many opportunities the chance to improve themselves.

THE SERVANT AND THE SCARECROW

Fran Walsh broke into scriptwriting thanks to a servantwoman, a talking scarecrow, and a producer named Grahame McLean.

Grahame McLean came to producing after working as a production manager during the New Zealand film renaissance in the late 1970s. He would later become, like Peter Jackson, one of the few New Zealanders ever to direct two movies back to back.

In 1982, McLean produced a 50-minute television programme called *A Woman of Good Character*, about a young English servant (brilliantly played by Sarah Pierse) who travels to New Zealand in the 1800s. 'It was a very difficult script, and it wasn't cutting particularly well,' says McLean. Feedback at overseas film markets convinced him that by recutting and adding in some of director David Blyth's old material, he would be able to sell the piece to cable television as a movie. Editor Jamie Selkirk suggested bringing in Fran Walsh, whom McLean had never heard of, to help write the extra material. 'She came back within a day, with an idea of restructuring it. I thought she was just amazing . . . she had an immediate hook on it.'

Two years later McLean produced two series of *Worzel Gummidge Down Under*, with *Doctor Who* star Jon Pertwee playing the fictional talking scarecrow. McLean had arranged New Zealand funding to relocate the popular show to New Zealand.

McLean argues that many films could be made more efficiently by cutting scripts down to size in pre-production, thereby saving the expense of filming scenes that will never be used. In the case of *Worzel*, he enlisted Fran Walsh as go-between with British director James Hill, making sure that Hill shot no more material than necessary on each week's episode. Walsh sometimes rewrote scenes overnight during filming, to bring the script up or down to size. The job, says McLean, demanded skills as both writer and diplomat. When it came time to film the final twelve episodes, McLean dumped the show's English writers, got Walsh to write most of the rest, and took over direction himself (by this point, Hill was having cataract problems). 'Fran just came up with some magic stories, she had a marvellous wit. And she's incredibly talented at fixing things.'

McLean argues that an extra level of energy and enthusiasm can be found through giving people their first crack. 'I'm a bit strange like that. Once I dragged a mechanic out of a local garage and made him a camera grip. Now he's probably the top grip in the country.'

STEPHEN SINCLAIR

During her stint at the Arts Centre, Fran Walsh met a writer named Stephen Sinclair. Soon they were living together as a couple. A child prodigy and something of a dab hand at languages, Sinclair would later help write a series of plays that brought middle-class New Zealanders back to the theatre in droves. Creative multi-tasking ran in the Sinclair family. Sinclair's father Keith, an occasional poet, wrote the bestselling and widely respected *A History of New Zealand*, while younger brother Harry would make music with multimedia duo the *Front Lawn*, and as a movie director.

Sinclair came to Wellington to escape home town Auckland and try to live out the romantic dream of a poet — which in reality meant alternating writing while on the benefit, with stints working as a postie. Increasingly he began to think that the theatre might be the way to connect to a larger audience. In 1986 he wrote *Big Bickies*, a musical satire about a working-class couple who win the lottery (Walsh composed the songs). The play was rejected by an Auckland theatre for political reasons, Sinclair later claimed, amid criticisms that it was 'ideologically unsuitable'. He began to wonder if many of those in the Kiwi theatre world were operating like mind police, 'telling us how to speak, how to behave'.

Sinclair, whose laugh has been compared favourably to a Gatling gun, was about to develop a gift for collaborations, controversy, and popular success. In 1987, he joined playwright Anthony McCarten to write *Ladies Night*, one of the most successful plays in New Zealand history. The story of a bunch of unemployed men who find success as strippers, *Ladies Night* spawned productions across Europe, a successful sequel, and a lawsuit in which Sinclair and McCarten accused the British movie *The Full Monty* of copying their plotline (Sinclair has long refused to comment on the outcome of the case).

Sometime in 1985 or 1986, Wellington film critic and filmmaker Costa Botes popped over with Jackson to show Walsh and Sinclair an early cut of a movie called *Bad Taste*. The pair thought it was great. 'I was impressed by how focused and driven he was,' Sinclair later said of his first meeting with Peter Jackson. 'Film was his life.'

Later, Sinclair rang Jackson and mentioned a story idea he had been playing around with, involving a monster in suburbia. The Sinclair/ Jackson/ Walsh trio quickly set to writing a script in Walsh and Sinclair's apartment above a Chinese restaurant on Wellington's half-bustling, half-flattened Courtenay Place. When cars roared by below their living room, the front windows often joined in in sympathy, making strange rattling noises of their own. The crumbling apartment would later be Mission Control for the writing of *Meet the Feebles,* only not quite yet. The monster script which had brought the group together was called *Braindead,* and that is another chapter entirely.

THE BIRTH OF THE *FEEBLES*

The idea for the *Feebles* was born during Jackson's first film *Bad Taste,* on an evening when Jackson and Cameron Chittock were taking a break from working on the movie's special effects. The original press material for *Feebles* puts it like this: 'One evening over a few beers (and probably suffering the effects of using solvent-based glues all day long) they talked about the idea of making a puppet film — "But one where they're dirty little creatures, taking drugs and all that stuff."' Continues Chittock:

> We talked about how it would be fun to do. It was something that hadn't been done before, I think. Just the idea of very basic, very cartoony characters doing things that if you got real actors to do, you would never get away with it. When it's a puppet or a cartoon character you're one step removed, so it makes it easier to absorb. We thought it would be fun to have puppets being blown to bits and shot. Also, we had the idea of doing a piss-take on the Muppets.

One of the questions motivating Jackson and Chittock was what really happened with Miss Piggy and Kermit once they got into their dressing room and closed the door behind them. Yet Jackson was aware that comparing the *Feebles* to Jim Henson's highly successful *Muppet Show* could be opening a legal can of worms. 'The *Feebles* certainly owe a lot to Jim Henson,' he later said. 'But basically the *Feebles* isn't satirising the *Muppets,* it's satirising humans.'

The idea of mixing puppets or monsters with adult-themed material is such an obvious one, it is surprising how few people had already tried it. In 1976, *Deep Throat* director Gerard Damiano unveiled *Let My Puppets Come,* a forty-five-minute comedy starring a cast of puppets and porn actors who make a porn movie. The movie has never been released in New Zealand, and reviewers generally give the impression that the film is a great idea going nowhere very interesting at all. The 1972 adult fantasy *Flesh Gordon,* a homage to comic-strip science fiction, combines stop-motion-animated monsters with pantomime villains and nudity (the *King Kong*-inspired finale is the only scene worth waiting for).

While working on the script for *Braindead* in Walsh and Sinclair's flat, Jackson remarked to his co-writers that he wished he had another film to work on between writing sessions. Sinclair and Walsh mentioned their own concept of a late-night television series for adults called *Uncle Herman's Bedtime Whoppers*. Why not develop the puppet idea as the first episode? The show would be hosted by 'a cantankerous old bastard named Uncle Herman who tells a late-night fairytale just before bedtime'.

Creaturemeister Cameron Chittock drew up designs for twenty puppets, providing a drawing board for Jackson, Sinclair and Walsh to develop their storyline. 'I would meet with Peter and we'd talk about who the characters would be,' says Chittock. 'He'd just bought a house in Seatoun. We wandered up and down the beach there, and had a great time thinking of these outrageous characters.'

Aside from the escapades of Blerta in the mid-1970s, New Zealand television had little tradition of producing anarchic black comedy, let alone a spoof involving puppet massacres and knife-throwing Vietnam vets. (The antics of no-budget extravaganza *Back of the Y* lay more than a decade in the future.) The pilot episode of *Meet the Feebles* included scenes of a frog lying on a toilet seat, injecting drugs into its pencil-thin arm, and an enormously-breasted hippo clad in little more than a garter belt and a machine-gun. When they saw the completed half-hour script, neither Television New Zealand nor the New Zealand Film Commission were amused enough to offer any cash.

Chittock and the writers decided to finance the pilot themselves. Using volunteer labour and $12,000 of their own money, they began shooting in the top floor of a house on Hawkestone Street, close to Parliament. Jackson and Chittock masterminded most of the creatures and effects, and Jackson's mother helped with the costumes and the catering. At this point movie fan George Port wanders briefly into our story (in later chapters, he will return as the first staff member of Jackson's special-effects company Weta Digital). As *Feebles* began shooting in April 1988, Port was working at Gnome Productions, a Wellington animation studio. He remembers the first time he heard about the idea for *Meet the Feebles*:

> *That was the first day I walked into the set. I heard that morning that Cameron was doing a puppet film and I should go down and have a look at it. When I turned up they handed me an elephant suit and said, 'Here, put this on,' and I, being the obliging sort of chap I was, did. Good thing the boss was away from Gnome that week. There wasn't much on, so I just took a week off and went off to be a puppeteer.*

The scenes which Port wandered into were eye-opening, but they also provided conclusive proof of the inspired visions which hard work, $12,000 and a whole lot of free help can get you. The camera whirred on scenes of a creature with droopy little eyes, snorting a strange white powder through a nose that stretched longer than his face. One behind-the-scenes photo shows the curly-headed Jackson standing next to a makeshift urinal in half an elephant costume, waiting expectantly for the tube of pipe between his legs to burst forth and cover some smaller Feebles with fake urine. (In case any eagle-eyed reader wonders why this writer's name is listed in the credits of the finished movie, Jackson gave me some rolls of film and instructions to get snapping.) There are photos of an exhausted Chittock lying recovering by an alcove window, after rushing to ready yet another puppet for filming. Sid was one of the only Feebles for whom ingenuity failed to hide the lack of budget: the head of this gormless elephant pokes out from under a yellow-and-red striped raincoat, like a tragically underfunded hybrid of kiwi and Dumbo.

Filming on *Feebles* came to an early halt when Jackson travelled to the Cannes Film Festival to unveil *Bad Taste*. It was there that Jim Booth, the Film Commission boss who had first ensured *Bad Taste* funding, saw that Jackson could do with a helping hand. The young filmmaker was trying to interest potential investors in *Braindead*, and Booth offered to come along to meetings as a stand-in producer. Clearly Booth saw something in Jackson. A few months later, Booth suggested that he might be able to help him produce *Braindead*.

By the end of 1988, Booth had left the security of the Film Commission to set up his own company, Midnight Films, and began developing a slate of projects that would later reach as many as ten. Yet none of the films which Jackson and Booth worked on as directing/producing partners would come out under the Midnight Films banner. As Jackson has written, 'I wanted to hang onto my silly *Bad Taste* company name and insisted that *Braindead* be made under the banner WingNut Films.'

Plans to finish *Feebles* had been sidelined by what had always been the main priority, the zombie movie. In October, Jackson and Booth went looking for *Braindead* funding at a film market in Milan. On a whim, Jackson had also bought with him seven minutes of edited highlights from the *Meet the Feebles* footage. It was there that money fell from the sky — or more precisely, from Japan. A Japanese film company offered to invest in Jackson's zombie-fest, and thought *Meet the Feebles* would make a good feature film as well. The company offered $US150,000 as a pre-sale.

Yet *Meet the Feebles* was now less of a priority than ever, as preparations continued to begin filming *Braindead* in early 1989. But six weeks before the scheduled start date, one of the biggest investors pulled out. Booth broke the news to the crew that *Braindead* had been put on hold. Chittock remembers Jackson's reaction.

> That was another thing about Peter that I really respect, and use in my life today — his ability to bounce back from blows which would normally kill a director's career. But he just gets up, gives himself a day to feel sorry for himself, and then gets on with it. When that film ended I just felt terrible for Peter — he'd worked so hard to get this film off the ground. I drove around the next day to his little house on the beach in Seatoun, and knocked on the door. He was in there listening to the Beatles. I said, 'I just came around to see you,' and we were sitting there having a talk. I think he really appreciated me coming. Then there was another knock on the door. It was Jamie Selkirk — his old friend Jamie had come round to see him as well. And we had a beer, and then Jim Booth turned up. Before long there were about twenty people in his tiny lounge, which isn't much bigger than this little shack, full of his friends. All these people that had helped him over the years. Just a magical thing, and that really cheered him up no end. Then we got talking, and said, 'What the hell are we going to do, now that this is over?'
>
> All the materials needed to build a set were in that warehouse, ready for Braindead. I said to Peter, 'Why don't we finish Meet the Feebles *as a short?'* Then Jim Booth said, 'Why don't we do a feature?' The next day Peter rang me up and said, 'Look, I've been talking to Jim and we think, bugger it, let's make a feature film of Meet the Feebles.' I said, 'You're sure you want to do that?'

Before January was over, Jackson was telling the *Evening Post* that *Meet the Feebles* (at around a sixth of *Braindead*'s cost) would start shooting in March, with the zombie film set to follow around August. In anybody's books, the schedule was optimistic indeed. But the announcement also demonstrated that Jackson had already learned one of the major skills of being a movie director: help make the impossible happen, by acting as if it is already organised.

Quite apart from not having the money to make either movie, turning a twenty-four-minute script into a full-length puppet feature was a big ask. Said Jackson:

> We dreamed of the original idea of the *Feebles,* so the idea and the concept appealed to us, but we never would have dreamed of making a feature of it. So the initial reaction was we were dubious about whether we could pull it off. But then we started throwing ideas around. The first thing we did was junk the [original] script. Basically we just convinced ourselves that it would work as a feature. If we truly believed it would be a hopeless thing and a mistake, we

wouldn't have done it.

How opportunistic was it?

It was opportunistic in that somebody gave us an opportunity to make a feature-length puppet movie, but we did have the integrity not to have our names associated with a piece of crap.

In later years, Jackson's descriptions of *Feebles* would vary depending on the interview — on more than one occasion, he said that the film had been made partly because it kept people in work, and filled a gap.

Sensing that fresh blood might prove useful in starting over on the *Feebles* script, the writing trio enlisted Danny Mulheron to help out. The multi-talented Mulheron had played Heidi the hippo in the short version of *Feebles*, and worked closely with Stephen Sinclair while directing a production of Sinclair's *Big Bickies*. Mulheron's late-night cabaret show *Death of a Jazz Critic*, featuring detective Randolph Bebop, his 1.6-metre assistant Bastard the Gnome and some tap-dancing, probably also had a part in winning Mulheron the job on *Feebles*.

FINDING MORE CASH

That year, 1989, marked one of the lowest points for the New Zealand movie industry since the Film Commission first helped kickstart the Kiwi movie renaissance, eleven years before. When *Bad Taste* debuted in Cannes in 1988, it was one of seven new Kiwi features on offer. But the movies at Cannes were like a last splutter before drowning. Tax loopholes had now been nailed firmly shut, and the disastrous stock-market collapse the previous October had hammered another nail in the idea of private investment in local features. Director Geoff Murphy put two American co-stars in *Never Say Die*, his latest road movie, then left to find a new and less creative career in Hollywood. Not for nothing was the only New Zealand film on show in Cannes in 1989 called *Zilch*.

When Judith McCann succeeded Jim Booth as executive director in January 1989, she proposed that the Film Commission provide complete finance to a small number of films in the hopes of getting some movies rolling again. In mid-February the *Meet the Feebles* scriptwriting team joined the queue at the Film Commission's offices. Recalls Danny Mulheron:

We went in and we were greeted by a Maori elder. Stephen, being a wonderful scholar and speaking Maori fluently, responded and did a whole mihi. The protocol thing, I think that disarmed them — these young punk film people, it took the wind out of their sails. I remember Fran taking the high ground and saying, 'Listen, you fund people, not bits of paper. You've got a filmmaker here who's got a real future.' Thumping the table, a very impassioned speech.

Film producer Bridget Ikin (*An Angel at My Table*), then a member of the board which made final funding decisions, recalls a lot of anxiety and discussion about the *Feebles* project. 'They turned up with a whole room full of puppets and basically wooed us with the dazzling magic of these puppets. But there was no script.' Ikin thought the project 'a poor second cousin' to *Braindead*, and felt the Commission's resources should be devoted to supporting the stronger film. 'It seemed to be more a sense of wanting to support Peter through a difficult, frustrating time, when the film he really wanted to make didn't seem to be going ahead.'

Fellow board member John Barnett also felt sceptical about the project. 'I thought there would be potential for adverse legal reaction from Jim Henson. I was also unsure whether the film would attract a distributor, and an audience. But I was wrong.'

In the end the Commission agreed to lend $500,000 to WingNut to make *Feebles*. If the film industry had been in a healthier state, it is hard to imagine that a project lacking a complete script would have been allowed in the Commission's door. 'It was a scam, ' says Mulheron, 'and the best type of scam possible because we got a movie out of it.' He argues that the best thing about bullying the Commission into saying yes was that it gave Jackson the opportunity to continue evolving as a filmmaker, at a vital point in his career. The Film Commission later exercised their right to take their name off the movie's opening credits, while continuing to publicise *Meet the Feebles* in their promotional material.

DEPRAVITY ON A DEADLINE

The most important words to apply to the writing of *Meet the Feebles* are 'rushed' and 'disgusting'. The accelerated birth of the movie provides a good test of whether a certain warped brilliance can sometimes emerge from lunatic circumstances.

After the news about funding came through, producer Jim Booth brainstormed with Jackson. Together they calculated that for the film to be ready by the October 1989 delivery date demanded by the Japanese, the *Feebles* script would have to be ready three weeks before the first day of photography. That gave them only three weeks to write it, which meant churning out six handwritten pages of script a day.

Of course such deadline madness is far from unheard of in the movie industry, and not just on poverty row. A number of big Hollywood movies like *Gladiator* and *Gangs of New York* have gone into production despite agreement by many of those involved that the script still needed a lot more work. But in those cases, there was the knowledge at least that some of the plot problems could be ironed out during the extended process of filming and editing. *Meet the Feebles*, by contrast, had only seven weeks to shoot, and few resources to fix things up afterwards. So why was Jackson pulling the lever to go? Ever the optimist, the director argued that despite the time limitations, there were definite advantages to being financed before a script had been completed.

> *We knew that the cameras were going to be rolling in six weeks no matter what, so we had total and absolute freedom. Normally between what you write there's been about twenty people that have said 'Can you change this?' and 'We don't like that.' That's the kind of stuff that wears you down. It gives you an incredible enthusiasm to know that there are no obstacles between what you write and what's going to get up on the screen. [Feebles] has a spirit and spontaneity that only exists because of the way everyone involved chucked themselves into it. If the film had been made another way, it would be a lesser film. I'm sure of that.*

The aim was to make *Feebles* as disgusting as possible. Says Jackson: 'There was absolutely no reason to make that movie unless we could make a terribly depraved and gross puppet movie. We tried our very hardest to make that.' With the short version of *Feebles* in mind, Jackson was worried that the puppets might quickly lose their novelty onscreen. As a result, the scriptwriters tried to make the movie even blacker, adding in 'sex scenes, violence, drug stuff, rock 'n' roll'. The group devised a cast-iron working rule: if anyone thought of something, but then hesitated because it seemed too disgusting, 'it absolutely had to go in the picture'. Jackson adds: 'We sat around daring each other to let our imaginations go.'

For Sinclair and Mulheron, the *Feebles* scriptwriting sessions provided a welcome opportunity to indulge in bad taste, after recent experiences in the theatre world. Mulheron had been involved in a production which the theatre cancelled after unsubstantiated accusations of rape against the playwright, Mervyn Thompson, and an incident where he was chained to a tree by a group of vigilantes. 'That was a turning point for me, because it was a preposterous situation,' says Mulheron.

Sinclair was still bitter about the initial rejection of his play *Big Bickies*, supposedly for being ideologically unsuitable. 'I very acutely felt the liberal censorship that was prevalent at the time,' Sinclair later said. 'So it [*Feebles*] was a great . . . purge, shall we say.' Liberal notions of political correctness would come under further attack in the farce which Sinclair and Mulheron completed soon after *Feebles*, the highly successful *Sex Fiend*.

Realising that even a bad-taste comedy sometimes needs its limits, the writers decided to introduce two new characters, in an effort to retain some sympathy from the audience: the shy but likeable hedgehog Robert, and the apple of his eye, a chorus seal named Lucille.

For Jackson the film's final atrocity — the hippo star killing many of the *Feebles* cast — remained a key one. As Fran Walsh put it:

> It really shaped the story. The compelling idea that attracted Peter in the first place was blowing away a whole lot of Muppet-like characters. It was how we got there that created all these problems. He really wanted to get his hands on that huge gun — Arnie wields it in Commando.

Cameron Chittock, aware of the opportunity but initially a little dubious about the restrictions of a low budget, found himself agreeing to handle design and construction for a puppet cast that seemed to grow in number with every passing week. Soundtrack duties for this musical that lacked only time and money were taken by keyboardist Peter Dasent, kickstarting a composer-director relationship that would continue through at least three movies. Dasent won the job on the suggestion of Fane Flaws, his old bandmate in The Crocodiles, partly because he could write both music and lyrics. Dasent would also provide the musical backing for Danny Mulheron's climactic ode to 'Sodomy', sung by actor Stuart Devenie. The song had originally come to Mulheron while motorcycling towards Ngauranga Gorge, inspired partly by a memory of how New Zealand had 'a fixation with anal-sex videos'.

The voices of the *Feebles* were recorded in three days before filming began, then played back on-set for the puppeteers to mime to. A team of seven versatile actors provided voices for all the parts. Wynyard the frog, the fly journalist and the Peter Lorre-ish tones of Trevor the Rat, for example, all came from one man, Brian Sargent.

The legislation establishing the NZFC refers to the necessity of taking community standards into account in its funding decisions. When the Commission saw the completed *Feebles* script, there were concerns about the subplot involving Trevor the Rat and his porno movies. But after some long discussions, *Feebles* went ahead.

FILMING THE *FEEBLES*

You are approaching a metal roller door, on which the words 'Brain Dead' have been painted next to a long red arrow. Only *Braindead* is no longer. You follow the arrow inside. From a room on the second floor, the *Feebles* puppetmaking headquarters overlooks a cavernous, window-cracked railway shed. Down below, within a temporary enclosure of studio walls, the backstage puppet universe of the *Feebles* inhabits makeshift corridors and dimly-lit rooms. Peeling posters and hanging stage-ropes jostle with all the lights and paraphernalia that go into moviemaking. The sounds of hammering and orbital sanders fill the air.

Along a nearby corridor, past the elegant office of Bletch the walrus, walls, floor and ceiling come to an abrupt end in an explosion of maple-syrup blood. The blood is long dry; other massacres are now afoot. Dorothy the sheep has been waiting to die since 10.15am. And Dorothy is not alone. The entire movie is now weeks behind schedule. But the *Feebles* film crew have other worries. The smoke needs to be right. The ear-deafening M-60 machine-gun is loaded with blanks. From Dorothy's position on the stairs by the lift shaft, her explosive blood-bags must be rigged to bleed on cue. Puppeteer Eleanor Aitken half-kneels under the stairs as preparations continue.

Dorothy's murderer is sitting nearby, rocking gently left and right inside a massive, upright hippopotamus body. Aside from her insecurities, everything about Heidi the hippo is big, from her dress size to her bulging hippo-human paws. But the sight takes its last step into the surreal by the way actor Danny Mulheron's undersized head pokes out of the hippo's neck.

By 11.05 Peter Jackson is ready to shoot the scene. But when the camera rolls, there is not enough blood — only one blood-bag bursts. On the second take, the sheep's eyes are staring off in completely the wrong direction. As Dorothy is syringed full of blood again, the hippo inhabited by Danny Mulheron leans against a pillow, eyes closed, apparently dead to the world. But with a yell of 'Everyone in position' from Chris 'Shorty' Short, the perpetually loud and good-humoured first assistant director, the hippo lumbers over to take up the gun again. Afterwards Dorothy the sheep is bloodied up for her final death-roll down the stairs. A crew member picks up the crimson-splattered puppet and asks, 'Can you take that out to Doctor Cameron please?'

Ask for memories about working on *Meet the Feebles*, and the response from crew members runs the gamut. Peter Jackson, a man whose positive attitude rarely goes missing in action, has been quoted as saying the film was 'hell to make — a nightmare on earth'. Costume designer Glenis Foster talks of crew members being pushed 'to the absolute limit'. First-time puppeteer Justine Wright is one of a number who thought *Feebles* great fun. For supervising puppeteer Jonathon Acorn it was 'a gig from hell'.

On the good days, stress and laughter went hand in hand. Says Foster, who operated for much of the shoot as a one-woman clothesmaking department:

What amazed me continuously is that the script kept us laughing. It was so surreal, so ridiculous that you could pull out a piece of script and go, 'Oh God, we're doing this today' and laugh — it was still funny. It was also painstakingly hard work. It would take a day to get the bloody hedgehog to walk from one end of the hallway to the other. Long hours of hard slog and all the rest of it. But somehow we had a sense of the absurd that carried us through.

A railway track ran the length of the disused freight shed which was home to the *Feebles* shoot. Many of the sets straddled the track to create more space for the puppeteers to work. Recalls George Port:

The cold was one of the worst things. The doors didn't close properly so the wind would just whistle on down through the grooves in the tracks, where most of the puppeteering would be done. But unfortunately, because it was such a fast build time, they built it all as just one big floor and you couldn't move any of the walls. So basically whenever we wanted to have the puppet go from one place to another, usually there were 150 boards that had to be chainsawed out to have a hole that we could move through. There were times we were under the set scrabbling around in this old shed among the rats and the fleas, bending ourselves around the woodwork.

Jackson and producer Jim Booth hoped to pull off a production of immense complexity on a shoestring budget. As Jackson remarked at the time, 'Every single shot in the movie is a special effect.' A scene of a puppet walking across a room and picking up a cup of tea might easily require five different set-ups, each using different methods or trickery to pull off the illusion of life. 'We had this incredible job of making a naturalistic drama using non-humans,' explains Jackson. 'I had to use lots of shots and camera movements to cover it up. It's something that gives the movie a rhythm and a tempo which goes towards giving it a little life, where no life exists.'

Jackson decided the only way he could be sure that each shot had pulled off the illusion of reality was by operating the camera himself, and thereby seeing the results directly. *Feebles* director of photography Murray Milne was usually close by, either adjusting lights or training a second camera on the scene. The situation where a director operates his own camera has traditionally been rare in mainstream moviemaking, partly because of the unionised nature of the film industry, and also because the technicalities of getting a shot can distract directors from the subtleties of an actor's performance.

The shooting schedule quickly began to look wildly optimistic. By the end of the first ten days of shooting, *Meet the Feebles* was already at least five days behind schedule. Said Jackson later:

Within about two weeks we'd established a method which gave us decent screen value, and we never varied from the rhythm we'd got. We thought of a hundred and one ways to save time, and none of them ever worked. I drew the line when I knew it would reflect on the quality of the script.

In the puppetmaking headquarters, above the *Feebles* movie set, Chittock and his small team stood in a sea of foam rubber off-cuts, trying to ensure that ninety-six of his character designs were ready when required, from fist-sized guppies through to the eight-foot-high Bletch the walrus. Instead of the traditional method of pouring latex into moulds, Chittock saved time by cutting characters directly from foam rubber. Robert the hedgehog, one of the smaller *Feebles* stars, required up to five puppeteers. Jackson later received a call from two Los Angeles viewers who complimented him on the special effects used to levitate the film's muckraking fly: '"We were just assuming it was some really nice blue-screen work and motion control." Replied Jackson: "No, we just dragged it on the end of a piece of string."'

Costume designer Glenis Foster made most of the costumes herself, producing three-piece suits for an eight-foot walrus, full army fatigues for a platoon of frogs, and about eighty more besides. Fresh off the satirical puppet series *Public Eye*, partners Richard Taylor and Tania Rodger helped Chittock on the puppetmaking, and each evening Rodger tried to give the puppets some medical attention after a day of indignities and bad treatment on set. Taylor built a number of models for the film's climactic wharfside sequence, where Bletch's car drives inside a giant whale. Taylor later said that the fleas in the railways shed were so bad that a number of crew members wore rubbish bags on their legs and high-strength dog flea-spray in their hair. Long hours with chemicals and glues did not help the working environment, and there were running jokes about grabbing some glue sniffers off the street if more staff were needed.

Chittock had studied puppetmaking in Christchurch before helping out with the effects on *Bad Taste,* and a number of the department heads had experience in commercials and television. But from top to bottom, *Meet the Feebles* marked the first experience of taking on a feature-length movie for many. Production designer Mike Kane estimates that seventy percent of the crew had never been on a film set: 'It was like a film school.'

The puppeteering department was one of the most inexperienced. Veteran puppeteer Jonathon Acorn was charged with finding and training up a crew. But compromises wrought by the movie's low budget meant that tensions quickly arose when the shoot began. The film's finances did not stretch to building multiple puppets of each character. As a result, Acorn had to spend much of his time converting glove puppets to marionettes, by quickly adding or taking the strings off when they were needed for specific shots. Acorn also found himself having to fight to get the television monitors with which puppeteers normally monitor their performances.

Acorn admired Jackson's 'imaginative approach to directing, and his eye for detail', but admits that the two did not get on. 'I don't think he liked me — he'd get Shorty [assistant director Chris Short] to do the talking. In the end it was one of those situations where communication was not the easiest. I can't remember him ever saying thank you. However, the job did get done.' Later, when *Feebles* went weeks over schedule and Acorn was offered a big television project in Auckland, he left early. 'They got rid of quite a few people. It suited me just fine.'

George Port acted inside the ungainly suit of Bletch, the cigar-smoking *Feebles* producer with a sideline in porno movies and drug deals. Port recalls that in one vital scene he did such a bad job of trying to make the walrus look seductive, that he came close to being fired. Puppeteer Justine Wright meanwhile began a close working relationship with Port's armpit, as she concentrated on waggling Bletch's flippers. Wright's credentials for working on *Feebles* included a childhood of making puppets. Now she found herself crammed under a table, puppeteering the cat in perhaps cinema's only cat–walrus sex scene. 'I'd been accepted for journalism school,' remembers Wright. 'But Danny Mulheron was saying, "Why do you want to be a muckraker in the gutter press?" And I was thinking, Why indeed? This is much more fun.'

Wright is one of a number of crew members who recall Mulheron as 'a real motivator', despite his copious swearing. Acorn laughingly admits that the actor's intervention on one especially trying day probably helped prevent a fistfight.

Mulheron's enthusiasm turned to fear during a scene where Heidi the hippo had to sit on a swing, above the set. Cables ran from Heidi's head to the waist of a puppet operator below to control the character's mouth movements. But the operator was not aware that Heidi was about to be pulled up above the ground — as Mulheron rose higher and higher, the operator was pulled into the air by his waist, dragging Mulheron's head further back under the tightening pressure from the cable.

> No one knew what was going on. I was trying to scream, but when you're surrounded by fifteen tonnes of foam . . . I was carrying a man's weight on my neck. The only person who saw the puppeteer dangling by his hips was Peter. He leaped onto the stage and basically picked this guy up so the cables would loosen.

Mulheron was also charged with massacring most of the cast in the scenes where Heidi, driven to despair by her deteriorating relationship with Bletch, goes mad with a machine-gun. Says Port:

> *The machine-gun was a real M-60 firing blanks, and if you know anything about blanks, there is metal coming out of the barrel. We didn't quite take it seriously until one of the scenes where Heidi came through. She machine-gunned through some building paper, and it literally ripped the paper in half. From that time on we were a little more cautious. This fine dust of metal particles would come out, probably not enough to kill, but definitely enough to impact into you.*

Decent food is one of the things which stops badly-paid film crews from leaving for a better job. The *Feebles* shoot saw a number of cooks come and go. One knew only about vegetables, another spoke exclusively in the language of mince. Mike Kane remembers that one of the worst offenders on the catering front made a habit of dropping off the food, then disappearing again. 'One day I locked the doors so he couldn't escape. When he couldn't get out, he instantly worked out there was a problem. I wanted to make sure that people got an opportunity to actually question him, and abuse him about the food.'

DARKNESS FALLING

As the weeks wore on, and winter tightened its grip, *Meet the Feebles* rolled slowly past its scheduled finish date. Glenis Foster found her telephone calls being interrupted by the echo of machine-gun fire down on the set. She remembers Mike Kane lighting a piece of corrugated iron next to his desk in an effort to keep warm. By the time the budgeted-for seven weeks had become nine, the Film Commission was applying increasing pressure for Jackson to finish.

'It was hard when it got to that stage,' says Foster. 'Are we coming to work next week? We just couldn't commit to anything, and they wanted us to be available. It didn't have a natural conclusion, it just drifted on and on.'

Jackson has argued that there was a danger of him being sacked. 'I refused to speed up the film and they threatened to sack me. Eventually what we did is after eleven weeks when it looked like they were absolutely going to sack me from the film, I said, "Okay, we've finished filming now, we'll just cut the film."'

It is questionable whether the Commission would have been in a position to fire Jackson, considering at this point they had provided only a loan to get the film off the ground. They were also well aware that sales interest in the film was linked to Jackson's name and previous success.

The wharf sequences, some scenes with Bletch on the golf course, and half of the Vietnam war parody all remained to be shot. Chittock and the four writers pooled most of their earnings and financed a final, secret week of filming themselves. One day, Jackson met with the Film Commission to discuss how the shoot had gone, before sneaking back to the golf course to carry on shooting. For half of that week he would spend the day editing, then go down to the set and film until five in the morning. The secret footage was sent to the lab under the name *Frogs of War*, 'so it wouldn't look like we were still working on the same film'.

Jackson argued that the sequences were vital in helping 'aerate the film' from its studio setting, and talked at length about his desire to 'maintain the integrity of the script'.

> *This film is going to be seen all over the world. An audience in New York or London is not going to care a darn whether we had to stop shooting five days ahead — they're not going to know. The Film Commission were entirely within their rights; I understand why they did it. They got to the stage where they thought there'd be no end.*

Asked whether the rushed circumstances of writing *Feebles* had felt especially horrific at the time, Fran Walsh says:

> *I think what was more horrific was seeing the footage — seeing where we'd gone wrong, and having very limited options in how to fix things. That was difficult. It's always hard to look at a script which you know you could have made a better job of, and all you can see are the flaws. I feel that a bit with* Meet the Feebles. *The puppetmakers, the puppet-operators, the director — everyone did a great job, you know, and it was really unfortunate that the script wasn't developed to the degree where we could completely pull it off.*

SHAKING HANDS IN AMERICA

In the year between the completion of *Meet the Feebles* and its New Zealand release in September 1990, doors began to open for Peter Jackson in Hollywood. During this period he found an agent and a lawyer to represent him in the United States, turned down at least two offers to work there, and soon after co-wrote his first script for an American studio.

During the making of *Feebles*, there had been a desire not to allow any of the movie's characters to resemble the *Muppets* too closely. Said Jackson: 'We used to joke around the set, "Wait until Disney see it," because they apparently sue at the drop of a hat.' (Others joke that *Muppet*master Jim Henson passed away in 1990 from the shock of seeing *Meet the Feebles*.) Now Jackson found himself strolling Walt Disney Studios' corridors with *Meet the Feebles* as his calling card — and instead of suing him, the company was enthusiastically playing sections of this most offensive of movies to senior executives, and asking him about a possible directing job (one of the movie projects discussed in this period involved dinosaurs, but little else is known). As for adverse feedback from the makers of the *Muppets*, the most Jackson heard was that Henson's daughter Lisa had seen *Feebles*, and had been 'a bit aghast' by seeing a little frog on a cross, who looked suspiciously like Kermit.

That year *Feebles* co-writer Danny Mulheron travelled to Los Angeles with Jackson. Mulheron recalls going to a preview screening of *Feebles* in which many in the audience walked out halfway through, while others accused him and Jackson of having 'the morals of alley cats'. But there was life in puppets yet. That year Jackson was approached about working on *Only Puppets Bleed*, a proposed puppet show for the Fox TV network. When Jackson decided he didn't want to get involved, Mulheron came on board as co-writer (the show never secured finance to go ahead).

Mulheron's memories of his experiences in Hollywood are not all complimentary. He remembers a world where one movie executive wilfully humiliated his lawyer by making him sit on a box at meetings, and where potential agents would rave about another agent, then minutes later call the same person an asshole, depending on what seemed best to say at the time. One prospective agent kept mistaking Jackson and Mulheron for Australians.

Not every meeting was as bad. Early on, the two New Zealanders lunched with a likeable young studio executive named Mark Ordesky, who read scripts for independent film company New Line. New Line had found a key to regular profits in the shape of the *Nightmare on Elm Street* series, starring the dream-invading killer Freddy Krueger. Enthused by Jackson's movie work, Ordesky put them up for a few days in his apartment. 'Mark Ordesky really fought for Peter,' recalls Mulheron. 'He saw something in him, and committed us to write the *Freddy* film.'

As a result, Jackson and Mulheron managed a short meeting in a corridor with longtime New Line boss Robert Shaye — one of those meetings, recalls Mulheron, consisting largely of comments like 'Nice to meet you' and 'Maybe we'll work together one day'. In the short term, the association between New Line and Peter Jackson went nowhere fast. Jackson and Mulheron's *Elm Street* script, in which Freddy's own traumas go under the microscope, was paid for but never used. Yet years later, Shaye would act on the same kind of instincts that had led him to *Elm Street* when no one else was interested, by signing the director of a raft of tasteless New Zealand splatter movies to helm one of the largest movie gambles in history.

For now, though, Jackson was just trying to find a way to get his next movie off the ground. Alongside the zombie epic *Braindead*, Mulheron and Jackson hoped to win Hollywood interest in their own fantasy script, *Blubberhead*, set in a *Lord of the Rings*-style universe of giants, dwarves and castles. Jackson often described the film as *Indiana Jones* mixed with Monty Python. In October 1990, shortly before the Wellington opening of *Feebles*, Jackson told the *Dominion* that he had won 'interest' from New Line in the script. He hoped to shoot in New Zealand, creating a big-budget fantasy for $10–$15 million, a fraction of normal blockbuster prices.

When I interviewed Jackson a few weeks later, he sounded increasingly frustrated by the gap between his own movie ideas and the ones Hollywood wanted to finance. The director was clearly growing tired of commands by financiers to adapt characters and storylines to an American setting. 'If you're expecting them to pay that amount of money, they're going to want everything done their way, which is not the way I want to do it,' he said. 'This last trip I started to set up the situation where I can get finance to stay in New Zealand, to make films here. If I do leave, it will be out of financial need — I'm not making any money, and I've got a mortgage to pay. I'll see how it goes. I'm doing my best.'

Amid the pressures of finding finance, there were still moments of laughter. In late 1990, Jackson, Mulheron and Heidi the hippo were shouted an all-expenses-paid trip to a fantasy-film festival in Japan. The audience responded enthusiastically to *Feebles,* clapping, according to Mulheron, each time 'terrible things happened'. Mulheron was introduced to *Halloween* and *Cul-De-Sac* star Donald Pleasence backstage. 'He was looking at me, and I was looking at him, and I'm in a fucking hippo suit . . . it was like *Cul-De-Sac*. He said to me, "Bet it's hot in there." I said, "Mmmmm."'

While in Japan, Mulheron was keen to check out some of the local sex shows. 'Peter was more interested in collectables from McDonald's. His interests are really strange. He would go into all the toy shops and model shops. He's like a ten-year-old like that, and it takes a big ten-year-old to make movies really.'

Jackson's travels also allowed treasured opportunities to meet some of his childhood special-effects heroes. In 1990, *Bad Taste* team-members Craig Smith and Ken Hammon joined Jackson at a film festival in Hamburg, where Ray Harryhausen and Jackson were both guests of honour. Craig Smith's recollection is that the meeting did not go as well as it might have. Over dinner, Smith says, Harryhausen began talking about an awful, terrible festival movie he had just been shown a little of, in which someone got their head blown off. Realising that Harryhausen had probably seen a section of *Bad Taste*, Jackson tried to explain that such horror movies were one of the only ways that young filmmakers could break into the film industry. (Hammon cannot remember this conversation, but says he was not at the table for the entire meal.)

Jackson also met special-effects man Jim Danforth, this time in California, concerning a proposed dinosaur project. Danforth, whose résumé included the 1970s pictures *When Dinosaurs Ruled the Earth* and *Flesh Gordon*, had become one of Ray Harryhausen's main successors in the world of stop-motion effects. The day after meeting him, Jackson received a phone call. Mulheron, under the impression that he was talking to producer Jim Booth, grabbed the phone off him and let loose a stream of invective, joking that he was swanning around Hollywood while Booth was stuck back in New Zealand, shagging sheep. He also told the producer to save the fake American accent for another day. But eventually Mulheron realised that the caller wasn't putting on an accent at all: his name was Jim *Danforth*. After the phone was safely on its hook again, Jackson and Mulheron started laughing, and found it hard to stop.

PARTING WAYS

For the four writers who had rushed to complete the script for *Meet the Feebles*, the year following the end of filming would see the creative and the personal intermingle in complex ways. Sinclair, Walsh, Jackson and Mulheron were working in different combinations on at least five different scripts for stage and screen. With *Feebles* out of the way, Sinclair joined Mulheron to finish drafting the play *The Sex Fiend*, sending up political correctness. It opened to enthusiastic audiences in Wellington in October 1989, the same month that Jackson flew to Italy with the completed print of *Meet the Feebles*.

Mulheron and Jackson had formed a writing team of their own, as they worked on the *Nightmare on Elm Street* script and their own fantasy *Blubberhead*. The original group of Jackson, Sinclair and Fran Walsh also met occasionally to continue the project that had first brought them together, the zombie movie *Braindead*.

Despite the productivity, post-*Feebles* tension lay in the air. Mulheron feels that before his arrival to help out on the *Feebles* script, the trio of Fran Walsh, Stephen Sinclair and Peter Jackson had formed a very secure and effective creative unit.

> I think I came along and kind of unbalanced it. I unbalanced Stephen and Fran's relationship with Peter, because I suddenly became Peter's new scriptwriting partner. I think Peter really wanted to work with Fran, but that was not available to him at that point in his life.

According to Mulheron's account, such tensions may have been exacerbated by Sinclair and Walsh's reaction to the finished version of

Meet the Feebles, and the fact that once filming began, they were the only writers of the group not required on set. 'I don't think they were impressed,' says Mulheron, recalling the first screening. 'I remember shaking Peter's hand and being very congratulatory, and them being rather quiet.' After *Feebles,* Mulheron, then friendly to both groups, was working with Jackson on projects which the director wanted to write separately from Walsh and Sinclair. As a result, Mulheron found himself at times acting as a middleman between the two sides, not wanting to betray any confidences, a situation he felt uncomfortable about.

Things came to a head in May 1990. Mulheron was in Christchurch, starring in a production of *The Sex Fiend,* and the actors had just gone on strike. In many regards Mulheron's life, he admits, was a mess.

> *I heard some comments made about my personal life, and I jumped to the conclusion that Fran was the source of them. I told her to piss off in the dumbest possible way. Like anything that destructive, it's really about destroying yourself. I was going through a very stressful time, and I took it out on Fran. My life was littered with casualties of my stupid outbursts at the wrong time, but that was one of the worst.*

As a result of the bad feeling that resulted from Mulheron's actions, Sinclair and Walsh were no longer talking to him. The lack of communication with Sinclair did not help when it came to discussing future productions of the much-in-demand *Sex Fiend.* Yet over coming months, Mulheron and Jackson continued to work and travel together with *Blubberhead* and their *Elm Street* script.

Thanks to the fallout in the group, the movie that had first brought the Sinclair/Walsh/Jackson writing trio together would now help to reunite them. This was the long-delayed *Braindead,* in which Danny Mulheron was meant to be playing the lead role of Lionel. Jackson now had an actor who was unpopular with two-thirds of the writing team. Says Mulheron:

> *We'd have these phone calls where he'd want me to pull out, and I'd say, 'No, why should I? So what if they don't want me in it — do you?' He never said he didn't want me in it. He said, 'Well they don't want you in it.' Peter was in an utterly invidious position. I eventually bowed to the inevitable and resigned.*

There was also another tension, arguably the most important one of all.

> *When we were writing together, Peter revealed his feelings for Fran to me. I remember looking out over Seatoun ... It was the only time I've ever seen him emotional. Peter and Fran were destined to be together. I lost touch after that.*

But essentially Steve and Fran split, and eventually Fran and Peter hooked up.

Jackson was in a relationship with a woman from Australia during the making of *Braindead*. He and Fran Walsh finally became a permanent couple sometime in 1992 or early 1993.

CONTROVERSY AND BOX OFFICE

According to an article written by Jackson's friend Costa Botes, Jackson was nervous about how the film's Japanese investors might react to *Feebles* war scenes in which slant-eyed Vietcong mongooses spout Communist dogma and generally act somewhat rudely. 'The screening went well, and everyone seemed happy,' wrote Botes. 'So Peter asked the investors what their favourite sequence was. To a man, the Japanese reached up, pulled their eyes into slits, and made chattering noises like the Mongooses!'

'The Japanese like anything with fantasy and imagination,' Jackson later told the *Melbourne Herald*. 'I think they need it as a release from their repressed, conformist existence.'

In July 1990 came one of the first public signs that Jackson's belief in his own talents was keeping pace with his fame. The cause: Bill Gosden had failed to include *Meet the Feebles* in New Zealand's yearly film festival programme, which began each year in Wellington and Auckland. On hearing the news, Jackson called Gosden's decision 'very mean-spirited', and later accused the festival of being more 'a Bill Gosden film festival than a Wellington Film Festival'. In more than one interview he expressed surprise that the only Wellington film made that year had not been included in the Wellington festival — an argument not dissimilar to saying that *Ghostbusters* or *Death Wish* should have won a place in the New York Film Festival merely because they had been made in New York. Gosden replied:

This is by no means the first New Zealand film I have declined to screen in the festival, but Peter Jackson is the first filmmaker to publicise such a rejection. If I am to be drawn into debating my decision I have no choice but to denigrate the film in detail, and at length, which I have no desire to do.

Feebles was not exactly new to controversy. The previous year the film had won more headlines when Motion Picture Distributors Association vice-president Timothy Ord commented that *Meet the Feebles* bordered on soft-core porn. Jim Booth must have been rubbing his hands in glee. 'I think it's funny to even think about it in those terms,' he said. 'It's a parody, and people are not getting the joke.' It is doubtful that Peter Jackson was very annoyed either:

If people come out of this film dazed and shell-shocked, that's great — I've got people to take puppets seriously, which I think is a big joke. However people feel about it, they're going to come out of it having seen a film like no film ever made before. I might possibly not make another film in my life that's as original.

Meet the Feebles failed to prove that controversies, even small ones, are always good for business. Two weeks after finally kicking off in Auckland, the movie opened in its home town at the Embassy Theatre (ironically the film festival's Wellington home). Though Wellington's first late-night Friday screening won a large audience, things went downhill from there. *Feebles* would go on to play in seventeen locations, but the final New Zealand box-office gross came to a disappointing $80,000. Scott Blanks of exhibitors Pacer Kerridge, put things in a nutshell: 'In years to come it will become one of those cult Kiwi films . . . whereas I don't think it did quite as well as *Bad Taste*, which caught everyone by surprise.'

Local film critics showed considerably less sympathy for *Meet the Feebles* than they had for Jackson's cinematic debut. While many praised the inventiveness of the puppet characters, the words which emerged most often in reviews were overkill and excess. *Listener* writer Chris Hegan, who had named *Bad Taste* one of his ten best films of 1988, expressed enthusiasm for Cameron Chittock's puppets, Peter Dasent's score and the ambitious camerawork. 'Once you get over marvelling at the imagination and the craft,' he continued, 'you start looking for a plot, but there is none. Just one episode after another, while the jokes wear thinner and the gross excesses grow humdrum through repetition.'

Meanwhile *Dominion* film critic Costa Botes wrote that despite an overly episodic structure, *Feebles* was 'a triumph of ingenuity and commitment over extreme adversity'.

Jackson's comments on early reaction to *Feebles* by New Zealand distributors are worth repeating here:

They say it's going to be very difficult to find a market for the film. One of them threw his arms up in despair and said you've got wonderful puppets, and the production values are great, and if we'd used any other script we would have had a huge success, a family movie. These people are all market-driven, and they can't see anything that is nothing to do with money. This is something which is completely off the wall.

Though *Feebles* finally sold to more than 30 countries, in many cases it went straight to video. There were high moments, like a packed midnight screening at the Toronto Film Festival of Festivals, and a special prize for the most distinctive unreleased film of 1990 from a group of French film critics. None of it was enough, though, to turn *Feebles* into a money-spinner.

In the US, the company that had bought rights to *Meet the Feebles* went bankrupt after the movie had played only in a small number of North American film festivals. For the next two years, Stateside rights to *Meet the Feebles* were trapped in legal no-man's-land. In 1992, David Whitten entered the ring. His company Greycat Releasing had won controversy with *Henry: Portrait of a Serial Killer*. In 1995, Greycat finally arranged a limited American release for *Feebles* and *Bad Taste*, on the back of Jackson's fourth feature *Heavenly Creatures*. At this point a critic from the *New York Post* did no good for the reputation of either Jackson or her newspaper, by declaring that *Meet the Feebles* was 'a must for anyone who admired' *Heavenly Creatures*. Critic Janet Maslin meanwhile predicted that *Feebles* would become 'an unfortunate footnote for Mr Jackson's career'.

The 'she'll be right' attitude which Peter Jackson had brought to bear in making *Meet the Feebles* helps to explain the movie's immense achievements and also its considerable flaws. *Feebles* joins Jim Henson's fantasy *The Dark Crystal* as one of only a handful of live-action movies in cinematic history to be populated entirely by non-humans; and *Feebles* is the only such film to merit a restricted rating (*Let My Puppets Come* and *Flesh Gordon* are both out of contention here, due to the many naked humans in their casts). That *Feebles* was made for less than New Zealand $1.5 million, so far from the world's traditional centres of puppetry, makes its achievement all the more eye-opening.

Computers have now opened up a new age of creature magic, which perversely only helps make *Feebles* more unique. These days the wires that hold up puppets can be digitally painted out, or an entirely new creature drawn in. But the animal cast of *Meet the Feebles* came to the screen the old-fashioned way. When producer Jim Booth argued that there had 'probably been no other film like it in the world', he spoke the truth.

The downside of Jackson's 'she'll be right' attitude was a script that was never given the chance to match the inventiveness of the creatures themselves. Aware of the tight deadline to meet the demands of his investors in Japan, Jackson cleverly harnessed this sense of urgency to help turn a difficult, far from ready project into a 'go' movie. But for all the freedoms gained along the way, he appears to have been temporarily blinded to the fact that writing a script in twenty days inevitably causes at least as many problems as it solves. Possibly he thought that lightning could strike twice. His first movie had managed to find success without having any script at all — the improvised, wandering tone of the narrative had actually worked in *Bad Taste*'s favour. By comparison, for many viewers *Feebles* achieves its originality at the expense of enjoyment. After about an hour of these amazingly disgusting creatures, admiration is replaced by gross fatigue.

Asked two years after its New Zealand release how she looked back on *Feebles*, Fran Walsh said that, worried that the puppets wouldn't engage the audience, the writers had gone overboard on satirical situations at the expense of character development: 'That was a mistake, but it wasn't one that we really could have known before we started, because we hadn't seen any other puppet films.' Walsh felt also that some segments of the audience were repelled by the very elements that attracted others: many splatter fans were annoyed by the love story, while viewers who enjoyed 'the novelty of the puppets, and the cute storylines' felt confronted by what they considered obscenities — a theory given credence by the *Village Voice* reviewer who compared *Feebles* to the feeling you might get from 'downing alternating glasses of Manischevitz and Zima'. Said Walsh:

> *I feel it's a really brave film in that it's bold and uncompromising. It wasn't at all geared to the market. But I think with a film of that type it probably should have been. It really was new territory for everybody. Nobody knew what kind of effect ninety minutes of puppets would have on somebody's brain. Right up until the editing stage, we didn't realise just how choppy the storyline was.*

If the *Feebles* have indeed found heaven after their unfortunate onscreen massacre, then that heaven is probably across the ocean in Australia. The movie critics there who found *Feebles* 'brilliant', 'extraordinarily funny', and 'enchantingly gross' were not alone — the movie has continued to rent to a devoted group of fans.

Peter Jackson has often talked in interviews about the movie's humour being for 'the naughty child at heart'. When pressed, he once said he felt *Feebles* was safe for children over the age of twelve. Australian censors gave *Meet the Feebles* only a recommended M15+ rating, allowing all ages to watch it, making this possibly the only occasion where Jackson appears to have desired a harsher censorship rating than the one actually imposed.

Even before his puppet movie had hit cinemas down under, Peter Jackson sounded as if he had put the whole *Meet the Feebles* experience behind him.

> Feebles *is virtually history now. It's nice for people to enjoy a film you've made, but in a way it's almost the least important thing for me. You don't stop caring about it. I'm proud of it now, and will be in ten years' time. Whether it's successful or not won't alter the fact. You've learned an awful lot, and you're eagerly looking forward to applying it to something else. It's a strange business, because you do spend a very long and intensive time doing one thing. Then you apply yourself to a very different idea.*

DANNY MULHERON

Was almost arrested in late 1989 for advertising half-price sex over a megaphone, during Wellington street promotions for the play *The Sex Fiend*. Mulheron and Stephen Sinclair's farce about proper behaviour proved so popular that it transferred to the State Opera House. Since then Mulheron has appeared in the sketch show *Away Laughing* as the politically correct Phineas O'Doodle, directed episodes of the hit television series *The Strip*, and the acclaimed Tom Scott play *The Daylight Atheist*. In October 2003 he worked with Stephen Sinclair on a production of Sinclair's new play *The Bach*.

HEIDI THE HIPPO

Was nominated for best female performance at New Zealand's 1990 Film and Television Awards, even though her quickstep and voice had supposedly been the work of two male actors. After Heidi was beaten to the award by *Angel at My Table* actor Kerry Fox, she exited the country for Europe, disguised as a checkout operator. There her work in *Feebles* was finally recognised, with a best female performance award at Rome's Fanta Film Festival. Heidi was last seen entertaining tourists at Disneyland in Paris.

JUSTINE WRIGHT

Followed her stint as a puppeteer on *Feebles*, and journalism training in Wellington, by joining the *Levin Chronicle* newspaper. There she wrote stories about beached whales and escaped frogs before escaping herself to become a guinea pig on her father's African safari-tour operation. Arriving in London in 1990, Wright managed to talk herself into a receptionist's job at an editing company run by Kathy O'Shea, daughter of New Zealand film legend John O'Shea. Since becoming an editor she has worked on dozens of commercials and a number of features. In 1999 she edited the film *One Day in September*, about the Munich hostage crisis, which later won the Academy Award for best documentary.

CHAPTER FIVE

BEATING THE CURSE OF THE ZOMBIES: *BRAINDEAD*

'We really liked the idea of inverting the story and having the zombies within the house, having to be looked after, sedated, and ultimately rehabilitated.'
WRITER FRAN WALSH, DISCUSSING THE GENESIS OF *BRAINDEAD*

'This isn't violence. This is splatstick. It's totally different.'
PETER JACKSON, DURING THE FILMING OF *BRAINDEAD*

You are watching a movie. On one side of the cinematic divide, lies the stuff of horror — that delicious feeling of tension and unease, of all the hairs on your back rising as one. On the other side lies comedy — where any tension is laughed right out of your system again, with each burst of laughter. And if there is a creature in horror which demonstrates just how close those two states of tension and laughter can be, that creature is the zombie.

Forget about demons, serial killers and chainsaw maniacs: zombies provide the litmus test of whether horror movie-makers really know their game. In the right pair of hands, the image of a person reduced to a shuffling, decaying shell can make for the perfect nightmare. But too often zombies shuffle right on over the cinematic divide, and become laughable for all the wrong reasons.

Zombies provide a challenge for storytellers because of two simple things: stupidity and walking speed. Serial killers, by contrast, normally have the advantage of swiftness and functioning brains (even a little intellect counts for something here). For filmmakers, this combination of velocity and smarts makes suspense that much easier to tap into. But when the lead villains have a top cruising speed of five kilometres an hour, and are interested only in finding more human takeaways, there is a danger that any tension will be drowned under a sea of audience guffaws.

Perhaps nothing tests horror movie-makers more than the tradition for zombies to have only one cruising gear. Slow-moving zombies are more than just a bad joke. They threaten to expose the engine humming just inside the horror/suspense movie, by revealing the essentially mechanical nature of the chase scene. Next thing, the script has to tie itself in circles and have one of the goodies unable to walk properly, in a desperate effort to equal the odds against the undead. ('Quick! We've got to drag ourselves across to that tank of ignitable petroleum, before those zombie extras get across the lawn and eat us all!')

These days zombies have become clichés, which makes them an obvious target for parody. Yet it is surprising just how rarely moviemakers have taken advantage of their comic potential. The video-store shelves are piled high with stalkers, slashers and sundry monsters, but unless you happen to live in Italy, the body of zombie pictures is relatively small. And the body of zombie comedies adds up to little more than a small gash on one arm.

Alien co-writer Dan O'Bannon's *Return of the Living Dead* (1985) — still one of the best-known zombie comedies — provides some clues as to why the genre can be such a challenge. The film acknowledges its debt to the mother of modern zombie movies — George Romero's tense, trapped-in-the-house chiller *Night of the Living Dead* (1968) — by cleverly mixing *Night's* plotline into the back story (indeed, horror writer John Russo worked on the scripts of both films).

In *Return*, some corpses left over from a previous plague of zombies have ended up locked away at a medical supply warehouse, and soon the local cemetery gets infected. The film provides some genuinely inspired moments and works a nice line in comic hysteria, mostly courtesy of the poor stiffs who work at the medical warehouse. But as *Return of the Living Dead* continues, the spotlight moves increasingly towards an abrasive bunch of young outcasts caught up in the pandemonium. It is a sign of how good *Return* is in other ways that these squabbling rebels do not ruin the movie entirely. Accountants are always on the lookout for a franchise: two sequels followed, the second likeably silly, the third a case of style over content. Complicating still further this multiple pile-up of *Living Dead* movies with long names, zombie-master George Romero has managed two follow-ups to his original *Night of the Living Dead* (the best sequel to date, *Dawn of the Dead*, mixes horror, splatter, and the inspired satire of the undead stumbling endlessly around in an abandoned shopping mall).

When a zombie comedy is really firing — as in the first half of *Return of the Living Dead* — the nasty and comedic elements work to complement one another. Just when there is that worrying feeling you might be about to vomit or jump out of your seat, something silly happens to remind you that none of this is really worth worrying about. But these movies require a delicate hand. The danger of fusing horror and comedy is that each element can work to undermine the other, and then the film will seem neither funny nor shocking, but merely contrived — like a wind-up toy trying desperately to please. Add zombies into the cinematic equation, and it can get even more delicate — these creatures often drift off into bad comedy, even in so-called 'serious' horror films.

Peter Jackson's first attempt at a zombie movie remains the bloodiest piece of cinema he has yet given us, but it is also one of his most endearingly romantic. The zombies in *Braindead* are rarely terrifying, but they are often comical and childlike, and sometimes even rather sad. The film finds time to both parody and re-energise the clichés of the living dead, without losing any of the excitement that can result when a piece of disembodied zombie intestine is trying to choke you to death. That *Braindead* is now routinely held up alongside such comedy/horror classics as *Re-Animator* and *The Evil Dead* provides testament to what can result when a gifted moviemaker manages to grab hold of two of cinema's holy grails: a decent script, and the means to properly realise it.

Everything about Jackson's movie is so inspired and perfectly pitched one could almost imagine it arrived direct to celluloid from on high. But then even a case of divine inspiration can gain immeasurably from a couple of good rewrites. If there is an explanation to *Braindead's* magic, it goes back not to a word like inspiration, but that dreaded 'rewrite'. Like everything else, slaughter works so much better if you tell a decent story first, and provide viewers with some characters to care about.

It is probably a testament to Jackson's raw talent that he had managed to direct two films without getting to know the word 'rewrite' very intimately. In all the years of working on his debut feature *Bad Taste*, the script never stretched beyond anything more than some occasional notes scribbled onto paper. *Meet the Feebles* marked an abrupt introduction to the vagaries of the movie industry, a world where sometimes the cash only arrives if the script is ready by yesterday afternoon. With *Feebles*, there was never time for the writing team to stand back and take a breath between drafts, before going back to the grindstone. This syndrome of creation by ticking clock is hardly unique to Hollywood; the promise of ready cash too often breathes life into movies which needed much more time to develop back at scriptwriting stage.

Braindead, by contrast, provides a case study which many budding scriptwriters aren't going to want to hear: a study in how long months of work can prove the safest route to arriving at a story worth having. It would be easy to say that when it came to this zombie opus, Jackson put to good use the lessons learned from the pressure-cooker writing of *Feebles*. Easy, only the chronology doesn't quite support it. As it turns out, the gradual perfection of *Braindead* owes as much to the unpredictable and capricious ways of the movie business as does the rush-job that was *Feebles*.

A MONSTER IN SUBURBIA

One thing is for sure: were it not for Stephen Sinclair, it is unlikely that *Braindead* would ever have come to the screen. Fran Walsh, talking before *Braindead*'s international release, described the story's genesis.

> *What happened was Stephen had an idea he wanted to develop for a play. It was about someone who metamorphosed into a monster in an upstairs flat, but he never developed it. Stephen liked the idea of somebody becoming kind of rancid within the confines of suburbia — that was the guts of the idea. Stephen then approached Peter with his idea, and said, 'Let's develop this into a screenplay.'*

The team began working on the script in Walsh and Sinclair's decaying apartment on Courtenay Place. Occasionally as they worked, the electric poles of passing trolley buses would bang into the front of the building on their way past. Says Walsh:

> *[The movie] was a bit like with the* Feebles. *We always planned it with carnage at the end. Peter's chief interest in the stories originally was that there was going to be lots of room for blood-bags and severed heads. What we didn't know was the most interesting way to get there, and we realised pretty quickly that having that at the end wasn't going to be any reason for people to watch.*

An engaging story and characters were clearly required. For the trio of writers, the movie's basic story elements were established fairly quickly. A shy young man named Lionel lives with his domineering, over-possessive mother, who becomes jealous of the relationship he is tentatively developing with a young woman who lives nearby. Mother gets bitten by a contaminated rat monkey, and begins to decay into one of the undead. Says Walsh:

> *We were really interested in the central idea, which was the inversion of the classic zombie story, where you've got people in a house being attacked from the outside. We really liked the idea of inverting the story and having the zombies within the house, having to be looked after, fed, sedated and ultimately rehabilitated. Also, it worked on another level, in that it was all about what's going on in the suburbs behind the net curtains — keeping up appearances.*

This desire to turn zombie clichés on their head would ultimately prove key to the project's appeal. But, as Walsh points out, it would also be responsible for some of the writing team's biggest nightmares.

> *We got to the point where all the zombies were rehabilitated, and the story ran out. The source of conflict in the story, which was the mother, had become so*

inert as a zombie that she ceased to be exciting as a threat to Lionel. We turned
a corner when someone came up with the idea of making Uncle Lesley a much
bigger character. Originally he got bumped off early on. We decided that he
would take over the role of villain.

Though many reacted to the first draft with enthusiasm, some were not so sure about Lionel, the henpecked main character. According to Walsh, they said, 'How on earth can you get an audience to sympathise with someone who's a bit retarded?' Lionel and his romantic interest would be the focus of many script alterations, including the late idea that their relationship was fated in the tarot cards. In the process the larger-than-life, theatrical nature of some of the characters and dialogue was getting toned down, and the script was moving closer towards comedy. As Jackson later said:

The film is basically like a theatrical farce in many ways. Lionel ends up with
a problem of having all these zombies in his house, without wanting anyone
else to find out about it. And every possible thing that could go wrong, does go
wrong. He has to cope. It's a classic farcical situation.

In a later interview, he discussed the film's treatment of Lionel's mother.

We wanted to have some fun with it. It was like we had this great opportunity
to do some really twisted stuff with the whole Freudian thing. It's all being
done in a naughty, subversive way, rather than making any serious statement.
My relationship with my mother is perfectly all right.

LEARNING TO DELEGATE

Many directors find themselves trapped in offices and development limbo after completing their first film, far from the process which actually got them into the game. But as *Bad Taste* finally saw completion and the writing sessions for *Braindead* continued, Jackson engineered a chance to get behind the camera again. In April 1988 he shot two-thirds of *Meet the Feebles*, the puppet television project which the trio of writers had been developing on the side.

When Jackson flew to the Cannes Film Festival the following month to promote *Bad Taste*, everything seemed to happen at once. At Cannes, *Bad Taste* proved a minor sensation, and a Spanish producer expressed keenness for the *Braindead* script. But for the Spaniards to commit some finance to the project, they wanted the storyline to incorporate a Spanish lead in the female role (at this point, Lionel's romantic interest was still written as a young New Zealander).

Jackson met Spanish actress Diana Peñalver in London, after seeing her performance in Fernando Trueba's civil-war comedy *The Age of Enlightenment*. By October she had been offered the role. Dissatisfaction with the terms of the Spanish deal would later see the co-production idea fall through, but by then the writers were rather enamoured of a Spanish love interest. They decided to keep it anyway. That same October, Jackson turned up at the yearly MIFED film market in Milan with a new, improved version of the *Braindead* script. It was there that a Japanese film company hit Jackson with a double-whammy: not only were they keen to invest in his zombie-fest, but they were interested in *Meet the Feebles* as well.

Braindead remained the main course on Jackson's menu. Danny Mulheron, who had shown his acting chops (after a fashion) from deep inside a hippo suit during the short version of the *Feebles*, was to play the hapless Lionel. Peñalver would play Paquita. The Film Commission promised to put up half of the New Zealand $3 million budget.

Jackson not only wanted to handle the directing, but also supervise all the special effects — a mammoth job in its own right, considering the sheer quantity of violence promised by the script. Jackson went to the boyish Cameron Chittock, who had arrived from Christchurch to help him construct the alien heads on *Bad Taste*. The two had got on well while building puppets in a cramped, periodically flooded basement, for *Feebles*. Now Jackson asked Chittock if he would be his right-hand man on the effects for *Braindead*. Says Chittock:

> At that point in his career things probably had to change, and it took Peter a while to realise that. Things didn't go very well with his first attempt at Braindead. But it was good in a way that Peter realised he couldn't be in the [special-effects] workshop and be a director. For the first time in his life he couldn't do all the jobs himself, even though he knew he could do them better than anybody else. He had to give it up.

What made him realise that, do you think?

Just time. It was simply time.

For Jackson and producer Jim Booth, the last half of 1988 proved a time of dramatic change. Suddenly they were dealing with the conflicting interests of overseas investors, and the complications of setting up their own film company. Booth brought in another producer to help him organise *Braindead*, but the new producer did not work out. Meanwhile some of those working with Jackson tried to persuade him that handling both special effects and direction would be too much, and that he should bring in someone more experienced to command the effects. In the period before filming on *Braindead* was first set to begin, Jackson reluctantly handed over the effects to Australian-based prosthetics expert Bob McCarron, whose CV included Mel Gibson's swollen eyelid in *Mad Max 2*, and the marsupial werewolves in *Howling III*.

Talk to a special-effects expert and it becomes obvious that there are many possible ways to achieve any onscreen illusion. In the case of the Sumatran rat monkey in *Braindead*, Jackson wanted to create the character using stop-motion animation, while McCarron felt it was better to handle it through puppetry. In the end, the monkey would be achieved through stop-motion, and special effects would be shared between McCarron and Richard Taylor, who had worked on *Meet the Feebles*.

In January 1989, six weeks before *Braindead* was due to begin filming, one of the film's key investors pulled out. With the Film Commission unable to take up the rest of the budgetary slack, the *Braindead* crew were called in to learn that the movie had to be put on hold.

As Chapter Four showed, Jackson quickly found a way to turn disaster into success. Before the end of January, and without even a completed script, he had announced that *Meet the Feebles* would begin shooting in March, with *Braindead* set to follow around August. In the end, 1989 was not to be the year of the zombie, but the year of the puppet. By November, *Meet the Feebles* had run its high-speed arc from mad idea to finished movie, and Jackson could turn his attention back to his beloved zombie movie.

Cameron Chittock recalls a conversation with Jackson that took place before either *Braindead* or *Meet the Feebles* had got off the ground.

> Peter said to me, 'I'd really like to have my own special-effects company — why don't we form a company?' I was really flattered. I said, 'I really think you're a great director, and you should stick to that.' There just wasn't the work in New Zealand to justify setting up a special-effects company. I think at the time maybe he was feeling a bit insecure about his directing career.

The art of creating believable special effects involves a skill unique to filmmaking, and takes it to an extreme — that skill is editing, which is partially the art of making sure that audiences are not able to see the joins. Where exactly is the best point in a shot to cut from an actor hanging from wires, to a shot of a doll filmed against a painted sky? To be an effective special-effects person, you need to have an instinctive grasp of how different types of illusion cut together.

Making *Meet the Feebles* likely heightened Jackson's awareness of his own natural ability at hiding the joins. But it may well have demonstrated that special effects were not enough for him, and confirmed that his path lay in storytelling more than in throwing monsters at the screen. *Feebles* had been a nightmare to make partly because every single shot was a special effect. During the long development of *Braindead*, the director began to realise anew the importance of story.

Back in early 1988, Jackson and Walsh were among those who lined up in Wellington to take a three-day seminar by American script analyst Robert McKee (who made clear his enthusiasm for Jackson's *Bad Taste* during his visit). The Film Commission had flown in McKee to talk about the importance of story structure in writing screenplays. He has long argued that writers need to master the basic structure of classical storytelling — and by that he means not classical Hollywood, but something predating cinema itself — before they get on to anything more experimental. (Incidentally Robert McKee, as played by British actor Brian Cox, turns up in *Adaptation*, that notoriously experimental movie about scriptwriting.)

'Attending his conference was a major change for me,' Jackson later said. 'I've never looked back since in terms of writing.' Perhaps remembering his own experiences with *Meet the Feebles*, he then attacked the naive view that someone could just sit down to write a feature, and that a good movie would result. 'It won't. It has to be a very very carefully structured document.'

The late New Zealand movie producer Murray Newey once said that every script needs four or five drafts just to get up to speed. Walsh, Sinclair and Jackson continued to work on the seventh draft of the *Braindead* script. Seven drafts is not an unheard of number, but in Hollywood, one writer or group of writers working alone to produce so many drafts on a project is less common. There, rewrites often involve a script passing through many hands, with each draft trying to satisfy the competing needs of a series of potential directors and stars. Sometimes this 'many writers' approach helps bring out the best in a story; at others, the script gradually loses the very elements that originally made it worthwhile.

In the case of *Braindead*, the extended search for funding had only one positive effect — the long timeframe was allowing the writers to develop their skills, and apply them to tightening and improving the script.

Braindead had now been in development for so long that the writers found themselves having to one-up their own gags — some of them, like the idea of a zombie cut in two, had begun turning up in other movies, like the sequel to *Return of the Living Dead*. But as the improvements continued, enthusiasm was in danger of dropping entirely away. Says Walsh:

> *There was a feeling at one point that it would never get made. It was shelved, and things can stay shelved. I think there also comes a time when people lose the desire to see projects made. That was rapidly approaching.*
>
> In terms of all of you?
>
> *Yeah. I think for Peter especially.*

Though Jackson's path to fame has not been without its moments of remarkable luck, you will find little of it during this period of his career.

After two ambitious, visually confident movies made on skeleton budgets, Jackson's strongest script yet had been cancelled weeks before going into production. Over a period of another two years, it now failed to win the interest of a host of companies in England and America (including, it seems fair to assume, New Line Pictures).

In 1991 *Braindead* finally rose again from the dead. At that point, the New Zealand Film Commission was set to provide most of the budget, with top-ups from the recently privatised Avalon studios in Wellington — where most of *Braindead* would be shot — and the film company back in Japan. By now, Chittock was in Auckland designing sets and puppets for the children's arm of TV3, and decided to stay on up north. Instead Richard Taylor, who had helped build models for *Meet the Feebles*, would work alongside McCarron to supervise the extensive special effects. Danny Mulheron, having been exiled from the *Braindead* team, was no longer starring as Lionel; instead Jackson had taken up Mulheron's suggestion and enlisted young theatre actor Tim Balme for the role.

Draft nine of *Braindead* involved one last major alteration, one which Jackson felt added a touch of naivety to the story, and at the same time helped take an edge off all of the gore.

> *The biggest change came about six weeks before we were due to start shooting, when out of the blue I suddenly came up with the idea of setting the whole film in the '50s. Before that it was a contemporary film. And the '50s period seemed to suit the mood and story of the film. It was something we'd never even dreamed of before, but suddenly it just seemed like the right thing to do. It gave the project a real breath of fresh air just before we were going to shoot. From memory, the only line of dialogue we altered was with Uncle Les, at one point when he's talking about how to kill zombies. He says, 'I've seen the films, I know how it's done.' So we changed that to 'I've read the comics, I know how it's done.' And of course that fits in with the period of EC comics.*

Tales from the Crypt, and other horror comics put out by EC, won controversy and censorship in the mid-1950s, when they were blamed by many for the corruption of American and English youth.

SPLATTER

American author John McCarty — who wrote a book on the subject — defines splatter movies as those whose main aim is not to scare, but to *mortify* audiences through scenes of explicit gore. Where exactly horror crosses over into the sub-genre of splatter can prove something of a grey area (McCarty argues for example that *Halloween* is a splatter movie, despite

its relative lack of gore). But certainly the majority of zombie movies —
especially those made since *Night of the Living Dead* — fulfil the conditions
of McCarty's definition of splatter: namely ample gore and entrails, low
budgets and implausible, often absurd plotting.

Whether Jackson's new zombie epic was primarily splatter, horror,
comedy or romance seemed to depend on which *Braindead* crew member
you spoke to, and what day of the week it was. In the middle of filming,
Jackson came up with another word to describe *Braindead*: 'splatstick'.
Jackson claimed it at the time as his own invention (the first use of the
term is unclear, although England's *Sunday Correspondent* had used it in a
review of *Bad Taste*, two years before). The root word 'slapstick' gets its
name from the two pieces of wood traditionally used by clowns to make a
loud clapping noise each time they appear to be hitting one another.
Jackson's appropriation of the term moves on from slapstick's basic idea
of aggressive or violent humour, and takes it somewhere even more
extreme. Instead of the sound of a punch or a slap, the sound of someone's
arm getting ripped off, perhaps. Said Jackson:

> *The biggest aim is to make people laugh, and give them an enjoyable time. I*
> *guess I'm trying to make a film that if you don't like gory splatter films you'll*
> *still like. Enjoyable splatter. Splatter for all the family.*
>
> *The* Feebles *was dark and cynical and vicious in terms of its comedy and*
> *satire, and* Braindead *is much more like* Bad Taste *was, in a sense that it's*
> *not a biting satire on anything, other than just being an enjoyable comedy*
> *with some gory effects. Laughter and horror I think are very close — you can*
> *be horrified one moment, but then given the slightest opportunity that can*
> *quickly turn into laughter when you realise how ridiculous it is. I think that*
> *in every sequence that we have horrific things happening, I'm always trying*
> *to put in these opportunities for laughter, something in there that takes the*
> *edge off it.*

The time had now come for me to speak up, as resident journalist
representing the easily offended:

Some would say that by combining the two, you're cheapening the
violence.
Well, it is cheap. I mean, they're zombies. Who's ever going to make a serious
zombie film? You're talking about how I would cheapen something if I'd made
a serious film that had a horrible car crash in it. Making that humorous would
definitely be cheapening car crashes, which are horrific and violent by their
very nature. But God knows, zombies chewing on somebody's leg . . . I don't
see how you can cheapen that, it's already pretty cheap to start with.

This isn't violence. This is splatstick. It's totally different. Violence is a psychological thing. I don't think it's a physical thing. And the psychology is totally dependent on the situation, and the context in which it's portrayed in a movie. You can punch somebody in the face in a drama, and it's an incredibly violent act. Then you can rip somebody's head off in a zombie film, and it's comedy. It's totally dependent on the context. Violence is such an emotive word, but it's used much too easily by people. Any discussions about violence in a movie should be totally within the context of what the film is, what genre it is, and what it's trying to achieve.

There will still be people who say that regardless of the fact that the film is being done for laughs, the essential reason for the film is to show gross acts of violence.

No, the essential reason for the film is to make people laugh. You know, Monty Python used violence. I mean even the old silent comedians — some incredibly violent things happened to people like Buster Keaton, Charlie Chaplin, the Keystone Cops. People whacked over the heads with frying pans. Violence is part of comedy — it always has been.

Yes, but obviously there's a jump between Keaton falling off a train and really gross comedy.

Yeah, but the grossness is what makes it harmless. The more gross you are, the more harmless it becomes, because you go so totally over the top that people will have to laugh. They can't possibly believe it. That is really the key point: the only harmful violence is believable violence, realistic violence, and there's nothing in this film that's realistic at all. It's fantasy.

In early September of 1991, the cameras finally rolled on Peter Jackson's third feature film. The floors of the studio had never seen so much blood.

RICHARD TAYLOR

Richard Taylor grew up on a farm south of Auckland, and taught himself to sculpt with mud dug from a creek behind his house. The child of an engineer and a science teacher, Taylor made toys out of cotton reels and rubber bands. Keenly interested in art at a supportive but mainly rugby-orientated high school, he had little idea that his path lay in moviemaking; he was seventeen before realising that local soap opera *Close to Home* was filmed in a television studio rather than in someone's house.

Taylor met his partner Tania Rodger while both were still in their teens, and the two later moved to Wellington. Rodger began an English degree. Meanwhile Taylor got in the wrong enrolment line at polytechnic, but stayed on in the graphic design course, too shy to point out the error. He wore his redband gumboots and Swanndri to polytechnic the first day it rained, 'only to be frowned upon by the cashmere-jersey brigade'.

Soon after graduating, Taylor got a job creating board games, but quit within weeks to make props and sets for television advertisements and the occasional stage play. When he heard that Wellington producer Dave Gibson was planning a *Spitting Image*-style puppet show satirising local politicians, he made a puppet of Gibson, and got the job. Over the next year Taylor, Rodger and another staff member created more than seventy puppets for *Public Eye*, sculpting everything in margarine (some of their puppets are still in the Backbencher pub near Parliament). Then they were introduced to Peter Jackson and worked on *Meet the Feebles*, making puppets and models alongside puppet-designer Cameron Chittock. The reborn *Braindead* marked Taylor and Rodger's baptism by fire. Although Australian-based prosthetics expert Bob McCarron created some of the more complex makeup effects, the lion's share of the work was handled by a nine-person group led by Taylor.

In the years following *Braindead*, Taylor and Rodger joined Jackson among the original partners in Weta: one arm was devoted to digital effects, while Taylor's Weta Workshop handled virtually every other type of movie illusion. Taylor and Rodger continued to alternate work on Jackson's movies with other projects: from fake cows and dead aliens to tidal waves and monsters for the television series *Hercules*. After nine moves in as many years, the couple made a permanent home for their workshop in Miramar.

On some projects, Weta Workshop's staff has expanded as high as 200, among them designers, makeup experts, blacksmiths and armourers. Many come from rural backgrounds. The glue holding the operation together is the lead-by-example work ethic and endless good humour of Taylor and Rodger. In interviews, Taylor extols the virtues of New Zealand talent, and an inventive, number-eight fencing wire approach to problems. Rodger gave birth to their first child shortly after Taylor won two Oscars at the 2002 Academy Awards.

CHAPTER SIX

THE UNDEAD ON SET

'Frying pan, fire, large knife, stream of bile, shards of wood, Void's guts, Mum monster, Edmonds baking powder, bag of onions.'
FROM THE DAILY CALL SHEET, DETAILING SOME OF THE ITEMS NEEDED FOR FILMING ON DAY 32 OF
BRAINDEAD

'We basically turned Avalon into a bloodbath.'
BRAINDEAD SPECIAL-EFFECTS DESIGNER RICHARD TAYLOR

7.14AM INTERIOR, AVALON STUDIOS

Two stained-glass windows cast a gleam of light down the wide, dark Victorian staircase that dominates the *Braindead* set. In the gloom at the bottom of the stairs, a line of doors can be seen running off along each wall. On the top floor, behind two long lines of banisters, lie more doors and rooms.

Below the stairs, in the middle of the tiled foyer, sits a movie lamp. The doorway to the nearby dining room is half-open, and in the light from the window one can just make out the outline of a polka-dot-covered body, wrapped carefully round with a length of power cord.

Now imagine you are a motion-picture camera, one of those gliding, float-anywhere machines that are so often ready on movie sets to follow innocent victims to their death. The imaginary camera takes you out the dining-room window and down onto the floor of Avalon's Studio 11, before gliding a couple of metres up the corridor: just in time to follow three crew members of *Braindead* into the makeshift kitchen, to join those already partaking of the first meal of the day. The meal is cereal, toast and some heated buns containing sausage and an indeterminate cheese-egg mixture. The scene ends with the camera closing in on Gemma, *Braindead*'s lovable German Shepherd, lying on the floor lapping up donations.

7.43AM

Crew members begin to assemble at the bottom of the stairs in the house set, while Peter Jackson, first assistant director Chris Short and endlessly calm director of photography Murray Milne plan the morning. 'Let's leave the Jed shots till later, and do the tearing shots now,' says Jackson. Today, roughly two-thirds of the way through the eleven-week shooting schedule, two camera crews will again be operating simultaneously — something of a scheduling nightmare, though hopefully by the end of the day it means twice as much footage in the can.

The daily call sheet is the film crew's Bible of what shots need to be filmed on any given day, and exactly what actors and materials are going to be required. The call sheet for day 32 has the second camera unit down in the bathroom set for most of the day. For example, there is Scene 156, described succinctly as 'Void severed in two'. Or Scene 56A: 'Lionel kicked by Void's legs'. Scene 158: 'Void loses guts, thrown in toilet, Lionel escapes'. Unit 1, meanwhile, will be alternating between a number of other rooms. Scene 155A is in the cramped pantry: 'Paquita nearly kills Rita'. Or Scene 161 — in both the kitchen and laundry: 'Mandy's head becomes a lantern'.

8.19AM

Preparations continue for the day's first shot. Resplendent in a yellow strawberry-dotted dress, Spanish actor Diana Peñalver has been carefully splattered over her face and neck with blood — today a mixture of maple syrup and food colouring — before entering the confines of a kitchen cupboard to await final lighting and camera preparations. Peñalver plays Paquita, the 'vivacious young Spanish woman' who romances Lionel Cosgrove, victim of domineering mother Vera Cosgrove. It is Mummy Cosgrove's kitchen which we are currently occupying.

Peñalver's shot requires her to stab violently towards the camera with a knife, fearing she is about to be attacked by a zombie. Watching rehearsals on the black-and-white video monitor in the kitchen, the flash of knife against strips of light and shadow puts one in mind of an old film noir. But off-camera the scene is as cramped as it is ridiculous: Peñalver shut in at one end of the cupboard, and three people peering back at her from the other. As well as camera person and sound, the bearded, tousle-haired Jackson is also inside, throwing pieces of tomato up at Peñalver's face. 'When the tomatoes hit you don't touch them with your hand, just ignore them,' he tells her.

The second camera unit are ready to film an unspeakably violent act in the bathroom. Jackson tells them to go ahead without him. After watching the playback later on video, he decides they should film it again.

Shooting of the second pantry shot requires adding another actor to the one already inside. 'Okay, turn over. Speed, 809, 2.' 'Mark — set.'

'Action.' Six crew members stand outside the cupboard watching, temporarily unable to add anything more.

In this shot, Paquita's only line of dialogue is 'It's okay, it's okay'. Afterwards the director tells Peñalver, 'Just a little bit more of a whisper — just a little bit more caring.'

In spite of outward appearances, the rooms inside Studio 11 at Avalon are not really rooms. They are individual sets, built over the period of a month in the rough shape of the 'real' Cosgrove house, so that the crew can film in any room at any time. (On many feature films, each separate room is broken down and replaced by another, once filming has been completed on it.)

The Cosgroves' bathroom is not at the top of the stairs on the left — where it will be in the completed movie — but at the bottom of the stairs on the right, because otherwise the bathroom floor would get ruined during the scene where someone crashes down through the ceiling of the kitchen. The darkened basement, supposedly below the stairs, is actually next door to the main 'house'. Also, the whole set is elevated off the actual floor of the studio, so that puppeteers can work their magic through special holes, which are drilled into the floor when required. As production designer Kevin Leonard-Jones — who masterminded it all — says, many of the rooms have breakaway walls, 'and the top floor has to stay up as well, which is a bit of a brain strain'.

9.45 AM

No brain strain here — but then no brain either. On the workshop floor which adjoins Avalon Studio 11, Richard Taylor is applying a section of shirt to a torso that has no arms or legs, plus a grievous bodily wound where its middle would normally be. 'You never know whether it's you bleeding, or false blood on a job like this,' says the boyish, curly-haired Taylor cheerfully, as his maple syrup-coated fingers rip into the cloth.

This particular appliance could be needed on set in anywhere from twenty minutes to an hour. 'You can't complain about it,' says Taylor, who in his mid-twenties is in charge of a team of nine. 'Schedule changes are part of the job. The less money you've got, the less schedule you've got.'

10.57 AM

Taylor has enlisted me to command one of the movie's most taxing effects shots. I sit on the sticky, dust-soaked floor of the cramped bathroom set with six crew. My job is to make sure that three lengths of plastic tubing don't fall off the end of a foot-long syringe filled with blood. I know I can do it. The tubes lead directly into the zombie torso, which now lies halfway through the bottom panel of the bathroom door, as preparations continue to pull him apart.

When it comes time to film, the syringe, which looks suspiciously like a detonator, does not want to budge, but the camera crew are more worried that there will not be enough light to show the crime. When the shot is shown at rushes (screenings of each day's footage) the next evening, Taylor is pleasantly surprised. 'I'm a great believer in film magic pulling you through on these cheapies,' he says. But he doesn't mention all the preparation time.

12.24PM

On the kitchen set, the scene is controlled pandemonium, as the crew prepare to film a scene in which Paquita and her friend Rita (Liz Mullane) rush around madly, barricading themselves against zombies. Behind them, against the wall, stands an actor with two heads, playing a character who has had an unfortunate encounter with a light socket.

Tina Regtien leans her own head back into a special cavity built into the wall, and the fake head takes its place. When plugged in, this substitute face glows orange all over, like a cheap circus decoration. After 'action' is called, Regtien begins flailing her legs and arms around wildly — part human puppet, part human firework. It is one of those absurd moments in filmmaking which would probably have half the crew in stitches, if they hadn't been working so long to make it happen.

12.37PM

Lunch, in the Avalon cafeteria — even the dead have to eat. There have been days when busloads of elderly residents from a retirement village are forced to join the zombies for lunch, before joining the audience of a local television game show.

2.00PM

Jed Brophy, arguably the most disgusting-looking person on set today, is lying close to the ground, his body halfway through a bathroom door. He has been lying in this position, supported partly by a special harness, for around twenty minutes, talking little. In situations like this, Brophy — playing the zombie Void, and soon to become a regular Jackson cast member — tends to switch off. 'I used to joke around a lot and get people amused, but then I realised that it doesn't help people to get the job done. You just have to switch off and try not to get bored or frustrated,' he says. 'Then it's a matter of being ready to go.'

Most of Void's insides appear to be on his outside. The *Braindead* makeup crew spend two hours each morning applying special prosthetic appliances to his face, before adding layers of fake blood, dirt and pus.

2.18PM

Preparations complete, Peter Jackson is called over from the other unit to check the shot. Jed advances towards the low-angle camera on his hands, growling, giving the illusion that there is nothing left of him below the waist. 'That's great — excellent,' comments Jackson.

2.29PM

Makeup artist Debra East inserts special, all black contact lenses in Brophy's eyes, completing his transformation into one of the undead. Richard Taylor applies to Void's spine a handful of Ultra-Slime — the viscous, non-toxic ooze used on the stars of *Aliens* and *Ghostbusters* — and retreats to the bath. Take one ready to roll.

2.42PM

Third and final take complete. Brophy can get out of his harness. 'I wouldn't say it was terrible,' he tells me later, 'but I was glad to get out of it.'

4.33PM

Editing suite 12, up the stairs at Avalon. Peter Jackson's longtime editor Jamie Selkirk sits at a Steenbeck editing machine with assistant Eric De Beus, making a rough cut from some footage shot on the house set a few weeks before. In the scene being worked on, Lionel (Tim Balme) is rushing to the door of the basement, trying to convince his sleazy uncle (Ian Watkin) that the noises coming from the other side are anything but zombies. For each section of dialogue from Lionel and Uncle Les, there are two or three different shots to choose from: a close-up of each character, plus a two-shot of them both — and multiple takes of most of them. You don't have to watch the process for long to realise that the number of possible combinations for the completed scene is rather large.

Selkirk's editing decisions are partially determined by the scene's major focus. 'Quite often the scene is one person's or another's,' he says. 'This is a bit of both.' The sequence is also made more complicated by small variations in the actor's performances between shots. In the two-shot, Les drops his arm from Lionel's shoulder before he walks off. But in one of the best close-ups, Les's arm stays by his side throughout. When Selkirk wants to make a cut in the film, he marks the point with a white china pencil, which shows up like a dark tire-mark on the TV-sized viewing screen.

As the footage spins back and forth endlessly under his hand, the editing suite becomes an aural nightmare of deep, bassy moans and overspeed tenors. Helped by De Beus, Selkirk juggles the two pieces of film until the action between the two discontinuous shots flows seamlessly. Rough cut of completed scene, just under a minute in length: work time, just over an hour.

TIM BALME

Playing the lead character in *Braindead* meant jumping into a world Tim Balme hardly knew. 'I've never been initiated into the horror genre,' he said shortly before the movie's release. 'If I wasn't in this film and it came out, I would not go and see it, but I'd be wrong in doing that. Sure, there's lots of gore, but there's also the hilarity in it.' Balme found his own acting niche very quickly indeed. After graduating from New Zealand Drama School in Wellington in late 1989, his first two professional acting roles won him an award for best newcomer and — even better — seven months' regular work. The award was for his performance as one of the Everly Brothers in *Blue Sky Boys*, the regular gig a national tour of Stephen Sinclair and Anthony McCarten's hit play about male strippers, *Ladies Night*. The following year he worked on a TV sketch show, played the unlucky husband in McCarten's play *Via Satellite* and, in early September, arrived at Avalon Studios to play Lionel.

'He's a social cripple really. I'm asking the audience to see this guy who is essentially clumsy, who's suffered from an over-protective mother, and is the most unlikely person ever to become the hero. He operates on survival, and also he's working on a level of guilt he feels towards his mother. She's had him under her thumb for twenty-five years.'

For Balme, the most difficult part of the transition to film was giving up the control that comes with being onstage. 'You are constantly having to compromise what you would normally do before the camera rolls — compromising for lights, for camera angles. The compromise is giving it over to someone in control, who's got a way of making it work. It's not a bad thing — it just means that actors have to bite the bullet.'

He is glad that Peter Jackson was the one behind the camera. 'It was my first feature, and the first time he was directing professional actors. I think it was good for both of us. We were meeting on common ground, and got on with it, invented the relationship.

'Peter never left me up in the air. He constantly had *Braindead* running in his head, so he was quite clear about everything. The best thing is that he's completely approachable at any period of the day, very calm.'

The day after the *Braindead* wrap party, Balme auditioned for a series of commercials while feeling very hungover, and somehow managed to get the part. Then he took a very long rest.

6.13PM

As the beleaguered Lionel, Balme is in the bathroom set, battling it out arm and arm with the upper half of Void the zombie. The latter appears remarkably dangerous considering he is a lifeless combination of foam and fibreglass.

Made-up by 8am, then waiting around for most of the morning, Balme has since had a busy afternoon, including acting out one scene — a zombie jumping for his neck — by filming it in reverse. Working with all that blood is not easy. 'It's pretty unpleasant,' he says, 'a sweet sticky feeling all day, for twelve hours. I guess it's a lot better than acting with the real stuff. I remember running out of [a screening of] *Flesh for Frankenstein*, but now I'm dealing with something worse. I guess I've got too much else on my mind to think about it.'

6.19PM

Supper on set. Croissants stuffed with tomatoes and ham. Then back to the gore.

DIANA PEÑALVER

The situation was simple: a movie director had arrived in London, keen to meet a prospective actor about a role in his next film. The problem was that the pair hardly shared any words in common. Spanish actor Diana Peñalver decided that the best way to get around her ignorance of the English language was not to allow time during their first telephone conversation for Jackson to ask any questions. After practising with her English teacher, the call went largely as follows: 'Corner of Tottenham Court Road and Oxford Street. Six o'clock. Bye bye.'

Peter Jackson and Diana Peñalver bonded over a few concentrated days of museum visits, with help from a small bilingual dictionary. Peñalver's introduction to New Zealand was watching *Bad Taste* on video. 'I didn't understand anything,' she recalls. 'I only saw that he moved the camera very well. I like it when the camera is another role, another person.'

Peñalver had been appearing in small roles in Spanish films, mostly comedies, and had also done a lot of theatre. Jackson noticed her in the rite-of-passage romance *El Ano de las Luces* (*The Age of Enlightenment*) directed by Fernando Trueba (*Belle Epoque*). Trueba warned Jackson that she spoke no English. Nonetheless, the director told Peñalver in London that he wanted her to act in *Braindead*.

Two years later, Peñalver heard that the much-delayed *Braindead* was finally about to go ahead. At the time, she was filming the role that would bring her to a large Spanish audience: as an actor in the television series *Las Chicas de Hoy en Dia* (*The Girls of Today*).

Diana Peñalver's first leading role on the big screen meant a new country, and a different language. On set in Wellington, she found herself concentrating so much on pronouncing her English correctly, she worried at times her performance was suffering as a result. The shy, reserved man she had met in England seemed surprisingly relaxed on a film set. 'I've never met a filmmaker who could be so demanding and so generous at the same time,' she later wrote.

Though some of the scenes made her squeamish, Peñalver found the violence was offset by the comedy in the material. She admitted later that not everyone shared her keenness for the film. 'I think there are a lot of good things in *Braindead*, but I don't feel free to show this movie to everybody. My big problem is with my family. They like to see my movies, but they don't feel well about the blood.' After the final, bloodsoaked weeks of killing zombies on *Braindead*, Diana Peñalver went home and took a long holiday. 'To come back to yourself,' she says simply. 'You take your normal life back.'

7.32PM

The day's final shot is complete. Balme emerges from the bathroom into the lobby, sleeves soaked in blood. By now he looks a little like a zombie himself. Meanwhile bored crew members sit around on the stairs, trying to comprehend tomorrow's schedule. For all its mobility, today's shot list has been a success. Working with one camera, the production normally averages around fifteen shots per day. Today, with two crews operating simultaneously, they have managed forty-one, many of them involving time-consuming special effects.

7.53PM

In a darkened screening room roughly the size of a large family lounge, the previous day's rushes are shown for what remains of the *Braindead* team. On the screen in front of them, the illusion is halfway to becoming complete: characters miraculously live, scream and violently die. Then suddenly reality intrudes: actions repeat themselves, characters turn to stare into the camera, or an offscreen voice angrily yells, 'Cut'.

Occasionally the crew laugh quietly, or look a little revolted. But the actors share an enthusiasm for the rushes. 'If you've had a hard day and you're feeling really whacked, they can be just the release you need,' says one. 'You end the day feeling you've done a good job.'

For editor Jamie Selkirk, the screening of the previous day's footage offers a rare chance to consult with the director over which particular takes he wants to use. But then everyone keeps an eye on Jackson during rushes. 'He's like a little kid, chuckling away to himself,' says actor Liz Mullane. 'That enthusiasm is what keeps everybody going.'

8.10PM

Rushes finish.

8.14PM

White paper cups litter the otherwise empty staircase. Nearby, special-effects wrangler Tania Rodger is packing up for the night. The production office is still occupied, and the effects department will be working for at least another hour, preparing for the next day's shoot. In the bathroom, the smell of maple syrup fills the air. There is still blood in the bath.

BLOOD

Talking about *Braindead* without mentioning blood is like remembering the movie *Titanic* without mentioning all the rooms that end up underwater. The dark red stain began in Avalon's Studio 11, but within a short time a coating of maple-syrup blood had attached itself to the shoes of many of the crew members, from where it spread down the corridor to the sofas of the green room and beyond. Avalon, the studio facility that had helped finance *Braindead* to the tune of half a million dollars, was now witnessing its generosity rebounding onto its own carpet. In between being called on set, zombie extras would sit around watching back-to-back sessions of *The Simpsons* or admiring *Braindead*'s 1000-page illustrated script. At night-time, some of them stood in the shower and had flashbacks to *Psycho,* as they watched all the fake blood running off their bodies. The teddy-boy jacket worn by actor Ian Watkin got so coated in it that it stood upright unaided.

When upwards of twenty bloodsoaked extras began arriving at the studio to shoot the movie's zombies-in-the-house finale, something had to give. The next day, long sheets of board sprang up to cover the corridor. The sequence that would earn *Braindead* an enduring place in horror history was rapidly approaching. Like many a classic moment in cinema, this scene drew inspiration from one especially absurd image, an image whose simplicity proved a nightmare to get onscreen. It was of a man, his lawnmower ('an essential New Zealand killing device', as Jackson joked) and a lawn made up of a writhing carpet-pile of zombies.

Two cameras were set up side by side in the main lobby of the house set to film the first take. Twenty-plus zombie extras waited at the foot of the stairs as the special-effects team continued preparations with Tim Balme and the fake lawnmower. Jackson, the camera crew and director of photography Murray Milne got into hooded white protective suits and gumboots, as did many of those in the crew with experience of Jackson's previous work.

Recalls one witness to what followed:

Everyone who was on set got completely saturated with blood, because they had this industrial-strength pump from a forty-four-gallon drum pumping out the whole time. The blood was going up from the lawnmower and hitting the roof, two and a half storeys away. The zombies were throwing themselves onto it, so it was more like fire-hose pressure. But it was great.

Paul Shannon, one of the extras in the scene, later wrote a magazine account about his experiences as a *Braindead* zombie. After this one shot of Balme mowing his way through the crowds of zombies, lawnmower in hand, the extras were so drenched in blood that Shannon was at first unable to open his eyes. He stood at the top of the stairs and watched the crew cleaning up for a second take, because the pump had not kicked in quickly enough on the first. After that, the crew clapped and cheered. Adds director of photography Murray Milne:

We were absolutely covered in this gunk afterwards. It's maple syrup and food colouring, so it is really sweet and sticky. There are scenes where there is so much blood lying on the floor that after each take the chippies would have to go around and cut holes in the floor, just like they did for the puppets with Feebles, *and then use great big rubber squeegees to wash all the blood down the hole underneath the set. They had big forty-four-gallon drums underneath to catch the stuff and recycle it.*

Were you shocked at how high the blood went the first time the machine was turned on?

Yes. And it had little chips in there as well. I don't know if they were real bone, or pretend ones, and it hurt when they hit you. It was just incredible. They had big hoses coming out underneath a mower so you couldn't see them and the amount of stuff that came out of there was just extraordinary. We'd all hoot with laughter afterwards, look at ourselves and go 'How disgusting'. And of course it would stain you. My light meter for a year afterwards still had the smell of this awful sickly-sweet maple-syrup stuff all through it.

The floor had fake tiles on it, and this maple-syrup stuff would go in underneath the tiles. Because of all the sugar it started to ferment after three or

*four days. And it became disgusting — the smell of it. I think at one stage they
ended up having to run heaps of disinfectant through it all, because of fears as
to what it might be breeding.*

One day Taylor and Rodger were washing out a keg of blood in Avalon's
main workshop area (these kegs could dislodge twenty litres of fake blood
in six seconds, which made Taylor very proud). Nearby, the sets used for
Sale of the Century had been stored, enabling the studio to be used until it
was time to record. While testing the pot to make sure it was clean, the top
blew off, resulting in twenty litres of blood going directly over the *Sale of
the Century* set.

In desperation, Taylor began directing a high-pressure hose across the
affected areas in an effort to clean off the red stain. That night, watching
the show on television, Taylor was sure he could still spot a touch of pink.

'No one complained, but it was so uncomfortable,' Jackson later told
Film Threat magazine of the shoot. 'By the end the main set where we shot
most of the carnage had this sweet, gassy atmosphere that was enough to
make you sick even if you weren't covered in blood . . . your feet would
stick to the floor like in a bad cinema.'

There were times for the actors when the fake blood got a little much.
For Diana Peñalver, newly arrived from Spain, her first day on set marked
one of them. Jackson later described the scene to Wellington student
magazine *Salient*:

> *Lionel has been grabbed around the throat through the door, with the zombie
> hands around the throat. Diana had to reach down and grab a pair of scissors
> and hack, chop and slice through the zombie's wrists. The camera was focused
> on the fake zombie wrists, and the effects guys were squirting fake blood through.
> I only realised when I'd yelled 'Cut!' that she was in tears. Because it was
> something she'd never experienced before. She said it was so realistic. She was
> very upset, but she was okay after that. She got used to it. (Laughs.)*

Braindead was far from the first time Jackson had worked with experienced
actors, but it was the first time they had made up a big part of his working
day. On *Bad Taste*, Craig Smith and lead alien Doug Wren had already
performed in a number of roles onstage, although the rest of the cast were
mostly friends. With *Meet the Feebles*, Jackson's dealings with the actors
largely involved the three-day period when he recorded all the voices for
the puppet cast (*Feebles* co-writer Danny Mulheron, playing Heidi, was
one of the only actors actually required on set). Jackson had more of a
pedigree in creating outlandish creatures than convincing human beings.
Now, casting director Fran Walsh had helped him assemble a cast that
included a female lead who was still learning English, a number of highly

experienced actors, and a young actor who had to find audience empathy while playing worried Mummy's boy.

Ian Watkin, whose acting résumé includes films with New Zealand legends Geoff Murphy and Roger Donaldson, recalls Jackson's work with the actors:

> He had the vision of what he wanted but getting that out of him wasn't always that easy. He was ultra-sensitive and trying to leave the actors room to do their thing, yet at the same time he had a very specific thing that he wanted them to do. And I think he was nervous about handling people, a little diffident. I think at that time he was going through the battle that a very private, introverted person has to go through to turn himself into an entrepreneur and a director. It was quite early in that process, really. In lots of ways it's not really fair to hold people's juvenilia up to them at a later stage. I thought he was definitely extremely clever, quite possibly something of a genius. As such you don't worry too much about their manner and their social graces, because you're into the project. Particularly when they're starting out, you know that'll change and they'll get those other skills at a later time. Just to be able to do that kind of work, which is really rare, is a bloody privilege. At the end of the day, once you've washed all the blood off and recovered from the post-traumatic stress, I have quite warm feelings towards Peter Jackson.

HOUSE CALL

The two-storey Cosgrove House at the centre of *Braindead* existed in three places simultaneously. Aside from the interior of the house constructed at Avalon, exterior shots were taken of a two-storey building that sits grandly on the lower slopes of Mount Victoria, close to the bus tunnel connecting Wellington's eastern suburbs to the city. The climax of *Braindead* features Lionel on the roof of the house dealing with his deceased mother, after she takes on monstrous Gerald Scarfe-like form. This scene required the construction of a fake upper floor further along Mount Victoria, allowing actors and monster mother to safely interact without falling so far to the ground.

When the crew arrived to film at a cemetery in the suburb of Karori, not everything went to plan. Worried by the lights and smoke rising up above the graveyard after dark, one local woman rang the police and fire brigade, in order to find out exactly what was going on. 'She obviously thought there was a fire or something happening there,' recalls Murray Milne. 'I think the fire brigade couldn't believe that we'd actually want to spend all night working in the graveyard.'

More was to come. One Monday late in September, a Wellington radio station made an urgent broadcast seeking the return of a decapitated head. Modelled on the face of actor Murray Keane, the head was being used for a cemetery scene in which Lionel's zombie mother bursts out of the ground, and starts throwing around some unwanted visitors. During one of the night shoots in Karori, the head had been left to dry under a street lamp. Fake heads can be difficult things to value, but Keane's was worth around $2000. (The real problem in such situations is not money, but time — fake heads are difficult to replace.) After the radio announcement a Wellington woman noticed the decapitated head among her son's possessions, and it was quickly returned.

Not for the first time, some of the grislier elements of Jackson's imagination were being committed to celluloid right next to where the actual dead lay in plentiful supply. Some crew members were surprised that the production had been given permission to shoot in the cemetery — especially when it came time to dig holes in the ground away from the graves, in order to hide actors for some of the special-effects scenes. But the most dramatic consequence of filming at Karori cemetery was yet to emerge.

BEATING THE BUDGET

The comparative cheapness of making movies Down Under bought Peter Jackson the time to take his love of special effects to a whole new level. As producer Jim Booth told *Fangoria* during the shoot, '$US1.8 million buys a lot of onscreen production values in New Zealand. Multiply that figure by ten to get a better idea of what we can do.' Even then, with more than two hundred different effects included in the schedule, the money on *Braindead* could only stretch so far.

Back at Avalon, one of the film crew told me that for *Braindead*'s first incarnation, the production had originally budgeted for six makeup people. But when *Braindead* finally came to shoot, there were only two. 'I've never worked on a film where you can't trust the call-sheet,' they said. 'And this one's always like that.'

Despite days that often ran to fourteen hours, *Braindead* was falling behind schedule. Says Milne:

> *I know I got spoken to by Jim [Booth] and [associate producer] Jamie Selkirk at*
> *one stage. I got summoned into the office and asked to compromise my work to*
> *make things go faster, because they were falling behind. I was taking so long*
> *with all this elaborate lighting, and Peter was not able to have as much time to*
> *do all the shots. I remember thinking I was doing so much, trying so hard, and*
> *things were going so well. I guess it was me just getting two hundred percent*

involved in this thing.

Jim must have been sitting there with the statistics, and he came to us and said, 'I've worked out that [the crew] only do a third of the amount of work in the morning, and yet you do two-thirds in the other half day, in the afternoon. Why is this?' I never quite figured it out, but for some reason it always seemed to take longer to actually get going. Then the panic sets in and things get humming.

Milne felt that for Jackson, the task of getting shots in the can was the most laborious part of the moviemaking process. 'He has the greatest fun actually writing it. It's like he's already seen it in his mind. To get it out on film is a hell of a long process.' Jackson is one of the rare directors Milne knows of with a ready answer for almost any question on set.

Though the main filming unit had finished shooting by November, a little over budget, a number of elements still needed further work. Jackson, never lacking good reasons why a particular scene might be pivotal to his movie, had long arranged with Booth that if the budget allowed, they would find time at the end to shoot a slapstick sequence involving Lionel walking the monstrous baby zombie in the park. Even Jackson would later admit that this scene, one of his favourites, was completely unnecessary. Shot with a skeleton crew, the scene features Fran Walsh sitting on a park seat with a blue pram, as the zombie baby goes wild.

A number of special effects also remained to be completed. Among them were stop-motion footage of the rat monkey's zoo attack on Mrs Cosgrove, and shots of a model DC3 flying through the clouds, for the film's opening montage. With the help of volunteer student labour the modelmakers created an elaborate model of 1950s Wellington, with trams running down the street, and tiny shop signs adorned with the names of those who had worked on the model. Meanwhile one of cinema's most ambitious zombie massacres needed to be painstakingly cut together in the editing rooms.

THE SOUND OF DEATH

In January 1992, sound designers Mike Hopkins and Sam Negri began working on *Braindead*'s sound mix at the National Film Unit, a short drive from massacre-central at Avalon Studios. Aside from laying on all kinds of day-to-day sound effects like chirping crickets and slamming doors, they were busy changing the pitch of the zombies, making them sound deeper and more terrifying, and adding a variety of near-subliminal sound cues to help build tension.

For the darkened cellar, which becomes the zombies' home inside a home, Hopkins and Negri conjured up a noise that was part drum pattern and part human voice caught between meditation and demonic possession. The cue combined a recording of Tibetan monks, Negri himself making a low 'Om' sound into a microphone, and Hopkins hitting a large steel plate with special drumsticks coated with Pink Batts. (Composer Peter Dasent was meanwhile shuttling back and forth between Sydney and New Zealand, preparing to record *Braindead*'s musical score.)

'Peter's an excellent director in that he knows pretty much what he wants, yet he's very open to new ideas,' said Hopkins. The sound designer could think of only one other New Zealand director he had encountered in eight years in the industry who maintained such a strong interest in the mechanics of the sound process, following after the ardous process of filming and editing: Leon Narbey, who that day was just down the studio corridor, putting finishing touches to *The Footstep Man*. Narbey's film told the story of a man who spends so much time inside a recording studio for a movie that he begins to lose touch with reality.

In March, as *Braindead*'s post-production continued, a man living in the coastal town of Waikanae opened his morning newspaper to an article about the new horror movie. Running along the top of the page was a picture of the *Braindead* film crew in Karori Cemetery, filming just a few metres from the marble gravestone where five of the man's extended family lay buried. In the photo, a crew member or actor could be seen sitting on a low wall which marked one edge of the grave. The first three letters of the gravestone were visible.

No one had told the elderly Waikanae man about the filming of *Braindead*. He felt the grave had been desecrated by filmmakers trespassing on it, and showing the grave onscreen. He wanted all traces of the tomb cut before the movie was shown, and an application was made to prevent any screenings of *Braindead* until his case could be argued in court.

By the time the application went ahead, Jackson was within weeks of finishing *Braindead* for its first trade screenings at the Cannes Film Festival. At the Wellington High Court, representatives of WingNut films argued that they had obtained proper permission to film in the cemetery, and had already spent $36,000 promoting it for Cannes. If the injunction was allowed, *Braindead* would not be in the festival. The judge allowed the film to go: though he could understand why the man was offended, the judge said, his feelings were not protected by the law. But he added that the full case should be argued before the film was distributed in New Zealand.

The first prints of *Braindead* emerged from the labs just days before Peter Jackson had to fly to Europe. Tim Balme was meanwhile approaching the festival from Paris, by train.

I was looking to see which of these little towns was going to be Cannes. I realised that I seriously believed that Cannes was a fishing village with a few cafés and a couple of movie houses. When I got off the train and people tried to rip my bags off and kill me, and I couldn't find a hotel and there were about a million people there, I realised I was wrong.

Amid the tumult and hardsell of Cannes, *Braindead* quickly made a name for itself. The film's three industry screenings won good turnouts. The crowds clapped and hooted, and buyers and film festival heads were soon lining up to get their hands on it. Director Jonathan Demme, recently arrived in Cannes, praised the movie's passion. *Screen International*, which published the first major review, argued that *Braindead* out-zombified all previous zombie flicks, calling the film 'hilariously sick' and 'technically accomplished'.

The weekend after Cannes, the print was screening at a Fantasy Film Festival in Nuremberg, north of Munich. Two extra screenings were hastily added to the schedule in order to satisfy all the fans. Soon after that came the movie's first awards at the Fanta Film Festival in Rome. Heading the Rome festival jury was Italian effects expert Carlo Rambaldi, who had created the aliens seen in the climax of *Close Encounters of the Third Kind*, and worked on the remake of *King Kong*. At Fanta, Tim Balme won best actor, while Richard Taylor took the special-effects award. Recalls Balme:

I walked into this theatre packed full of Italians. They'd seen it, they loved it, and they went wild about the fact someone from the film was there. When I went up and got the award, fortunately they were approving, so I got an ovation. The woman before me who was receiving some award, she got booed off. I was very thankful they liked it.

COURTING OFFENCE

In late July, with *Braindead*'s New Zealand premiere just over a fortnight away, the cemetery case went back to court. The Waikanae man sought an order that WingNut Films stop showing the film until the cutting of a fourteen-second scene that ended with Balme sitting on the steps of the man's family tomb. The man's list of claims included that WingNut had desecrated the tomb, trespassed on it, unintentionally inflicted emotional distress on him and his family, and defamed him because people might think he allowed the filming.

A run of newspaper headlines followed the case. When the man was ten, he said, his grandmother had asked him to look after the tomb, and he argued that it was part of his family heritage. By now he had watched

Braindead on video. He was quoted as telling the court it disgusted and sickened him: 'It's an insult to see a cemetery and the graves in it in such a violent film — it insults my ancestors.' His son, who had died aged only two and a half weeks, was buried in the cemetery. The man and his wife had found the film's scenes of the zombie baby particularly distressing.

Permission to film in cemeteries internationally varies wildly. Many allow no filming at all, while other cemeteries allow it often but draw the line at music videos or student filmmakers. A number make it a requirement of their contracts that details on gravestones not be readable onscreen. WingNut Films had paid the Wellington City Council $600 for the use of the cemetery, but there seemed to be disagreement among council staff over who had ironed out the final details. One parks and recreation manager said he wouldn't have given permission for the movie to film if he had known what the crew were planning, but agreed that he hadn't asked to look at a script. The cemetery's sexton thought that since permission had been given, it was understood what was going on. He agreed that people walked and sat on grave sites, and volunteered that he had sat on the Waikanae man's family tombstone himself.

One witness claimed to have seen dummy corpses and chicken offal being thrown around during one of the graveyard shoots. Location manager Anna Cahill argued that the chicken offal falling on graves was actually plastic scraps and maple syrup. It was always known that tombstones would be filmed, because that was the main point of filming in a cemetery. A Catholic herself, Cahill said that she had reminded the film crew to be sensitive of where they were filming.

One of the factors that appears to have helped decide the case was that the filmmakers had made sure that the name of the tombstone was not visible in the finished movie. Beyond that, each side had different views of what occurred onscreen during the graveyard sequences. As the *Evening Post* put it: '[Jim Booth] agreed an actor was filmed pretending to urinate on a grave but denied there was a scene of simulated sex with a corpse. He thought this must have been confused with a scene where an actor was pulled on to a grave, disembowelled and was shown writhing. He said it was a very funny film and well-made for its genre.'

Reading lines such as this, one begins to get a sense of how incredibly narrow is the line between comedy and offence. But in choosing to film some of his mayhem so close to cemetery graves, one has to ask whether Jackson fully realised that such divisions exist. Two days before the movie's scheduled premiere, the Waikanae man's case failed. On one of the six causes of action, trespass, the judge recognised that the man had sufficient rights to support the action but could not see how an injunction on the film would provide any remedy. He said that there was no evidence that the filmmakers had trespassed during filming. He agreed that graveyards and tombstones are sacred places, and that the man and his family found the appearance of their tombstones deeply disturbing, but that did not justify granting an injunction.

AMERICA CALLING

As the trial came to a close, *Braindead* was continuing to sell around the globe. But the sale which meant the most commercially was to the US. In mid-June, Jackson screened the movie in Los Angeles to representatives of a number of interested parties. By mid-year Universal, Warners and 20th Century Fox had seen it, along with independent distributors New Line, Miramax and Trimark. According to Jackson, Universal president Tom Pollock took *Braindead* home one weekend and loved it. 'We're in the middle of orchestrating a bidding war,' Jackson said at the time.

Jackson and Booth signed with Trimark. The independent company had begun in video as Vidmark, before moving into filmmaking and distribution. Trimark was beginning to make a name by handling hard-edged movies like Ken Russell's *Whore*. When it came to its latest acquisition, Trimark's advance for English-speaking rights in America and Canada came in at twice the figure that any New Zealand film had previously managed. Though one of the conditions of the sale was that *Braindead* be released uncut, the company were keen to tighten it a little, and the director first removed five to six minutes, increasing the movie's pace.

One thing Jackson could do little to change was Trimark's new title for the film. In 1988, *Basket Case* director Frank Henenlotter had released an American movie called *Brain Damage*, featuring a sluglike creature that latched on to people's brains. Late that year, Jackson told *Gorezone* magazine that he had originally wanted to call his own movie *Braindead*, 'but that's too close to *Brain Damage*. My alternative was *Housebound*, but that's too similar to *Hellbound*. So I have no idea what to call it right now.'

Other titles considered over the years included *Unstoppable Rot, Cranial Blowout* and *Bubonic Basement*. Jackson's favoured title became even less viable with the release of the delightfully twisty Bill Paxton horror / comedy *Brain Dead*, filmed in the US in April 1989. (Ironically, this *Brain Dead*, developed from a script by late *Twilight Zone* writer Charles Beaumont, had itself begun under another title: *Paranoia*.) Yet for Jackson, *Braindead* it long remained.

Staff at Trimark were aware of the American *Brain Dead*; they decided that Jackson's splatter-fest would become *Dead Alive*. Former Trimark distribution executive Tim Swain is unsure exactly who came up with the name change. 'It was such a good film you wanted it to have its own identity,' he says. 'This issue came up, and it just seemed to be the better way to go ahead and change the title.'

Jackson did not appreciate the news. Talking to *Fangoria* reporter Michael Helms in late 1992, he insisted on calling his movie *Braindead* for the entire interview, knowing that it would annoy Trimark executives. In another interview, he said Trimark had insisted on the name change: 'It's a kind of clunky, slightly ugly name, but we can't do anything about it.' At the same time, he expressed enthusiasm with the company's efforts to promote the film, and their courage in releasing it unrated.

A new Los Angles design company called Dawn Patrol was enlisted to come up with a selection of possible poster images. Dawn Patrol founder Jimmy Wachtel says that the extreme nature of *Braindead* meant 'we could go as far out as we wanted. Once you saw that movie you knew that Peter was somebody. Something was going on in New Zealand.' One proposed poster featured sandwiches with eyeballs and fingers sticking out of them. The final image, which would launch a thousand video boxes, showed an eye-opening image of a woman (in real life the photographer's girlfriend) holding her mouth wide open to reveal a tiny zombie skull staring out.

After watching *Dead Alive*, the American critics reacted with a mixture of shock and praise. *Village Voice* reviewer James Hannaham singled out the film's climax for containing 'some of the most excessive evisceration I've seen outside of snuff films. That it's hysterically funny shows how comedy is really tragedy with its limbs ripped off.' In the *Los Angeles Village View* Tom Crow praised the film's slapstick, its Keatonesque contortions and the physicality of Tim Balme's performance. Crow speculated that Jackson had taken the work of previous zombiemeisters 'and decided to carry it to the most excessive and absurd extreme possible.' *Dead Alive*, he wrote, 'builds its carnage with such wit and invention that disgust gives way to an acknowledgement of — if not admiration for — Jackson's wild set pieces.'

Though some reviewers questioned the point of the film, they were in the minority. *The Hollywood Reporter* writer Jeff Menell predicted that *Dead Alive* would become a cult favourite among gore fans, and called it 'one of the bloodiest films in cinematic history'. (The German censor evidently agreed, banning *Braindead* outright, although a version shorn by twenty minutes was eventually passed.) Despite all the rave reviews, *Braindead* failed to catch fire at American cinemas. At the widest point of its American release, it was playing in only seventeen theatres. 'The people who saw it responded to it,' says Trimark's Tim Swain. 'But we were hoping that it would break out a little bit, and it never really did.'

In Australia, mirroring the reaction of many in the audience (some of whom were reported rushing to the toilet), a number of critics found the film's gore-stained climax far too much. Though enthusiastic about *Braindead's* first half, *Age* reviewer Neil Jillett wrote that 'the film's last fifty minutes virtually abandon parody or any other comic impulse'. The onslaught of carnage appears to have rendered a number of the critics senseless: more than one would try to persuade readers that the lawnmower massacre lasted for more than thirty minutes of screen time (in the uncensored version, the lawnmower shots run to a little under three minutes).

The zombies fared better in Europe. In Hungary, recently emerged from behind the Iron Curtain, Jackson's gore-fest managed to get as high as number three in the box-office top ten. When it came to its video release in England, it managed similar feats. In January 1993, shortly before it opened in France, *Braindead* took away the Grand Prix at the Avoriaz Film Festival. The prize was one of Jackson's most prestigious yet — past winners of the top prize at Avoriaz included *Carrie*, *The Elephant Man* and *Blue Velvet*.

FACING THE CENSOR

When it came to American video release, Trimark / Vidmark pulled out all the stops. Gina Draklich, then Trimark's vice-president of marketing, remembers sending out rubber body parts in boxes to promote *Dead Alive's* arrival on video. 'We sent out arms, fingers, teeth . . .' Special candy dispensers imprinted with the screaming poster began appearing in video stores: when you reached inside the woman's mouth for a candy, the dispensers let out a scream.

Though *Dead Alive* did well on video, the price of American success was a savaging like nothing else in Jackson's career. The main reason: many of the big video chains refused to stock unrated movies unless they were cut to a softer certificate. Says Draklich: 'If you wanted to maximise your sales, you had to make it available in two formats.'

At the time the Blockbuster chain of video stores represented a little under half of the national market, and would no longer accept unrated movies. Says one former Trimark staff member, who worked on the video release of *Dead Alive*:

> They [Blockbuster] were huge — the difference between whether you were gong to make money or lose money that year. They weren't saying, 'You have to cut the film — but if you want us to buy it, you need to.' Everything was changing in home video at the time, with home video becoming the bread and butter of a film company — especially an independent film company, without lots of other revenue sources.

In the late 1960s, the Motion Picture Association of America (MPAA) established a movie classification system, partly to avoid the looming possibility of government censorship. The MPAA trademarked a whole series of voluntary classifications, failing to do so only with their new X rating, which limited movies to audiences aged over sixteen.

For a while, the system seemed to work for everybody. *Midnight Cowboy* and *Last Tango in Paris* were released with an X, and became mainstream successes. But makers of hard-core sex films were bypassing the MPAA and hijacking the X label as a way to market their own product. Though the MPAA later tried to remove some of the stigma of the X certificate by renaming it as NC-17, the change has been largely cosmetic. Some newspapers refused to carry advertising for X-rated or NC-17 movies, and these days a number of cinemas and video chains refuse to deal with them at all. The MPAA's R rating is similar to New Zealand's old RP rating — those younger than seventeen are allowed in, as long as they are with a parent or adult guardian.

In an effort to avoid the deathknell sound of an X certificate, distributors occasionally bypass the MPAA and release their films unrated, though usually with a note that the film can only be watched by specific ages. When it came to video release, Richard Jordan, then Trimark's head of post-production, was one of those charged with cutting *Dead Alive* down from the unrated form shown at cinemas to an R-rated version that would satisfy Jackson, the MPAA and the video stores. 'The original version was pretty gruesome. There's an amazing amount of fluids,' says Jordan. 'The MPAA was just mortified at all the body parts and ooh and gooh coming out of all these different orifices. It was like Peter was going left, and the MPAA was going right.'

Adding to the complications, time was against both Trimark and Jackson. 'I was in the middle, and probably a little green to be honest,' says Jordan, who remembers the *Dead Alive* situation as one of the least enjoyable assignments of his entire career. 'We were just trying to get the film as hard as we could. My bosses at the time were saying you have to get this done in this amount of time . . . But as an older wiser person today, I would probably have done it differently.'

An ex-Trimark staff member involved in the recut offers another perspective.

> *Hindsight is twenty-twenty. Maybe if we'd started the process sooner, been more forceful with the MPAA, and been a little more brutally honest with Peter . . . We should have said, 'Peter, these guys are going to ruin your fucking movie. You're going to be unhappy no matter what happens, because we have to cut arguably the best stuff out of the film to get the thing to R.' It didn't help*

*that Trimark was kind of on probation with the MPAA at the time. We had
been pushing the envelope a little bit with some of our unrated independent
movies.*

The former staff member feels strongly that a major studio has more
clout in the MPAA cutting process than an independent. 'If Peter Jackson
today had *Dead Alive*, and he was dealing with the MPAA, all I can say is
I guarantee they would not have made us cut as much out of the film as
they did.' The final R-rated cut of *Braindead* emerged a full twelve minutes
shorter than the original.

And what of its home territory? Uncut, *Braindead* lasted in New Zealand
cinemas for a more than respectable four months, and won the best reviews
of Jackson's career to date. A number commented on the film's effortless
evocation of the 1950s, and complimented Jackson's ability to tell a New
Zealand story in a way that appealed to an international audience. Though
the film was never a local phenomenon, profits generated from the film
per screening at times beat blockbusters like *Batman Returns*. But in the
great tradition of underfunded releases for New Zealand cinema, two of
Braindead's available prints had to be pulled while the movie was still going
strong, so it could open elsewhere in New Zealand. For *Braindead*, as with
so many lesser horror movies, the true saviour would be home video.

There was one more controversy to come. The following year, at the
New Zealand Film and Television Awards, *Braindead* was nominated in
almost every major category. When it was announced as the winner of
best film, as well as best director, best screenplay and best male actor, one
of the judges made it clear he did not agree with the decision at all. Author
John Cranna told journalists that *Braindead*'s win made a mockery of serious
filmmaking in New Zealand: 'If the rest of the world takes this as evidence
of the level of cultural sophistication here, we will further develop our
reputation as a cultural Albania — a bit retarded and with one foot in the
last century.'

Cranna thought the film crude and 'stupefyingly dull'. By his account,
two of the six judges on the night had thought *Braindead* the worst film on
show, and they had won agreement from the award organisers that the
split decision would be mentioned. Since nothing had been said, 'I feel no
longer bound by the majority decision.' Robert Boyd-Bell, the head of the
awards society, later argued that was not the case at all. 'You don't give a
decision and say, "Oh, by the way, only five of the judges agreed with it."'

As for Peter Jackson, he refused to comment about the controversy.
The director was in Christchurch. He had other things to worry about.
The morning after the awards ceremony, Jackson began work on a project
that offered a challenge he had not yet dealt with: real life.

TIM BALME

Despite failing his truck driver's licence three times running, Tim Balme's acting career has hardly slipped a gear. In the years following his star turn in *Braindead*, Balme took a long-running role as the Harley-driving sleazeball Greg Feeney in New Zealand's most popular soap opera, *Shortland Street*, and had a memorable first scene as the sexually harangued husband in *Via Satellite*. His solo performances of the self-penned *The Ballad of Jimmy Costello*, based on the exploits of a New Zealand crime legend, have won acclaim here, in New York and at the Edinburgh Festival (the *Scotsman* called it 'a breathtakingly energetic tour de force'; a movie version is in development). In 2000, Balme teamed up with a group which included his actor wife Katie Wolfe, to tour three productions with the New Zealand Actors Company. He continues to act in television and film, most recently *Mercy Peak*, and finally has his truck driver's licence.

CAMERON CHITTOCK

As a child, Chittock once made a Plasticine man and stuffed it with the insides of some shellfish, then waited for the man to come to life. Years later, after studying puppetmaking at the Canterbury School of Fine Arts, he helped Jackson create the alien heads for *Bad Taste*, worked on the first, abandoned version of *Braindead*, and designed and helped build more than ninety puppets for *Meet the Feebles*. As *Feebles* finished production, Chittock rushed to Auckland to design creatures and sets for the children's department of new network TV3. The Claymation series *Oscar and Friends*, which he directed and designed, continues to screen in New Zealand, the UK and the US. In late 2003 Chittock moved to Singapore to lead the team producing the $7 million animated series *The Adventures of Bottle Top Bill*.

CAMEOS

Those who work behind the camera on Peter Jackson's films often find themselves being given roles onscreen as well. *Braindead* is absolutely stuffed with them: apart from Jackson's own cameo as the half-witted undertaker's assistant, look out for the following: Walsh cooing over a baby in a blue pram, during the zombie baby in the park scene; Jim Booth playing Lionel's father (seen mostly in photographs); Jackson's longtime editor Jamie Selkirk is seen during the zoo scene, trying to take a photograph when Lionel's mother ruins the picture; Tony Hiles, who helped out on *Bad Taste*, has a memorable cameo here as a gormless zookeeper with a penchant for telling gory stories. *Braindead*'s zombie finale also sees priceless moments from two future founders of the Weta effects company —

a bespectacled Richard Taylor turns up in a green waistcoat, for just long enough to lose his scalp, while George Port loses his head and gets it repeatedly kicked around the floor. Future *Lord of the Rings* casting director Liz Mullane, playing the cheerful Rita, strikes zombie problems of her own during this sequence. For the crowning touch, cameo king and *Famous Monsters of Filmland* editor Forrest J Ackerman is also seen during the zoo sequence, taking photographs of all the mayhem.

CHAPTER SEVEN

A DIFFERENT KIND OF MURDER:
HEAVENLY CREATURES

'The girls believed in survival after death. Heaven was for happiness,
paradise was for bliss. There was no hell.'
JOURNALISTS TOM GURR AND HH COX, WRITING ABOUT PAULINE PARKER AND JULIET HULME

'I don't think Pauline and Juliet are so very different from anybody else.'
HEAVENLY CREATURES SCRIPTWRITER FRAN WALSH

Cities are melting pots of everything contained within them, the sum of history, architecture, and personal memory. But try to reduce a city to a single event, and it is surprising how often memories can end up in the same place. Think of Wellington, and it could easily be the sinking of the ferry *Wahine* in Wellington Harbour, and the passing of 51 lives. Think of Christchurch, and the tragedy that most often rushes to mind is just one life; but the tragedy is so famous that there are people thousands of miles from New Zealand who know only one thing about Christchurch — that it is the place where a woman was killed by two teenage girls, one of them her own daughter.

On a June day in 1954, Honora Parker was found dead in a hilltop park overlooking the city. Around 3.30 that afternoon, dark-haired Pauline Parker and her English-born friend Juliet Hulme ran from the edge of Victoria Park, clothes covered in blood, claiming that Honora Parker had slipped and hit her head on a rock. That night, Pauline admitted killing her mother, and said her friend Juliet had not been involved. Soon after, the police found fourteen exercise books of the girls' writings, including Pauline's diaries, which described plans for the murder. The next morning Juliet changed her story and confessed to her part in Honora's death. She described seeing Pauline hit Honora Parker with a brick wrapped in a stocking, adding that she had hit Honora as well. Juliet's statement to the police included the words, 'I was terrified. I thought that one of them had to die. I wanted to help Pauline.'

The nature of the relationship between Pauline — then aged sixteen — and fifteen-year-old Juliet fascinated New Zealand at least as much as the murder itself. The two girls had formed an extraordinarily close bond, and arguments over whether their relationship was a lesbian one have continued over four decades. The teenagers invented their own imaginary worlds, complete with temples and saints, and wrote letters to each other under fictionalised personas. The imaginations of two intelligent teenagers somehow combined with circumstance, and helped send them into a realm where murder could seem a logical answer.

The Parker–Hulme case has become one of the most talked-about murders in New Zealand history. Matricide has never been the most common of crimes, and it is even more rare for the murderer to be female. But fascination with the Parker–Hulme case is also about the durability of myth, reflecting how a tragedy can be moulded to suit the mindset of those retelling it. The story has been retold in many ways: as a warning against a lack of parental discipline, of parental affection, of the 'evils' of a homosexual lifestyle, and of a society too repressed for its own good.

Decades after the events chronicled in the following pages, writers in four nations began work on their own cinematic version of the Parker–Hulme story. The man who won the race to bring the tragedy to the screen would inadvertently take his career to a whole new level in the process, and find fact and fiction feeding off one another in unexpected ways.

PAULINE PARKER AND JULIET HULME

Juliet Hulme's parents left England for Christchurch in late 1948, so that scientist Henry Hulme could take up a position as head of Canterbury University. The Hulme family soon made their home at Ilam, a large university-owned mansion in one of Christchurch's more affluent suburbs. Pauline Parker and her sister Wendy lived a more humble existence — another sister spent much of her childhood at a nearby centre for the intellectually disabled, and the family took boarders into their house in the central city to supplement her father's income as a manager at a fish shop. Privacy was difficult to find, so it is not surprising that Pauline found herself attracted to the liberal, affluent household of the Hulmes, with their extensive gardens and many rooms. Pauline's diary indicates that Hilda Hulme may well have over-egged her welcome, on one occasion calling Pauline her foster-daughter, and implying that Pauline would one day come to England with the family (Hilda later denied this account in court). Pauline's diary mentions her joy at once being taken to be English.

Pauline's admiration of the very British Hulmes mirrors the history of the city in which she lived. Christchurch was founded on an idea of upper-class England which had been distorted in the process of transplantation. The town's English founders planned that Anglican religion and a superior education would be central to the new city. But as religion declined and universities sprouted elsewhere, Christchurch instead began more and more to market the Englishness of its buildings and gardens.

Christchurch has long faced accusations of being New Zealand's most class-conscious city, a view which certainly held some truth at the time of the murders. Socially a big gap existed between the rundown flats and boarding houses where Pauline lived, and the famed gardens of the Ilam homestead. Actor Sam Neill, who grew up in Christchurch in this period, has described it only half-mockingly as a place where teenagers modelled themselves after the American teen idols they saw at the movies, and the authorities occasionally brought in truckloads of soldiers to round up anyone congregating in Cathedral Square who 'didn't look exactly four-square'.

The Red scare was still in full swing; a few years before, the government had used censorship and scare tactics to try to halt a divisive waterfront dispute. In 1954, the censor's office banned the Marlon Brando motorcycle movie *The Wild One*, worried about potential social effects. That year, a special government committee into delinquency and immorality blamed recent incidents of teenage sexual behaviour on everything from lack of parental supervision and the decline of religion, to 'precocious girls' who corrupted boys.

ISOLATION

The legend of Pauline Parker and Juliet Hulme is of an attraction of opposites: Pauline the slow, sullen, ugly duckling from the colonies; Juliet the bright, confident English rose. But the truth is less clear-cut. Pauline was a bright teenager, with a strong wit and an imaginative mind. As for the ugly-duckling tag, psychiatrist Reginald Medlicott and some of Pauline's schoolmates have described her differently. One classmate said she had a 'wild gypsy look with dark flashing eyes'. Both girls appear to have stood out in their disregard for authority, amid a class which hardly lacked in high achievers. Like Hilda Hulme, Pauline's mother Honora hailed from England, and for a few years as a toddler she had lived in the same Birmingham street known earlier to a young schoolboy named Ronald Tolkien.

At the age of five, Pauline spent almost nine months in hospital after being diagnosed with osteomyelitis, a condition in which bones become infected and inflamed. Her leg required several operations and a two-year period of daily dressings, limiting her participation in sports. Juliet herself spent extended periods living apart from her parents and her younger brother, due partly to a serious bout of pneumonia and other respiratory illnesses. Hoping a warmer climate would aid her health, the Hulmes sent her away first to the Bahamas, followed by the Bay of Islands. After time away at a private boarding school in the North Island, she returned home and began at Christchurch Girls High, befriending Pauline Parker towards the middle of the year.

Worries about the closeness of Juliet and Pauline's relationship first surfaced in 1953. One Christchurch Girls High teacher has recalled cautioning both families that year about the 'unhealthy' nature of the relationship. Soon afterwards, Honora Parker discussed the matter with Henry Hulme. Honora was later told by a doctor that her daughter's relationship with Juliet was probably homosexual, and that she would likely grow out of it. Pauline's diaries, quoted from during the trial, seem to indicate the two were romantically and sexually involved, though some argue the latter was primarily a form of heterosexual play-acting. After the murder, a psychiatrist famously asked Juliet if her relationship with Pauline had been sexual. She replied, 'But how could we? We are both women.'

By April 1954, Juliet and Pauline's bond was arguably the only sure thing in their lives. The girls made plans to go to the US together, where they might become famous writers and travel to Hollywood. Pauline's relationship with her mother had broken down, partly due to conflicts about her close friendship with Juliet. Pauline left school in her School Certificate year, beginning a secretarial course on April 21. Over the next few days, Juliet discovered that her mother was having an affair, that her father was about to resign from the university, and that her parents were about to divorce. Soon it became clear that this meant Juliet would be going overseas with her father. The possibility that Pauline might travel with Juliet was rejected by Pauline's mother. Pauline's first explicit diary reference to the idea of murdering Honora occurs on April 28, an entry in which Pauline also mentions the possibility of suicide.

Parker and Hulme: A Lesbian View, the first non-fiction book on the case, cites studies supporting the theory that many murders by adolescents occur over long-standing conflicts with parents. Authors Julie Glamuzina and Alison Laurie suggest that such murders are often triggered by a series of events which are mistaken by others as the cause. The book argues that tensions in Pauline and Juliet's families had been building up for some time before the murder, with an acceleration of events that April.

In June, both families allowed Pauline to spend ten days with Juliet at Ilam, knowing the girls were about to be permanently separated. Accounts of a plan to murder Honora Parker begin appearing regularly in Pauline's diary from June 19 — the day before she left Ilam — until the entry for

June 22 marked 'The Day of the Happy Event', when Honora Parker died. After the murder, Pauline wrote a note which included the words 'I have taken all the blame'. The note was taken from her by police. Later Pauline managed to throw it into a nearby fire, where it was partly destroyed.

THE TRIAL

When the case came to trial in August 1954, the defence lawyers for Pauline Parker and Juliet Hulme had few options. Since both girls had made full confessions, their only defence was for lawyers to prove they were insane. Psychiatrist Reginald Medlicott, the chief defence witness, argued that Pauline and Juliet were suffering from *folie à deux*, a form of communicated insanity existing between two people. Medlicott had interviewed the girls three times since the murder, and argued that their delusions included 'their own paradise, their own god and religion, and their own morality'. He thought that there were similarities between the Parker–Hulme case and that of Americans Leopold and Loeb, the homosexual teenagers who had murdered a young boy in the 1920s. The two were later saved from the death sentence by a defence of insanity — the movies later inspired by Leopold and Loeb include *Rope* (1948), *Compulsion* (1959), and *Swoon* (1992). In later years Medlicott commented on the 'extraordinary similarity' of the two cases, as did many crime writers. But *Parker and Hulme: A Lesbian View* argues persuasively that the Leopold–Loeb case shows many differences, including that the threat of separation had no part in Leopold and Loeb's motive.

Pauline's diaries and the girls' stories were mined extensively by both sides during the trial (references in the diaries indicate that Juliet kept her own diary as well, but, if so, it has never been found). Medlicott argued that the violence in Pauline's stories rose in proportion to the time she spent with Juliet. Key to Medlicott's evidence was a diary entry Pauline wrote in April 1953, the famous 'Port Levy revelation'. There Pauline wrote of seeing 'a gateway through the clouds', and the girls' discovery of a key to the Fourth World — a paradise open only to a small number of people.

Medlicott found further proof of their 'extraordinarily exalted state' in Pauline's poem 'The Ones I Worship', which describes two glorious daughters, 'understood by few', who 'reign on high': Jackson's movie of *Heavenly Creatures* takes its name from a line in Pauline's poem, and has a long quotation from it at the point where Juliet is driven home from the sanatorium. Psychiatrists at the trial gave widely differing points of view on the argument that 'homosexuality and paranoia are very frequently related'. (Many New Zealanders first heard about ideas of same-sex relationships through newspaper accounts of the trial.)

A later medical witness echoed many of Medlicott's theories, but in the process undermined the defence case. He said that the girls had been aware that the murder was contrary to the moral values of the community, thereby placing their mental states outside the legal definition of insanity. After the defence case had been completed, judge Justice Adams came close to stopping the case early, because he considered that the defence lacked enough evidence to raise even a possibility of insanity. The defence did not have an easy task — there were few legal precedents for two insane persons combining to commit a crime. At this point, prosecution lawyer Peter Mahon cooperated with the defence lawyers to ensure the case continued.

At times there was a sense that three couples were on trial simultaneously. By the moral standards of the 1950s, it could be argued that both sets of parents had dared to transgress the accepted rules. The trial revealed that Pauline's father was technically still married to someone else. Although Herbert Rieper and Honora Parker had lived together for twenty-five years, they had never officially married. But Christchurch was probably more shocked by Hilda Hulme's affair with Walter Perry. Prominent in the recently-formed Christchurch Marriage Guidance Council, Hilda had regularly appeared on a local women's radio show to discuss issues such as the best ways to bring up children.

Theatre director Elric Hooper has been quoted as saying that at the time of the trial, he heard university academics gossiping that the Hulmes had got what they deserved. Hilda was subpoenaed and had to stay in New Zealand for the trial, while Hulme, who had taken the girls home on the day of the murder, was allowed to leave New Zealand with his son before the trial began.

In his closing address, Crown prosecutor Alan Brown talked of a premeditated murder conducted by 'dirty-minded little girls', and argued that Parker and Hulme were not incurably insane but incurably bad. The jury agreed. Parker and Hulme were found guilty but, as they were still under eighteen, escaped the death penalty. After spending five years in separate prisons, Juliet was released in November 1959, and within days had left New Zealand to join her mother overseas. Pauline's jail term ended later that month, though she remained on probation until 1965. Both were given new identities, and one of the conditions of Parker and Hulme's release was that the two never meet again.

FASCINATION AND OBSESSION

The Parker–Hulme murder has been a staple in crime books for decades. The accounts of many writers often carry an unspoken implication that the girls' crime was that much greater, not just because the killing was one of matricide, but because females were responsible. Just a year after the trial, one American book had already predicted that the case would come to be remembered as the most dreadful crime of the century.

Most of us are loath to admit any kind of fascination with murder, despite the popularity of detective stories, horror movies and racks of books concerning true-life murders. Such true-life stories allow a glimpse into the darker aspects of human nature and the opportunity to judge others in the process, a combination which many find difficult to resist. Yet the Parker–Hulme murder continues to fascinate people today thanks not just to a sensationalist interest in all the taboos that it broke, but also to a measure of empathy and a desire to know why. Many can see the shadow of their own puberty in the girls' story.

In many ways the Parker–Hulme case sounds like a piece of fiction. It was probably inevitable that it would become one.

After reading about the case in a newspaper feature in the 1970s, Wellington teenager Fran Walsh grew fascinated by the Parker–Hulme murder. She tracked down a novel called *Obsession*, a melodramatic, doom-laden account of the murders written in the 1950s by British journalists Tom Gurr and HH Cox, who had reported on the original trial. In real life, Pauline and Juliet had revelled in play-acting, giving each other a series of fictional identities. In *Obsession*, they now became Alison and Susan, and Pauline's social status was upgraded so that her home was no longer a boarding house. The book used many of Pauline's diary entries verbatim. Its main argument appeared to be that the only thing that had turned the girls into murderers was the fact that they had met each other.

The fourteen-year-old Walsh lapped *Obsession* up. Years later, she told a journalist:

> *I've had very intense adolescent friendships — they were very positive, affectionate and funny — and I understood to a large degree what was so exciting, so magical about the friendship. And though it ended in a killing, the friendship itself is something people would identify with, particularly women. . . Adolescence is that weird time — you find someone who represents everything positive and wonderful in the world, and you grab on to them and reject everyone else.*

In 1986 Alison Laurie and Julie Glamuzina began research for their book *Parker and Hulme: A Lesbian View*. Soon after, American-born playwright Michelanne Forster began her own investigations. *Daughters of Heaven*, the play she later wrote based on the murder, would win good audiences and admiring reviews, and is now often studied alongside

Jackson's movie in New Zealand high schools. (Ironically, Jackson was among the minority who publicly accused Forster's play of being unsympathetic towards Parker and Hulme, by portraying them 'as psychos'.)

Before *Daughters of Heaven* opened in October 1991, the subject matter was criticised by some in Christchurch, including several members of the Court Theatre board. Forster says she stepped knowingly into controversy:

> *Great stories attract strong feelings and passions. That's partly why I chose it. My biggest worry was the fear of inadvertently hurting people who had suffered through this tragedy. But I was deeply moved afterwards when a lot of people wrote me personal letters saying, 'I didn't think it was a good idea that this play be done, but your play's been a cathartic experience for me.' They praised it.*

Many women, she argued, could relate to the idea of an adolescent girl feeling 'so angry that she could throttle her mother'. But the Parker–Hulme case was partly about how a run-of-the-mill adolescent conflict had ended in two people acting out their feelings and breaking the taboo of matricide.

PARKER AND HULME ON FILM

Certain events — the sinking of the *Titanic*, the murderous escapades of Ed Gein, the mutiny on the *Bounty* — provide the kinds of tragedy which filmmakers repeatedly turn to. Proposals to make a movie about the Parker–Hulme murder had been turning up periodically at the Film Commission offices since the first half of the 1980s. But by 1990, interest in the case had stepped up a gear. Among those who had already tried to turn the murder into a workable script were Australian playwright Louis Nowra, who looks to have been the first to manage a completed draft, and Jackson's old filmmaking friend Costa Botes.

Sometime early in 1991, before filming began on *Braindead*, Peter Jackson and Walsh started writing a script about the Parker–Hulme murders, fuelled by the idea of a murder story which 'had no villains'. By the time *Braindead* was completed in May 1992, Jackson felt ready for a rest from splatter movies, and *Heavenly Creatures* felt like the perfect change. Initially, however, he took some persuading that Parker and Hulme might be his kind of movie. 'The film only got made because of Fran's enthusiasm for the subject matter,' he told *Premiere* magazine. 'I said, "It's two girls murdering one's mother. I mean, where's the story in it?" And she just hammered it into me.'

As the director read more about the case, his curiosity rose. The girls' love affair with storytelling and the imagination struck chords in Jackson's own adolescence. At Pauline's age, when she was filling exercise books with tales of murderous royals, Jackson had spent long hours working on ambitious movies populated with winged creatures and death-dealing Cyclopes. 'I could relate very much to how they had this love of creating fantasy worlds and stories.'

Another thread linked Parker and Hulme's imaginary kingdoms with Jackson's childhood. It could be argued that, in both cases, the excitement of creating imaginary worlds had been co-opted partly to help survive the trials of puberty. Jackson, by his own admission an unconfident teenager, found some of his closest friends through a shared love for making fantasy films. If the young Peter Jackson had honorary saints, they were not the romantic figures of James Mason and Mario Lanza, but monstermakers like effects man Ray Harryhausen.

Much of what Walsh and Jackson read about the Parker–Hulme tragedy seemed to them to be advancing a specific agenda or political angle. Said Jackson: 'What interested us was to show these two fifteen-year-old girls with no other agenda than to be as accurate as we possibly could, and to somehow imagine what was going on inside their minds.'

The couple began tracking down everyone they could think of who had known the Parker and Hulme families. As for earlier researchers like Laurie, Glamuzina and Forster, reactions from those the couple approached ranged from cooperation to denial of all knowledge. Walsh and Jackson managed to find at least fifteen of the girls' former classmates (a tough job considering how many had married and changed their names) and a number of former university staff and students who had come into contact with the Hulmes. The fact that Jackson was the man who had perpetrated *Braindead* appears not to have counted against him — few of those he spoke to were younger than fifty, 'so usually people had never heard of me'.

Canterbury University would later allow them to film at Ilam mansion itself, still under university ownership. But Christchurch Girls High, where Juliet and Pauline had met, was a different story. Some of the ex-pupils spoken to by Walsh and Jackson recalled that the day after the murder, the headmistress had told the assembly that 'no girl is to discuss a certain matter' — in forbidding it, effectively making the discussion more likely to occur. In 1972, the school won headlines again when two students walked out on hymns at morning assembly, protesting that time allotted by the Education Department for music was being used on compulsory religious studies. The girls were expelled, although the Supreme Court (as the High Court was then known) later ruled that the expulsions were contrary to the rules of natural justice. They lost their case regardless, as the board was within its powers under the Education Act.

In 1991, Christchurch Girls High allowed the launch of *Parker and Hulme:*

A Lesbian View to go ahead in the school auditorium. Principal Dawn Lamb was quoted as saying, 'We live with our history. I think there would not be many institutions 115 years old who could get by without having someone less than perfect attend them . . . It was nothing to do with the school, really.'

But when Jackson asked Lamb if he might film some scenes from *Heavenly Creatures* at the school, she refused, and encouraged her students to have no involvement in the movie. It is hard to say whether Lamb imagined that any film would only fuel more interest in the scandal of the case, or was offended by Jackson and Walsh's planned approach. She later told the *Christchurch Star* that Jackson had shown her a copy of the script, and she 'didn't like it'. Jackson would get the final laugh — the school had moved locations in the interim, and the original buildings were now under the jurisdiction of Christchurch City Council, which gave permission to film in one of the original classrooms.

Jackson has said that Lamb's only comment after seeing the script was, 'Why can't you make a film about pupils of whom we are proud.' Such reactions only strengthened his belief that making a movie about the Parker–Hulme case was a good idea.

> *We found that a lot of the people we interviewed, even though forty years had gone by, were still presenting attitudes of the fifties: this was some dark, sordid little thing that was best kept quiet and should never be mentioned. Many times we got, 'Why on earth would you want to make a film about this?' We should just forget about it, and hope it will somehow disappear. And we actually thought about doing that. But within twenty or thirty years most of the people connected with it will be dead, and at that point in time we'll never know anything about it. We felt it was a good time now, while there were still quite a few people alive, to do the interviews and try to get something accurate, for the record.*

During the research process, Jackson and Walsh went to the Justice Department and asked to look at their files on Parker and Hulme, which included mention of the girls' new identities. Both signed agreements that they would never divulge these details. Sometime during this period, either Jackson or Walsh was also accidentally shown some documents they were not meant to see. A staff member is said to have arrived, and taken the documents back. Jackson mentions in a number of interviews having looked at Parker and Hulme files that 'no one had seen for forty years' — one of the clues that they saw extra information, as it was on the public record that Laurie and Glamuzina had requested and seen the complete trial and prison files back in 1987.

Some have speculated that Jackson and Walsh saw Pauline's original diaries, although all evidence is that these diaries no longer exist. The voice-over in *Heavenly Creatures* is based entirely on the diaries, and only a small number of quotations in the movie appear to lack known sources. However, it seems more likely that the forbidden documents related either to Pauline and Juliet's period in prison, or the period shortly after their release. Laurie and Glamuzina were permitted to look at most of the files concerning Parker and Hulme's incarceration, although under strict conditions. In 1997 Pauline Parker herself threatened to take a legal case against Jackson. Her lawyer in London claimed that Jackson and Walsh had seen diaries she wrote while incarcerated, and had based the film on these diaries. Jackson replied that he had 'never heard before that she wrote diaries from prison', and *Heavenly Creatures* itself ends at the point before she went to jail. The case never went to court.

THE RACE TO THE BIG SCREEN

By mid-1992, at least four other Parker–Hulme scripts were in various stages of development. Michelanne Forster handed in a draft for a telemovie based upon her play to Television New Zealand in April 1992. A few months later, actor Dustin Hoffman's production company Plumb Productions began seeking directors for a Parker and Hulme script by New Yorker Wayne McDaniel.

When moviemakers are in a race to make a film based on a particular event or topic, it is rare for more than one winner to emerge. The other versions either don't see completion, or if they do, usually fail to find an audience. Heard of *Valmont*, or the second 1970s version of *King Kong*? The first film used the same source material as *Dangerous Liaisons*, and the second, *The Legend of King Kong*, was abandoned before reaching a cinema screen. Disaster movies, which rely on spectacle more than concept, are rare exceptions to the 'one winner' rule: the competing meteor movies *Armageddon* and *Deep Impact* both had respectable commercial success.

While Jackson and Walsh were working on their script, a formidable team of New Zealanders were beavering away on a Parker–Hulme movie of their own. Working partly from the research of Laurie and Glamuzina, Wellington actor, playwright and director Fiona Samuel wrote a script called *The Pursuit of Happiness*. It won the interest of producer Bridget Ikin, who had recently had international success with Jane Campion's *An Angel at My Table*. Enthused, the two spent a year working on drafts of *The Pursuit of Happiness*, eventually hooking up with director Niki Caro. Ikin says the script offered a somewhat 'darker vision' than what Jackson finally put onscreen, 'a different, female take on it, I suppose. We had something more subtle and psychologically truthful, for me more interesting. But a lot of people love that film.'

Work on the Jackson and Samuel scripts continued under a Film Commission scheme that gave producers funding to develop their own scripts, without having to announce them publicly. (Samuel's project had been mentioned in the media as early as February 1992.) News that someone else had quietly been writing about Parker and Hulme came like a 'bolt from the blue' to the Samuel team. For Ikin it would provide a lesson in dealing with material in the public domain: 'You have to expect that you're not the only person working on it.'

ANOTHER ANGLE ON PARKER–HULME

Abandoned scripts based on the Parker–Hulme case can be found in filing cabinets across four nations. The earliest script known to the author is by Australian playwright Louis Nowra (*Radiance*), and dates from 1987. Having first learned about the case after picking up *Obsession*, the fictionalised account read by Fran Walsh as a teenager, Nowra saw the makings of 'a great script', and flew to Christchurch to continue his research.

Australian Stephen Wallace made plans to direct Nowra's version, called *Fallen Angels*, in Canberra. Intrigued by accounts of the girls' telepathic communication in the courtroom, *Fallen Angels* ended with 'Juliet' and 'Lisa' in different jails, communicating via the Fourth World. After Wallace was forced to withdraw from the project, Nowra tried to find another director, and considered directing himself. His plans were delayed when director Vincent Ward enlisted him to help write *Map of the Human Heart*.

In September 1987, English novelist Angela Carter was commissioned to try her hand at adapting the Parker–Hulme case. The second draft of her script, *The Christchurch Murder*, was completed in August 1988 (the script can be found in her posthumous collection *The Curious Room*). England's Euston Films and Auckland company South Pacific Pictures, both had a hand in developing it, but Carter's script failed to satisfy all parties.

New York scriptwriter Wayne McDaniel, inspired partly by a nonfiction account of the murders written by *Obsession* writers Gurr and Cox, rang court authorities in New Zealand and arranged for a copy of the trial transcripts to be sent to New York. He had a first draft of his own script *Sugar and Spice* finished by August 1990. In 1992, *Sugar and Spice* won the interest of Dustin Hoffman's company Plumb Productions. Memories differ as to the level of Hoffman's involvement, although McDaniel says there was talk at one point of him playing the role of chief prosecutor.

Plumb staff member and splatter fan Tim Meyers added the final twist to the saga, when he suggested approaching Peter Jackson, then winning acclaim for *Braindead*, as a possible director. Meyers's efforts to track down a copy of *Braindead* led eventually to the New Zealand Film Commission. But when the Commission learned that Plumb was considering asking Jackson to direct, it broke the bad news: Jackson was within weeks of shooting his own version.

Having learned that Jackson was set to ask for production funding at the next Film Commission meeting, the Samuel/Caro/Ikin team rushed to put in their own application. By then, Jackson was close to securing international investment and had a number of cast members in place. 'It turned into a race,' Ikin says simply. 'I suspect that they just went for the one that was more developed. He was the golden boy, someone the Commission wanted to support, and rightly so. He's extremely talented. But my personal doubts at the time were about whether it was his kind of story.'

In late 1992, the Film Commission promised *Heavenly Creatures* conditional funding of around $2 million. Samuel's script was abandoned soon after. Niki Caro later went on record to say that the Film Commission's choice of director was 'wildly inappropriate'.

How had Jackson leaped to the front of the line? The answer involves a mixture of luck and determination. By the time Jackson and Walsh began writing in early 1991, two of the earliest Parker–Hulme projects were effectively comatose — Angela Carter's had been abandoned, while Louis Nowra's had been put aside. Of the other projects, only one of them, Samuel's, appears to have had a director assigned. Niki Caro's second film, *Whale Rider*, has become one of the most successful films in New Zealand history, but in late 1992 she was yet to make her feature debut. Jackson, though, was riding high on the success of *Braindead*. And for many months he said nothing publicly about his plans.

Asked on the eve of the film's release how he dealt with the pressure of all that competition, Jackson gave a revealing reply: 'It made me aware of the responsibility we had. There was only going to be one film made, and we had to do it right.'

Caro and Ikin were not the only people in New Zealand wondering if Jackson was the right person, and the right gender, for the task. Five years earlier, movie critic Stephen Ballantyne had written that the majority of New Zealand films were the work of middle-class liberals, whereas *Bad Taste* marked the welcome arrival of 'a bunch of rowdy young hoons'. This particular hoon — a shy, polite one, perhaps — had gone on to prove his talent. Yet judging by his movies to date, Jackson's interests lay much more in the comic delights of ripping his characters' limbs off than in investigating the human psyche. The potential for a movie that was all stylish bluster, and no brains, loomed large.

THE GERMAN CONNECTION

According to Jackson, *Heavenly Creatures* was written with a New Zealand audience in mind. But even before cameras rolled, the film was winning interest in the country where Jackson's movies had previously been known almost exclusively to video recorders. After reading the script, American film company Miramax, then one of the hottest independent distributors in the US, bought sales rights to *Heavenly Creatures* for much of the world. But Miramax were second on the scene — German producer Hanno Huth (*Enigma*) had beaten them to it.

Back during the hubbub of the Cannes Film Festival in 1992, Huth sent a team of staff members out to hunt for movies his company could distribute in Germany. Later, back in his office in Berlin, he read a rave review from Cannes of a new horror movie named *Braindead.* When he asked his staff if they had seen it, they tried to persuade him that the film had not been at the festival at all: most of *Braindead*'s screenings had been in the evening, when many Cannes-goers are off at parties.

Huth finally caught up with *Braindead* in Los Angeles, fell in love with it, and bought the rights. 'After seeing this movie I thought I might have made a big discovery,' he says. 'I wanted to produce the next Peter Jackson movie.' Armed with a thriller script he was trying to find a director for, Huth met Jackson in London. The director showed little interest in the script, but spoke instead about a story in which two girls form an extraordinary friendship. Says Huth:

> You meet people, and you get the feeling these guys are talented or less talented.
> I don't know how it is, you develop a feeling for it. I had the feeling I shouldn't
> question and doubt too much that this movie was going to be fantastic. I was
> fascinated by the story, and the people were very down to earth and real.

Huth's company Senator Films agreed to put up just over sixty percent of the *Heavenly Creatures* budget. Jim Booth spoke at the time about how the film's financing reflected the increasing globalisation of filmmaking: 'The original negotiations for *Heavenly Creatures* were held in London and finalised in Milan, with a German company which has its head office in Munich but signed the contract with a subsidiary in Ireland. The lawyer was in LA.' In months to come Huth would sell the completed movie on to the US, and lose a talented movie director through no fault of his own.

LONDON

Heavenly Creatures was obviously going to live or die on its casting. Jackson and Fran Walsh flew to London, having enlisted English casting agents

John and Ros Hubbard (*The Commitments*) to help fill out the English half of the *Heavenly Creatures* cast. Finding someone to play Juliet Hulme proved relatively easy. Jackson and Walsh quickly settled on seventeen-year-old television and stage actor Kate Winslet, who worked part-time in a deli in her home town of Reading.

Among those auditioning for the role of Juliet's mother Hilda Hulme was theatre actor Diana Kent. Having been informed that *Heavenly Creatures* was based on a true story, she assumed at the time of her audition that the real Hilda Hulme had already passed away. As for meeting Jackson and Walsh, she remembers them as 'very accessible, relaxed and unthreatening'.

Kent had learned about Peter Jackson's growing reputation from some New Zealand-born friends, and was aware that his experience lay more in special effects than in working with actors. But the real problem was that Kent was in the midst of an ambitious production of *An Inspector Calls*, directed by Stephen Daldrey (later to helm the movie *The Hours*). 'Contractually I was open to leave, but in terms of my feelings, my commitment to the piece, it was huge.' Attempts were made to work the *Heavenly* schedule around gaps in the play's performing season, but to no avail. In the end, the originality of Walsh and Jackson's script made the decision for her. 'It was really on the strength of that rather than asking much about the director. I decided that one should be having new experiences, so I thought, blow it.'

Veteran film and television actor Clive Merrison's resemblance to the real-life Henry Hulme is so strong that in the scene where he stands by a painting of his character, the painting is one of the actual Hulme, rather than of himself. Called before Walsh and Jackson, Merrison played a few scenes with an Australian actress trying out as Hilda Hulme. If his account can be trusted, the New Zealanders were dumbstruck at his resemblance to the real Hulme. 'Peter and Fran were just staring at me thinking, fucking hell — if this guy can put two words together, we'll be okay.'

Merrison was keen. 'You've got to be on for adventure. Besides, my sister lives in Melbourne, and I thought I could see her at Easter.'

All engines were go on possibly the strangest film of Peter Jackson's career — a movie whose main interest was not zombies, bloodthirsty aliens or homicidal puppets, but the extraordinary friendship of two teenage girls.

HENRY HULME

Henry Hulme and his son Jonathon sailed from New Zealand for London in July 1954, before the trial of Juliet Hulme began. On the sea voyage he was quoted as saying, 'My only concern now is for my son. I want to spare him all I can.' In the next few years Hulme divorced, remarried and became a key member of the British scientific team designing a thermonuclear hydrogen bomb. He died in 1991.

HILDA HULME

Sailed for England with Canadian Walter Perry, after both went on the stand at the trial. Perry had originally met Hulme in her capacity as a counsellor at the Christchurch Marriage Guidance Council, and moved into an adjoining flat at Ilam in December 1953, an aspect of the Parker–Hulme story which remains unclear in some overseas cuts of *Heavenly Creatures*. After the murder, a public auction of the Hulmes' personal effects attracted a large crowd. Hulme married Walter Perry in 1955.

HERBERT RIEPER

Father of Pauline Parker, died of pneumonia in Christchurch in 1981, aged 92.

HONORA PARKER

Was born in Birmingham England, and despite all the writings and research about the Parker–Hulme murder, much remains unknown about her. No photographs of her have ever been published. After arriving in New Zealand at the age of eighteen, she met Australian book-keeper Herbert Rieper while working in Raetihi. In 1936 the couple moved to Christchurch, and had four children, but the first died of a heart defect shortly after birth. Honora Parker was murdered on June 22, 1954.

CHAPTER EIGHT

PUTTING IT ON FILM

'To take a risk on somebody who could be extraordinary was worth it, because the film was so important.'
PETER JACKSON, ON THE CASTING OF *HEAVENLY CREATURES*

'I remember walking away from the track after the second day, and being very aware of the sunlight and how important it was to be walking towards it.'
ACTOR SARAH PEIRSE, ON FILMING THE MURDER SCENE IN *HEAVENLY CREATURES*

For every movie ignited by showcasing the first appearance of a new acting talent, another is sunk on delivery, due to risky casting that did not quite work. With *Heavenly Creatures*, Peter Jackson knew that whatever abilities he might demonstrate behind the camera, if he got the wrong actors to portray Pauline Parker and Juliet Hulme, the film was effectively sunk before it left port. By February 1993, preparations were continuing for *Heavenly Creatures* to begin shooting in Christchurch in less than five weeks. The actor to play Juliet Hulme had been organised for months, in the shape of English unknown Kate Winslet. Jackson had auditioned 500 women in his search for Winslet's counterpart — someone who could pass for sixteen years old, who looked like the real-life Pauline Parker, and who could act. Only a small number of professional actors fitted the bill. Perhaps remembering the largely amateur cast of *Bad Taste*, Jackson was wide open to the idea of using someone with no acting experience.

During his search, the director had found two young women in their early twenties whom he felt could take on the role.

> They were very talented, but I felt very reluctant to cast somebody that age. Fran said, 'You're not really happy with the choices, are you?' This was like four weeks out from the shoot. I said no. She said, 'This is crazy — we're about to go into this movie we spent two years writing, and we haven't got someone who's right for the role yet. This is unbelievable madness.'
>
> I said, 'Yeah, but blowed what I can do about it.' She just jumped in a car

and started driving up through the North Island stopping at schools, going up to principals and saying, 'We're making this movie, here's a photograph of Pauline Parker, is there anyone in your school we could look at?'

Walsh later recalled that the mode of transport for the casting expedition was a rusting old Ford Cortina. She and her casting assistant were often asked why, as moviemakers, they weren't driving a Porsche. 'So then I would pitch the story to the entire classroom, scanning the room the whole time, looking for sullen, brooding schoolgirls, all the while thinking, what would she look like with her hair dyed black?'

Meanwhile in Christchurch, Jackson was being pressured by producer Jim Booth and key crew members to decide which of the actors on his shortlist had the role.

The wardrobe department needs to start to measure, they can't make a single Pauline costume until they know who's playing the part, and here we are going to start shooting in three weeks. I was saying, 'No, no, just give us another few days — Fran is trying to find somebody, just wait.' And finally I got this call from Fran one night. She was in New Plymouth. She said, 'I've seen someone today who I think is really interesting. I think you should fly her down straight away — she's got an amazing face, amazing presence, she really jumped out of the class and she's done a bit of school acting.

Melanie Lynskey had auditioned with some of her friends from New Plymouth Girls High School. Though she had been doing drama training for five years, the sixth former's performance experience was limited to some school plays and a couple of musicals with the local opera society. After meeting her for the first time in Christchurch, Jackson was immediately impressed by her presence. 'If she's just standing there doing nothing she's still interesting to look at, which is a bit like what Tim Balme's got. That's a gift that not many actors have.' But Lynskey was so nervous at that first audition that 'it was hard to get anything out of her'. After she flew back to New Plymouth, Jackson was worried that her acting experience wasn't up to taking on a feature.

A couple of days later, he flew Lysnkey back to Christchurch for a second audition. This time actor Miranda Harcourt was on hand, with just a few hours to try to put Lynskey at her ease and help determine whether she had the natural acting talent to pull off a major role.

'I was young, but I wasn't stupid,' Lynskey later recalled. 'I knew they were a bit nervous. In my mind I was an actress, because it's all I've ever wanted to do. And I was naive enough to think, well, I've done so many plays, I guess I can be in a movie. But it's a whole other thing.' Adds Jackson:

She [Harcourt] brought her into the audition, and Melanie was incredibly brave and poured on this really powerful performance, which convinced us she was definitely worth the risk. I think that to play it safe you're actually undervaluing the film in a way. You're not entirely happy, you're not allowing the film to reach its full potential. But to take a risk on somebody who could be extraordinary was worth it because the film was so important. It was an unbelievable pressure at the time — I was losing sleep over it, and I don't usually do that.

Later, Jackson would argue that Lynskey's lack of professional experience helped make her the right person for the role.

IMAGINARY WORLDS

Pauline Parker and Juliet Hulme created imaginary kingdoms complete with elaborate networks of royal families. And like many teenagers, they idolised certain celebrities with near-religious strength.

Though the girls invented two kingdoms, Volumnia and Borovnia, much more is known about the latter. When Juliet was confined in a sanatorium with tuberculosis, the girls began to write to each other in the voices of two of their favourite Borovnian characters, letters later described by Juliet as 'a lifeline'. Pauline wrote as Charles, the king of Borovnia, while Juliet replied as Charles's wife Deborah. This habit of assuming new identities and calling themselves by different names crossed into real life. Pauline often imagined herself as a gypsy girl named Gina, and by late 1953 preferred to be addressed as such. Her family continued to call her by her middle name of Yvonne.

Diello was another favoured Borovnian character. Son of Charles and Deborah, Diello has been described by scriptwriter Fran Walsh as 'a murderous teenager who'd kill anyone who was a problem to him'. As *Heavenly Creatures* progresses, Diello increasingly pops up in the girls' imaginations to dispatch those who irritate them. Walsh and Jackson chose to give Diello the intense features of actor/director Orson Welles, feeling that Diello shared many of the qualities the girls feared in Welles, who was at one point in the girls' pantheon of saints.

The girls built a shrine in the back garden at Ilam to worship their own shifting set of saints and gods, and spoke about religious matters more often than *Heavenly Creatures* implies (later they decided to break all ten Commandments, but appear not to have got very far).

Pauline's 1953 diary lists a series of saints, each with their own special code: singer Mario Lanza was 'HE', British heart-throb James

Mason 'HIM', and Harry Lime 'IT'. Harry Lime is the shadowy character Orson Welles played in the classic 1949 thriller *The Third Man*, which is recreated in *Heavenly Creatures* (Canadian actor E Jean Guerin, who met Jackson and Walsh while driving for them at a film festival in Toronto, flew to New Zealand to take the role). Mention of Lime caused confusion in court, as a number of medical witnesses appear not to have been movie fans. The girls' most important saint was apparently James Mason (Diello's name may even have been inspired by one of Mason's roles). Pauline wrote in her diary after one movie, of Mason being 'far too wonderful to attempt to describe'.

Two weeks before filming, Jackson rang Lynskey's mother Kay, and told her he wanted to offer Melanie the part of Pauline Parker in *Heavenly Creatures*. Kay had worries about the emotional demands of the movie, but was also conscious of the opportunity being offered. It was a Friday night, and by Sunday, Melanie Lynskey was in Christchurch.

At times over the next fortnight of rehearsals, a strange sense of *déjà vu* hangs in the air. A teenage girl with a distinctively New Zealand accent watches at Christchurch airport as a confident, glamorous young actor arrives on the plane from England, and feels instantly a little outclassed. Within days rehearsals are in full swing, and the two teenagers are fast becoming friends. Yet even before the shoot begins, the making of *Heavenly Creatures* feels at times as if someone has injected life and laughter into a ghost story. Melanie Lynskey and Kate Winslet are running through the grounds of Ilam mansion together in a state of mingled joy and concentration, trying to recreate the conversations of two people separated from them by forty years, and a murder.

PLAYING JULIET

It was clear to me that a strange alchemy was occurring in the Christchurch warehouse where *Heavenly Creatures* was being made — the process of recreating another person's life was helping an actor define her relationship to the world, so that the act of moviemaking became something special in itself, whatever might end up on celluloid.

A seventeen-year-old actor had travelled 20,000 kilometres from her home in England, to recreate part of the life of Juliet Hulme, an English teenager who had once dreamed of Hollywood, only to spend four years of her puberty in an Auckland prison cell. Seven weeks into the film shoot, Winslet had no idea that playing Hulme was going to provide her own launch-pad into acting stardom, but she knew already that the role had changed her. 'I just think I'm going to be more understanding,' she said, a few minutes after our interview was supposed to have finished and the film crew had called wrap for the night. 'I feel I've crossed this barrier. I've suddenly left being a child behind and stepped into this adult body.' Unprompted, she then made a list of the ways she planned to be a better person to a number of those close to her, once back in England. Cynics would ascribe such sentiments to some kind of temporary hysteria caused by overwork, which is just one example of why cynics are worth avoiding; if getting inside the skin of a tragedy can help us to embrace life and other people more fully, then I was hearing the evidence firsthand.

Winslet's view of the young Juliet Hulme that evening in May was of a person whose upbringing had bred insecurity, thanks partly to a lack of parental love, and also to a childhood spent living under a succession of nannies, relatives and boarding schools. In Winslet's opinion, the insecurity had bred a front of great confidence, and a degree of self-dependence.

She was tall and slim and very above herself. Her head was just totally in the clouds. I think Juliet was attracted to this kind of a funny little creature which was what Pauline was, so different to her. We met quite a few of their old school friends. One of them was from England and said she was very arrogant, very very English for England, incredibly posh. She had to learn to cope so much on her own, and so therefore she made everyone beneath herself, and many people were in awe of her. At school she would make the teachers feel like children because she was downright rude. Half the time she got away with it because her father was the rector of Canterbury College. She played on that all the time. She and Pauline together were always scheming to do naughty little things and fantasising about other worlds. I think she was a lovely person but that never showed because she never had anyone to show it to, and so she met Pauline.

She had this amazing ability to shift her mind and her soul into another world, make everything happy, and just detach herself from what she didn't want to see. When she met Pauline, it gave her the confidence to make her whole imaginary unreal world bigger, because at last she could share it with someone. I think she lost all sense of her identity the minute her parents sent her to live with far-off relations in the Bahamas when she was eight years old. She lost all sense of who am I, and where are the people that love me. That's when it all began because she'd never had anyone to cling on to. She had to create the magic of warmth for herself, which is why she was so selfish. She'd never had the chance to share. And that's why the intensity between her and Pauline was so great — because she just threw her whole being into this friendship.

When Winslet first read the script for *Heavenly Creatures* in England, she knew nothing about the Parker–Hulme case. Yet she 'totally clicked' into the girls' story, and the sadness of the murder. Later, an acting friend of Winslet's went along to an audition, and told her that a photo of the real Juliet Hulme looked exactly like her.

In one of Winslet's auditions, she was asked to act out a scene with Diana Kent playing her mother. Kent remembers the audition well. 'I thought, gosh, she's very young. We did one scene which wasn't in the film, where I'm going to a party and she's trying to stop me going. She throws her arms around my legs and holds on to me. After the audition Kate asked me on the street, "Did that feel all right? I practised on my mum in the kitchen." I said it was great. She was just a very immediate performer.'

Like the soon-to-be-discovered Melanie Lynskey, Winslet had been acting for a number of years. By the time of her *Heavenly Creatures* audition (joining over 150 others), she already had ongoing roles in two television series behind her, plus a host of musicals and theatre roles, and voice work dubbing foreign-language films. Winslet had grown up in Reading, to the west of London, and gone to a nearby theatre school. Acting was part of her life: alongside her father's acting work in television and theatre, her grandparents ran a small theatre in their back garden, and an uncle had appeared in West End musicals for many years. Like many in her family, she expected her acting career to be in television or theatre.

On one of Winslet's final auditions for Jackson and Walsh, Walsh filled in by reading out Pauline's lines of dialogue. Winslet recalls taking control of the audition, asking if Walsh could sit in a certain position while they went through the scene: 'I just felt determined to show them I could do it.' Winning the part of Juliet brought on 'a thousand different feelings', among them excitement, disbelief, and utter panic. Soon after, Jackson and Walsh began sending her photos and information about the real Juliet Hulme (the lead cast received packs about the person they were playing, including extensive information from the trial). Though Hulme had been slightly thinner than Winslet, the resemblance between the two would prove unnerving to some of those on set. When a makeup artist was about to apply fake moles to Winslet's face for the sake of accuracy, she was surprised to discover that the actor had many in virtually the same place already. Says Winslet:

I met one woman who was a very close friend of the Hulme family. She had these letters Juliet had written to her from prison, and she put them down on the table. I knew she had them, Peter had told me, and I was looking at these letters. It was like Juliet was creeping into my brain. Then she said, 'Would you like to hold the letters? Would you like to look at the letters?' I took them, and it was like electricity going through me. I was touching her handwriting. I just couldn't believe how I felt so incredibly sad. I was sitting there in front of this woman who I'd known for five minutes, crying these huge heaving sobs. She put her hand on my shoulder and said to me, 'You must be totally devastating as Juliet, you must be arrogant, but you must have a certain finesse that is incredibly rare. And you must be totally like her. I know you can be. You look exactly like that dear child.'

When filmmakers work from real-life tragedy, the moral dilemmas spread outwards like a spider's web. When does empathy cross unconsciously into insensitivity, and storytelling become invasive? Well-meaning actors and directors do their best to get inside the minds of those who have undergone life-changing horrors, and when they do their job well, can become famous in the process. With *Heavenly Creatures*, Winslet and Lysnkey were in the position of trying to get inside the minds of two people who had done their best to move on from tragedy, and no longer wanted the world to know about their pasts. The Department of Justice had made sure that Parker and Hulme were given new identities after their release from prison in 1959. Yet Jackson and Walsh had no desire for Parker and Hulme to be found. They had gone ahead with their project partly due to an awareness that if they did not make the film, others were likely to make it regardless.

Though people tried to steer clear of the topic during interviews, it was clear that a number of those on set were aware of Parker and Hulme's 'new' identities at the time of filming. Some of those I spoke to let slip that the two were still alive. At this point Winslet already seems to have felt uncomfortable about her level of knowledge of the 'old' Juliet Hulme.

If someone made a film about me, and dug up all of this truth about my life, knew exactly the things I did, exactly how I walked, moved, laughed, I would just be freaked out.

If I had something to say to her, I would say 'I just want you to know that I really do feel so much for what you went through, and I don't want you to feel that I've dug up your past. I'm sorry if this film being made does hurt you, but I hope that it's been done with no offence meant.' I think I'd like to meet her, really, and tell her that myself.

That Peter Jackson had a strong emotional investment in telling the Parker–Hulme story is clear. One day Jackson and Walsh and the two lead actors visited Victoria Park, to find the point on the track where Honora Parker had died. Says Winslet:

We just stood there when we got there. I basically freaked out, crying and going, 'Why did they do it?' Peter walked down to me, hugging me and quietly crying himself. We all just sat there for about half an hour on this track like lost, devastated souls, sobbing. I think that says enough about who he is, that he is not a guy who just directs splatter films.

Work I've done before has been hard, you have people rushing around all over the place and half the time the director is God knows where, so you don't have that intimate thing with the director you have with Peter. He can say three things to me and have me in tears. There was this one scene I did on a telephone talking to Pauline, and Peter said to me, 'Do you feel okay about doing this, do you feel ready?' and I said, 'No, I don't.' He took me off into a room and said three things to me and I came back and I was just a mess. It's just amazing the kind of effect he has. He said, 'Just remember who you are, how you feel about Pauline at this stage, that you're totally in love with her and this friendship, and also remember that you are going to kill her mother.' And then he said, 'How are you going to kill her?' And I said, 'With a brick.' He said, 'You're going to kill her with half a brick at the top of Victoria Park. You're going to kill this woman.' And he was holding me really closely to him and I think he was nearly in tears himself. That was it. He knows what to say, what to do.

GETTING IT RIGHT

Jackson's concern for historical accuracy meant that many scenes in *Heavenly Creatures* were shot on actual locations. The mansion at Ilam where the Hulmes had lived was now a university staff club; Jackson filmed in Ilam's grounds, and also made use of the bottom floor of the building. But the upstairs rooms had changed so much since the 1950s, that they were rebuilt in the production's warehouse studio (production designer Grant Major used architectural plans from the period to ensure accuracy, although the Ilam sets were shrunk by around fifteen percent from their original size). The upstairs balcony at Ilam had since been glassed in. A replica balcony was built, and computer whizz George Port later digitally pasted the fake balcony over the real one.

Jackson managed to persuade a local embroidery guild to remove a large tapestry so that he could film in the classroom Juliet and Pauline had shared as schoolmates: there were identical classrooms along the corridor, but Jackson wanted the actual room. Plans to shoot scenes in the Cashmere Hills sanatorium where Juliet had stayed were abandoned after the filmmakers discovered the building was going to be demolished. Major salvaged a number of doors and window frames from the site and used them in the building of Pauline Parker's house, one of the only interior sets which had to be designed more by guesswork. The filmmakers' research went as far as finding the original doctor's surgery where Pauline had been interviewed, the make of car driven by Dr Hulme, and the probable colour of the family's beachside bach.

After two movies in which director of photography Murray Milne had performed creative miracles on 16mm, *Heavenly Creatures* saw Jackson collaborating for the first time with cinematographer Alun Bollinger and shooting on 35mm. Bollinger, often referred to as Al Bol, is one of New Zealand's most respected cinematographers, having survived tough shoots with his old Blerta mate Geoff Murphy and provided the extraordinary images of *Vigil* alongside director Vincent Ward. In a strange fluke, Bollinger had even shot a movie for Australian Stephen Wallace, one-time likely director of arguably the earliest Parker–Hulme project, *Fallen Angels*. Jackson, who had spent three movies mining increasingly ambitious imagery from tight budgets, no longer had to worry about the multiple complications of filming around puppets and extensive on-set effects. With a movie based largely around humans, Jackson had the chance — and the budget — to go a little mad. And so he did, encouraging Bollinger and his camera crew to one of the most fluid, swirling pieces of cinema in New Zealand movie history.

FILMING THE MURDER

After three movies featuring violence as a major element in their comic armoury, *Heavenly Creatures* marked the first time Peter Jackson had chosen to treat murder seriously onscreen. 'Fran and I felt that we identified strongly with Pauline and Juliet and we wanted to make an audience identify with them,' he says. 'Yet it was a very fine balance, because ultimately we didn't want to condone what they did. The film hopefully explains what was going through their minds at the time — it gives some explanation which has never been given in forty years of people writing about this case. But I was not going to take their point of view on the day of the murder. I just pulled right back and said, okay, we're just going to watch what happens here, but we're not going along with what they're doing, because it's unforgivable, an atrocious thing to do.'

Jackson was able to film in the tearooms where Pauline, Juliet and Honora Parker had stopped in real life, before going into Victoria Park on June 22, 1954 (the tearooms were pulled down a few months after filming). But when it came to recreating the murder, Jackson's desire to make as much of *Heavenly Creatures* as possible on real-life locations failed him. As he told *Scenario* editor Tod Lippy:

We went to the murder site, and we just felt uncomfortable about filming there. It was very strange, and maybe it was just our imagination, but it was very quiet, very tranquil. I mean, all the way down the path you hear the wind and the birds, and suddenly when you arrive at the spot, you hear nothing. So we filmed the murder scene at Victoria Park, but it was on a different track, about a hundred yards away.

According to Jackson, the film crew were 'in a state of trauma' while shooting in Victoria Park. Sarah Peirse, who played Honora Parker, has spoken of filming the scene where her character receives repeated blows to the head with a brick, at the hands of Juliet and Pauline:

It's the sounds you make which are so evocative and difficult to deal with — the sounds of pain, anguish, distress and fear, and the sounds of the girls and their breathing. I remember walking away from the track after the second day and being very aware of the sunlight and how important it was to be walking towards it. I was very upset and I wept for Honora. It took me some time to get back to the top where we were based . . .

In some ways the story is honouring the fact that she didn't deserve it. I feel sure that it was the very quietness of the woman that contributed. The plainness and horizons of the parents were so limited in relationship to what Pauline wanted — the sophistication of what was occurring at the other home. I think Nora was symbolically the easier mother to kill. She represented reduced horizons, and domesticity in all of its negative aspects, whereas Hilda Hulme was powerful and potent. Honora must have been so bewildered and terrified when it happened.

When asked if she ever worried about identifying too closely with the role of Pauline Parker, Melanie Lynskey spoke immediately about Victoria Park.

We filmed the murder scene over about three days and it was so hard to get into that frame of mind. I thought, I'm not going to let myself get out of this for a while. So for those whole three days I just tried to stay in that.

At times, Lynskey found herself watching Sarah Peirse closely in between scenes.

Not like stalking Sarah or anything, but just . . .
Thinking you could kill someone?
Yeah, because there are some things I think you can't pretend to be thinking.

When the scene was finally completed, she 'went off and cried'.

Though Jackson understood how Parker and Hulme could have thought that murder was the only solution, he has never known why, on the day, they actually went through with it. He must have wondered at times why he was asking someone else to recreate the experience.

> *Melanie is so sweet, you know, yet you're having to transform this girl into a murderer. It's not good. What Melanie learned very quickly is that it's no good to pretend. She can't sit there and pretend to be a murderer, she actually has to be a murderer because that's the only way you're going to see it in her eyes. She had to become this person that was so alien to her. She was utterly traumatised by it at the time. Kate had to do exactly the same thing, but she at least had the training to be able to switch in and out of that a little bit easier than Melanie. Melanie had none of those techniques. She was just bullied and coerced into becoming this murderer, without the ability to fall back on the techniques of the acting profession.*

Jackson's comments paint an unfairly negative picture of Lynskey and Winslet's overall treatment on set. Every *Heavenly Creatures* cast member I interviewed has spoken of the care taken of the movie's two leading actors during filming. 'I always felt really safe,' Lynskey later said. 'We were very protected from the pressure.' Lynskey has talked of how producer Jim Booth and his partner Sue Rogers acted like surrogate parents to her during the shoot, while 'Peter was like . . . big brother or something.' Lynskey also enjoyed a very close relationship with Sarah Peirse, who doubled playing her mother by being Lynskey's acting tutor.

And how much of herself did Melanie Lynskey see in her role? Like Pauline, Melanie Lynskey, interviewed at the time, writes poetry and has 'relationships that sometimes mean everything'. She adds: 'I can just see how if you met someone you connected to that strongly, how important it would be. Sometimes I think there is quite a lot of me in the role, but then I remember how hard I had to work to get to where she was.'

Lynksey and Winslet both tell stories of how Jackson liked to act out scenes in character before a take, becoming a teenage girl before their eyes. Merrison (Henry Hulme) offers a different spin on the habit: 'People who can't talk to actors do that.' He felt that Jackson's background in special-effects-dominated films showed through on set. 'He didn't really know the language of actors. Peter's direction was like, "Clive, just one thing, can you be funnier?" It's not really the way to go towards it. But you don't make a film that good by accident. He's awkward with people, but that didn't stop him communicating what he wanted. His perseverance and determination and stamina were huge.'

Merrison remembers feeling privileged that he was on the ground at an exciting time for New Zealand's film industry. 'There was a real buzz around. I've never been to rushes like it. Everyone was there, down to the catering staff. We were betting on takes. I never watch rushes, but it was extraordinary, so I went every night. I didn't look, but I joined the party.'

Some US film industry visitors could not believe that each day's footage was being seen by more than just the director, producer and writer. 'Often [in the US] the crew are banned from watching the footage,' said Jackson. 'To me, that's just a crazy way of working.' He spoke of the family atmosphere on set, where crew members were encouraged to speak up if they had any good ideas.

There were moments of comedy, too. Merrison can laugh now about the day he arrived in Christchurch airport after a particularly nightmarish flight — no one was there, he had no idea where he was staying, and his luggage had all gone on to Bali. Later, during shooting of the high-school scenes, the film crew spent the day dressed in girls' clothes. A sequence with *Braindead* actor Elizabeth Moody playing a terrifying French teacher had to be filmed again partly because it was so much fun to shoot that it came across as too comic in the rushes.

JIM BOOTH

Heavenly Creatures is dedicated to producer Jim Booth, who died of cancer on January 4, 1994. Over a nine-year period he had gone from being the man at the Film Commission who turned down Peter Jackson's requests for movie funding, to being one of his closest collaborators. Since leaving the Commission, Booth had produced two movies for Jackson, but admitted to him at one point that *Meet the Feebles* and *Braindead* were not really his cup of tea. In 1993, as cancer continued to ravage his body, Booth supervised the making of the film that would take Jackson's career to a whole new level, and show the world that the director was as masterful at handling tragedy as comedy.

After Booth's death, Jackson wrote a long account of his relationship with Booth for the next issue of industry magazine *Onfilm*. 'I still can't believe that Jim's gone,' the article began. 'His presence in my life over the last few years has been so great that to think I'll never see him again is just too awful to contemplate.'

In between post-production duties on *Heavenly Creatures*, Jackson worked with Booth in the last months of 1993 on a host of scripts and movie proposals. The meetings began at WingNut's office, and as the cancer reached Booth's lungs, adjourned to his bedroom. During this period, Jackson wrote that he had never heard a word of self-pity from Booth, who continued to make jokes about his condition.

In the *Onfilm* obituary, more than one acquaintance spoke of how Booth had been an inexhaustible source of good ideas and a lover of fun. Once, before joining the Film Commission, he had gone into the office of a workmate and said, 'That tie will simply not do,' before taking a pair of scissors and cutting the offending tie in two. Booth is probably one of the only people so well liked that he could have got away with it.

BREAK ON THROUGH TO THE OTHER SIDE

For Peter Jackson, Jim Booth's passing marked the worst possible beginning to what would be a very strange year, a year in which Jackson's new film would win acclaim throughout the world, along with the kind of newspaper headlines he dreaded.

Sometime in the first few months of 1994, a print of *Heavenly Creatures*, without music or subtitles, was rushed to the selection committee of the Cannes Film Festival, to see if it might win a place among the films in competition. In the end, *Heavenly Creatures* was offered an out-of-competition screening at midnight (Madonna's *Truth or Dare* had been offered a similar slot three years before, before it was successfully negotiated back to 11pm — but that film wasn't looking for any awards). *Heavenly*'s out-of-competition offer was turned down. Some said that French cable television had been playing Jackson's *Braindead* on a nightly basis during the selection period, and that had an influence. Jackson commented that Cannes festival head Gilles Jacob 'kept muttering about *Braindead*' when he spoke later with Film Commission staff. 'Perhaps he didn't want to be seen to be supporting a splatter director,' Jackson wondered. Taking a gamble, Miramax decided to hold the film in the hopes of winning a spot in September's Venice Film Festival.

Miramax was now handling the film in most territories of the world. Once Miramax saw the completed film, it was given fourteen days to decide if they wanted it for the US as well. Negotiations were completed mere hours before the expiry period.

The American company had established itself as a master at marketing risky and foreign films to stateside audiences — where, in the xenophobic American market, the two words had long been seen as interchangeable. In May 1993, when Miramax executives flew down to New Zealand to take a look at how the *Heavenly Creatures* shoot was going, the company was in the midst of evolutionary change. That month, Miramax bosses Harvey and Bob Weinstein prepared to sign a contract which meant that the company would become an independent subsidiary of Disney.

In July 1994, Miramax announced that it had signed Peter Jackson to an exclusive first-look deal. 'New Zealand has proven itself recently to be a country with a lot of talented filmmakers,' said Miramax executive David Linde, possibly remembering the company's recent success with *The Piano*. 'We can't have offices everywhere, and [Jackson] is a key person in the New Zealand film business.'

The deal involved an 'exclusive first look at anything Peter writes, produces and directs'. It also called for Jackson and Walsh to act as the company's eyes and ears in New Zealand, helping bring new filmmakers and projects to the attention of Miramax. In one stroke, Jackson's power in the New Zealand film industry had been doubled. Jackson himself described the deal like this:

> *Any time I want to seriously do something like write a script or make a movie, I have to give them a first look at it. They have seven days or something to decide if they want to do it. If they pass then I'm free to take it to anybody else I want to. So it doesn't tie me down at all. Obviously, if they like something then it's a fairly easy route to finance, and I don't have to go through any of that agony about trying to get money.*

There seem to have been a few speed bumps in the early days of the Miramax deal. Despite having won attention from Hollywood, the notoriously loyal Jackson felt he still owed something to German producer Hanno Huth, whose original investment had helped get *Heavenly Creatures* off the ground. A few months after signing with Miramax, *Variety* reported, Jackson was giving Huth's company Senator Film first look at two of his new projects, *The Black Max* and *Jamboree* (see Appendix 4). Jackson insisted that this did not conflict with his renewable deal with Miramax. Asked about this period later, Huth was philosophical.

> *I would have liked to co-produce more Peter Jackson movies. Once you discover someone, then the big companies from America come and seduce the talents to work with them, and give them monthly payments and development deals. These companies are so big and they have enough people to travel a lot. But it is like it is.*

By the time *Heavenly Creatures* got to the Venice Film Festival in September, much had happened. For starters, the movie had lost around ten minutes of its original running time. Miramax, in the midst of establishing a reputation as a company that liked to buy films and then either shorten them or leave them sitting on a shelf for long periods, sent 'hatchetman' (Jackson's humorous description) Charlie McClellan to New Zealand to help the director come up with a shorter cut. (Miramax has won little positive publicity for this habit — but then it should be remembered that filmmakers are reluctant to admit that cuts made in a movie by executives might actually improve it.) Miramax, long a fan of test screenings, was uncomfortable with some scenes, including the comical moment at the dinner table where Pauline imagines her parents dying. 'We had final control over the film, but they pleaded with us to take out about ten minutes' worth of footage,' Jackson later said, adding that he now preferred the shorter cut of *Heavenly Creatures* which had resulted.

Yet the movie was originally released in New Zealand in its long form. England and many other countries saw a version which was somewhere between the two cuts. And Miramax staff member Charlie McClellan left his job at Miramax, to begin working for Jackson.

THE RISE OF MIRAMAX

The two brothers who run Miramax films have long been aware that the US is not the only place that produces moviemakers. Famous for the passion and bluster of co-founder Harvey Weinstein, Miramax grew from tiny maverick to Hollywood powerhouse in only fourteen years.

Miramax was founded by New Yorkers Harvey and Bob Weinstein in 1979 to distribute concert movies, after older brother Harvey had begun by promoting rock concerts. In 1989, Miramax started to make its mark in a crowded independent marketplace, after buying American rights to three highly-successful movies: *Sex Lies and Videotape*, Ireland's *My Left Foot* and Italy's *Cinema Paradiso*.

Miramax was simultaneously making a name for itself by waging a series of campaigns against America's MPAA ratings system, challenging the X (or NC-17) ratings given to some of its movies. Such campaigns underscored the company's shrewd marketing, which helped win large audiences for difficult foreign and 'art house' titles such as *The Crying Game*.

In May 1993, Disney paid between $US60 million and $US80 million to buy Miramax, in a contract that Harvey Weinstein noted contained multiple mentions of the word 'autonomous'. The deal provided substantial capital, but also prohibited Miramax from releasing NC-17 movies, since it was now a subsidiary of Disney. In 1995, Miramax released the controversial *Kids* as NC-17, establishing a special company solely for the purpose.

Since then, Miramax has moved increasingly into more mainstream film production. Its 176 Academy Award nominations include having made or distributed *The Piano* (1993), *The English Patient* (1996) and *Shakespeare in Love* (1999). In 1994, Bob Weinstein established the Miramax subsidiary Dimension Films, which helps buffer some of Miramax's riskier projects by developing mainstream franchises like the *Scream* trilogy, *Scary Movie* and *Spy Kids*.

Nicknamed 'Harvey Scissorhands', Harvey Weinstein is famed

for wielding a strong influence in the editing room, thanks partly to *Cinema Paradiso*, which Miramax shortened by thirty-three minutes and turned into a box-office success in the process. Director Jim Jarmusch later said that Miramax bought his 1995 film *Dead Man* after completion, then told him it needed re-editing. According to Jarmusch, when he refused to make any cuts, arguing that the contract was on his side, *Dead Man* was given a limited release and little publicity. Harvey Weinstein's 'creative disagreements' with a number of producers and directors (including three of 2003's Oscar nominees for best picture) are legendary. His strong opinions are a tonic to some, and an embarrassment to others.

DISCOVERY

For thirty-five years, Juliet Hulme's and Pauline Parker's whereabouts had been unknown to the public at large. In late May 1994, a few months before *Heavenly Creatures'* premiere screening at the Wellington Film Festival, *Sunday News* journalist Lin Ferguson was at a party. Some of those around her began talking about Peter Jackson's movie, and the original Parker–Hulme court case. Ferguson recalls that an elderly Cantabrian woman in pearls, slightly the worse for alcohol, then said the following words: 'I believe the Hulme girl is an author called Perry — and she's very successful.'

Back in her office, Ferguson had a copy of *Parker and Hulme: A Lesbian View* on her desk. Flicking through the book one day during a phone call, she found a reference to Walter Perry, the man whom Hilda Hulme had married shortly after the murder trial.

'I just started looking in reference books,' says Ferguson. 'When I opened this book called *Contemporary Authors* . . . it's like she wanted to be found. She left all the clues. Same birthdate. Mother's name. Stepfather Walter Perry. There was nothing hidden.'

Anne Perry wrote Victorian murder mysteries, and lived in a small village in Scotland. Ferguson began reading all the Anne Perry novels she could find. The first one she looked at included a scene where someone was hit over the head by a blunt instrument; another alluded to a character writing romance novels under another name. When Ferguson talks about Anne Perry, it becomes clear that her own justification for 'outing' the author's long-hidden past is somehow tied into the fact that Perry writes murder mysteries. That aspect helped sell the story to Ferguson's editor Sue Chetwin, but Ferguson argues that it also demonstrates on some level that Juliet Hulme/Anne Perry wanted to be discovered. 'She was writing all about it, disguising it, putting it into a different era.'

Having gained confirmation of Hulme's new identity from three different sources, Ferguson was still unsure whether to go ahead with the story. 'I had nightmares over exposing this woman after forty years,' she says. 'I didn't sleep. I must have asked all my friends about 900 times, saying, "I don't know if I should do this." No one said don't do it. And the friends were not journalists.'

She rang Peter Jackson, who urged her not to publish, and called her some 'not very nice names'. By this point, Ferguson knew that the cat was out of the bag — after telling her editors of her discovery, the story would run whether she wrote it or not. The day before the story was due to appear in the *Sunday News*, Ferguson and some of those around her had a final attack of nerves over whether they might have the wrong woman. On July 31, Ferguson's story appeared under the front-page banner headline 'Murder She Wrote!'. On the next page, Ferguson quoted a spokesperson for Anne Perry's literary agent, upon hearing the news: 'We're all reeling from shock. Are you sure you're right?'

Considering how she must have been feeling, Perry handled the situation with grace and courage. Five days after the appearance of the *Sunday News* story, England's *Daily Telegraph* published an extended interview in which she gave her account at last.

Perry argued that her parents would have taken Pauline overseas with them, but Pauline's mother would not allow her to go.

> *She felt her mother was the only thing stopping her from leaving a situation she felt was intolerable.*
>
> *She wished me to join her in this act and I believed that if I did not she would take her own life. I thought it was one life or the other. I couldn't face the thought of being responsible for her dying. I made a foolish choice.*

Pauline was 'literally wasting away' — journalist Sarah Gristwood mentions the word bulimia. Perry said she had 'completely blocked out' the murder — 'All I can say is that it was violent and quick' — and also 'chosen to forget' a great deal of her later three-month period in solitary confinement. She said that in the months before the murder she had been treated with drugs for a chest ailment, drugs that she claimed tended to warp judgement. 'But obviously I was an accomplice. I was party to this act and I never pretended otherwise.'

Claims of a sexual relationship with Pauline were 'completely untrue', she said. Her discovery meant that she was frightened for her family. Her mother, who lived in a nearby village, had a heart condition. 'She doesn't deserve this.'

Soon after the interview, Television New Zealand reporter Cameron Bennett knocked on Perry's door in Scotland accompanied by a camera crew, and was told by one of her friends that the author was unavailable, after advice not to speak to the media. Bennett asked the woman somewhat desperately whether Perry might be able to come out and provide the film crew with her refusal in person.

Jackson clearly felt regret that his film had caused the pair any distress. 'We were wanting to get in and out of this film with the least amount of disruption to their lives,' he told the *Sunday Star-Times* in October. But he also expressed some surprise that Perry's secret had not emerged earlier. According to Jackson, her new identity had been common knowledge in Wellington theatrical circles and among actors on the set of *Heavenly Creatures*, after a friend of Perry's had told an actor from the cast of the Parker–Hulme play *Daughters of Heaven* back in 1992.

But one comment from the *Sunday Star-Times* interview made one wonder if Jackson was forgetting at times that the movie had sprung from real-life events and not vice versa. 'It's a shame because we feel the film doesn't need this kind of publicity,' he said of Hulme's discovery. 'It stands quite by itself. We actually feel really sad the film has never had an independent life from a writer who lives in Scotland. We'd much rather it had a sense of mystery — you come out of the movie and say, "Wow, I wonder where they are now?"'

In later interviews, Kate Winslet no longer sounded comfortable about the idea of meeting the real-life Juliet Hulme, and expressed guilt at having known so much about her life.

FLOATING IN VENICE

So this is the Venice Film Festival for a New Zealander in 1993. Melanie Lysnkey stands before a crowd of eager Italian paparazzi, rocking back and forth on her toes with an embarrassed grin before turning on an expression of serene friendliness that would do any superstar proud. Just before that, she joins the *Heavenly Creatures* press conference with Peter Jackson and Sarah Peirse, sitting 'on one of those little stages like you always see Rachel Hunter sitting on', terrified that someone will ask her a question.

The official screening of *Heavenly Creatures* wins an extended standing ovation, and some tears from the lead actors. Kate Winslet has jetted in from a film set in Hungary, just in time to join in. A few days before, Venice looked like a distinct impossibility for her. Lynskey has already watched *Heavenly Creatures* on Jackson's television set and had time to adjust to it. But for Winslet, watching *Heavenly Creatures* for the first time in the midst of all the festival hoopla is 'like someone had just punched me in the heart. It all just came belting back in with a great big slam.'

Peter Jackson's jump into mainstream acceptability began next to a cloud-covered ocean in Venice. *La Republica* critic Irene Bignardi found *Heavenly Creatures* 'one of the most unique films of the festival'. *Variety* reviewer David Rooney said the film showed 'a drop-dead command of the medium', and was both 'a dazzling, kinetic techno-show and a complex, credible portrait' of an out-of-control relationship. At the closing ceremony, a jury headed by American director David Lynch awarded *Heavenly Creatures* a Silver Lion, one of the festival's major prizes that year. A week later, a poll of 600 international writers at the Toronto Film Festival presented Jackson's fourth movie with the Metro Media Award for best movie at the festival.

Time critic Richard Corliss was an important early convert to *Heavenly Creatures*, joking that viewers should move to New Zealand in order to see it. It was Corliss who wrote one of the most memorable lines of all — that Jackson 'is like a physician who assumes a patient's fever in order to understand her illness'. The movie, he wrote, communicated the creepy excitement of its main characters with 'urgency and great cinematic brio, while neither condescending to the girls nor apologising for their sin'. Thanks partly to 'perfect' casting, the sad creatures that Pauline and Juliet must have been in real life had been 'alchemised into figures of horror and beauty' onscreen. 'They become the stuff of thrilling popular art.'

A survey of nine Australian critics later put *Heavenly Creatures* at the top of the twenty-six films on release that month — the only movies which came close to its average rating were fellow New Zealand sensation *Once Were Warriors* and the Chinese film *To Live*. The end-of-year lists continued in a similar vein. At least thirty American critics named *Heavenly Creatures* one of the ten best films of 1994. The *Sydney Morning Herald* found it the best movie of 1995 (again, *Once Were Warriors* also made the top ten). *Heavenly Creatures* also made it onto top-ten lists for Richard Corliss at *Time*, *Guardian* critic Derek Malcolm, and critics Peter Calder and Harvey Clark at the *New Zealand Herald*.

Critics praised the acting of *Heavenly*'s two leads. Some saved most praise for Kate Winslet; others preferred Melanie Lynskey. Both received awards for their work. *Sunday Star-Times* critic Russell Baillie called the film 'an original and a stunner', arguing that it proved that Jackson could direct actors 'just as well as he once could craft comedy out of carnage'.

Although rave reviews massively outnumbered all other varieties, not all critics were enraptured. In a mixed review, *Pavement* editor Bernard D McDonald felt that the film's generous portrayal of the girls helped 'align the audience more with their plight than with the ultimate fate of Parker's mum . . . Should we be moved by two premeditated murderers with sociopathic leanings? Probably not, but it makes for engrossing cinema.' *New Statesman* critic Jonathan Romney accused Jackson of overloading the film with whimsy, and failing to take audiences inside the girls' heads. 'He simply makes it look as if the girls are fleeing one world of irreducible weirdness for another. There's no sense of a revolt against dead suburban banality — Jackson can't do banality except through the filter of the bizarre.' But Romney felt the film was on surer ground with its handling of the run-up to the murder. A number of other critics argued that Jackson's focus on capturing the girls' fantasy life was achieved at the expense of emotional depth.

Heavenly Creatures opened in America in November 1994, a few weeks after its New Zealand release. Miramax made sure to capitalise on the recent discovery of Anne Perry. 'Murder she wrote!' ran one advertisement. 'The *true* story of the mystery writer who committed murder herself.' On learning of the campaign, Jackson and Walsh were 'disgusted'. Jackson has spoken of ringing Miramax on the day the film premiered in the US, asking that the publicity make no mention of Perry. His protests appear to have been ignored — the following February, the 'Murder she wrote' advertisement was still in print.

On its opening weekend in New York, *Heavenly Creatures'* per screen average was higher than any other film showing in the city. The film's American theatrical gross would later reach $US3 million, a solid yet far from stunning figure, considering the media coverage won by the film. In New Zealand, it became the seventh most successful locally made movie in history, just six weeks after release. In some countries, *Heavenly Creatures* had mainstream commercial success, while in others it remained in the arthouse. But the media interest in the film and in Parker and Hulme helped establish Peter Jackson as an important name to watch, as did admiration from critics who would normally have avoided his movies. About this time, with the help of contributors from around the world, a Canadian-born chemistry professor named John D Porter began assembling what remains the single most extraordinary information source about the Parker–Hulme case, and the movie which followed. (Porter's FAQ can be found on a number of *Heavenly Creatures*-related websites, including The Fourth World (www.geocities.com/Hollywood/Studio/2194/).

FICTION AND FACT

Heavenly Creatures ultimately tries to incorporate two kinds of truth — the known truth of events leading up to June 1954, and the psychological truth of Juliet and Pauline's world view at the time.

Jackson has spoken of trying to depict all the people portrayed in the film as accurately as possible, and refusing to tidy up reality. He argues that 'we couldn't have invented anything that was more extraordinary than what happened'. Yet Jackson did not want to stay 'totally tied to real life, and totally dull', and endeavoured to 'have a little bit of fun' by taking a less naturalistic approach to the film's authority figures, such as Francis Bennett, the general practitioner who saw Pauline.

I guess if you were trying to justify it you could say we were presenting them from the girls' point of view, but that's not strictly true. I just think that there were really only two people who we needed to be realistic with, and they were Juliet and Pauline, both of whom were slightly larger than life anyway.

Jackson's comments highlight the complications of telling a story which aims for factual accuracy, while simultaneously presenting many of its events through the emotionally-heightened prism of two imaginative teenage girls. The opening titles of *Heavenly Creatures* contain the following lines. 'During 1953 and 1954 Pauline Yvonne Parker kept diaries recording her friendship with Juliet Marion Hulme. This is their story. All diary entries are in Pauline's own words.' This preamble helps give the impression that the movie was either authorised by Parker and Hulme themselves, or is based on their own accounts. To some degree the latter is true. But inevitably *Heavenly Creatures'* view of reality is highly selective. As in almost every account of the murder, the reliance on Pauline's diaries means that the scriptwriters know much more about Pauline's story than Juliet's. Pauline's diary entries have been edited for the screen, sometimes with lines missing within entries (journalists and authors commit the same potential sin on a regular basis, in the act of trying to balance fairness and brevity in quotations). Peter Jackson has admitted that the film tends to emphasise the diaries' more dramatic aspects, at the expense of some of the more humorous entries.

A number of important lines from the diary, for example the one where Pauline declares she could fall in love with Juliet, are not included onscreen. Such decisions reflect Jackson and Walsh's stated view that the relationship was not sexually based — Walsh has said that they 'did not want to lumber the film with a lesbian label when it was at best open to speculation'.

Vital elements of many of the fantasy versus reality scenes, such as the one where John first has sex with Pauline while she mentally escapes into the kingdom of Borovnia, appear to be largely speculative. The decision to bring the inhabitants of Borovnia to the screen as clay or Plasticine figures is an inspired creative leap. Yet its basis in the girls' actual stories is tenuous: Jackson's jumping-off point was learning that the girls sculpted Plasticine figures.

The Parker–Hulme case is so complex that turning it into a film requires some degree of 'editing' in order to create an accessible, unconfusing narrative. But part of what makes *Heavenly Creatures* such an arresting movie is the scenes where Walsh and Jackson stray furthest from what is agreed on in real life — notably the scenes where the girls hover between their real lives and Jackson's vision of their imaginative kingdom, seemingly losing touch with the boundaries at vital moments. In the opinion of the author, Jackson and Walsh's account would be that much easier to admire if Jackson had not downplayed their own imaginative contribution by insisting so often on the film's accuracy. Much of the criticism that can be directed at *Heavenly Creatures* would be rendered meaningless if they had prefaced the movie with the far safer words 'based on a true story', or changed the names of Juliet and Pauline.

For Jackson and Walsh, the intense journey taken with Parker and Hulme reached an extreme in February 1995, when Jackson was woken by a call from Miramax co-boss Harvey Weinstein, who excitedly told him that his and Walsh's script had just been nominated for an Academy Award for original screenplay. 'Wow, that's fantastic,' replied Jackson.

That week, the couple also learned that Anne Perry had accused *Heavenly Creatures* of creating a grotesque, distorted portrait of her. Perry questioned the acceptability of making a film about 'people who are still living, because of the damage it can do. It can ruin lives.'

Perry's comments came as she prepared to begin a twenty-three city tour of the US to promote her latest novel. But she said that her only desire in speaking was to try to clarify the truth, since 'other people have made such a noise'. Though Perry still refused to see *Heavenly Creatures*, she disagreed with the idea that the murder had been motivated by Juliet and Pauline's imminent separation. 'I mean certainly we were good friends, but it was a debt of honour,' said Perry. 'It wasn't a great "I can't live without you" business that these idiotic moviemakers are making out of it.'

In an interview a few days later, Walsh argued that everything in the movie was well researched, and that Perry was trying to protect her career. The blow-up quickly died down when Perry replied that her 'idiot' comment had been an unfortunate one, likely made in the heat of the moment: 'From what I've been told, I don't feel the movie was grotesque and distorted at all.'

In a later interview, Perry said that her rediscovery had been far from desired. But in some way it marked 'the last stop as far as healing is concerned. Because I'm finding that now practically everybody in the world knows who I am — and they still like me.'

Jackson's prediction that Quentin Tarantino's movie *Pulp Fiction* would take the best screenplay Oscar in 1995 turned out to be correct. 'The real award for Fran and me is just the fact that we have been nominated for one of the five best screenplays of the year,' he said. While Jackson took a seat in Los Angeles for the Academy Awards ceremony, the woman who had for so long wanted to bring the Parker–Hulme story to the screen made do with watching the awards back in New Zealand. Fran Walsh was just a few weeks away from giving birth to her and Peter Jackson's first child.

JULIET HULME / ANNE PERRY

Left New Zealand for England after being released from jail in 1959. In the late 1960s, she finally got to travel to the US, where she found herself attracted to the 'inherent kindness and fairness' of the Mormon religion. Between stints as a secretary and a flight attendant, she began to write historical novels, but did not find a ready market until she incorporated murder into her plotlines. Her first published novel, *The Cater Street Hangman*, was released in 1979, and later adapted for television. Perry has since published more than thirty-five novels, a number of them American bestsellers. Her William Monk series revolves around an amnesiac detective who may have committed a murder, but is not sure. In recent years Perry has begun to venture into fantasy, with the religiously-themed *Tathea* series. She lives in Scotland.

PAULINE PARKER / HILARY NATHAN

Travelled to England in 1965 after her probation was complete, and spent time as a librarian. In 1997, journalist Chris Cooke tracked Nathan down to a small village in southeast England, where she was running a riding school for children. Nathan had no comment to make.

KATE WINSLET

After completing her role in *Heavenly Creatures* as Juliet Hulme in June 1993, Kate Winslet went back to her deli job until the following September, when she had a minor role in the little-seen *A Kid in King Arthur's Court*, one of her only career mis-steps to date. After winning acclaim for *Heavenly Creatures*, Winslet appeared in period pieces *Sense and Sensibility*, for which she was Oscar-nominated, *Jude* (contributing one of cinema's more horrifying birth scenes) and *Hamlet* with Kenneth Branagh. Won over by the vision of *Terminator* director James Cameron, she signed on to the seven-month shoot for *Titanic* without a completed script, and became a star in the process. Winslet then flew to Morocco for the under-rated *Hideous Kinky*, where she met future husband Jim Threapleton and to Australia for Jane Campion's schizophrenic *Holy Smoke*. Winslet's role as writer Iris Murdoch in *Iris* (2001) earned her a clutch of best-actor awards and another Oscar nomination. Recent roles include *Neverland* with Dustin Hoffman and *Eternal Sunshine of the Spotless Mind*, in which she plays a woman who seeks to erase her bad memories. Winslet has one child to Threapleton, who she left in 2001. In mid-2003 she married British director Sam Mendes.

MELANIE LYNSKEY

Constantly and unfairly found wanting by many when her career is compared to the meteoric rise of Kate Winslet, Lynskey is one of New Zealand's few female actors to have found regular work in the US. She left for Los Angeles straight after high school in 1995, found the experience terrifying, and returned to New Zealand to study drama in Wellington. After life-changing advice from director Gaylene Preston, Lynskey returned to Hollywood in 1997, was offered the lead role in the little-seen independent movie *Foreign Correspondents*, and since then has shown her gift for comedy in *But I'm a Cheerleader* and Cinderella fantasy *Ever After,* played cute in *Detroit Rock City*, and flew to Greece for *The Cherry Orchard*. Much of her work as the best friend in *Coyote Ugly* ended up on the cutting-room floor in favour of shots of models dancing on top of bars. Lynskey narrowly missed out on playing the romantic interest in Adam Sandler's big-budget bomb *Little Nicky*, and later continued her luck by winning the lead role in New Zealand road movie *Snakeskin*, one of her most enjoyable experiences to date. She appeared in the Stephen King mini-series *Rose Red,* starred in indie horror film *Claustrophobia* (2003), and is third-listed behind Hayden Christensen and Chloe Sevigny in *Shattered Glass*.

JIM BOOTH

Peter Jackson's longtime producer passed away on January 4, 1994, after a long battle with cancer. Later that year, his sons Nick and Simon joined his partner Sue Rogers to accept the Silver Lion award for *Heavenly Creatures* at the Venice Film Festival. Rogers later took over the running of Booth's company Midnight Films. Simon and Nick Booth both worked on *The Lord of the Rings*.

CHAPTER NINE

EMPIRE-BUILDING: *FORGOTTEN SILVER* AND THE BIRTH OF WETA

*'It is deceitful and dishonest to claim documentary status
in order to perpetrate a joke.'*
A LETTER TO THE EDITOR ABOUT *FORGOTTEN SILVER*, NOVEMBER 1995

*'The art of storytelling is the art of spinning a convincing lie.
I'm not going to apologise for doing my job well.'*
FORGOTTEN SILVER CO-DIRECTOR COSTA BOTES, REPLYING TO ANOTHER LETTER, NOVEMBER 1995

Let's play a little game, a game that involves travelling back in time. Back past the release of *Devil Girls from Mars* to that first, hand-cranked age of cinema: an age when the rules of the movie game were still being invented. Imagine a young New Zealand filmmaker named Colin McKenzie, a man with big dreams and little cash. After Colin completes his first film, his grandfather offers him money to burn it. Later, when times are tough, Colin is forced to travel from town to town around New Zealand, where he remakes the same story for local audiences in each place he stays. Eventually McKenzie begins work on an epic movie featuring ambitious battle scenes and cross-cultural love affairs. He falls in love with one of his lead actors and asks her to marry him. But on the first day of filming it starts to rain, and all the extras enlisted to play warriors run off. Colin is in a pickle. Will he ever finish his beloved movie epic?

The above story may sound a lot like the one told in Peter Jackson and Costa Botes's *Forgotten Silver*, a film that has been accused of having only the dimmest relationship with truth. Yet although *Forgotten Silver* may be a tissue of lies, a surprising number of those lies pay homage to genuine local film pioneers. In fact everything mentioned in the above paragraph did occur — the only lie was the sneaky insertion of the fictional name of Colin McKenzie. The opening of this chapter actually retells events in the life of New Zealand filmmaker Rudall Hayward.

Hayward really did marry one of his lead actors, his extras really did run off, and his historical epic — *Rewi's Last Stand* — did eventually make it to cinema screens. If you have not heard of Rudall Hayward and other cinema pioneers like Ted Coubray, you are far from alone: New Zealand's widespread ignorance of its own cinematic history helps explain why thousands turned on their televisions one Sunday late in 1995 and fell hook, line and sinker for a history lesson whose lies fly very high indeed.

This chapter is about two different varieties of lying. The first type involves the kind of extraordinary lies which result when real-life filmmakers stand in front of a camera and praise people who never existed. The rest of the chapter involves the birth of Weta, a special-effects company whose deceptions are born from silicon chips, foam latex, and hard work. Though some of the company's work can be as down-to-earth as removing television aerials and installing new verandahs, the Weta effects empire has found most fame for creating visions that defy rational belief. The period of *Forgotten Silver*'s making saw Weta in the midst of phenomenal growth, and Peter Jackson finding a home base he could call his own.

FORGOTTEN SILVER

Perhaps more than for any other film in this book, the lies of *Forgotten Silver* should be witnessed firsthand, before letting a biographer spill any of their secrets. Applying a microscope to *Forgotten Silver*'s making feels somehow contrary to its spirit of storytelling, like trying to describe a friend's amazing imitation of Sean Connery — one really needs to be there, listening to the burr in person. But the bare facts are these: *Forgotten Silver* tells the story of a young inventor named Colin McKenzie, born late last century in the South Island rural town of Geraldine, who fell in love with film at an early age. Later, he became the first man in the world to bring sound, colour and full-length movies to the screen. In spite of this, to many he remains a failure — his greatest work, an adaptation of the Biblical epic *Salome*, never saw completion, his love life was a tragedy, and he remains best known for a series of repetitive pie-in-the-face comedies.

The idea for *Forgotten Silver* had its inspirations in *Alternative Three*, a British television mockumentary which Wellington film director Costa Botes saw back in the 1960s. (Though the mockumentary term was not invented at the time, it is now routinely used to describe a fictional film or programme that pretends to be real.) But *Forgotten Silver* is very much a collaboration between Botes and Peter Jackson. 'Most of the original story ideas in *Forgotten Silver* are mine,' Botes later wrote. 'But I can honestly say there isn't a single moment in the film that wasn't revisited, overhauled, or somehow radically influenced by Jackson.'

Botes first met Peter Jackson back in the mid-1980s while working as an assistant director on the television series *Worzel Gummidge Down Under.* At this point Jackson was still trying to get his first movie *Bad Taste* off the ground. When Botes saw some footage, he found Jackson's movie 'extraordinary'. It was Botes who first introduced Jackson to scriptwriting partners Fran Walsh and Stephen Sinclair, and over the next seven years he would become an unofficial part of the WingNut creative family, working separately at various times on film scripts with Jackson, Walsh and George Port.

Forgotten Silver was one of many projects being developed under the wing of Jim Booth. TV3 showed little interest, fearing that the show would not rate. The project got its chance at glory when the Film Commission joined with public funding body New Zealand On Air and Television One to commission a series of one-off dramas for television. After the success of the computer effects in *Heavenly Creatures, Silver's* grand visions of ancient cities and epic battle scenes suddenly seemed a lot more economically viable. The *Montana Sunday Theatre* funding committee was looking for contemporary dramas. So Jackson and Botes decided to send them a period 'documentary' instead.

Forgotten Silver quickly rose onto the preferred list from more than 300 submissions. Jane Wrightson, then New Zealand On Air's television manager, remembers that the project met with universal enthusiasm. 'We thought it was a bloody good idea, a really good boundary-pushing piece. We said, "Hell yes".'

COSTA BOTES

Born on the Turkish isle of Imbroz in 1958, Botes emigrated to New Zealand with his Greek family when he was just three years old. He began dabbling in filmmaking while still at school in Wellington, using the Bolex camera of a family friend. Unsure how to go about getting a job in the film industry, he began an English degree at Victoria University but spent most of his time in the library, reading about movies. When someone dropped out of a filmmaking course at Canterbury University's Ilam School of Fine Arts, Botes was accepted just a few days before the course began. After leaving Ilam he directed his fourth short film *The Lamb of God* (1985), about a meat-eating couple who find themselves trapped with a butcher after a revolution staged by sheep.

In his last year at film school, Botes read a Michael Morrissey story in which a young Catholic boy imagines that Stalin lives in his street. His adaptation of *Stalin's Sickle*, co-written with Anne Kennedy, showed a confident handling of mood and point of view, and later won him the jury prize at the Clermont Ferrand short film festival in France.

Botes met Peter Jackson in the mid-1980s, and took a cameo role in *Bad Taste* as an alien who refuses to die even after being cut in two by Jackson's car.

In between a long stint as film critic for the *Dominion*, and a period working as a storeman, Botes taught himself film editing, when he could not afford to hire an editor. He has since directed a number of works for television, including episodes of *The Ray Bradbury Theatre*, and co-wrote with George Port the hippie versus hoon short film *Valley of the Stereos*.

'I think the mainstream narrative film is more artistically challenging than any avant-garde film,' Botes said before the first screening of *Forgotten Silver*. 'The only truly avant-garde things in film were done by people such as Buster Keaton, Eisenstein and Murnau back in the twenties. All we can do now, really, is find our own unique voice.'

'I don't ask myself the question "Why do I do it?" any more,' he told writer Douglas Jenkin in 1987. 'I feel really bad when I'm not doing it. That's probably a better answer.'

DISCOVERY

During the Second World War, the New Zealand government built a series of gun emplacements overlooking Wellington's Miramar Peninsula, in the hope of heading off any attacks from the sea by the Japanese. Years later, Peter Jackson used a former army base in Seatoun, close by one of the emplacements, to film some scenes for *The Lord of the Rings*. While spying on a night shoot of *Rings* for a later chapter of this book, I discovered in one of the abandoned bunkers a metal cabinet that was empty but for two documents, along with some old folders of Weta telephone bills. One of the documents, an early *Forgotten Silver* script, is attributed to Jackson, Botes and Fran Walsh (in the finished film, Walsh is mentioned only as script consultant). The second document is even more fascinating — a funding proposal for an earlier version of *Forgotten Silver*, subtitled *The Extraordinary Life and Death of Colin McKenzie*.

The earlier treatment is undated. But it reveals that at one point Jackson and Botes were not to appear onscreen in *Forgotten Silver* at all. Instead, the search for the lost history of Colin McKenzie would be undertaken and narrated by a postgraduate film student named Sarah Blanks.

Botes had long envisaged that at a certain point in the story, Colin McKenzie would go bush, disappearing from view to begin work on some great epic. But it was Jackson who came up with the image of an abandoned film set hidden in the forest, where the remains of McKenzie's moviemaking efforts would finally be discovered. Jackson felt that for all the comedy and visual trickery, he and Botes should work to highlight the story's drama, and make the characters as believable as possible.

Careful examination of the *Forgotten Silver* script and treatment reveals a sequence that appears to have been progressively excised from the script, possibly due to worries about cultural sensitivity. The missing sequence argues that when Colin was trying to find funding to continue making the epic *Salome* in 1927, the Ministry of Native Affairs contacted him about recording an important gathering hosted by the Tainui tribe. Colin got the job. But when he arrived with his camera, Tainui elders, offended by previous photographers having stolen their images with little thought to context, asked that he record all the speeches at the gathering with respect, and in their entirety. The finished silent movie, *Hui*, ran for twenty-three straight hours and came with a 500-page transcript, which would rank it just behind Chinese epic *Burning of the Red Lotus Temple* as the fourth longest film in the history of cinema. Unfortunately all but a few minutes of *Hui* perished in a mysterious fire, just before its second screening. It appears there are few people alive who witnessed *Hui* in its full glory, partly because of the unexpected fire, and partly because hardly anyone stayed awake long enough to make it through that pivotal screening.

The proposal for *Forgotten Silver* script funding mentions other classics of the mockumentary genre: probably 'the closest of all in form and spirit to what we want to achieve is Woody Allen's *Zelig* — a dramatic and unforgettable merger of history and illusion'. The filmmakers also cite another classic of fake documentaries — New Zealand's long-running rural series *Country Calendar*, which famously broadcast an episode showing farmers who gave their turkeys miniature gumboots. In fact Australasia as a whole has a solid tradition of stories that lie at the border between documentary and comedy — including Fred Dagg, John Clarke's Olympics parody *The Games*, selected fraudulent episodes of *Havoc and Newsboy*, and Australian mockumentary *Bigger than Tina*.

MAKING IT REAL

While in the US to talk about his next movie, Jackson grabbed a camera crew, having persuaded Miramax boss Harvey Weinstein and film critic Leonard Maltin to join the *Forgotten Silver* cast. Weinstein even agreed to make a joke about Miramax having cut an hour out of McKenzie's epic *Salome*. Maltin had memorably cameoed in *Gremlins 2* as a film critic who is attacked by most of the cast. Like Jackson himself, whose scenes in *Forgotten Silver* are a model of persuasiveness in acting, Maltin proved to be one of the project's aces in the hole.

Though *Forgotten Silver* was made in conditions of secrecy, accounts differ as to the level of knowledge of *Silver*'s lies on set. Actor Peter Corrigan, who played silent comedian Stan 'the Man' Wilson, has said in interviews that he was told the character had really lived.

'A lot of people were told that it was fake,' remembers production designer John Girdlestone. 'But even the crew were a bit confused. You had to remind people that Colin McKenzie wasn't actually a real guy. Everyone was too busy.'

Part of the beauty of making *Forgotten Silver* was doing all the things you are not normally allowed to do when making a film — like talking during filming, and treating your film stock very badly indeed. Cinematographer Alun Bollinger used every trick in the book to create the many different looks of Colin McKenzie's mythical lost films — deliberately filming some scenes out of focus, leaving the camera door open, and undercranking the camera. Once the film had been processed at the National Film Unit, staff threw it on the floor and coated it in oil, in order to make it look old.

Judging by some of the outtakes, Jackson's recreations of the Spanish Civil War had to be pruned because some of the footage was too dramatic. Jackson, who has a war movie inside him waiting to get out, filmed execution scenes, and made use of a prop armoured car built by the production on the body of an old Model T (neither made it into the final cut). Many of the film's props were begged and borrowed from specialist collectors.

While Jackson concentrated on bringing the many recreations of old film footage to life, Botes would periodically drag cast members off in between scenes, to supervise the 'period' photographs used extensively throughout *Forgotten Silver*. Wellington photographer Chris Coad, who took three-quarters of the film's stills, estimated that he took around twenty rolls of film a day during *Forgotten Silver*'s production. (Botes handled most of the onscreen interviews, apart from those done in the US by Jackson.)

'It was incredibly ambitious for what the budget was,' says John Girdlestone. 'You're shooting Roman times, the Spanish Civil War, World War Two, Richard Pearse, all that Chinese stuff. I'll probably never work on anything as good again.'

Ambition was certainly the order of the day when the crew filmed at the Wellington cenotaph in front of the former National Museum, which would be glimpsed in the museum sequences of *The Frighteners*. The crew piled fake foliage and dirt over the cenotaph steps, close by a small patch of trees. Some of the scenes where Jackson and Botes discover the lost city of Colin McKenzie in the forests of the West Coast forest were shot there, within a stone's throw of a busy street. The Jerusalem battle scenes of McKenzie's *Salome* used the same location. A group of 200 extras were filmed fighting at various points around the cenotaph, and the shots later digitally combined to create a scene in which people swarm over every available space. In *Behind the Bull*, his documentary on the making of *Forgotten Silver*, Botes reveals that this one wide shot of the battle scene took up twenty percent of the entire budget.

Forgotten Silver cost around $650,000, more than any of the other six episodes in the *Montana Sunday Theatre* series, and required a funding top-up from New Zealand On Air and the New Zealand Film Commission. Executive producer Caterina De Nave estimates that Jackson would have contributed at least half of that budget again in terms of uncharged Weta resources and his own time.

Forgotten Silver was a throwback to the past, but at the same time it provided a signpost to Jackson's future. In one sense the *Salome* scenes marked a return to the no-budget days of *Bad Taste*, where scenes began with a rough story outline before being improvised on set. At the same time, *Forgotten Silver*'s recreations of the past made use of the expensive computer equipment that had recently arrived for Jackson's big-budget movie *The Frighteners*.

For Jackson, *Forgotten Silver* offered a chance to indulge his love of film history while putting a little of himself onscreen, disguised by the mantle of documentary. He was faking war scenes in a Wellington quarry with an old Bolex camera, just weeks before beginning work on his first big-budget Hollywood movie. Many of the conflicts present in McKenzie's story — the pressures of balancing filmmaking and family, and keeping the moneymen happy — were present in Jackson's own life.

SHOWING THE AUDIENCE

Jackson apparently felt sure that *Forgotten Silver*'s lies would be revealed before it screened, even though he and Botes asked cast and crew to say little about the project. An article in the *Listener* the week before the first screening helped keep the secret alive. Journalist Denis Welch played along with Jackson and Botes's ruse, even including interviews with the fictional Hannah McKenzie, said to have fallen in love with Colin after he left New Zealand for Spain. Jackson was quoted as saying that researching McKenzie's life was 'the most exciting thing' he had ever done: 'In a feature film you can tell a story, you have a lot of artistic licence to invent things, but when you're telling the true story of a man's life you have to honour the facts.'

Asked what a documentary, 'however sensational', was doing in a

Sunday Theatre slot, Jackson could not resist bringing *Silver*'s part-financers the Film Commission into the story: '. . . they felt that the *Montana Theatre* would be just right for it.'

In fact, Film Commission marketing director Lindsay Shelton had spoken to Jackson a few days before *Silver*'s television premiere, asking whether the film should have an explanatory title added to the start or end, warning viewers of its fictional nature. According to Shelton, Jackson believed there were sufficient clues and jokes throughout the programme to make it unnecessary.

On Sunday October 29, 1995, an estimated 440,000 New Zealanders began watching the story of an unknown filmmaker called Colin McKenzie (*Forgotten Silver* rated equal first that night with the movie *Power of One*). Exactly how many of that television audience finished *Forgotten Silver* in a state of belief, and how many were in hysterics, is unclear. But judging by what occurred over the next few days, the tide of the converted appears to have been high.

Among those who are said to have fallen for Botes and Jackson's deception are senior members of Television New Zealand and arts-funding body Creative New Zealand. A staff member from a museum in Wellington rang WingNut asking about putting on an exhibition of McKenzie artefacts. Telephone calls about *Forgotten Silver* came into radio talk shows, TVNZ headquarters, New Zealand On Air and a number of newspapers. Some sounded confused, some angry. A tourist operator telephoned the *West Coast Times*, excited about the tourist potential of a film set hidden away in the wilds of the West Coast. TVNZ spokesman Roger Beaumont said that Television One had decided not to give the game away in their publicity, and revealed that the programme was 'all really a bit of fun'. Beaumont's words were like petrol poured onto the fire.

Jackson found himself appearing on the mid-evening news to defend his decision. By the end of Tuesday, an anonymous source at TVNZ revealed that the station had received close to a hundred calls. Some 'were very very angry and bitter. They said they would never trust us again.' Others enjoyed the joke, or wondered whether the show was real or not. Later a survey of letters to the *Listener* found that a majority of three to one disapproved of the show. One writer felt so annoyed at the damage done 'to true documentary' that after a lifetime of interest in film, they had resigned their membership of the Film Society. A second felt that Jackson and his conspirators 'should be shot'. Another called *Forgotten Silver* 'the best New Zealand entertainment in ten years'.

Whangarei television reviewer Joanne McNeill wrote that all but one person she spoke to the day after the screening thought *Forgotten Silver* was true. When she questioned them about some of the holes in the plotline, a number replied, 'But Leonard Maltin was in it'. *Taupo Times* reviewer Val Smith found her belief in the show was shared by her daughter, 'a high-ranking, retired police officer, a deputy headmistress and an ex-hospital matron puffing next to me at the heated pool'. Added Smith: 'I did wonder about the 200 dozen eggs, and the fact that none of the descendants of the massive army of film extras ever claimed that grandma was once a seductive dancer and grandpa a Roman solider. But I wanted to believe this marvellous story of ingenuity, courage and tragedy so much that I pushed such churlish ideas away.'

As the story blew higher, Botes assured journalists that there had been no intention to trick the audience. 'To my mind a hoax is something you keep up, and we never had any intention of never coming clean. We thought the next day it would all come out. And it's actually come out with very little help from us.'

Forgotten Silver executive producer Caterina De Nave's defining memory of this period is finding herself bailed up by six very annoyed documentary filmmakers at a film screening. 'They were saying I'd single-handedly killed the documentary, and how could the public ever trust the documentary again,' she says. 'I just thought it was a really arrogant attitude. I've probably had more abuse about that show than anything I've done. Many of the professionals didn't get it, but the public did. My mother knew it wasn't true. One guy who is a carpenter knew that at that time of our history there was not enough concrete to build those sets.'

Botes's only regret about *Forgotten Silver* was for descendants of pioneer Kiwi aviator Richard Pearse, some of whom were unaware the programme was a fraud. According to *Forgotten Silver,* a computer blow-up of a small newspaper seen in the home-movie footage provided proof that Pearse had flown nine months before the Wright brothers.

Otherwise, Botes felt that many viewers were in denial that many 'genuine' documentaries were also constructed views of reality that could not automatically be trusted. He wrote in reply to one particularly angry newspaper correspondent: 'I suppose Mr Martin is still wondering how Steven Spielberg managed to train the dinosaurs in *Jurassic Park*? The art of storytelling is the art of spinning a convincing lie. I'm not going to apologise for doing my job well. If *Forgotten Silver* causes people never to take anything from the media at face value, so much the better. Our film was better researched, and, on the whole, more "true" than most products of the "infotainment" industry.'

Much of the public's annoyance at having been fooled seemed to reflect how strongly viewers wanted to believe that Colin McKenzie was actually real. The romantic appeal of an unknown New Zealander having beaten the world to so many cinematic breakthroughs appeared to have temporarily dissolved the logic stem in many otherwise functional brains.

Botes argued that the film was 'a full-blown celebration of Kiwi ingenuity, asking people to wake up and see what's in their backyard'. Jackson went even further, arguing that many of those that had criticised *Forgotten Silver* were the very same people who would have put down Colin McKenzie, had he existed. 'There's a lot of Colin McKenzies out there, and a lot of such backyard people are nobbled in New Zealand. They're nobbled by the "go out and get a proper job" brigade. The negative reaction to our programme seems a very good example of that.'

The following year, the Broadcasting Standards Authority rejected three complaints from viewers that TVNZ had tried to mislead and deceive in its showing of *Forgotten Silver*. Complainant Brent Proctor called TVNZ 'the getaway driver in this stick-up of the collective conscience . . . as culpable as gunman Jackson and cohort Botes'. But the BSA argued that since the programme was a drama, neither factual accuracy or balance were relevant. They added that *Forgotten Silver*'s spoof came with many clues disclosing its fictional nature, and did not have the potential to alarm viewers, unlike for example Orson Welles's *War of the Worlds* radio drama decades before (which had dramatised the arrival of alien beings).

Later in 1996, Botes and Jackson accompanied *Forgotten Silver* to the Venice Film Festival, where it won a special critics prize. Most of the international rights had already been snapped up by European company Pandora before a packed screening at Cannes back in May. Botes's worries that *Forgotten Silver* would not play to an overseas audience were swiftly abated by the laughter and applause he witnessed in Venice. He found that a number of the more obscure political and cinematic jokes that had won little comment in New Zealand got fulsome laughter.

Just before the start of the film's first public screening at Venice, Botes was telling something to one of the festival staff, and missed hearing his name when it was announced over the loudspeakers. Wondering where his directing partner had gone to, Jackson stood up and acknowledged Botes's applause. When Jackson's own name was called straight after, he got up again. Despite the comedy of the situation, the moment had some symbolism: since then a number of the overseas video releases of *Forgotten Silver* have neglected to mention that two people made this film, rather than one.

Internationally, *Forgotten Silver* has won largely admiring reviews. Judging by the number of votes posted on the International Movie Database website, it remains something of an oddity: *Silver* is one of the most admired films Jackson has ever been involved with, despite fewer people having seen it than any other that he has had a hand in directing.

From time to time, university students continue to send enquiries to the offices of the New Zealand Film Archive from across the globe. They want more information about a legendary filmmaker named Colin McKenzie . . .

THE BIRTH OF WETA

The story of the special-effects company named Weta is that of a talented child who is forced to grow fifty limbs to keep up with its homework. All those extra limbs have enabled Peter Jackson's cinematic visions to grow increasingly ambitious with each succeeding movie. The phenomenal pace of Weta's expansion has at some points outpaced the infrastructure needed to run it, which only makes the company's creative achievements all the more remarkable. The full tale of Weta's many comings and goings may well never be told, but for now, some insights into the company's early days should be manageable.

Tempting though it is to declare that the Weta special-effects empire began with a man, a computer and an instruction manual, that would be perpetuating the myth that Weta exists only to create computer effects. Though Weta did not officially come into being until the making of *Heavenly Creatures* in 1993, its origins lie with Jackson's previous movie *Braindead*, whose bloodsplattered last half-hour contains more special effects than five or six average feature films. It was here that modelmaker Richard Taylor came into his own. Having first come on board to design and build many of the models and props used in *Meet the Feebles*, Taylor headed the team handling *Braindead*, working in tandem with Australian expert Bob McCarron.

Along with scale models of 1950s Wellington streets, the job involved coming up with articulated zombie babies, zombies with no legs, and mountains of fake limbs. Taylor's pragmatism and good humour proved a valuable asset, as did his ability to work for extraordinary periods without complaining or falling over. Later Jackson enlisted Taylor and his partner Tania Rodger to take on a very different job for *Heavenly Creatures*, their main task being to design and build seventy latex suits for the scenes set in the imaginary kingdom of Borovnia.

Heavenly Creatures marked the point where Jackson discovered the virtues of computers. Until then, his experience lay mainly in physical effects, an extension of his own hands-on work during the home-movie days of *Bad Taste*. Physical (or mechanical) effects essentially mean that the illusion has been captured by the time the camera stops running — and can vary from miniatures and puppets, through to the fans used to pump out fake wind at the end of *Bad Taste*. Where New Zealand lacked experience was in the other major branch of screen illusion — optical or photographic effects.

Key to pulling off many special effects is the ability to combine different pieces of film in one image, usually through a photographic process known as a matte or travelling matte. An example of this is a scene combining a shot of a miniature monster and live-action footage of someone cowering at the monster's foot. The gluing together of such images normally requires an optical printer, which at its core is a combination of cameras and projectors working together. Creating mattes on an optical printer is an expensive, inexact process, sometimes leading to a telltale blue line that makes the matte look like a bad cut-out. According to Jackson, in the heydays of the 1980s only three or four labs in the world 'could do good blue-screen mattes — one in London and two or three in the United States'.

The late 1980s and early 1990s marked a revolution in the art of special effects. The floating water-alien in James Cameron's undersea epic *The Abyss* (1989) and the morphing villain in Cameron's eye-opening *Terminator 2* (1991) showed the way. But the movie that signalled an evolutionary change in special effects was *Jurassic Park* (1993), because its creatures were not liquefied, out-of-this world creatures, but living, breathing dinosaurs. George Port, who would be charged with the task of starting the digital-effects arm of Jackson's operation, was in Los Angeles at a computer conference around the time Steven Spielberg's epic first began to conquer audiences:

> *The first thing I did when I got off the plane was walk to the nearest cinema in Anaheim. I watched* Jurassic Park, *called Pete and said, 'We're onto a winner, Pete.' Any doubts that you had before that time that computer animation would take over the world were quickly swept out the window. Because you saw the dinosaurs, and you thought, this is it.*

The computer-generated stars of *Abyss*, *Terminator 2* and *Jurassic Park* were all developed at Industrial Light and Magic, the special-effects company originally created by George Lucas for *Star Wars*. ILM's dinosaurs in *Jurassic Park* essentially eclipsed at a stroke one entire branch of special effects — the traditional method of animating creatures used by stop-motion experts Willis O'Brien and Ray Harryhausen (though it also made extensive use of physical effects for many of its close-ups, thanks to animatronic dinosaurs and puppets). 'When I saw the computer-generated T-Rex in *Jurassic Park*, I felt as if I was twelve years old again,' Jackson later told *Cinefex*. 'I had feelings of awe and wonder watching that movie that I hadn't had since I was a kid watching the original *King Kong*.'

The man who had harboured dreams of making a feature film involving stop-motion creatures realised he needed to give the new computer technology a try. 'I'm the least computer-oriented person in the world,' he told an interviewer in 1994. 'I can manage to turn on my laptop and press the Save button, but I can't really go beyond that . . . but I felt I had to investigate this further.'

The advances signalled by *Jurassic Park* were about more than just believable monsters. The rumble that you heard was the deathknell of the optical printer. Computers now allowed different shots to be precisely combined (or composited) digitally, and then transferred back onto film. 'This stuff is much simpler to use, and much easier and cheaper than optical effects ever were,' said Jackson before *Heavenly Creature*'s release. 'We can do perfect blue screens in the room next door at a press of a button . . . I don't see the new technology as meaning everybody is going to make big effects movies. It just means filmmaking has become a lot easier.' (Optical printers are still sometimes used to produce fades and dissolves, and for opening titles, but in the field of compositing they have now largely been replaced by computers.)

Jackson had known George Port ever since the time he turned up and donned an elephant suit for the first, abandoned version of *Meet the Feebles* in 1988. Port was a film nerd from way back: as a child in Wellington's Hutt Valley, he watched many movies for free because his grandfather ran a shop next to the local cinema. Later he discovered the monster movies of Ray Harryhausen during Sunday double features at the Majestic. By the time Jackson met him, Port had abandoned his university film studies to work for a Wellington animation house, where he continued to dabble in stop-motion and primitive computer animation. He joined the *Feebles* team as a puppeteer, had a cameo role as a decapitated head in *Braindead*, and simultaneously became one of Jackson's first historians — it was Port who grabbed a video camera and shot extensive behind-the-scenes footage of both *Feebles* and *Braindead*. (A nearly-completed cut of a *Feebles* documentary has existed for years, but as yet none of Port's material has ever been seen publicly.)

'It wasn't a big gamble in terms of the whole film resting on their shoulders,' recalls Port of the computer effects in the *Heavenly Creatures* script. 'As they had written it, if you couldn't afford to do them, they could be simplified. But because of my computer animation background, we started discussing whether I could get this stuff together.'

Shortly before filming began on *Heavenly Creatures*, three boxes of equipment arrived at WingNut's offices on Tasman Street: a prototype film scanner, which converted negative film into digital data, an SGI Indigo computer, and a film recorder, which transferred the digital data back onto film again. The scanner came with just two pages of instructions. 'I was a little surprised,' says Port. 'I believe now they have quite a considerable handbook — very friendly software. But in those days the software was neither friendly nor helpful.'

Port spent the next few months trying to get the three pieces of equipment to communicate with one another, and finding a way to store a little more than the ten seconds of footage that the system could handle. The film scanner was one of the first available on the open market, and Port's efforts exposed some flaws which he then fed back to the scanner's American manufacturers, allowing them to improve the design. Finally, after around four months, he got his first usable shot.

At this point, WingNut could not afford the $80,000 that many 3D software programs sold for. 'So we went after this nice cheap one which was only $6,000. The trouble is, the company fell over before we even started doing the butterflies. In those days that was what happened. Companies would run out of money.'

That year, Port worked for at least seven months without taking a day off, readying the forty or so digital-effects shots required for *Heavenly Creatures*. Port's work ranges from the invisible — altering the balcony of the Hulmes' house to make it more historically accurate — to sequences where entire landscapes morph onscreen into a garden paradise, and imaginary movie stars stalk the girls by night, drained of all colour. On Christmas Day, Jackson dragged Port over to his house, forcing him to take half a day off.

Having leased the minimum of computer equipment needed for *Heavenly Creatures*, a group of WingNut staff decided to use future Weta profits to buy it. The group was Peter Jackson, Jim Booth, Jamie Selkirk, Richard Taylor, Tania Rodger and George Port. Says Port: 'We went into a room and batted about a whole bunch of ideas, and ended up with *Weta*, as an acronym of WingNut Effects and Technical Allusions.'

Taylor has said that the company's name was chosen 'because we didn't have any other ideas, and we really like it now because it's provided us with an easily identifiable label'. Wetas are large, cricket-like insects, often found in dark caves — in Taylor's words, the closest thing New Zealand has to genuine monsters.

In 1994, the digital arm of Weta gained its second staff member, Matt Aitken. And over the year leading up to the start of shooting of *The Frighteners* in May 1995, the company as a whole found that rarest of things in the New Zealand film industry: near-continuous work. That year Weta provided 150 effects for the romantic fantasy *Jack Brown Genius* (at which point the company's digital-effects staff had grown to seven, with Taylor's staff now at twelve) and supervised the more taxing sections of *Forgotten Silver*. Much of the *Forgotten Silver* work was subcontracted to a small Wellington company called Pixel Perfect, whose staff were later employed by Weta on a permanent basis. Weta also supplied effects for a number of

RIGHT: Joan and Bill Jackson in 1993, outside the basement room where their son worked on special effects for *Bad Taste*.

BELOW: A view looking southeast over the town of Pukerua Bay, taken in the mid-seventies. The clifftop battle scenes in *Bad Taste* were filmed on the cliffs stretching off to the right of frame.

© IAN PRYOR

© DOMINION POST COLLECTION / ALEXANDER TURNBULL LIBRARY (ATL)

OPPOSITE: Peter Jackson striking a pose in 1988, the same year his debut feature film *Bad Taste* was first unleashed upon the world.

RIGHT: The group of friends who doubled as both film crew and main cast members on *Bad Taste*. From left to right: Craig Smith, Peter Jackson, Pete O'Herne, Dean Lawrie, Mike Minett, Terry Potter, and Ken Hammon.

BELOW: Peter Jackson wearing the homebuilt camera rig used to film parts of his debut movie *Bad Taste*. In the background, Terry Potter readies another poster.

TOP: Some of the cast of *Meet the Feebles* pose alongside the humans who helped create them. From left to right: puppet designer Cameron Chittock, co-scriptwriter Fran Walsh, Peter Jackson, and producer Jim Booth (February 1989).

BELOW: Perhaps channelling the monstrous star of his favourite film *King Kong*, Jackson poses above a scale model of Wellington in the 1950s. The model was built for Jackson's third movie *Braindead*, largely by design students working under the supervision of Richard Taylor (February 1992).

TOP: Two actors near the beginning of their careers: Kate Winslet and Melanie Lynskey at the Venice Film Festival in September 1994, where *Heavenly Creatures* first began to attract international acclaim.

BELOW: Frank Bannister (Michael J Fox) and Lucy Lynskey (Trini Alvarado) in a moment of tension from Jackson's *The Frighteners*: Peter Jackson's first movie made for a Hollywood studio.

TOP: Filmmaker and film critic Costa Botes, whose friendship with Jackson stretches back more than fifteen years. In 1996, the two collaborated to make the pseudo-documentary *Forgotten Silver*.

RIGHT: Writer Stephen Sinclair, who has worked on the scripts of three of Jackson's films: *Meet the Feebles*, *Braindead* and *The Two Towers*. Sinclair's long list of plays includes collaborating with Fran Walsh to turn *Braindead* into a bloodsoaked stage musical.

TOP: Camperdown Studios, Peter Jackson's base in the Wellington suburb of Miramar.

BELOW: Some of the cast and crew of *The Two Towers* at the film's Wellington premiere. Billy Boyd (who plays Pippin) and Karl Urban (Eomer) are standing on the far left. Directly to the right of Peter Jackson is effects wizard Richard Taylor (in spectacles) and New Line executive Mark Ordesky (in profile).

TOP: Gollum makes his first live appearance in Wellington, during the Australasian premiere of *The Two Towers* (December 2002).

BELOW: Peter Jackson displays his Companion of the New Zealand Order of Merit, and Fran Walsh her Member of the Order of Merit, awarded in the New Year's Honours for 2002.

other productions, beginning a long association between Taylor's monster-making team and the *Hercules* and *Xena* television series being shot around Auckland. Other productions included a Jean-Claude Van Damme film shot partly in Queenstown, and helping out on *Napoleon*, 'the other talking animal film from Australia'.

Napoleon is an Australian/Japanese movie starring a small white dog. Port remembers it as a nightmare. 'The dog goes up in this balloon basket and floats over Sydney, and also travels in the pouch of a kangaroo. But everything had been shot wrong — we were trying to put together shots that were never meant to be put together. They had some stock footage of a kangaroo from Qantas, and wanted this dog to be put in the pouch. Crazy stuff.'

But Weta's small staff and comparatively low wages meant that the prices charged per completed computer-effects shot could be as low as twenty percent of competitors in America. What few profits remained were ploughed straight back into the company. By the time American director Robert Zemeckis popped by to take a look at Weta Digital's operation, something had to give. The company's fast expansion had taken over every centimetre of the house in Tasman Street where WingNut was based. A malfunctioning air-conditioning unit meant that for a period in the afternoons, work had to be stopped because the computers got too hot.

MOVING TO MIRAMAR

As you drive around the harbour-edge from Wellington city towards the airport, the suburb of Miramar lies hidden behind the hilltops of the Miramar Peninsula. Imagine the peninsula as a foot connected to Wellington: if someone tried to saw the foot off, the runway of Wellington airport would mark the line of the saw. The suburb of Miramar (which means wonderful sea) sits in a long valley in the middle of the peninsula, closer to the toes than the ankle, but never far from the roar of aeroplanes.

The warehouse bought by Peter Jackson in 1993 is at one end of Miramar's main road, just at the point where the industrial buildings run out and middle-class suburbia takes over. The building now known as Camperdown Studios once manufactured batteries and, later, Max Factor cosmetics. For many years, the area edged onto a petrol-storage facility. But Miramar's history is not entirely industrial: back in the 1900s, the Wonderland amusement park sat close by, its attractions ranging from an artificial lake to distorting mirrors and fireworks.

'I figured I want to stay here, and make films now and again,' explained Jackson about the purchase in early 1995. 'So why not buy one of these old warehouses — and right now it's a great buyers' market for old warehouses — and just call it home.' Over the next few months, the Weta Digital staff began to move into their new base, along with $6 million worth of new computer equipment, in readiness for *The Frighteners*. At Camperdown, Richard Taylor and Tania Rodger now had a very big workshop indeed.

It is tempting to imagine the purchase of Camperdown as the first stage in the kind of dream Francis Ford Coppola had attempted to realise in New York in the 1970s with his company American Zoetrope — a place where directors might escape the pressures of the corporate system, and make movies their way. But the idea of Jackson using his name to help others make cinema had faded with the passing of Jim Booth. 'That was a scenario we did discuss, and it was exciting,' Jackson told the *Listener*. 'We had the ability to get money because of the things I'd done. With Jim's death, the path to the future has altered a bit. It is very difficult for me to concentrate on anything else than what I'm doing.'

A FAVOUR OWED

If there is a movie in this book whose reputation precedes it in the worst way, that film is probably *Jack Brown Genius*. Tony Hiles calls it 'the worst job as a director I've ever done'. Jackson, who is listed in the movie's credits as co-writer, second-unit director and executive producer, tends to distance himself from the movie in his rare comments about it. 'I kind of inherited the job of producing it,' he later said. 'It's not my film.'

Jack Brown Genius began in the mind of Hiles, the director and producer first brought in by the Film Commission to help see *Bad Taste* through to completion. The plot follows an inventor (played by *Braindead*'s Tim Balme) whose brain becomes home to the spirit of a monk who is sure that he has discovered a way to make humans fly. Hiles began developing his 'bizarre', essentially special-effects-free romantic comedy with Booth in 1992. Later Booth thought the film might have a better chance of securing funding if it was made under the WingNut banner, rather than by Booth's own company Midnight Films.

After Booth suggested that Jackson and Walsh take a look at Hiles's script, the three ended up getting together to do some rewrites. As the process continued, the more visually fantastic aspects of the storyline began to assume increasing importance. 'We worked together well,' says Hiles. 'The script got swallowed up in a process which was very invigorating. But at the end I was looking at something that wasn't what I started out to say. If I'd recognised it, I would have done something. After all, I was the one who had the right to pull stuff out.'

Before Booth died at the beginning of 1994, he asked Jackson to do what he could to help make *Jack Brown Genius* happen. Booth's wish meant that Jackson's name helped secure finance for *Jack Brown* from German company Senator Films (which had helped fund *Heavenly Creatures*). With Jackson signed on as executive producer, the tables had turned — Jackson was now helping oversee the first feature film directed by Hiles, who had once done the same for Jackson on *Bad Taste*.

Hiles first had to decide whether to stay with the project after the death of the producer he had known for ten years. 'I'm sure that everyone who's made a film with Peter knows that his input is what you might call boisterous,' says Hiles. 'But in the end I decided if you don't go down the river, you don't know what the banks are like.'

Jack Brown Genius was the first feature film to be shot at Jackson's Camperdown Studios in Miramar. 'It used to rattle like buggery in the wind,' says Hiles of the building. 'The weather was terrible.' On top of that, Hiles, long a believer in live synchronised sound, found himself working around the noises of aircraft from Wellington airport.

The director likens the *Jack Brown* production to a bunch of virgins getting into bed together, and says that there were strong tensions between crew and management, partly thanks to disagreements over overtime contracts. Hiles says he spent too much time worrying about the lack of a firm hand over the movie's unrealistic budget, and not enough time bringing the story to the screen.

Hiles decided to 'shoot to cut' — essentially filming only the footage required to complete a scene, thus allowing fewer creative choices later in the editing room. Part of his reasoning was that Jackson, who was directing the second unit, was going through so much film on his own. 'You could argue that what Peter was trying to do was absolutely right, but under the circumstances, I knew I had to start economising. I remember saying to one of the producers, "Put a lock on the stock cupboard door." He said, "You know what Peter's like." Without Jim Booth, the group of us were like a cartwheel with the hub missing — all the spokes crashed together. Jim was a great manager. He could create cohesion among disparate people.'

While no classic, *Jack Brown Genius* is not nearly as bad as its reputation might suggest. The main problem is that the quirky plotting ultimately comes across as more interesting than the characters, many of which feel underwritten or act in contradictory fashion. Senator Films eventually requested that *Jack Brown Genius* be recut and *Bad Taste* composer Michelle Scullion's score replaced. Despite promises to the contrary, none of the producers could bring themselves to break the bad news to Scullion. In 1996, Tony Hiles's work on *Jack Brown Genius* controversially took the best director prize at the New Zealand Film and Television Awards. Later, one of the voting panel told Hiles he had got the award because *Jack Brown Genius* had been such a hard shoot. 'The film didn't work,' says Hiles, 'so it couldn't have been for any other reason.'

COSTA BOTES

Followed his work on *Forgotten Silver* with the arresting short film *Original Skin* in 1996. His feature-film debut, a low-budget adaptation of the Duncan Sarkies play *Saving Grace,* was a critical and commercial failure upon release in 1999. The film chronicles the relationship between a street kid and a man who may or may not be Jesus Christ. Botes later shot extensive behind-the-scenes material during the making of *The Lord of the Rings* trilogy: portions of his footage have been used among the supplementary material included on the DVD editions of the movies. It is rumoured that Botes's original, feature-length documentaries may be included on a future DVD release of the trilogy.

COLIN McKENZIE

Lies buried in Spain, close to the Mediterranean Sea. But his grave is very difficult to find.

CHAPTER TEN

FINDING HOLLYWOOD WITHOUT REALLY LOOKING: *THE FRIGHTENERS*

'. . . the big studios play the destructive game of developing dozens of projects with the intention of making only one in ten or one in twenty. At any one time in Hollywood, ninety percent of the writers and directors are busy working on scripts that will not get made.'
EXCALIBUR DIRECTOR JOHN BOORMAN

'People were slapping me on the back. People were jazzed. Very, very jazzed.'
UNIVERSAL STUDIOS VICE-CHAIRMAN LENNY KORNBERG, HOURS AFTER A SCREENING IN LOS ANGELES OF EARLY FOOTAGE FROM *THE FRIGHTENERS*

By night, the ghosts of a hundred horror movies wander the back lot of Universal Studios, searching in vain for the castles and ruins of earlier Universal glories. Some mill hopelessly in front of the courtyard where Lon Chaney made his star turn as *The Hunchback of Notre Dame*. Others stand crying on a darkened soundstage, awaiting the return of Frankenstein's monster. The ghosts of Universal are freshly run over each morning by the first busloads of tourists, come to take the studio tour. The tourists measure history by a different timescale. They want to see *Shrek* and go on the *Jurassic Park* ride, although the familiar outline of that spooky hotel from *Psycho* still wins some gasps.

Hollywood's oldest studio began flirting with horror as early as 1913, and has gone through a number of periods since, when horror movies were the only things keeping the wolf from the door. By the 1930s, the studio's biggest stars were monsters like *Dracula, Frankenstein* and *The Invisible Man*. Universal first began to wake up to the audience for horror when Lon Chaney appeared in two of the studio's earliest hits, *The Hunchback of Notre Dame* and *The Phantom of the Opera*. But at the time, the studio was not exactly famous for rewarding its talent. After acting in dozens of minor roles, Chaney had to leave Universal to find stardom elsewhere, and he asked for a hefty wage rise before he would return to the lot to make *Notre Dame.*

Still, the studio had no illusions that Americans would have a monopoly on horror. Like Carl Laemmle, the German-born founder of Universal, the key talents of many of the early Universal horror classics come from Europe — people like British director James Whale (who brought Boris Karloff and other English stage actors to work on *Frankenstein* and *The Invisible Man*), and innovative German cinematographer/director Karl Freund.

In the 1940s, after money troubles saw Laemmle's ousting, Universal turned to horror again and again, only with tighter budgets, less respect and more double-bills. They raided their old classics, reusing footage and film sets. Horror met comedy in a series of tired yet moneymaking bouts between Universal's horror stars and comics Abbott and Costello. By the 1950s the mating process was one of horror and science fiction, and the setting was no longer a bunch of castles somewhere in Europe. An American desert town saw the arrival of Jack Arnold's *It Came from Outer Space*, while the radioactive star of Universal's classic *The Incredible Shrinking Man* found that the backyard provided the most terrifying landscape of all.

In the 1970s, the old Hollywood studio system collapsed. Universal survived by keeping a strong hand in television production, and putting its special-effects staff to work on a run of successful disaster movies. Budgets had shot up, and advertising. Universal's sales and merchandising efforts for Steven Spielberg blockbusters like *Jaws* and *ET* sometimes went so far overboard that they threatened to tarnish the qualities of the films themselves. At one point during the campaign that accompanied *Jaws*, the Universal Studio shop in Los Angeles began selling foetuses of dead baby sharks. The company that made a long-running franchise out of *Frankenstein* had not forgotten the moneymaking potential of sequels, as evidenced by the three increasingly lame shark tales that followed *Jaws*.

In the 1980s and early 1990s, the company also financed or distributed movies by such key horror directors as Tobe Hooper, John Carpenter, Wes Craven and Sam Raimi. 'We picked up a lot of them,' recalls Tom Pollock, studio chairman for ten years during this period. 'I have a fondness in my heart for horror movies.' In the early 1990s, acquisitions staff sat down to look at *Braindead*, a film Pollock remembers fondly as 'Grand Guignol in the highest tradition'. But nothing came of it.

THE LURE OF LOS ANGELES

The American movie industry is like a funnel through which the world's movie talent continues to pour. New Zealand directors Lee Tamahori, Roger Donaldson and Vincent Ward have all left for extended stays in

Hollywood after completing only one or two feature films in New Zealand. Geoff Murphy managed to stay on for five, before doing the same. When he began shooting movies in America, the famously straight-talking director sometimes found it 'almost impossible to make a directorial decision without it going before some sort of committee'. He managed at least one good American film, *Young Guns 2*, and stayed on for a number that proved more mediocre. Other New Zealand directors, like Roger Donaldson, have managed solid work in Hollywood over a long period.

By the time Peter Jackson completed his fourth feature in 1994, he had become that rare thing: a New Zealand filmmaker who had won Hollywood's attention, but taken none of its cash. Sure, he was represented by an agent in Los Angeles, and had turned down a number of offers to direct American movies, including horror pairing *Freddy and Jason*. But Jackson has always been stubborn: the idea of gaining a million-dollar budget in exchange for surrendering control of the final shape of his movie has never appealed.

Despite his stubbornness, Jackson is also an opportunist. As *Heavenly Creatures* neared completion, he took a telephone call from one of the US's most successful filmmakers, asking if he might want to direct something on a Hollywood-sized budget for Universal. The man who thought of Hollywood as a place obsessed with fame and money had been invited in, to make a movie. Eventually Jackson said yes, but with one small proviso: 'How about doing it in New Zealand?'

PUTTING A GHOST IN THE HOLLYWOOD MACHINE

The idea for a new twist on ghost movies was born one Sunday afternoon, on the way to buying some milk. Thirsting for a break during the scriptwriting for *Heavenly Creatures*, Jackson and Walsh set off on a walk to the shops, and on the way, came up with the idea of a conman who hires himself out to clear ghosts from people's houses. The twist would be that the ghosts are real — the conman lives with them, and uses his spirited friends 'to scare up some business'.

The ghost story was just one of many script ideas Jackson and Walsh were considering trying to sell in Hollywood. 'We wouldn't have anything to do with making them,' Jackson later said of the idea. 'They'd just be a bit of work we could do in between movies.'

Jackson and Walsh bottled the ghost idea in a two-page outline, named it *The Frighteners* after an English expression which Jackson likely heard from his parents, and sent it off to their agent in Los Angeles. At this point, the rotting, skeletal head of the Crypt Keeper rises into view. Inspired by the darkly humorous EC comic stories of the 1950s, the anthology cable

TV series *Tales from the Crypt* was hosted by a wisecracking skeleton, and executive-produced by a powerhouse Hollywood team that included filmmakers Robert Zemeckis (*Who Framed Roger Rabbit?*), Richard Donner (*Lethal Weapon*) and *Die Hard* producer Joel Silver.

Jackson had heard that the team were looking for scripts to turn into a series of *Tales from the Crypt* movies, with one star director commanding each film — 'and all had scripts except for Bob'. Jackson and Walsh's agent duly forwarded the *Frighteners* outline to Zemeckis. Thanks largely to the massive success of the *Back to the Future* trilogy, Zemeckis had his own office at Universal and a deal allowing the studio a first look at any projects he might want to produce or direct. In early 1993, a few months before Jackson began shooting *Heavenly Creatures,* the two moviemakers met in Los Angeles. Though enthused about the ghost outline, Zemeckis argued that it didn't fit the (fairly wide) *Tales from the Crypt* brief. Did Jackson want to develop the script with him as a separate project?

Whether Zemeckis ever had designs to direct *The Frighteners* himself is unclear: he declined to be interviewed for this book. Longtime *Crypt* producer Gilbert Adler, who played a big hand in the first two *Crypt* movies *Demon Knight* and *Bordello of Blood* and directed the latter, has no memory of Zemeckis ever mentioning the Jackson script as a possible *Crypt* project. Adler also dismisses talk of the show's series of star directors ever planning to take on *Crypt* movies of their own.

Zemeckis was more than aware that getting a foothold in Hollywood is about lucky breaks as much as talent — his own Hollywood debut had occurred thanks largely to the power of Steven Spielberg, while his breakthrough hit *Romancing the Stone* only came his way because star Michael Douglas insisted that the then-unknown director was the man for the job. Watching the confidence displayed in *Heavenly Creatures,* Zemeckis likely thought: time to pass it on.

Having a script in development in Hollywood can be a valuable foot in the door, but getting one's name up on a cinema screen is another matter altogether. In his book *Money into Light, Excalibur* director John Boorman has put it succinctly: 'At any one time in Hollywood, ninety percent of the writers and directors are busy working on scripts that will not get made.' Whether Hollywood's habit of extensive script development drains the life from scripts, or helps perfect them, remains hotly debated.

As 1993 came to an end, Jackson and Walsh finally had the chance to get stuck into their Hollywood writing assignment. *The Frighteners* was intended as a rollercoaster ride, a movie that balanced shocks and laughter. At the centre of the ride is Frank Bannister who, since losing his wife in a car accident, has the ability to see ghosts. Frank now shares his half-completed house with three ghosts of varying temperament, and regularly sends them off to do some haunting to create demand for his fraudulent ghostbusting business. But with the discovery that something is squeezing the life out of a succession of townspeople, the authorities suspect that Frank might be the culprit.

Zemeckis read the completed script while toiling on the edit of *Forrest Gump*. He asked Jackson if he wanted to step up to the plate and direct *The Frighteners* himself. Perhaps in agreeing to the offer, the opportunist in Peter Jackson, and probably the patriot, won out. He later admitted that when Zemeckis asked him, he had never imagined the possibility of directing the movie himself. The unexpected offer potentially gave him the chance to use major-league Hollywood resources on his home turf, and show the world what New Zealand filmmakers were capable of. And by stepping in as executive producer, Zemeckis could provide him with a buffer against the possibility of interference by studio executives.

A throwaway remark that Jackson made during *The Frighteners* shoot is worth repeating here. 'While *The Frighteners* is more mainstream, it's a good logical progression if I want to get my hands on the sort of budget to make *Blubberhead*.' This is the closest thing to a career-based comment that I have yet read from Jackson, a man who has declared on many occasions that his next film is the one he feels like making at the time. It may well demonstrate his growing realisation that some degree of compromise was necessary if he was ever to find the finance for the comparatively expensive left-field movies he hungered to make.

FROM SPIELBERG TO JACKSON

Perhaps the best thing about Jackson's entrée to Hollywood was that director Robert Zemeckis was opening the door, and the studio was Universal. To find the reason, one needs to turn the clock back to the early days of a certain Steven Spielberg. As an unknown filmmaker in the late 1960s, Spielberg spent extended periods hanging around the Universal studio lot in Los Angeles, and won his break there, after an editor friend, Chuck Silvers, saw an early Spielberg short. The editor phoned Universal executive Sidney Sheinberg, who quickly signed the young filmmaker to a seven-year contract. Asked how Spielberg could ever pay him back for making the phone call, Silvers asked only for an occasional hug. But he also made Spielberg promise that on finding success, he would 'pass it on', by helping others to enter the film industry.

Thanks to *Jaws*, *ET* and two *Jurassic Parks*, Spielberg went on to bring Universal four of its biggest hits. And as he began to find success, Spielberg passed it on. A young working-class filmmaker called Robert Zemeckis had begun sneaking onto the Universal studio lot, hanging around the film sets. Impressed by a student film Zemeckis had made, Spielberg persuaded Universal chairman Sidney Sheinberg to let Zemeckis direct his first feature film, the low-budget comedy *I Wanna Hold Your Hand*. The movie tanked. But thanks partly to Spielberg, Zemeckis later got the chance to earn millions for Universal through directing the trilogy of *Back to the Future* movies. And Zemeckis in turn would pass it on by leading a New Zealand moviemaker inside the gates of the same studio to start the tale over again.

Some have argued that Spielberg's sideline in producing films by quirky talents like Robert Zemeckis and Joe Dante (*Gremlins*) has allowed him to explore darker aspects of his creative personality without the risk of compromising his own filmmaking career. The same argument may apply to Zemeckis himself. A horror fan, Zemeckis directed a number of episodes of the *Tales from the Crypt* television series, and executive-produced the movies that followed ('executive producer' is an all-encompassing job description whose meaning can range from 'made one telephone call' to 'stopped the whole thing falling apart'). But in his own directing career Zemeckis increasingly tended to the more serious: he did not begin making his own horror movie (horror/thriller *What Lies Beneath*) until 1999. Helping Peter Jackson may well have allowed Zemeckis, like Spielberg before him, to keep his hands in darker themes without putting his mainstream career in any danger.

Five years before, an unexpected opportunity had encouraged Jackson to turn a little project on the side into the feature film *Meet the Feebles*. But once he decided to do it, Jackson's commitment to that project had been total, and the same would be true with *The Frighteners*. Jackson was suddenly in demand in the US. As work continued on the next *Frighteners* draft, he signed a separate first-look deal with Miramax, which offered another potential source of stateside funding. After the complications of telling the Parker–Hulme murder story as accurately as possible, and the subsequent discovery of Juliet Hulme/Anne Perry, *The Frighteners* was a chance to do something 'much more crazy and out there'.

Then Universal chairman Tom Pollock believes that *The Frighteners* would not have got the go-ahead from the studio without the involvement of Robert Zemeckis. 'Studios are not designed to have an easy "yes" for any movie to get made,' he says. 'Somebody has to keep pushing, to overcome all the hurdles that the studios put in the way. Bob was the person pushing. He strongly felt that Peter Jackson was a big talent.'

According to Jackson, when he asked if he could make the film in New Zealand there were two reactions. Zemeckis replied, 'Okay, if you can make it look like Middle America.' One of the Universal executives said, 'Is that a good idea?'

Says Jackson: 'Somebody said they were looking at rushes from *Babe*, and *Babe* didn't look like America at all.' The studio was keen for the farm in *Babe* to look archetypal, rather than specifically Australian. A photographer was sent off to take a series of photos of buildings and towns around New Zealand for Universal to show that the country could fill in for the US, and then the deal was done. The fictional North Californian town of Fairwater would be stitched together from location filming around Wellington, interiors in Camperdown Studios, and three weeks in the South Island town of Lyttelton, where Jackson had filmed the holiday scenes of *Heavenly Creatures*.

CASTING AMERICAN-STYLE

When Michael J Fox read *The Frighteners*, he thought it was one of the weirdest scripts he had ever seen. Though it possibly had the makings of something brilliant, he was also worried that it might turn out 'really stupid' like *Ghostbusters*, or degenerate into an 'over-the-top gore fest', which held no interest for him. Still, Zemeckis had shown him strange scripts before: one of them, *Back to the Future*, had turned Fox from a popular television actor into a movie star. Zemeckis suggested that the actor go and meet Jackson and catch his latest film, *Heavenly Creatures*, at the upcoming Toronto Film Festival.

Fox loved *Heavenly Creatures*. When the two met, he told Jackson 'I think you're a twisted genius bastard. If you want me to take the boat, then I want to go.' As Fox has said, 'There was a sense that he was a kid waiting for the right toys to play with, and I wanted to be there when he got them.'

Fox had topped Jackson and Walsh's wish list to play psychic conman Frank Bannister. They felt his sympathetic qualities and gift for comedy would help make the character a little more likeable. For the role of Lucy Lynskey, the doctor who finds herself falling for Bannister, the couple went with Trini Alvarado, whose résumé included Australian director Gillian Armstrong's acclaimed remake of *Little Women*. The daughter of a Spanish singer and a Puerto Rican flamenco dancer, Alvarado had been performing since joining her parents onstage at the age of seven. On the set of *The Frighteners*, she would get to do more than her share of bopping people over the head and running for her life. 'It was like heaven, you couldn't get me to say a bad word about it,' Alvarado told the author in the few minutes we spoke by telephone (she later cancelled our planned interview).

Horror fans could comfort themselves with the presence of other names: names like Jeffrey Combs, John Astin and Dee Wallace Stone. Combs made his name as the disturbed scientist Herbert West in *Re-Animator*, one of

Jackson's favourite horror comedies, and followed it with many more. His portrayal of the disturbed FBI agent on Bannister's tail would squeeze many people's hearts in just the right way. Astin remains best known for introducing the destruction of toy trains to American television, through playing the charming father in cult 1960s comedy *The Addams Family*. He also fathered a future star of *Lord of the Rings* (Sean Astin), and survived appearances in three movies starring killer tomatoes. As the bedraggled, gunslinging ghost with a detachable jawbone in *The Frighteners*, Astin is nearly unrecognisable. As for the normally blonde-haired Dee Wallace Stone, her career in horror is testament to the fact that there are worse things than acting with children and animals — on top of playing Elliot's mother in *ET*, she has appeared onscreen opposite werewolves, alligators, a rabid dog and a band of mutant savages. Her part in *The Frighteners* as the much-harangued past lover of a serial killer gave her a chance to subvert her typical role as everywoman caught up in terror.

When Jake Busey auditioned for the role of serial killer Johnny Bartlett in a room on Sunset Boulevard, it was for him one of around a hundred auditions that year. After enjoying *Heavenly Creatures* and the craziness of *The Frighteners* script, Busey knew he had to 'go meet this guy'.

> *One of the audition scenes has Michael J Fox standing over me and I'm screaming and pleading and angry and all these things at once. So I did it in this little office. I wound up harming myself with the wall and all the falling on the floor. Peter had this kind of shocked smile on his face.*

It was only after hearing he had the role that Busey realised *The Frighteners* was being made in New Zealand, rather than Jackson coming to Hollywood. 'When I found out I had to go to New Zealand I thought, "Holy shit! Fantastic."'

'It was one of those great times,' is Busey's description of working on *The Frighteners*. 'I would do it over again in a heartbeat.' He counts Jackson as a rare director who is technically adept, yet able and patient with actors. As for Jackson's fabled habit of acting out scenes himself for his cast, Busey found it happening often. 'He'd very much get into it, which was fun. In my opinion it's the ultimate form of a director expressing their vision. They've got the whole idea in their head. The frustrating thing is amateur directors who give you line readings [instructing the actor in exactly how to say a particular line of dialogue]. It's an unspoken law that you don't give line readings, and Peter doesn't do that. Sometimes he would act it out, but then say, "Don't say it like me."'

For Fox, making *The Frighteners* appears to have been both a joy and a trial. He later told interviewers that halfway through the shoot he was 'away from home, missing my family and working myself to death'. But claims that the trials of *The Frighteners* are to blame for Fox quitting movies and returning to television should be taken with a grain of salt. In fact, Fox mentioned the idea of returning to television to the New Zealand press before filming even began.

Fox has spoken about how the cast of *The Frighteners* was invited over to Jackson and Walsh's house and asked if they wanted to throw any ideas or lines of dialogue into the film. The actors were 'stunned at first', because it was a question they were so unused to. 'Then this idea festival starts up and they're throwing stuff out. I was amazed because, days later, we got back these pages directly reflecting our ideas.'

Walsh and Jackson's script continued to undergo rewrites for the duration of filming, partly to maximise the contributions of the actors and partly, one suspects, because Jackson had been so busy working on *Jack Brown Genius* and co-directing *Forgotten Silver* that a number of plot holes remained to be filled in. 'Just about every week we've been adding new pages,' he said at the time. 'The guys at Universal say this is the first time it has ever happened. Usually they don't rewrite much because if they finance a film, that is the film they wait to see.'

Jackson claimed that despite some tensions, Universal were pleased with the improvements. 'I've had total freedom.' Universal vice-president Lenny Kornsberg later put it somewhat differently while telling the *Listener* about the rewrites that kept spilling from his fax machine during filming. 'If it was anybody less affable than me, any normal executive would have been freakin' out.'

KEEPING BUSY

In the months before *The Frighteners* kicked off, Jackson's life might have been easier if he could have cloned extra versions of himself, so that he could work in two places at the same time. As he rushed to shoot his final scenes for *Forgotten Silver*, Universal executives arrived from Los Angeles to discuss the *Frighteners* shoot and tour Camperdown Studios. Jackson continued to work on *Forgotten Silver* during much of their visit, all the while trying to give the impression that his debut movie for Hollywood was the only thing on his mind. As *Forgotten Silver* co-director Costa Botes has written:

> . . . the Universal men found themselves being escorted around exotic places of great interest around the Wellington area, while Peter was 'taken ill'. There was also an 'emergency gas leak' around Camperdown Studios which meant the whole facility had to be 'evacuated' for three days (actually, we were there filming).

As late as a fortnight before the beginning of filming for the most expensive movie Jackson had yet made, he was on location around Wellington, shooting scenes for *Forgotten Silver*. At one point, while following some soldiers around with a camera during the shooting of the Spanish Civil War scenes, he injured his knee, and wondered for a moment whether *The Frighteners* would have to be delayed.

Weta's recent glut of work meant that the digital arm of the company was far from prepared for the phenomenal demands of *The Frighteners*. As pre-production began, the special-effects company rushed to get two other commitments out of the way — completing the flying scenes of the Tony Hiles fantasy *Jack Brown Genius*, and the fake footage of *Forgotten Silver*. A number of the *Silver* effects shots were contracted out to a small Wellington company named Pixel Perfect, home to John Sheils, who would be a key member of the *Frighteners* effects team. Aside from easing the workload, the hiring of Pixel appears to have been partly an attempt to disguise the fact that Weta had been using expensive new computer equipment, intended for *The Frighteners*, on another project. 'The Americans were not happy with anyone spending any time on any other project than *The Frighten*ers, because for them it was a gamble,' says George Port. At last Weta Digital was able to move base from its overcrowded Tasman Street home and join the rest of Jackson's team at Camperdown Studios, along with a pile of new Silicon Graphics computer technology.

In May, the latest horror movie from Universal Studios began filming in an old perfume factory near Wellington airport. Interviews for *The Frighteners* would cite the roughly 130-day shooting schedule — almost the same number of days as later epic *Gangs of New York* — as the longest that the studio had ever pre-approved. (A number of other Universal films had ended up running even longer — Spielberg's problem-plagued *Jaws*, for example, started at fifty-five and finally ran to more than 150 days.)

Was the studio worried about letting a moviemaker loose for so long, so far from Universal's Los Angeles headquarters? 'We didn't have a problem,' says Pollock. Apart from having completion-bond insurance, the studio had taken steps to check that Jackson had no reputation for going wildly over-budget. 'Days in New Zealand are cheaper than days in Hollywood,' explains Pollock, 'because people get less money. I made *12 Monkeys* with Terry Gilliam right after he'd made [wildly over-budget] *Baron Munchausen*. I was much more nervous about that. In fact, Terry Gilliam brought it in on-budget.' *The Frighteners*' long schedule was also misleading: many of the days were set aside for special-effects and blue-screen work, which used a much smaller crew.

Pollock places *The Frighteners* firmly into the category of movies over which Universal had little control. 'Our control was the decision to make it,' he says. 'If we saw dailies [rushes of recent footage], they were days late. You didn't really have a lot of input into things.' Nonetheless Universal paid for a staff member to stay on in Wellington and keep an eye on how things were going.

Almost all of the heads of department on *The Frighteners* were New Zealanders, apart from American composer Danny Elfman (*Beetlejuice*). Six weeks into the shoot, three-time Jackson cinematographer Alun Bollinger had a serious car accident — his replacement John Blick later alternated duties with Bollinger for much of the rest of the shoot. Jackson's keenness for camera movement and wide-angle lenses required some clever hiding of lighting sources on set.

SPECIAL EFFECTS

The following year marked Weta's rushed, somewhat haphazard growth to adulthood. Richard Taylor's team in the Weta Physical department worked on around forty effects. Their work ranged from the exaggerated makeup required for the ghosts to a complex animatronic dog and some superb miniatures of the town of Fairwater. Perhaps their most eye-opening creation was the Gatekeeper, a winged cherub that helps guard the cemetery. Worn by an actor in a suit, complete with a computer-controlled face, the Gatekeeper did not make the final cut. The movie's search for an appropriate mixture of comedy and horror saw other casualties — American actors Chi McBride and Jim Fyfe are fondly remembered for their comic antics on set, but much of their acting work ended up on the editing floor (some of it can be found on the laserdisc).

The Frighteners also offered a chance for the fanboys in Jackson and Taylor to work, however briefly, with legendary American makeup artist Rick Baker (*An American Werewolf in London*). Baker was enlisted to design the makeup for John Astin's decaying ghost the Judge (his detachable jawbone was later added digitally). But in the end, Baker was too busy working on turning Eddie Murphy into *The Nutty Professor* to be able to fly over and apply Astin's five hours of makeup himself.

The Frighteners' extended schedule owed much to the fact that scenes where ghosts and human characters interacted had to be filmed twice — once with the human characters acting on set, and then with the ghost characters acting against a blue screen. The two elements would later be digitally composited into one shot. Such sequences required precise timing from the cast as they traded dialogue with characters who were merely blank air.

The task of adding glows to the ghosts and compositing them into scenes fell to George Port and his digital-effects team. But perhaps the biggest visual challenge was creating the villainous spirit who is responsible for a run of deaths in Fairwater. Most often, the ghost appears in classic Grim Reaper form — a tall, hooded figure darting about with a large scythe. The Reaper went through many transformations before finding physical form. 'We set out with the intention of doing the Reaper as a rod puppet,' Jackson told *Cinefex* magazine, 'maybe shooting it in a water tank. We even thought of shooting someone, dressed in costume, at different camera speeds.' Test footage was shot with puppets and a man in a Reaper suit. But in the end, the Reaper would be created almost entirely on the computer, thanks to valuable input from New Zealander Gray Horsfield and the team of digital artists.

When a small organisation is forced to rapidly upsize, organisation becomes the key word to surviving the process. Early in what was originally meant to be an eighteen-month period for completing *The Frighteners*, staff in the computer arm of Weta committed themselves to a tight schedule for completing digital effects, which quickly became a noose around their neck. As supervisor of digital effects, Port spent most of the six-month shoot supervising effects work on the film set.

> *The catch was that I was doing all the on-set stuff, so somebody else got to set up the schedule. And we hadn't planned it to the level that it needed to be planned. At the end of the day it was my fault, because I still had to approve it. We were supposed to be delivering finished shots six weeks after the film had begun shooting, and that was crazy. The trouble is that you do the schedule like that, you publish it, the studio reads it, then suddenly people started holding it up and saying this must be obeyed, coming to Peter and saying, 'Look it hasn't been done, it hasn't been finished.'*

Progress on digital-effects shots was also slowed by Jackson's immense workload. Though the director often visited Weta Digital during breaks from filming, he was not always keen to give final approval for particular effects shots until he saw how they fitted into the completed scene. Indecision about the final look of the Grim Reaper character also delayed the completion of many effects, a number of which were later revisited and improved.

'We wanted to put more things in, because Peter had fantastic visions as always,' says Port. 'We were thinking, "Okay, so if we can get more money, we can get a couple more staff in and make it better."' Towards that end, Port agreed to put aside a couple of unused Weta computers for a few days to do a washing-machine commercial. Though word of Weta's earlier under-the-counter work on *Forgotten Silver* appears not to have reached Los Angeles, Port now quickly got a call from Zemeckis, reminding him that Weta had contracted to work on only one project. 'Having Bob

Zemeckis yelling at you on a Saturday morning is not great at all,' says Port. 'Especially since he was one of my favourite directors. We wanted to roll the money back, so we could make the film better.'

With so many ghosts among its main cast, *The Frighteners* required more digital-effects shots than almost any movie made up till that time. For a special-effects company that had been in existence less than three years, the project defined the very word ambitious. Says Port:

> *None of us had worked on a film of that scale before. Not producing, directing, certainly not effects-wise. So all we had to go on is what we knew from research and seeing other films. There was still a sense of being able to get by on the Kiwi number-eight wire mentality. In the past Richard and I had worked together, with Peter overseeing the effects. But with a big effects movie, you normally have a visual-effects producer and a supervisor as well, someone who takes things down to the physical side and the digital side, and ties it all together. We never had that. These are things that I was a little worried about, and started mentioning to Jamie [Selkirk, producer] and Peter. But at some point they didn't want to hear it any more, because they had other things to worry about. They had some ideas for getting money to the film, but they weren't sharing them with me. At the end of the day, the communication didn't work any more. Well, not for me, as digital-effects supervisor.*

In the period before March 1996, when George Port left the company he had helped create, Weta underwent another major burst of expansion. The search began for a supervisor of visual effects, and ex-Miramax staff member Charlie McClellan, who had helped coordinate the completion of *Forgotten Silver*, moved over to become *The Frighteners'* digital-effects producer.

It is difficult to say with absolute certainty how Jackson's first Hollywood film came to receive a substantial cash injection and an accelerated release date. What is clear is that executive producer Zemeckis flew down to *The Frighteners* set during the closing days of shooting, and was given twenty minutes of footage to show to Universal executives in Hollywood. After the November 16 screening in Los Angeles, reactions from Universal staff appear to have been enthusiastic. 'People were slapping me on the back,' Universal vice-president Lenny Kornberg told the *Listener* hours after the screening. 'People were jazzed, very very jazzed.'

With the studio's Sylvester Stallone disaster movie *Daylight* running behind schedule, someone suggested bumping *The Frighteners* forward from its October 1996 release date (Halloween) to take *Daylight*'s prime-time slot.

In the months before Zemeckis flew to New Zealand, he contacted Wes

Takahashi, former animation director for George Lucas's Industrial Light and Magic, to show him some of the special-effects scenes which Weta had done to date. Takahashi had supervised the effects animation for a run of Zemeckis movies, including *Back to the Future 2* and *3*. 'The shots I saw were pretty remarkable,' says Takahashi, 'but Bob noted that there were about 400 still to do, so he was kind of worried.' Takahashi was quickly drafted in as *The Frighteners*' visual-effects supervisor, and began looking at the schedule, trying to work out whether the film could be finished in time. 'There was no way we'd make the deadline. I was asked to figure out what it would take,' he says. Takahashi speaks of 'a concerted plan' involving Jackson and Zemeckis to 'convince Universal it was worthy of sinking more finance into'.

The executives at Universal proposed farming out some of the shots to special-effects companies in the US. Jackson, for whom the film was a chance to show that New Zealand filmmaking could stand alongside anything from Hollywood, is unlikely to have responded enthusiastically. Instead *The Frighteners* got an accelerated release date, four months earlier than planned, a $6 million budget top-up, and at least fifteen new staff and computer workstations, some of them borrowed from Universal.

'At that stage we didn't have enough money to finish it,' says Port. 'Well, we always would have finished it off, but the way that we wanted it to look, the quality we wanted . . . If they hadn't brought the schedule forward, hadn't poured the extra money in, there would have been problems.'

Takahashi rang around the major effects houses in Hollywood, asking if he could borrow some of their digital-effects staff to finish *The Frighteners*. 'I would say the major draw was the film itself,' he says. 'But one of the things we used as bait was large salaries. And also nice houses.' Jackson had got the go-ahead to make *The Frighteners* on the promise that New Zealand's comparatively low wage rates would make the movie's effects cost-effective; now the production had been given the go-ahead to import expensive Hollywood labour to meet the new deadline. Once the new staff had arrived, the disparity between the two sets of pay rates made for some tension. As one Weta crew member puts it: 'Often you'd see the situation where a Kiwi would be supervising people who were paid double what he was, and having to pick up the slack when they went off skiing instead of hitting their deadlines.'

Takahashi claims he wanted to 'bring everybody's pay up to an equal level', but that others were against it. In the end, arrangements were made for local effects staff to receive a small bonus if they stayed on till the end of production, and efforts were made to bring in a fairer payment system on future Weta films.

Takahashi found that many of the American staff, despite impressive production credits, had quite a narrow range of skills, whereas the New Zealanders, perhaps because they had come from jobs in small companies where they needed to handle a variety of tasks, proved 'amazingly well-rounded . . . From that point on I certainly didn't have the impression that ILM has the most talented staff of people. I was really impressed with the New Zealanders.'

Even with its budget top-ups, at around $US30 million the effects-heavy *Frighteners* remained a bargain for Universal. Weta had shown that large quantities of digital effects could be created at a fraction of what most American companies would charge. The challenge now lay in persuading Hollywood that ringing the other side of the planet was worth the bother.

In 1996, Weta Digital joined nine companies to supply effects for the Robert Zemeckis science-fiction film *Contact*, which remains one of Weta's few major non-Jackson projects since completing *The Frighteners*. The company's roughly forty effects shots make up the bulk of the eye-opening 'Wormhole' sequence late in the movie, during which Jodie Foster's character journeys in the pod and finds reality starting to do some very strange things.

Though many of the key staff from *The Frighteners* period have now left Weta, friendships live on across the globe. 'I think everybody gelled pretty quickly,' says one former Weta staff member. 'A number of lifelong friendships were born on this production that continue to this day between Kiwis and Americans. The extended *Frighteners* family is still very healthy.'

GETTING THE SCISSORS OUT

Jackson made it a condition of his *Frighteners* contract that Zemeckis had right of final cut. 'Final cut' is a term which turns the concept of artistic freedom into something that can be legally enforced. Final cut simply means that the director of a film has ultimate control of its final shape. Traditional thinking is that only a handful of people in Hollywood have it. In New Zealand, it is the norm.

Tom Pollock, who now co-heads a production company, thinks that final cut is more common in Hollywood than many think. 'It's not as rare as it ought to be, let's put it that way. Practically anyone who has a hit gets final cut. We financed over 200 movies at Universal in the time I was there. I can only think of one case where the studio made a change over the director's objection. In effect, the director had exercised final cut in 199 movies, whether they had it legally or not.'

However, Pollock freely admits that even with those major-name directors who insist on getting control of their movie down on paper, a give-and-take process occurs between studio and filmmaker. US-based director Roger Donaldson (*Smash Palace, 13 Days*) feels that demanding final cut can work against one's career, in making a director less appealing to a studio: 'You've got to be able to get people on your side so they'll support you and finance you, and ultimately look after your movie when it's made.'

Sometime in the first half of 1996, Zemeckis flew to New Zealand to watch Jackson's first two-hour cut of *The Frighteners*. The next day, they went through it again and came up with ideas as to how the film could be tightened. 'We didn't cut any film,' Jackson told writer Philip Wakefield. 'He said, "Finish the film as you want. I've given you my comments."'

Only battles with the ratings board of America's MPAA remained. Aware that he was meant to be delivering Universal a PG-13 rating, Jackson had cut back on the fluids and onscreen violence as much as possible. But he says that the film's climactic scenes in the hospital pushed the MPAA film over into R-rated territory: 'I said, "But you don't see anything!" but they kept insisting, "No, it's the tone."' Jackson tried to trim the material back, but the rating did not change. In the end, much of the stronger footage was restored, and the climactic hell sequences were beefed up.

SOMETHING TO CROW ABOUT

New Zealand filmmakers have a dismal record when it comes to talking up their own movies in the media. The problem is partly that journalists would rather talk about celebrities and spectacle, whereas low-budget moviemaking lives or dies on boring old intangibles like scripts and performances. In a country where the average film budget does not even cover a Hollywood special-effects bill, claims that a local movie is loaded with excitement and glamour are usually taken with a pinch of salt. Lacking the obvious selling tools such as the presence of a major-league movie star, directors are reduced to vague bragging, not an obvious Kiwi strength.

With *The Frighteners*, Jackson found himself finally able to indulge in the kind of hype that helps keep movies in newspapers and cinemas. His natural, unforced showmanship had been in evidence for years; he once informed me, matter-of-factly over a plate of won-tons, that his latest film featured 'definitely the funniest script that's been written in New Zealand' (*Meet the Feebles*), while the mock-documentary *Forgotten Silver* provided a licence for him and co-director Costa Botes to claim one of the discoveries of the decade. Having managed the miracle of bringing *The Frighteners* in on time, Jackson now argued that the movie featured more computer-generated effects than anything in cinema history, and that the computer-animated cloak seen on the movie's Grim Reaper was a cinema first, making it even more of an amazing achievement than computer-generated dinosaurs. (The last statement was likely news to Los Angeles company Pacific Data Images, which had created Batman's CGI cloak in *Batman Forever* the previous year, or the *Jurassic Park* team over at ILM.) Jackson crisscrossed the US on Universal's executive jet, talking up his movie to legions of American journalists, arguing that *The Frighteners* was a New Zealander's failed attempt at an American movie, and all the better for the fact.

When Peter Jackson's sixth film opened at 1669 American movie theatres on July 19, 1996, German director Roland Emmerich's *Independence Day* was beginning its third week atop the box office. Nine movies opened in America that week: their major competition was not each other, but the twin behemoths of *Independence Day* and the Olympic Games that had just begun in Atlanta.

Success is where you find it. In its first week out, Jackson's movie took in $US8 million, making it the week's biggest new release. For some reason *The Frighteners'* main competitors out of the opening gate — *Kazaam, Fled* and the cloning comedy *Multiplicity* — formed a tight scrum directly behind it on the box-office charts. But *Independence Day* was one of the few films not affected by the Olympics. Unluckily for Jackson, the alien-invasion tale coined more on *The Frighteners'* first weekend than his ghost story would gross on its entire North American theatrical run.

Universal distribution head Nikki Rocco argued that the company had gone in hoping *Frighteners* would make 'great counter-programming' against the Olympics. 'We tried to give it its best shot, but hey, sometimes you make mistakes, and hopefully you learn from it.' Compared to the planned opening on Halloween, the release date had been risky. However, Universal's marketing campaign, which included eye-opening 3D posters and a trailer that honestly related the film's twin urges towards comedy and horror, won praise from film industry magazines.

'I remember reading somewhere that Peter said I hated the movie, and I killed it,' says Tom Pollock. 'I didn't, but there's nobody to write to, saying you got me wrong. Actually I liked it. I think the failure economically had to do with it being a cross-genre movie, and they are tough to do, and tough to sell.'

Though *The Frighteners* failed to set the American box office alight, press reports in New Zealand put all kinds of spin on it. Early reports noted that the opening weekend alone had made more money in the US than any other movie directed and produced by a New Zealander, encouraging the question of how other New Zealand films might have gone had they also benefited from a 1600-print opening and an advertising campaign. A number of journalists quoted an early review in *Variety* which called *The Frighteners* facetious, 'aggressively jokey' and over-reliant on special effects. The *Hollywood Reporter*'s reviewer, who the same day had found the film inventive with 'skilled, whiz-bang moviemaking', did not get a mention.

The *Reporter* was not alone. At the *Washington Times*, Gary Arnold described the film's mixture of supernatural suspense, comedy and spectacle as 'impressive and satisfying', with a sophistication missing from many of the season's blockbusters. *Chicago Tribune* critic Michael Wilmington praised Peter Jackson's dynamic, hyper-kinetic action and outlandish comedy, as well as his ability to move far beyond what few other directors were willing to try. Wilmington felt that the film sets out 'to be the horror thriller to end them all — taking most of the horror movie conventions of the past thirty years far past cliché into a kind of delirious crescendo'. *Kansas City Star* writer Calvin Wilson found that *The Frighteners* managed to be 'funny without losing its mood of foreboding', and praised Michael J Fox for a subtly-layered performance that 'seems so effortless that it's no doubt been taken for granted'.

Truth is, critical reaction to *The Frighteners* in the US can be turned any way you want it to. Roughly half the reviews tend towards the highly positive, but the negative reviews were very negative indeed. The elements that some reviewers praised — notably the script, the deluge of special effects, and the performance of Michael J Fox — were the things which others had most problems with.

With the American press for *The Frighteners* out of the way, Jackson could finally take a rest. The two-year-long rollercoaster ride of signing with Miramax, winning Oscar nominations, producing *Jack Brown Genius*, co-directing *Forgotten Silver* and finishing *The Frighteners* had come to a halt. That winter, Jackson and Walsh scaled back their work to three hours a day as they began writing a little something called *King Kong*.

KONG

The offer to remake *King Kong* had come from Universal executives, months before they saw the final cut of *The Frighteners*. Someone at the studio clearly had faith in Jackson's talent: at this point, for all his acclaim, the director had not managed a hit on American soil.

Initially Jackson turned the *Kong* offer down, before realising that to remake the film that had started him on the path to being a movie director was to allow somebody else to do a worse job. 'The fact it's my favourite movie is of some comfort to me,' he told the *Observer* in January 1997, 'because at least I'm remaking something that's close to my heart.' Again the plan was for all filming and effects to be handled within New Zealand. Late in 1996 Jackson stopped off in Mexico to discuss the part with Kate Winslet on the set of *Titanic*. Other possible casting names mentioned included Minnie Driver and George Clooney.

The Frighteners opened in New Zealand on Boxing Day, 1996, to mixed reviews. The days when Jackson's latest movie was nudged towards cult status thanks to the fact that the distributors could afford only a small number of prints, had long gone: this time United International Pictures opened on thirty-seven screens, and *The Frighteners* became the biggest film of the summer. Within a few short weeks, it had moved past *Heavenly Creatures* as the fifth most successful New Zealand movie to date.

Then Universal announced that *King Kong* had been put on hold. A gaggle of upcoming creature movies — including Roland Emmerich's *Godzilla* remake and an expensive version of RKO's other gorilla classic, *Mighty Joe Young* — had given Universal executives the spooks. But there was likely another reason: at the time of the announcement to cancel, Universal had just finished an expensive race to beat the disaster movie *Volcano* into cinemas with its own entry *Dante's Peak*. Some estimates say that the rush cost them an extra $US20 million.

So Peter Jackson had finally arrived in Hollywood, where his movie had been a commercial loser, without being a financial disaster. But his own career was now caught between two worlds.

MICHAEL J FOX

Finished shooting *The Frighteners* in late 1995, then returned to his wife and family in New York. The following year he fulfilled his desire of returning to television, starring as deputy mayor Mike Flaherty in the highly successful *Spin City*, which he also co-produced. In November 1998, with the press threatening to break the story, Fox told *People* magazine that he had been diagnosed with Parkinson's disease seven years before. He continued to star on *Spin City* for four seasons, until an emotional farewell episode which included appearances by some of his former *Family Ties* co-stars. Since then Fox has written *Lucky Man*, a book about his life and experiences with Parkinson's, campaigned for increased research into the disease, appeared occasionally onscreen, and provided voice-overs for the movies *Atlantis: The Lost Empire* and *Stuart Little*.

GEORGE PORT

Left the digital-effects company he had helped create just a few months before completion of *The Frighteners*. He moved to Auckland with *Frighteners* costume designer Barbara Darragh, and later joined the effects staff at Pacific Renaissance Pictures, makers of cult television series *Xena* and *Hercules*. Later Port and a team of as many as thirty New Zealanders took over the creation of most of the computer-generated effects for *Xena*. After Pacific Renaissance shut up shop in 2001, Port bought most of the company's computer equipment and set up the effects company PRPVFX, whose credits include an Emmy nomination for the mini-series *Superfire*, a film about Polynesian migration playing at Auckland's National Maritime Museum, and the television show *Power Rangers*.

CHAPTER ELEVEN

THE POLITICAL ANIMAL

*'Perhaps all works of art that necessitate a collaboration
between an artist and his patron contain within them the seeds of enmity.'*
DIRECTOR MICHAEL POWELL, 1986

'Let's just say that it's time for fresh blood.'
PETER JACKSON, CRITICISING THE NEW ZEALAND FILM COMMISSION IN 1997

In 1997 Peter Jackson was suddenly in fighting mode. Early that year, the director's opportunity to remake *King Kong* was abruptly cut from under him, and the Weta special-effects team went overnight from busy to virtually unemployed. Meanwhile, an uncomplimentary review of *The Frighteners* in the *Listener* so incensed Jackson and Walsh that they decided to take legal action. By December, the director was calling the Film Commission misguided, directionless and indecisive in an attack precision-timed for its twentieth anniversary; talking again about going to the lawyers; and telling *Variety* that he was considering leaving New Zealand.

In the end, nothing came from Jackson's talk of joining the creative brain drain. Instead, he found his life overtaken by a movie project whose complications left little time for worrying about his relationship with the Film Commission, the organisation that had funded his first three movies. But five years later, as the second *Lord of the Rings* episode had its Australasian premiere, Jackson's feelings towards the Commission had reached the point where he labelled them 'aggressive and vindictive'. Meanwhile, Walsh had taken a case against the *Listener,* for publishing an article by someone with a similar name to her own, and not alerting the public to the difference.

Alongside his partner, the man whose unflappable yet slightly shy manner had helped make him a media favourite, appeared to have found a new way of making himself heard. This chapter is an attempt to make some sense of Peter Jackson's complex relationship with the New Zealand media, and his even more up-down relationship with the guardians of the country's film funding. Hang on — it's going to be a bumpy ride.

THE MEDIA

There is a saying in Hollywood that the movies with the best chance of getting made are those whose storyline can be summarised in one sentence. These days, movies with simple hooks and outlandish creatures have a built-in advantage in winning public attention. If one of the protagonists in your sensitive romantic drama is played by an alien with eight limbs, so much the better.

In many senses, Peter Jackson is a walking hook machine. Each of his movies, even the ones hardly anyone saw at the time, is a magazine headline waiting to be written, whether it be pornographic puppets (*Meet the Feebles*), outrageous lies (*Forgotten Silver*), or teenage murderers (*Heavenly Creatures*). And thankfully his films tend to be as much fun to watch as to read about.

Jackson's unforced knack for showmanship, and homemade abilities with special effects, helped capture the attention of the media from early on. Newspapers in Wellington began to publish photos of him standing by the motorway in a homemade gorilla suit, or wielding a chainsaw amid the alien cast members of his first low-budget film. Having won a prize from a local newspaper for a film made as a teenager, and later working as a newspaper photolithographer, Jackson got an inkling for the power of the media. Casts of zombies, aliens and oversexed puppets helped win him generous media coverage. In a country where many local films fail at the box office partly because no one has heard about them until they hit cinemas, Jackson's approach was somewhat revolutionary: invite some journalists onto your film set, show them a monster or two, and grab some free publicity.

Quotability helped too. Jackson spoke unpretentiously about telling Kiwi stories that made him laugh, and how their success was a good thing, because it enabled more New Zealand films to get funding. Jackson's air of openness, and love for cinema, has helped convert many a journalist to the cause. At the same time, the director has capitalised on the near myth-like aspects of his story in many of his press releases and interviews — the birthdate on Halloween (in a country that rarely celebrates the event), the childhood viewing of *King Kong* that turned him overnight into a filmmaker, the idea he is so grounded that he never gets angry or annoyed. Though Jackson's early films failed to break out much beyond film festivals, you cannot blame that on any lack of facing up to the press.

Around 1994, Jackson's dream relationship with the media finally began to fray, just as his fame reached a new height. *Heavenly Creatures* marked the turning point. By the time he got round to recreating one of New Zealand's most famous murders, Jackson realised that he was no longer subject to the media's every beck and call (and by now, their calls were many). Aware of the sensitivities of filming the Parker–Hulme tragedy on location in Christchurch, Jackson chose for the first time in three movies to keep his set largely free of journalists. Interviews for the film found him trying to balance his positive feelings about two misunderstood teenagers with sensitivity to the tragedy they had caused.

When, shortly before the release of *Heavenly Creatures*, journalist Lin Ferguson revealed that the real-life Juliet Hulme was now an author named Anne Perry, Jackson and Walsh found themselves defending the accuracy of their account against one of the actual participants — a woman who felt that *Heavenly Creatures'* very existence was morally questionable.

From that point on, secrecy began to take increasing precedence in Peter Jackson's career, often with good reason. There followed the carefully managed lies of the fake documentary *Forgotten Silver*, for which at least two publications published articles pretending that fiction was truth. When it came to the legislated secrecy of *The Frighteners*, a number of journalists entering Camperdown Studios had to sign non-disclosure agreements ensuring they wouldn't write about anything they saw inside — for example, the then-unannounced *King Kong*.

The media's unveiling of Juliet Hulme made Jackson acutely aware that media attention can be a double-edged sword. He has spoken of feeling guilt for the part *Heavenly Creatures* played in Hulme's rediscovery, and also expressed his anger at the journalist who found her (Ferguson, on the other hand, insists she refused to cash in on her scoop by selling the story overseas). The act of revealing the identity of someone who once murdered, and paid for their crime, is arguably more questionable than Jackson's own actions: making a movie which quotes often from the personal diaries of a murderer. But balancing such ethical questions requires knowing exactly why Ferguson, Jackson and Walsh decided to tell the stories they did — and untangling any desire they may have had for success or fame from a possible desire for good.

My own belief is that Jackson took much of his own guilt at having turned the Parker–Hulme murder into a successful movie and laid it at the door of the media. This theory would help explain why Jackson allowed himself to throw a photo of Parker and Hulme onto the screen in the midst of *The Frighteners*, as if it was a kind of in-joke, just months after having been criticised in real life by Hulme/Perry for exploiting her story. The scene in *The Frighteners* (with Trini Alvarado's character watching a video about a serial killer) appears to be attacking media sensationalism of tragedies. But including an image of Parker and Hulme, however briefly, comes across as somewhat hypocritical, especially in a film which itself plays murder largely for sensation and entertainment.

Still, you could argue that a certain blindness to the opinions of others forms part of the armoury of the genuinely courageous filmmaker, and *Meet the Feebles* and *Lord of the Rings* certainly place Peter Jackson in that category. The director occasionally sounds surprised in interviews that people could find certain of the more extreme images in his films offensive, although he had long been aware that negative reviews come with the territory. When I criticised *Meet the Feebles* in print in 1990, Jackson alluded to my negative review with a grace I would have been hard pressed to match in his place.

HITTING THE JUGULAR

By 1996, as Jackson's movies drifted closer to the mainstream and his power in the industry grew, his sensitivity to criticism appeared to have grown also. Late that year, he argued that several American film critics felt they had discovered him through their positive reviews for *Heavenly Creatures*, and this in turn had been a factor in their overly negative reaction to *The Frighteners*. 'They didn't like the fact that I turned on them and did what they see as a lowbrow, brainless kind of horror movie,' Jackson told *Listener* journalist Gordon Campbell. 'I was being punished. Most of the time the film wasn't being reviewed, it was my career.'

Yet Jackson sounded somehow freed by the negative reviews for *The Frighteners*, telling Campbell with a laugh that he no longer had 'anything to lose'. He was mistaken. Shortly after the interview, *Listener* writer Philip Matthews gave a thumbs-down review to *The Frighteners*. Two months later, Jackson and Fran Walsh launched proceedings for defamation against Matthews and the magazine.

Matthews's review moves from criticising the lack of originality of the big-budget *Frighteners* to arguing that the charms of earlier Jackson movies had more to do with financial necessity than choice. Matthews thereby manages to simultaneously attack both *The Frighteners* and the earlier films he claims to prefer. *The Frighteners*, he writes, makes Jackson's best film *Heavenly Creatures* 'seem like an aberration'.

Though Michael J Fox's performance wins praise, as do the special effects, the review also argues that *The Frighteners* is built so completely from references to other movies that 'if one brick came out, the whole structure would collapse', and goes on to list seven of the films by name. *The Frighteners*, 'is a fairly shaky piece of architecture built from the rubble of other people's movies, scattered with what film bores call homage and what real people call stealing'.

In late February 1995, Jackson's lawyers issued proceedings against the *Listener* and Philip Matthews for defamation. According to the statement of claim, Matthew's review alleged that 'they had stolen the entire film *The Frighteners* from other films'. Lawyers for the *Listener* filed a statement of defence disputing the claim and arguing that Matthews's review represented his honest opinion. In the end, Jackson and Walsh did not pursue the case further.

Cases of directors or studios threatening to take legal action against reviewers are rare — though undoubtedly many directors have thought about it, and been persuaded against the idea. In the 1930s, 20th Century Fox took a case against Graham Greene for a *Spectator* review in which he wrote of sexualised images of Shirley Temple having been exploited for an audience of middle-aged men (Greene lost the case, and was forced to pay damages). In 1998, director James Cameron published a letter in the *Los Angeles Times* accusing critic Kenneth Turan of disliking movies and their audiences, after a controversial column in which Turan reiterated his distaste for Cameron's *Titanic*. In Jackson and Walsh's case, it seems surprising that their annoyance at the review of *Frighteners* ever came close to legal action — especially when one considers that film criticism is partly about the expression of opinion, one of the key defences used in cases of defamation.

In the weeks before lawyers took proceedings over *The Frighteners* review, another *Listener* story caused Jackson annoyance: this time a fairly neutral piece by Gordon Campbell about the cancellation of *King Kong* and the mystery project that had replaced it on the drawing board. The story mentions the 'poor reviews and box-office take' of *The Frighteners* in the US, and puts forward some theories, including Jackson's own, as to why Universal chose to cancel *King Kong*. 'I talked to a few other sources and added some analysis about the likely contributing factors,' recalls Campbell. 'Afterwards, to my amazement, one of his underlings contacted me to say that by talking to anyone else, I was implying that Jackson had been lying, and so all communication with Jackson would now cease.'

My only negative experiences with Peter Jackson before writing this book occurred with a story I wrote in 1994, which mentioned a key international screening of *Heavenly Creatures*. The article correctly stated that reaction to the film had been mixed, but questionable editing at the newspaper made the piece sound far more negative than originally intended. Attempts to talk about the matter with Jackson were diverted to one of his staff, and a number of discussions followed. After finally being told by the staff member that the issue was now behind us, I discovered many months later that Jackson was still too annoyed about the article to allow me to visit the set of *The Frighteners* (though in later years, my impression was that the story was no longer an issue).

By October 2000, when Gordon Campbell wrote the first major feature on the tax breaks used for *Lord of the Rings*, he was still on Jackson's *persona non grata* list. Some of those working on *Lord of the Rings* came under suspicion of leaking core information about the tax breaks, a suspicion Campbell claims was unfounded. Among other sins, Campbell was now one of the few journalists in the country who had dared to point out that even if it went into profit, *Lord of the Rings* might well cost New Zealand hundreds of millions of dollars in tax revenues.

Campbell argues that the stories in the *Listener* also contained strong arguments in favour of the tax breaks, and held positions that Jackson agreed with. 'In my experience, Jackson appears to object to any media that is not palpably positive, or that doesn't function as a fairly passive vehicle for the messages he wishes to promote,' he says. 'I don't see in him much understanding — let alone tolerance — of the independent role of the media. This is not unusual in a celebrity, but the intensity of his response is a bit surprising, given that he projects an image of being the easygoing Kiwi bloke.'

During the filming of *Lord of the Rings*, Jackson's former employer the *Evening Post* also spent time in the media sinbin, after what *Rings* publicist Claire Raskind called 'problems' with the newspaper. For months, the *Post* had continued to publish occasional photos of *Rings* sets, taken from public land. In fact, a *Post* photographer had managed to grab some passable hobbit shots on the first day of filming, but the paper had been persuaded by the production not to use them, in exchange for promises of future interviews with the cast. As the months rolled by and *Post* staff began to realise that their place in the *Rings* interview pecking order was fairly low, the newspaper began visiting the film sets more often. But either Jackson or New Line were beginning to tire of all the people standing on hillsides with cameras. Although many of these photographers were actually reporting for Tolkien fan-sites, the message was delivered to the mainstream media instead.

In August 2000, lawyers for Jackson's company Three Foot Six claimed copyright on pictures taken by the Christchurch *Press* of the spectacular hilltop Edoras set. A $2 *Evening Post* poster of Edoras images and some shots from the movie trailer was withdrawn from sale after the threat of an injunction. When the *Evening Post* was banned from a press conference in Wellington a few months later, editor Suzanne Carty compared the move to Tom Scott's infamous banning in the days of Prime Minister Robert Muldoon. But by the time the *Post* devoted extensive coverage to the Wellington premiere of *Lord of the Rings*, relations were back on an even keel.

However much we might like to deny it, the relationship between public figures and the media is partly one of mutual exploitation. Despite all the efforts of company publicists and lawyers, one of the trade-offs of being able to make movies is that the curiosity of the media cannot always be controlled by a corporate schedule — and even when it can, there is no requirement in law for movie reviewers to like the result.

By 2002, Peter Jackson's fame had taken him to a place that no one deserves to be trapped in: the director had finally become subject to the kind of invasive journalism found in British tabloids and New Zealand women's magazines. Among other stories, editors at the *Sunday Star-Times* and the *Wairarapa Times Age* decided that photographs and stories involving renovations at one of Jackson's houses ranked as publishable news (one doubts whether the newspapers' editors would have felt their own homes merited the same treatment, had they been public figures). That year, Jackson was heard to comment that if anything drove him out of New Zealand, it would be the media's obsession with the private life of him, his partner and their family.

THE FILM COMMISSION

Imagine if you will a small hut in the middle of a landscape of gently rolling hills. Six times each year on a special day, hunters appear on horseback from all corners of the earth, and come racing across the hills towards the hut, seeking the treasure inside. The only entrance is a low, squat door.

Until very recently, this has been the landscape for New Zealand filmmakers, and the low-cut door marks the entrance to the offices of the Film Commission. The door is small because the Commission cannot afford a larger one. Its income derives largely from Lottery Grants Board funding and a small government top-up: the $10 million total remained virtually static for a seven-year period until 2002, when the government began announcing a series of substantial funding increases for New Zealand films. The door to the Film Commission remains key to the existence of New Zealand movies. Local production companies concentrate mainly on television programmes and commercials, only rarely dipping their toes into feature films. Private investors are hard to find.

Despite the increasing international interest in local directors after the success of *The Piano* and *Once Were Warriors*, overseas film companies are rarely able to shoulder the whole cost of a New Zealand director making a movie on their home turf (the Miramax-funded Martin Donovan thriller *Heaven* is a rare exception). Most often it is the Commission that takes up the funding slack. The organisation's power over which New Zealand movies get made is immense.

In his first nine years of filmmaking, Jackson often tried to get inside the Film Commission's door. Sometimes he had to knock a number of times before it gave him any money, but on four of those occasions he eventually walked out with a cheque. In three cases, the movie in question promised images of violence that many a government-appointed funding body might have found problematic. In a world where more movies are rejected than ever receive funding, this is a solid record of support.

However, it was only because of cash injections slipped through the system by then executive director Jim Booth that Jackson's first movie *Bad Taste* ever got made. At the time, some Commission staff questioned the value of an amateurishly-shot home movie featuring aliens and chainsaws. But market reaction to the film helped calm them.

Jackson's second movie, *Meet the Feebles,* marks the point where director and Commission first found themselves in major conflict. The original press kit for *Feebles* is something of an oddity. Its account of the film's journey to the screen reads a little like a game of Russian roulette played by the film's Vietnam-vet frog, with the frog aiming shots at the Film Commission, only to keep hitting himself in the head through his use of truth and misinformation. To quote from the press kit:

> *The writers and crew of* Meet the Feebles *represent the new-wave of New Zealand filmmakers — determined to make original, entertaining films for audiences they understand. The Establishment has had trouble coping. Less than a week before shooting started the polished script was presented to the New Zealand Film Commission. They hated it and withdrew their funding. Discussions with the full Board went on into the night and the money flowed again. The same was to happen twice more during the shoot. Throughout the shoot, the script was to be debated with the NZFC, scenes disapproved, challenged and quietly shot, until in the end the original script — as written — was in the can.*

Jackson's decision to switch to *Feebles* after the collapse of another project required meeting a tight deadline imposed by an overseas investor. The Film Commission's decision to lend money required its approval of the completed script, which at that point was still being written. Everything about the movie was rushed and under-budgeted, and the Commission board set itself up for a nightmare by offering funds in the first place.

The *Feebles* script, which would make *Bad Taste* look like an exercise in pastoral lyricism, had to be finished three weeks before shooting began. According to the press kit it was finished on time, with another week for a polish. Yet for reasons unknown, the Commission did not get to see it until 'less than a week' before the cameras were due to roll. The Commission's temptation to pull the plug at this point, or at least delay the shoot, must have been high.

Though all of the former Commission staff and board members interviewed remember discussion over the risky nature of the project, few are able to provide details of the script conflicts cited in the *Feebles* press kit. Still, when Jackson's name is mentioned to past and present Commission staff, diplomacy is often the second word that seems to come to mind. One person recalls worries that *Feebles'* porn-movie subplot might conflict with the Commission's legal requirement to reflect community standards.

The Commission enlisted board member John Reid (director of *Middle Aged Spread*) to monitor filming of *Feebles*. With the movie drifting further behind schedule every week, Reid was asked to stay on until the completion of the film. One day on set Jackson called a meeting in Reid's absence, and mentioned Reid's fee for staying on as an example of the Commission's gross misuse of funds. Reid feels that this may have been partly an effort by Jackson to create unity in his crew, by encouraging the idea of the Commission as a common enemy. 'The crew were determined that they were going to hang in there,' he says. 'They undertook to make a very ambitious film for a ridiculously small amount. I think they were of a mind that if they could get it going, they could somehow find a way of keeping it going.'

Reid left them to it. With the *Feebles* shoot continuing to go seriously over budget and schedule, the Commission eventually put its foot down. The *Feebles* press kit tries to paint them as the villain, for insisting that filming stop 'almost a week' before the scheduled finish date. In fact the scheduled finish date had by then long been left behind — by the time the Commission demanded the shoot must end, the challenges of the puppets, and Jackson's perfectionism, meant that *Feebles* had already gone a month over its original seven-week filming schedule.

Jackson has said in a number of interviews that he then came close to getting fired, and mentions in one that Booth was also in the Commission's sights. If such a threat was ever uttered by the Commission, it appears to have been a fairly hollow one. (Extended attempts to gain permission to look at the Commission's files on the making of *Meet the Feebles* had not met success as this book went to press.) As a former Commission executive, Booth would have known that firing a director in such a situation is extremely rare. Jackson stayed on and completed one last self-financed week of filming, while pretending to the Commission that the shoot had been completed. When *Meet the Feebles* emerged, it proved a box-office failure.

Feebles marks one of the darkest moments in Jackson's career, a movie whose tiny budget and all-puppet cast were more than likely incompatible from day one. Yet Jackson's early spin-doctoring here provides a fascinating insight into the development of his public persona — cleverly turning disasters to his advantage by painting himself as the filmmaker battling for perfection, with the Film Commission as resident villain. A moviemaker at the beginning of his career, he was already making muffled noises in the press kit implying the government moneyman was playing the heavy.

Jackson's next two projects were far more positive for all. *Braindead* got eighty percent Film Commission funding, and won acclaim around the world. *Heavenly Creatures*, forty percent funded by the Commission and sixty percent by German company Senator, did even better, its success opening promised avenues of German funding in New Zealand film.

LAUNCHING THE FIRST ROCKET

The Film Commission has often met criticism from within the film industry, with many accusing it of being bureaucratic and out of touch. By the late 1990s, some felt that it was becoming increasingly obsessed with the self-defeating idea of funding 'commercial' projects, though few were willing to go on the record with their criticisms.

In late 1997, after releasing his first Hollywood-funded movie *The Frighteners*, Jackson launched an attack on the Commission's competence at one of the only times that year the organisation was guaranteed some positive press. The skirmish began as the Commission prepared for its twentieth anniversary. New Zealand industry magazine *Onfilm* published a sponsored supplement to celebrate, and *Onfilm* editor David Gapes asked a number of local moviemaking figures to contribute a short piece about the Commission, perhaps including some personal anecdotes.

Gapes asked for pieces running at around 500 words. But when Peter Jackson's contribution arrived, it was 1800–2000 words long, and consisted almost entirely of an attack, accusing the Commission of being confused and inconsistent in its decision-making, riven by internal strife, and out of touch with the needs of filmmakers. Jackson argued that the majority of Commission board members who judged the viability of film projects had 'little understanding of film making'. He felt that it was time to get rid of 'the government-appointed seat-fillers' on the board, and replace them with people with experience in the film industry.

'I recognised that he was saying what a lot of people in the industry felt,' recalls Gapes. 'There's always been a pretty vigorous debate about the Commission. Having said that, I was surprised by the piece . . . It was fairly strongly worded.'

Though the anniversary supplement would include critical comments about the Commission from a number of other filmmakers, the tone and length of Jackson's piece posed special problems. The Commission was offering more than $10,000 worth of advertising for the special issue, and was a regular advertiser. After discussions with contacts at the Commission, Gapes was told that the decision over running Jackson's piece was his, but unofficially that going ahead with it would jeopardise the magazine's ongoing relationship with the Commission. Gapes says this comment marked the only time in his decade as editor that the Film Commission tried to influence the content of *Onfilm*.

Then *Onfilm* features editor Mike Wheeler feels that Jackson had every right to be critical of the Commission, but questions his timing: 'In my opinion, to have a rant at the Commission over its recent performance, when the issue was about the whole twenty years of the institution, was downright egocentric.'

After discussions at the magazine, Gapes told Jackson's assistant that the story could not run in its present form — it was too long, and also likely to be defamatory. 'In the end, Jackson said, "You must run it all, and with no excisions." Apart from not backing down at all, he was reasonably understanding about our position.'

Jackson's piece finally appeared the following month in *Metro* magazine, then edited by Bill Ralston, along with a feature about the state of the Film Commission. The version which appeared in *Metro* was around 300 words shorter than the version seen by *Onfilm*, and included the line 'individuals are not to blame'.

The timing of Jackson's article was complicated by a recent film proposal, and his partner Fran Walsh's own experiences on the Commission board. Walsh resigned from the board less than a year into her appointment, alleging to *Metro* that she was told to cite family reasons as her motivation rather than concerns with the Commission (concerns which have never been fully explained in the media). That year, wearing his executive producer's hat, Jackson tried for Commission funding for the cross-genre love story *Pink Frost*, to be directed by Harry Sinclair. The Commission offered conditional funding, and there was talk of *Pink Frost* going into production in June 1997. But the Commission withdrew its $2 million, after Jackson and Sinclair failed to find evidence of 'market support'.

In the *Metro* piece, Jackson talks of 'indecisive meandering' from the Commission, and goalposts shifting between progressive board meetings. He claims that the Commission allowed only three weeks to find market support before withdrawing its *Pink Frost* funding, and that he had considered taking legal action over the affair.

In terms of fair treatment, I would argue that Jackson's comments about *Pink Frost* were hardly setting much of an example. By refusing to drop a client-confidentiality clause, Jackson got to complain about the

Commission's handling of *Pink Frost* while refusing to allow the Commission to respond publicly to his allegations. In June, the Commission had agreed to a two-month extension to their original funding proposal, to allow more negotiations with potential overseas financiers. In August, Jackson and *Pink Frost* co-producer Tim Sanders asked for another two-month extension, this time for negotiations for possible financing by a New Zealand merchant bank. After 'considerable discussion' the Commission turned the extension down, citing a lack of market support.

Jackson went to legal firm Chen and Palmer over *Pink Frost*, and there was discussion of the firm conducting a legal review of recent Film Commission decisions. According to the *Metro* article, the lawyers told him he had grounds for suing the Film Commission over *Frost*, but he felt the idea was 'destructive and expensive'. Yet he spoke of keeping the firm on as he was 'using a legal approach to look at reform on a political level'.

Jackson sounded tired of asking for the money to make movies. 'I'm a guy who has worked in this industry longer than some of the board, and I object to the way I've been treated,' he said. 'I can't continue working in this country if that's what I have to face.' A few months earlier he had been quoted telling American entertainment Bible *Variety* that he had a choice — 'either try to do something about the NZFC's problems, or leave the country. I will put up a big fight before I come close to a decision because this is the country I want to live and work in.'

At this point Jackson was secretly working with partners in Hollywood on developing *Lord of the Rings*, to shoot back in New Zealand. You might argue that his various comments were meant to help other local filmmakers with far more to lose from sticking their necks out. Yet the way Jackson went about his attack, along with his threats to leave the country, make one wonder if he was starting to get a little carried away with his own success. Whatever the merits of his argument, the timing of the piece, and its heavy-handedness (not unlike sending in a scathing attack of Weta employment policies, just in time for *their* anniversary) probably only succeeded in making those at the Commission more defensive. The Commission's chief executive Ruth Harley had been in the job for only eight months, and as another critic of the Commission pointed out, it would be another two or three years before any policy changes were reflected in the movies that actually emerged.

There are a number of ways to interpret Jackson's many jousts with the Film Commission and the media. Here is mine. There are two sides to the public face of Peter Jackson. The face we see most often is that of the modest, laidback filmmaker, the unpretentious man of the people. The other face is of a Peter Jackson whose passion for filmmaking, and distaste for bureaucracy, can make him temperamental to the point where his solution is increasingly to bully, ignore or attack those who do not see things his way. Though Jackson's passion for a better way is obvious, his approach is more liable to create defensiveness and anger than open discussion.

In *The Fellowship of the Ring*, Bilbo meets Frodo again after a long journey and, in an unforgettable scene, Bilbo's gentle face suddenly reveals great wrath, as he reacts to the power of the Ring. Try to imagine Jackson as Bilbo, recently returned from Hollywood. What Jackson sees during these rare moments of wrath is not the lure of the Ring, but the stupidity of people who do not see his logic. It is almost as if there are two Jacksons: the one on the film set, who handles all the manifold stresses of moviemaking with diplomacy and Zen-like calm, and the one out in the world of media and film politics, whose response to events he cannot control is often either denial or attack.

Perhaps Jackson's particular brand of creative spark requires having someone to fight against. In the absence of a tyrannical or uninterested parent, the obvious psychological enemy is the Film Commission, the funding body that helped him into being — the body that appears so resistant to real change. Jackson's attack in *Metro* may also reveal some of the pressures of becoming an increasingly large fish in the tiny New Zealand film industry pond, yet not finding it any easier to get local funding.

The same month that Jackson attacked the Commission in *Metro*, he joined a small number of New Zealand producers and directors to form the Feature Film Group, which hoped to bring about policy changes to the Film Commission. The group met with Cultural Affairs minister Simon Upton in the weeks before Christmas 1997, hoping among other things to persuade him that the Commission needed more film industry expertise on its board. Upton had been in the job for only three months, and Jackson told journalists that the Minister was honest to the group about his lack of knowledge about the film industry, telling them, 'You're the first film-related group I've ever met. I know nothing.'

A few days after the meeting, an article appeared in the *Evening Post*, in which Jackson spoke of his feeling that Upton had a portfolio he didn't want or understand. Jackson's willingness to talk publicly about Upton's apparent lack of understanding did little to win the Minister's support. 'We all got a letter the next day from an outraged Upton,' recalls Ian Mune, another member of the group. 'He was basically saying, "You won't get any help from me."' Within a few months, the Feature Film Group faded from view.

KAHUKURA

Kahukura is a Maori word meaning rainbow. The pot of gold at the end of this particular rainbow would be a series of films trapped in limbo, and a new low in the relationship between New Zealand's most powerful filmmaker and the major funder of local films. Wellington producer Larry Parr began the Kahukura company in 1997, after selling the Film Commission on the idea of a series of low-budget movies. Parr's idea was that if the films were no good, there would be no requirement to waste more money on readying them for a cinema release. Mirage, the movie company he co-founded, had collapsed shortly after the 1987 stock-market crash, and since then Parr had continued to work in the film industry in a variety of roles.

In late 2002, Kahukura received $4 million from television funding body New Zealand On Air to make a comedy series called *Love Bites*. (A series, I might add, whose better moments have been unfairly buried in a rush of Kahukura-related bad feeling.) Kahukura also had four low-budget movies on the boil, including Parr's own *Crime Story* and Grant Lahood's *Kombi Nation*. In the first few months of 2002, the Kahukura rainbow began turning to custard. A mystery investor had suddenly withdrawn funding from *Love Bites* (some argue they never existed at all). Problems began when Parr allegedly used Film Commission payments for Kahukura's movies to make up the shortfall. Meanwhile bills were mounting for the movies at the Film Unit, the film laboratory now owned by Jackson.

After four months, the Film Unit began considering legal action to get payment from Parr for a $180,000 lab bill owed for *Kombi Nation*. (The Film Commission had already paid Parr the money, but it had never been passed on.) For a while a solution seemed possible, but then it became clear that Kahukura owed even more money, including some to Inland Revenue. The Film Unit called in the liquidators, the unpaid-for cans of film remained locked up, and Jackson later claimed that *Kombi Nation* had been 'sent into liquidation hell due to the ill-judged actions of the New Zealand Film Commission'.

By December 2002, a flurry of accusations and press announcements had succeeded only in creating confusion and distrust. But one thing was obvious: the Kahukura movies were still in limbo, and efforts to negotiate payment for the many creditors had gone nowhere fast. A key stumbling block was that the Commission and New Zealand On Air were trying to hold back $500,000 in Kahukura payments in order to pay off creditors. The liquidator argued that the money belonged among Kahukura's assets, which would have allowed the liquidators and Inland Revenue to get first share of it.

Grant Lahood made arrangements with the Film Unit to borrow the only print of *Kombi Nation* for some special screenings. He hoped to drum up some interest in distributing the film, and was angry that the Commission continued to show little interest in helping *Kombi Nation* out of the mess, despite positive responses at test screenings. The Film Unit made sure a security guard accompanied the print, so that no one ran off with it.

In December, Lahood went on National Radio and attacked the Commission for making so little effort to get the Kahukura movies out of liquidation. Lahood says he got a call from the liquidator after going off air, telling him, 'You've created a storm.' Suddenly the liquidator was ready to talk about selling him the rights to *Kombi*. Lahood offered $20,000, planning to embarrass the Commission by managing in a few phone calls what had taken them six months.

Instead, new Commission chairman Barry Everard sent out a press release claiming that 'six months of negotiation by the Commission' had secured the rights to three of four of the Kahukura films back to their directors. The liquidator announced that the Commission had had nothing to do with it.

Meanwhile Lahood had just paid $20,000 for the rights to a film that was still locked up at the Film Unit, owing money. But on the day of the Wellington release of *The Two Towers*, Jackson rejoined the attack. The Commission was not welcome at the *Towers* premiere, he wrote, because of his disgust at how Everard had 'attempted to wash his hands' of *Kombi Nation*. Jackson wrote of Everard's approach of 'fiscal irresponsibility and vindictiveness', and Film Commission spin-doctoring. The press release argued that the *Two Towers* premiere:

> celebrates the achievement of New Zealand talent behind and in front of the camera; in a year when film crews and suppliers of the independent film industry have been abused and vilified by these self-serving bureaucrats, it would be totally inappropriate for the Film Commission to be participating in this event.

That morning, Jackson went on National Radio to attack the Commission's 'aggressive' efforts not to pay any of the Kahukura debts, and their 'insidious' strategy for *Kombi Nation*: 'They're basically setting up Grant as the poor filmmaker who now owns his own film, but can't possibly pay the debt.'

The Commission, he said, failed to realise that the Film Unit was run 'on the smell of an oily rag' and could not afford other people's debts. The Commission had expected the whole film industry to subsidise the Kahukura low-budget model, and then abandoned it when things got tough. Considering Jackson's percentage points on *Rings*, some listeners might have wondered why he was trying to play the poverty card. His interview hardly even mentioned Parr, the man whose financial mismanagement had caused Kahukura's demise. Instead, he used the Kahukura fracas to launch a wider attack on the Commission, saying it was no longer run by risktakers, having become a 'very unimaginative, dull organisation' that no longer supported young filmmakers. He repeated doubts expressed earlier in the year that he would have won Commission funding, if he had come through the funding system now.

When Everard followed Jackson onto the show, interviewer Linda Clark's second question was: 'Can the Commission afford to be so offside with the country's most successful filmmaker?' Clearly goodwill for Jackson's achievements can go a long way. While Jackson repeated his mantra of Commission aggression, Everard's mantra was that paying Jackson's legal fees was 'an absolute misuse of public money'. His comments gave the impression that paying off small film-industry creditors was a much higher priority than playing 'nanny for a fully-established business'.

Each side accused the other of incompetent credit controls — Everard arguing that one phone call early on from the Film Unit would have prevented the debts racking up, Jackson saying that the Commission had gone ahead on making *Crime Story*, despite knowing that Kahukura could not pay its bills (the Commission had already spent a considerable amount by that point, and argued that finishing the film was preferable to stopping halfway through). In between the squabbling, each spoke sympathetically of their concern for the small man, and the many film industry people who had been caught up in the company's collapse.

Gordon Campbell has argued that the heart of the Kahukura wrangle is the Kiwi assumption that the state should always step in, to save everyone from the consequences: 'Making films is a chronically risky business, and who would want to send out a signal that any cowboy production house that gets into trouble can count on having their bills paid for them by the state?' The battle was also about strong personalities throwing apples at one another as the legal bills climbed, their antagonism having reached such levels that they appeared to be unable to sit down at one table to talk things through. (Jackson's disinvitation to the premiere was aimed specifically at Barry Everard and Commission chief executive Ruth Harley, whose voice had been conspicuously absent in the Kahukura debate. Some of the Commission's other staff were told they were still welcome.)

Jackson insisted that the timing of his Kahukura announcement — embargoed to the media until 2am on the day of the *Two Towers* premiere — was completely coincidental. Yet the timing encouraged the idea that

Jackson might be using international media interest in the premiere to embarrass the Commission on the world stage. If so, his flair for the dramatic moment may well have backfired. As a result of his public snubbing of the Commission, the shadow of domestic politics was cast over one of the film industry's most important days of celebration, with a number of overseas reports using the Kahukura bust-up as their angle on *Rings*.

The following March, the Commission and the Film Unit finally announced a 'commercial resolution' for the remaining Kahukura debt. The joint press release quoted Jackson as saying he didn't 'want to spend any more of my time on this subject' and ended, 'No further comment will be made by either party.' And by August, *Kombi Nation* finally got to the cinema, with the remaining Kahukura movies due to follow.

THE *LISTENER* AGAIN

In March of 2002, the *Listener* published an article about the challenges of making commercially successful New Zealand films, under the headline 'Lord . . . what next?'. Images from *Rings* were included in the illustrations. Written by an Auckland freelance journalist named Frances Walsh, the story had at least some members of the film industry wondering whether Peter Jackson's partner had written it. Soon afterwards, a press release from 'Frances R Walsh MNZM' (Jackson's partner) announced that defamation proceedings had been threatened. The press release spoke of the *Listener*'s deliberate attempt to mislead readers that Walsh's 'profoundly negative' views about the New Zealand film industry belonged to her, and argued that the article compromised Frances R Walsh's credibility with local filmmakers, her employer and the New Zealand government. 'It is sloppy journalism, mischief-making; or both.'

Instead of writing a letter to the editor as a way of making her case heard, Walsh and her lawyer gave the *Listener* seven days to apologise, publish a retraction and pay damages and costs. Editor Finlay Macdonald issued a statement disputing the charges, and expressing surprise that Walsh had made public her claims without waiting for a reply: 'What right does anyone have to demand that another discontinue using their own name or to make reference to another person, in the course of going about their lawful business?' Walsh was upset with Macdonald's response, and argued that she had never made such a demand. Instead, as the *New Zealand Herald* put it, 'she said that it should have shown that the writer was not her'.

The following week, the *Listener* published a note about the legal dust-up, mentioning that the co-writer of *Rings* was referred to in the movie's own website and publicity as Fran Walsh. The note ended: 'Readers may well share the view of the leader writer of the Christchurch *Press* that no one is entitled to believe that they have monopoly rights over their name and that it must be hoped the threat does not mark a new level of American-style litigiousness in New Zealand society.'

In May 2002 Walsh had three claims for defamation filed in the High Court against the *Listener*'s publisher and Macdonald. The case had not gone to a hearing as this book went to press.

CHAPTER TWELVE

FINDING THE RING

'Now that would make an interesting picture.'
DIRECTOR ANTHONY MANN, AFTER SEEING THE BOOK
THE DECLINE AND FALL OF THE ROMAN EMPIRE IN A SHOP WINDOW

'If you were entrusting $270 million to someone making three movies,
you wouldn't choose me.'
PETER JACKSON

*Once upon a time there was a man, and there was the word. In fact, a great many
words. The man's words spun every detail of another universe, of kingdoms
populated by creatures loathsome and well-meaning, all of them tied in some way
or other to the fate of one small object: a golden Ring. The wordsmith's name was
Tolkien, and though Tolkien did not like to travel far, his three tales of the Ring
journeyed for him. The power of the Ring grew.*

*Years later, in a land across a vast ocean, a man named Peter began to wonder
if that same power might lie within his grasp — if he might take the Ring and
forge it anew. This Peter possessed both determination and courage, though people
sometimes did not see it in his homely countenance.*

*By now Tolkien had passed on, and the tale of the Ring had long been under
the protection of a man with a generous white beard — a man known as Zaentz.
Peter sent emissaries to talk to Zaentz, and so began a round of discussions that
lasted many days. For in complicated times such as these, ideas can involve many
emissaries, magicians of thought and language who hammer out what words are
really worth, how they can be protected, and how the profits shall be shared. Peter's
emissaries on this mission were possessors of power and riches far beyond his
own. The brothers of Miramax had formed alliances with Zaentz before, and Peter
knew there was a possibility that they might win the Ring, only to keep it for
themselves.*

*Finally the brothers of Miramax won for Peter the right to hold the Ring. Yet
more trials remained. Long before, the tale of the Ring had been unveiled book by
book in three volumes of magic. Realising that one must bow one's head a little in*

order to win the main battle, Peter now agreed to reforge the tale in two smaller pieces.

But the brothers of Miramax feared that even two such giant Ring parts might well lead them to ruin, for it was their Uncle Walt's treasure that was paying for all the hammerwork. The brothers spoke; they said that the three great books must shrink in size until they were but three hours in total duration. And this was not a kind of magic that Peter wanted any part of.

Yet even as they turned away, the brothers showed some compassion; they also spoke the word 'if'. Before taking the Ring for themselves, they would provide Peter with one last chance: allow four weeks for him to find a benefactor who might be willing to remake the Ring in a form closer to its proper shape. If Peter failed in his quest, the brothers of Miramax could then take the jewel back for themselves, to do with as they willed.

Peter hurried back to the land of his birth. He reached for his camera, and rushed around filming everything in sight — elaborate visions of the Ring and the creatures that lusted after it, anything that might prove he was the man born for the task.

When Peter crossed back to the land of Miramax with videotape in hand, he found many doors had closed before him — for all the moneymen had video-recorders, but not all wanted to use them. Peter's dream was close to dying. Then he came to the castle of an empire named New Line, an empire that had built its riches upon a magical tale of a grinning demon with long fingernails. When Peter stood before the king of New Line, showing him all that had been done already on reforging the Ring, the king was quiet for a moment. Then he said, 'But why do you speak of two parts, when originally the tale of the Ring was that much bigger?' Peter felt suddenly as if spring had flowered in the graveyard of his dreams. Only one question remained: would he have to take Sundays off?

John Ronald Reuel Tolkien was born in January 1892 in a town called Bloemfontein, far from the English countryside he would come to love. His father Arthur Tolkien was manager of the branch of a bank in South Africa. Just weeks after turning twenty-one, Arthur's wife Mabel had sailed all the way from her home in Birmingham to marry him. Following the wishes of Mabel's father back in Birmingham, the couple had waited three years to tie the knot. The Tolkien family, though originally from Germany, had lived in England for generations.

The hot, dust-blown landscape of Bloemfontein did not agree with Mabel, but it was to be another four years before she and the family were able to return to England for a visit — minus Arthur, who was busy at the bank and planned to follow later. While the Tolkiens were in England, Arthur contracted rheumatic fever and, soon after Ronald turned four, died of a severe haemorrhage.

Mabel herself passed away after falling into a diabetes-related coma aged thirty-four, when Ronald was only thirteen. Ronald would later look back on the four-year period before she died as one of the most important of his life. The family left the poverty of Birmingham to live in a cottage in Sarehole, a village on the edge of the city. There Tolkien discovered his love for trees and the English countryside. Mabel's family had their origins in another nearby West Midlands town, and many of the elements that would become central to Tolkien's life can be traced back to this particular time and corner of England — including the rural Shire he would create in books about hobbits, the ancient languages he would later study, and the Catholic religion of his mother. In the house in Sarehole, she taught him Latin, French and botany. Already he loved words, as much for the way they sounded as for what they actually meant.

After Mabel's death, Ronald and his younger brother Hilary went back to Birmingham to stay with an aunt, before ending up eventually in a lodging house. Despite his skinniness, Tolkien became a keen rugby player. Later he tried unsuccessfully to blame his often indistinct, slightly muffled speech on an old rugby injury during which he had cut his tongue. Yet it was Tolkien's love of words that would come to define him. Not content with knowing a number of languages, he began as a teenager to invent his own. At Oxford University he would specialise in linguistic studies. His tutor for a time was a quiet but exacting New Zealander named Kenneth Sisam (ten years later, Tolkien would compete against Sisam for a coveted professorship at Oxford, and get the job).

On a Christmas holiday with relatives after his first year studying at Oxford, Tolkien found himself joining in the family play-acting. He wrote and starred in a play in which he portrayed a detective-cum-professor hunting for a lost heiress. But it was the romance that really mattered: the heiress in the play had fallen in love with a penniless student in the lodging house where they both lived, only she wasn't allowed to marry him until she turned twenty-one.

In reality, 'heiress' was a little grand. Edith Bratt was a beautiful piano-playing orphan whom Tolkien had fallen for three years before, at the lodging house they stayed at in Birmingham. But when the Catholic priest who was Tolkien's guardian learned of the romance, he forbade them to communicate until Tolkien turned twenty-one. Now three years of waiting were over. Weeks after turning their romance into a play, Tolkien wrote to Edith and redeclared his love. Some complications — Edith was now engaged to another — were sorted out within a few days.

Edith and Ronald finally married in 1916. A few months later Tolkien was standing in a trench in France, next to a no-man's-land awash with mud and decaying bodies. As a second lieutenant, he was involved on his first day of action in the launch of a major offensive on a town called Ovillers: many of his battalion were killed by machine-gun fire. A grim pattern of attacks, rests and then more attacks followed. Later that year Tolkien got trench fever and was sent back to a hospital in Birmingham.

The death of close friends in the First World War injected Tolkien with a sense of urgency in showing what he was capable of. Before the war, he had nursed the idea of connecting together a number of his poems under a common theme. Convalescing in the English countryside, the idea expanded. He wanted to create an entire mythology for England, an alternative history for the languages that fired his imagination. This collection of connected legends would be set in a world called Middle-earth — earth in some long-ago time, when the continents were in a different shape. The epic he was working on would become *The Silmarillion*.

Later in his life, when the Tolkiens had children of their own and they could not sleep, he made up stories for them, stories which allowed the Oxford professor to cultivate a sillier side: tales of Rover, the tiny dog who travels to the moon and meets a white dragon (Tolkien had long had a thing for dragons), and Maddo, an armless gloved hand that moved of its own accord (the Beatles movie *Yellow Submarine* would feature a similar image). Tolkien wrote some of the stories down, adding lavish illustrations, and sent elaborate letters via the chimney, signed by Father Christmas.

Sometime in the early 1930s, these two separate imaginative worlds began to fuse in Tolkien's mind. He began a story for children about a hobbit named Bilbo Baggins setting out on an adventure to kill a dragon. As Tolkien wrote, it became clear that Bilbo and the wizard Gandalf were walking in the same mythological landscape of Middle-earth that he had long been chronicling in *The Silmarillion*. He later described hobbits as 'just rustic English people made smaller', a people who made up for their limited imagination with their great courage. When a staff member of London publishers George Allen & Unwin got a chance to read the text, she encouraged him to finish off his tale. Company chairman Stanley Unwin, who felt that children were the best judges of children's books, showed *The Hobbit* to his ten-year-old son Rayner, who wrote a positive report. When *The Hobbit* saw publication in September 1937, most of the adult critics agreed. The first edition sold out in only three months.

Many have argued for the similarities between Tolkien, hobbits and Peter Jackson — all being creatures who prefer simple pleasures to the complications of leaving their home patch, and travelling out into the world at large. Costa Botes has recalled how after Jackson's trip to France to launch his first movie, his photos contained mostly pictures of McDonald's outlets, because he didn't like foreign food. But Jackson's interest in technology contrasts vividly with Tolkien, whose relationship with the motor car was one of passionate hatred.

THE NEED FOR A SEQUEL

Sometimes the forces of commerce can provide just the kick which a procrastinating writer needs. The most famous book in the history of fantasy owes its birth to the publisher's request for a *Hobbit* sequel — readers wanted more. At first, Tolkien brought back Bilbo Baggins as his hero, leaving home in Hobbiton with the magic Ring he had acquired in the first book. But Tolkien quickly began to wonder if the character of Bilbo had enough in him for another adventure. He crossed out Bilbo in the first draft, and replaced the character with Bilbo's young nephew Bingo (later, Bingo would become Frodo).

The Ring Bilbo had found in *The Hobbit* after a nightmarish underground encounter with the creature Gollum still offered lots of unexplored dramatic potential. Tolkien made some notes about the Ring having a power over whoever has it. As he began on the follow-up chapters, a sinister horse-borne Black Rider appeared in his story, as if from nowhere. But Tolkien liked it, and decided to keep it in. In such fashion *The Lord of the Rings* began its journey from the light, playful tone of *The Hobbit* to the vast, doom-laden epic it would become. By the following year many of the basics of the story had fallen into place. Bingo/Frodo learns from the wizard Gandalf that the Ring must be taken on a journey to the dark landscape of Mordor, and thrown into a dark crack in the earth. Sauron, the Dark Lord of Mordor, has the other rings, but he needs the final Ring in order to control Middle-earth. The hobbit's only alternative is to destroy the Ring.

As the Second World War raged on, Tolkien continued to alternate his duties as a professor of Anglo-Saxon with the mapping of a journey through another world, a world whose scale and complexity would have few parallels in literature. Epic movies are one thing, but this is another miracle: a man alternating lawnmowing and lecturing with the creation of an elaborate alternative history, a world of peoples, an entire landscape. The elaborate mythology which Tolkien had been working out for years in *The Silmarillion* was its backdrop, and the private alphabet he had once written in his diary was used for the elvish inscriptions. Tolkien's desire for perfectionism led to the creation of elaborate charts and maps to make sure Frodo's travels could actually have happened as written. At one point he even went back and corrected a number of chapters concerning Frodo's travels towards Mordor, after discovering that the moon rose and fell in the wrong direction.

Tolkien approached fantasy with the dedication of a historian researching another culture, which helps to explain why Middle-earth has a realism missing from so many other fantasies. But it also provides clues as to why the book's characters sometimes feel a little thin. Tolkien seems to have been more interested in the geography and languages of Middle-earth than the finer details of how his characters thought. The women came off worst of all: the author who had written love poems to his wife was working on an epic that largely relegated the women characters to minor players, and condemned its major romance to an appendix.

Tolkien hated the idea that people should look for any kind of deeper meaning or allegory in his books. Middle-earth gave him a place above all else to indulge his love of invented languages. The irony was that in the end he would have to cut back on using these languages too much in the text, to avoid alienating his readers. The author often spoke of events and characters from the book almost as if they were part of an actual history; in this way, he was able somehow to deny his own part in the creative process.

When Tolkien completed *The Lord of the Rings*, twelve years after beginning it in 1937, he was almost sixty. Two things now threatened to stop it from reaching the public. One was its thousand-page length, as publishers were still desperately short of paper in the aftermath of the war. The other was Tolkien's insistence that publishers buy his difficult, far from complete *Silmarillion* as part of the deal. This ultimatum scared off both of the prospective publishers. Tolkien had to abandon his *Silmarillion* demands, reluctantly agreeing to Stanley Unwin publishing *The Lord of the Rings* in three separate volumes. Days after the publication of part one, *The Fellowship of the Ring*, in August 1954, Tolkien's friend CS Lewis wrote one of the earliest reviews, proclaiming the book a major step forward for the heroic romance. Not everyone agreed. As the other volumes — *The Two Towers* and *The Return of the King* — followed over the course of the next fourteen months, critics ran the gamut from delirium to contempt. But the book was selling, and it was a trend that would never stop.

MAKING MOVIES

Tolkien was never much of a movie fan — most of the travels he took were in his own head. Introduced to film star Ava Gardner in the late 1960s, he had no idea who she was. When it came to the idea of turning his own books into movies, he appears to have felt conflicted. He disliked the idea of other people adapting his work for other mediums, believing it would reduce them to their most trivial level. But knowing that such offers were likely, he and publisher Stanley Unwin formulated an unusual policy over how to handle them. The two decided they would be most partial to two very different kinds of offer — those open to the author's input, and those that offered a lot of cash.

The same year that *The Return of the King* first saw publication, a radio adaptation of the trilogy began playing on the BBC. Tolkien was not pleased. Soon after that came one of the first movie nibbles: three Americans who hoped to turn the trilogy into an animated film. One of them was Forrest J Ackerman, soon to become known as the film fanatic behind *Famous Monsters of Filmland*, the magazine that would later help turn Peter Jackson and many others on to the delights of monster movies. The short *Rings* scenario which Ackerman and his cohorts showed Tolkien did not appeal to him. Keen to see cash, Tolkien tried his best to be polite. But when he wrote Ackerman a long letter about the proposed storyline, he found it hard to contain himself, complaining among other things about their shoddy treatment of Tom Bombadil, the orcs (who here had beaks and feathers) and an over-reliance on travelling by eagle. He added that the climax was 'totally unacceptable'. Negotiations were soon cut short.

Another of that unsuccessful trio of cinematic suitors was a New Yorker named Al Brodax, whose name opens a strange link between Tolkien and the Beatles. In the late 1960s, the Beatles were desperate to find a movie that would fulfil a three-film contract they had with United Artists. They were also equally desperate to fly to India and study with the Maharishi. Brodax solved both problems by proposing that they let him make an animated fantasy based around the Beatles and their songs. The resulting movie — which opened in London just weeks before the Beatles finally abandoned their attempt at a fashion store by giving the entire stock away — was the eye-popping masterpiece *Yellow Submarine*.

By this point world sales of *The Hobbit* and *The Lord of the Rings*, for so long on an upward curve, had begun heading ever more rapidly skywards. A new generation of American university students was embracing Frodo's story, helping speed two competing paperback editions of *The Lord of the Rings* to the top of the bestseller list (one edition was completely illegal, but that is another story). Tolkien's romantic epic, set in a world where nature itself appeared to be under attack, plugged directly into the spirit of change sweeping through the late 1960s. Some of the book's keener fans even began wearing Frodo Lives badges and organising costumed hobbit picnics; Middle-earth and hobbit head shops opened, selling more than just pipe tobacco.

It makes perfect sense that the band that helped set the decade's musical barometer would attempt to get in on the act. The Beatles approached director Stanley Kubrick about taking charge of a *Rings* movie. Under the

Beatles' bizarre plan, 'spiritual' Beatle George Harrison would play the wizard Gandalf, Paul would be Frodo, Ringo his trusty friend Sam Gamgee, and John Lennon would skulk around as Gollum. Lennon, who was a big fan of *2001: A Space Odyssey*, met with Kubrick, but the meeting did not go well. Some books claim that the Beatles then approached Italian director Michelangelo Antonioni (*Blowup*) to take on the project, and he proved keener. But it seems unlikely that the narrative complications of *Rings* would have been up Antonioni's alley. The story goes that when the Beatles approached Tolkien's agent, it came to nothing regardless: the rights had been snapped up a few days previously by United Artists.

The first genuine contender to get Middle-earth onto a cinema screen was English director John Boorman, who had broken into motion pictures from television and was soon to score a big international hit with the elemental backwoods thriller *Deliverance*. A man whose interest in myth was equalled by a gift for capturing arresting images and moods, Boorman was in many ways the right man for the job. As Michel Ciment points out in his book on the director, many of Boorman's films can be seen as versions of a quest, reflecting his long fascination with the legend of King Arthur.

As he had just completed a film for United Artists, the studio asked Boorman what he would like to do next. He suggested a movie about Merlin, the wizard from King Arthur's legend. The executives shook their heads, but mentioned that they had bought the film rights to *Lord of the Rings*. Was Boorman interested? As he writes in his superlative book about filmmaking, *Money into Light*, the project perfectly fitted his theory that filmmaking is about setting oneself impossible problems, then failing to solve them. Elsewhere he told Michel Ciment: 'I thought it was impossible to adapt to the screen, but United Artists were so insistent that I allowed myself to be persuaded.'

Boorman and his scriptwriting partner, architect Rospo Pallenberg, retreated to Boorman's home in a valley near Dublin and began condensing Tolkien's epic into one script. In six months they had covered the walls of one room with every page of Tolkien's book, and maps and diagrams of Middle-earth. Simultaneously Boorman began researching the extensive special effects the project required — there is every chance that the challenges of bringing Middle-earth to the screen would have resulted in a noticeable jump forward in special-effects magic, just as *2001* had done a few years before.

But when Boorman took the completed *Rings* script back to United Artists, things had changed — as they often do in Hollywood. The studio was now worried about the scale and expense of the project, thanks partly to a run of box-office bombs, Boorman's among them. The executive who had been keenest on Tolkien's book no longer worked for the company, and hardly any of the other executives had read Tolkien's book. After he showed the *Rings* script to a number of other studios, including Disney which years before had dabbled with the idea of animating Tolkien, Boorman's plans foundered. In an earlier letter to Boorman, the author expressed relief that Boorman planned to shoot the film in live action, having had nightmares of an animated version.

FINDING THE RINGBEARER

Not unlike Peter Jackson, the man who first succeeded in bringing Tolkien to the screen had a screen pedigree for tastelessness. Animator Ralph Bakshi's debut feature *Fritz the Cat* (1972) had won an X certificate, while *Coonskin* (1975), his satire of the Disney movie *Song of the South*, caused even more controversy. A fan of Tolkien's work, Bakshi approached United Artists, proposing that the best way to bring *Rings* to the screen was by staying as close to the original books as possible — by making the films in multiple parts, using traditional animation. Bakshi believed that trying to create live-action hobbits, elves and dwarves was an impossible task that would only undermine Tolkien's imaginative world. Bakshi has spoken of executives at United Artists showing him a script by Boorman that weighed in at 700 pages and telling him, 'We never read the books. We ain't got time to read it, you understand, Ralph, so go do it.'

RALPH BAKSHI

Born and raised in New York by Russian parents, Ralph Bakshi rose through the ranks of animation at remarkable speed. Soon after receiving his diploma in cartooning, he won a job on the production line at Terrytoon Cartoons. At twenty-eight, he became Terrytoon's supervising director, helping create the satirical series *The Mighty Heroes*, whose stars included Diaper Man and Cuckoo Man.

Bakshi hit pay dirt with *Fritz the Cat*, his first animated feature. The writer / director's X-rated riff on Robert Crumb's underground comic strip about a pseudo-hippie cat showed animators a new alternative to the cuteness of Disney animation. Crumb hated the result, and in revenge had his comic-strip character go to Hollywood and then get stabbed to death by a murderous ostrich, two months after the film's release. *Fritz the Cat*'s meeting points with Peter Jackson's *Meet the Feebles* are obvious — both take joy in simultaneously embracing the adult and the juvenile, pushing cinematic boundaries by showing animals copulating, urinating, and attacking one another. But *Fritz* is limited only by the fevered imaginations of its animators, resulting in a satirical portrait of life on the streets that transcends all the groping.

Freed by success, Bakshi followed *Fritz the Cat* with two highly personal films, the evocative *Heavy Traffic* and the racial satire *Coonskin*.

His first fully-fledged fantasy *Wizards* (1977) places classic fantasy elements — including elves and an evil ruler — on a post-nuclear earth, then throws wisecracking dialogue and Nazi imagery into the melting pot. In the film's climax, two movies collide onscreen as cute animated warriors face off against what are clearly human riders on horseback. By this point viewers will see *Wizards* as either an ambitious new benchmark in animation technique, or an awkward hodgepodge that takes some interesting imagery and coats it in clichés.

Bakshi's recent interviews betray a sense of wounded pride at being the first to put Tolkien's prose into pictures, and winning more criticism than credit for the achievement. Of the new film, he told the Jam! website: 'I wasn't contacted, I wasn't asked for the rights to do it, let's just put it that way . . . no one's ever spoken to me about it. I'm kind of stunned that they are doing it. Certainly I'm wishing them all the luck in the world on a visual level.'

By Bakshi's account, he then walked across a hallway from the United Artists offices to those of MGM president Dan Melnick, and persuaded MGM to pay out $US3 million so that Boorman's script could be spiked and Boorman could go swimming and laughing in the pool (Boorman's version of how he felt at this point is not quite so upbeat). Bakshi's *Lord of the Rings* was now go for MGM. But when Melnick left the company soon after, go turned to stop and the nightmare of Hollywood musical chairs began again.

At this point Saul Zaentz makes his first entrance. Today, Zaentz is known as the white-bearded producer who has produced and set up a number of challenging and risky literary adaptations — in twenty years, his seven pictures have snagged three Oscars for best movie: *One Flew Over the Cuckoo's Nest*, *Amadeus* and *The English Patient*.

In 1975 Zaentz was better known in music industry circles. In the late 1960s he and a group of investors took over San Francisco-based Fantasy Records, where he had worked as a sales manager. Soon to develop one of the world's most impressive jazz lists, Zaentz would find riches through Fantasy's contract with swamp rockers Creedence Clearwater Revival. His career then began to move along parallel lines — in one, he was becoming known as a music mogul caught up in extended legal spats with Creedence singer John Fogerty; in the other, he was increasingly seen as the epitome of the independent, the guy with the balls to stay in San Francisco and make the movies that Hollywood wouldn't.

Zaentz had been one of the silent investors on *Fritz the Cat*. Initially worried that this new proposal might harm their friendship, Bakshi asked Zaentz to help him secure the movie rights to *The Lord of the Rings* and *The Hobbit*. After winning the rights outright, the duo felt obligated to travel to England and meet Tolkien's family and the book's publishers to gain their blessing.

As they worked on the *Rings* script, classics scholar Chris Conkling and Peter S Beagle (author of *The Last Unicorn* and introductions for a number of Tolkien books) were asked to stay as faithful to Tolkien's words as possible, a desire some critics later argued was a path to madness. Like Jackson to come, one of Bakshi's overriding concerns was realism, and he recorded the soundtrack with a largely English cast (*Star Wars* fans will note the presence of C3P0's Anthony Daniels, who voiced Legolas).

Bakshi began shooting a live-action version of the movie in California, then relocated to Spain to capture the epic battle scenes of Helm's Deep. The press notes for *Rings* spoke of a 'breakthrough in animation' allowing epic battle scenes involving hundreds of participants. Such images had traditionally been one of the holy grails of animation, kept beyond reach partly by the sheer work needed to animate large groups in one scene. Bakshi's 'breakthrough' was actually a variation of a technique invented at least fifty years before. The rotoscope is a movie projector that shows a frame of film on a glass plate, allowing an animator to stand at a table, and trace over live-action footage frame by frame. The completed animation can be either an exact copy of the actor's movements in the original footage, or a stepping-stone to help bring an animated character to life. (Rotoscoping is also used in other ways — like drawing in the animated glows to the lightsabres in some of the *Star Wars* films.) Animators at Disney employed rotoscoping often, after rediscovering the technique while creating Dopey for *Snow White and the Seven Dwarfs*. When slavishly applied, this technique of copying life in exact detail can backfire: by dispensing with the artist's main point of difference — their very ability to be selective — rotoscoped images often seem stiff and unconvincing to the human eye.

Bakshi had played at the meeting point between animation and reality before. His second movie, *Heavy Traffic*, features animated cars driving through real-life streets, and in the battle scenes of *Wizards*, many of the villains are rotoscoped humans on horseback. But as the technique takes over *Rings*, one gets the impression that rotoscoping was used as much for time-saving reasons as creativity. There are even scenes where thinly-rotoscoped characters (looking like bleached-out photos) stand around in the same frame as traditionally-animated figures.

In his book *Masters of Animation*, John Grant writes that production on

Rings soon slowed to a crawl and there were constant changes of staff, as Bakshi watched his dream project go down in flames. As the release date drew near, hopes of treating Tolkien's material with respect faced further disappointment. Bakshi had set up his first movie to close halfway through the second book, at the end of the battle of Helm's Deep. But as the crew of 200 animators rushed to meet their deadline, it became clear that United Artists wanted to release the film only as *The Lord of the Rings*, shorn of the *Part One* subtitle. This is like releasing *Star Wars* without the attack on the Death Star. Bakshi's protests were ignored.

The finished film is not nearly as bad as many of its detractors make out — it is interesting to note the many similarities in how Jackson's scriptwriters and Bakshi's have adapted Tolkien's storyline. Where the animated version falls short is in its portrayal of Tolkien's more fantastic moments and characters. Though the Black Riders have some atmospheric scenes, and Frodo is likeably portrayed, neither Gandalf or Gollum create any excitement; the Mines of Moria and Helm's Deep fail to match the standards of animation established by less important scenes; and the cliché-ridden score should have been put out to pasture. On release, *Rings* was not a blockbuster, though it did make a slight profit. At that point, it was the US's fourth most successful animated film of all time, one of the only non-Disney animated movies on list.

At the 1979 Cannes Film Festival, between dodging all the new ripoffs of *Animal House*, Zaentz announced plans for a *Rings* sequel, and even an animated *Hobbit*. But in the end, Bakshi had no involvement in either: another company produced cheaper animated versions of both *The Hobbit* and *The Return of the King* for television.

Peter Jackson was the kind of teen movie geek who was more likely to know about the tasteless movies of Ralph Bakshi than the books of JRR Tolkien. When the animated version of *Rings* finally hit Wellington, Jackson got the train into town to watch it. According to Andrew Neal, the boyhood acquaintance who helped out on some of Jackson's short films around this period, Tolkien meant little to Jackson until after he saw the animated movie. Neal though was a big fan, and had spent hours copying a giant picture of Bakshi's Black Riders onto his bedroom wall.

Soon afterwards, Jackson took another train trip, this time on the main line that snakes up the centre of the North Island towards Auckland. The nine-hour journey passes through all manner of landscapes: snow-capped mountain peaks, yawning cliffs dropping away abruptly to foaming rivers, and later the rolling farm hills of the Waikato — in short, a treasure-trove of locations for a movie industry just waking up to what it might be capable of. Jackson picked up a copy of *The Lord of the Rings* and began to read of a dark power creeping across the many lands of Middle-earth.

SEARCHING FOR THE RIGHT CREATURE

By late 1995, Jackson was at a place where past cinematic inspirations seemed newly relevant, partly because they now lay within his grasp. Tight deadlines to complete his effects-heavy *Frighteners* movie were just beginning to raise their head. Yet Jackson's experiences of working with Hollywood money had so far not been the creative nightmare part of him had always feared.

Now Universal had asked him if he wanted to remake *King Kong*, the very movie that had inspired him to make films as a boy. Back then, carried away by the wonders of *Kong* and *Jason and the Argonauts*, Jackson had thrown his friends into cinematic battle against stop-motion animated monsters, using many of the same special-effects techniques that had brought *Kong* and the classic Ray Harryhausen creatures to life. The arsenal of computer equipment established for *The Frighteners* opened up the possibility of reinventing the monsters and adventures of his moviegoing past.

The idea of making a big-budget fantasy was about opportunity as much as inspiration. Though there had been major growing pains, a world-class special-effects facility was in the process of forming under Jackson's wing, and without the promise of some big projects to work on after *The Frighteners* there was a danger that much of the New Zealand computer talent would drift off into the ether.

As Jackson told horror magazine *Fangoria* in November 1995 on the set of *The Frighteners*, he was dabbling with the idea of applying Weta Digital to *Blubberhead,* the serio-comic fantasy project he had been trying to get off the ground for the last six years, which he had more than once described as Monty Python meets *Lord of the Rings*. But for one reason or another, he abandoned the idea. Jackson's career to date provided living proof of the worth of setting oneself impossible challenges — in short order he had followed one of the goriest films in cinema history with an acclaimed true story, a genre-twisting mockumentary and a big-budget Hollywood effects film. Now a landmark in fantasy had been offered to him as a viable movie project, powered by the kind of blockbuster budget that made even *The Frighteners* look small. Facing such an amazing possibility, it looks as if a switch clicked in Jackson's brain. The switch was marked, 'think fantasy, think big'.

Jackson put it another way in a later interview with *Pavement* magazine:

> *The thinking at that time was that we'd have to create an original fantasy film. But we kept referring to the fact it would be* Lord of the Rings-*like. I wasn't at the place where I had a life-long ambition to make a film of* Lord of the Rings. *I'd read the book once and really liked it. But I felt it would be out of my*

reach . . . You just naturally assume that it's an impossibility.

Nonetheless Jackson picked up the telephone, asking his American agent to make some discreet enquiries as to who owned the screen rights to Tolkien's work. Since Bakshi's attempt at filming Tolkien, those rights had remained with Zaentz. Over the years there had been many enquiries, but none of them excited Zaentz enough. (European plans to make a multi-part version of *Rings* — with a wish list that included Sean Connery as Gandalf — never went beyond the scripting stages.) After talking to his agent, Jackson also put in a call to Miramax boss Harvey Weinstein — under the terms of his deal with the company, Jackson was obligated to let Weinstein have first look at any new projects in case Miramax wanted to be involved.

At this point luck intervened, because the man who controlled access to two of the landmark works in fantasy owed Weinstein a favour. Weinstein had just stepped in to help resurrect Zaentz's *The English Patient*, after 20th Century Fox dropped it shortly before the start of filming — the studio did not consider Kristin Scott Thomas a bankable enough name for the leading role, but director Anthony Minghella wanted her regardless.

Jackson had loved epic movies for years. Ken Hammon recalls Jackson as a huge fan of period epics like Sergei Bondarchuk's *Waterloo* (1972), fond of quoting the number of extras used in some of history's biggest battle films. While making the abandoned vampire movie *Curse of the Gravewalker*, Jackson had spoken of using perspective tricks to create the illusion of a long line of soldiers fading off into the distance, by placing children at the furthest point from the camera and adults at the closest.

Weeks after the cancellation of *King Kong* in early 1996, Jackson and Walsh flew to Hollywood, carrying proposals for a number of movie projects. Jackson's Tolkien plans at this point look to have been to make *The Hobbit* first, and follow it with a two-part adaptation of *Lord of the Rings*. During a talk at Wellington's Victoria University in late 2001, Richard Taylor confirmed that *The Hobbit* was first on the director's drawing board. As he put it:

> At the tail end of King Kong *falling over Peter came to us all and said, 'Well, we are in the shit, but I think I've got something that we can do. I'm going to shoot for the rights to make* The Hobbit.' *And we fell over backwards! We were going to bring one of the greatest pieces of modern English folklore to the screen . . . This was overwhelming to us.*

According to Taylor, only a small amount of design work was done on the new project. But a few months later Jackson gathered the Weta crew together. He told them, 'Well, we're moving ahead, but guess what? It's not *The Hobbit*, it's *Lord of the Rings*.'

During Taylor's presentation at Victoria University, an audience member asked if Jackson's original *Hobbit* announcement had been partly a ploy to check Weta's loyalty. Taylor replied in the negative, then said:

> *I would never question him at that level. He had a reason to tell us initially, and maybe he could only visualise doing something that was as linear as* The Hobbit. *To try and bring those three massive novels into cinema was obviously a daunting thought.*

Certainly the more tightly-written *Hobbit* is the most obvious candidate of Tolkien's books for movie treatment, and it is easy to imagine Jackson's attraction to it. *The Hobbit*'s balance between comedy and adventure is closer to Jackson's past work than the darker feel and narrative complexity of *The Lord of the Rings*.

The rights to *The Hobbit* proved unavailable, caught up with United Artists. But rumours of a Jackson movie of *The Hobbit* continued to circulate right into May 1998, and Jackson seems to have used the confusion as a convenient cover for his plans. The swirl of Internet rumours about Jackson's mystery project may well have encouraged such practice. In January 1998, Jackson went on an Internet site to tell fans he had been asked to sign a confidentiality agreement about the film he was making with Miramax. He argued that most of what he had read about it on the net was 'total rubbish', and maintained Saul Zaentz was not producing and that he had never spoken to him. (Zaentz would later say that aside from watching *Heavenly Creatures*, it was meeting Jackson and Walsh, and seeing their intelligence and enthusiasm for *Rings*, that helped win him over. That meeting may have occurred after January 1998).

Once it looked as if the rights to *The Lord of the Rings* might actually be accessible, Harvey Weinstein gave Jackson and Walsh the money to go work on the script and the extensive process of deciding how Middle-earth might look onscreen. But it soon became clear that the double feature of *The Fellowship of the Ring* and *The War of the Ring* were going to cost more than Miramax could afford. At this point, Miramax had rarely dabbled in big-budget movies: the nightmares of funding Martin Scorsese's epic *Gangs of New York* still lay in the future. Weinstein went to his corporate parents at Disney, and asked if he might go higher than the projected cost of $75 million for the two *Rings* films. The Disney executives said no, and were not interested in becoming partners with Miramax either. In a strange way, the refusal may have been a blessing in disguise. As early as 1937, Tolkien had written of harbouring a 'heartfelt loathing' for the Disney studio's output. We can only guess, but based upon Tolkien's aversion to the idea of an animated version of *Rings*, a live-action movie funded by a

Disney offshoot might still have been the lesser evil for him, compared to an animated version made by anybody else.

Miramax went looking for partners at other studios, but none came to the party. Jackson's lack of blockbuster experience was likely seen as a liability at this point, considering that the *Rings* should have offered the kind of broad-appeal, ready-built franchise that Hollywood is normally crying out for. Factor in the likelihood that the films would be very expensive, and a director who was a relative unknown, and the franchise starts to sound a little more shaky: in Hollywood, nothing is a sure bet, not even a classic like *The Lord of the Rings*.

What happened next would become the stuff of moviemaking myth: news of a plan to murder Jackson's dream project by his supposed protectors, before last-minute resurrection at the hands of an unexpected saviour. This story has partly become myth because it offers something to please everyone — it confirms our worst fears about Hollywood's gutlessness and indifference in the face of genuinely grand ideas, while offering hope that in spite of all this, sometimes the jewels can still get through untrampled.

It is too easy at this point to paint Harvey Weinstein as the evil Sauron of the piece, leaning in to get his hands on the Ring so that he might crush it into a very boring shape. It was Weinstein and his lawyers who had won the rights to *Rings*, a task fraught with legal complexities. Also in Weinstein's favour, it appears that he could have abandoned Jackson and given the rights to another director after Jackson abruptly slipped a few notches back down the Hollywood ladder towards minor player, with the cancellation of *King Kong*. Instead, Miramax continued to pour significant funds into development of the movie.

In Hollywood, they say you are only as hot as your last movie. By this standard, Jackson was not really very hot at all. His last movie had been an American box-office bomb, and only one of his previous films (*Heavenly Creatures*) had made a major impact on American soil — and that in much more of an artistic sense than a commercial one.

Weinstein's failure to find further funds to bankroll *Rings* left him in a difficult position. In June 1998, he suggested to Jackson that the *Rings* project be reduced in scope to a single movie. A staff member at Miramax even prepared a list of scenes which might be removed without damaging the story — for example, the entire section in the first book in the Mines of Moria (the elf Galadriel had been taken out already). Perhaps the only thing Weinstein could have said which sounded more worrying than this was, 'Bugger off — the Ring is mine.'

When a long book is squashed in length in order to fit a contained running time, there is a danger of losing the very qualities that made it a classic (the movie of *Dune* is a good example). But try to tell the story over a series of films, and one of the basic rules of moviemaking can ultimately prove just as calamitous: no one likes being forced in advance to make a sequel, without any guarantee that the first episode has an audience.

Jackson and Walsh flew to the US to tell Weinstein that they could not be responsible for cramming one of the most famous trilogies in history into one movie. As Jackson told the *Hollywood Reporter*:

> *Harvey basically said, 'You're forcing me to have to hire another filmmaker. I'll take the project to another director and I'll get another screenplay written.' Harvey had spent a lot on the film at that stage. It almost got too far that Harvey couldn't afford not to make any film [of the book]. He now had us refusing to make the film that he felt that he needed to make. So it was a really difficult scenario. There was a day when we walked away from the project, when we literally just had to look Harvey in the eye . . . and say, 'Look, Harvey, we cannot be part of what you're proposing here and if you have to get another filmmaker then so be it. But it certainly can't be us.'*

The flight back to New Zealand took almost an entire day. As New York faded behind them out the aeroplane window, so did Jackson and Walsh's hopes for *Rings*. They had made it through all the hoops, only to fall in the last quarter. When the couple finally emerged from the aeroplane, they felt tired and depressed. But they were met with breaking news. During the flight, Jackson's agent Ken Kamins had called Weinstein and proposed that Jackson be given one last chance — a narrow four-week window in which to find someone willing to take *Rings* on as a two-film project, and pay Weinstein out on his expenses to date.

Weinstein agreed, but he set a hard deal. The $US12 million plus that Miramax had spent to date on the book rights, as well as script, design and technical development, would all have to be paid back within seventy-two hours of any signed agreement. Also the Weinstein brothers wanted an executive-producer credit on the finished films, and five percent of any gross earnings. From what Weinstein has said in interviews, he was fairly confident none of this would come to pass, with Jackson likely ending up agreeing to do the short version of *Rings* at Miramax.

Kamins began calling all the Hollywood studios and independent producers he could think of, to ask if they would meet with Jackson. One or two asked to look at the script. Most said no on the telephone. Others waited to say no until they had read it.

Back in New Zealand, Jackson began work on the most important short film of his career: a thirty-six minute promo for the *Rings* project, complete with test shots of computerised cave trolls, enticing glimpses of New

Zealand scenery, and interviews with Jackson and his creative team trying their best to sound excited and enthusiastic rather than desperate to hold onto their jobs.

When Jackson and Walsh arrived in the US with their video in hand, only two companies remained in the picture. One of them was Polygram, the other New Line Cinema — the latter the very company for whom Jackson and Danny Mulheron had long ago written a *Nightmare on Elm Street* script, in one of their first encounters with Hollywood. An emissary from Miramax had meanwhile arrived at Jackson's studio in New Zealand, preparing to pack up the *Rings* models and design work to take back to Miramax.

The meeting with Polygram began well. The company was interested. The only problem was that they were in the middle of being sold, ironically to Jackson's former *King Kong* backers at Universal. Polygram was not in a position to approve a mega-budget project, especially not when a $US12 million-plus cheque needed to be signed within a fortnight.

Jackson rang New Line, pretending he was trying to juggle a busy diary of appointments. He asked if their meeting could be delayed until later that day, in a desperate effort to make a rapidly cooling project appear in demand. If Jackson's old New Line friend Mark Ordesky had been in charge of the company, Jackson would have been less nervous: he knew that Ordesky was a big *Rings* fan (Ordesky had even written a letter to Zaentz years before, asking him if New Line might make a *Rings* movie). But there was one man to please: Bob Shaye, the man who had built New Line up from nothing.

The meeting did not begin promisingly. Shaye felt the need to tell Jackson that whatever was about to happen, he would love to work with him on other projects. He also mentioned that he didn't like *The Frighteners*. Jackson and Walsh sat nervously with their agent as the tape rolled, half-expecting Shaye to press stop before seeing any of the video. Here was Jackson, sitting next to a precipice, armed only with a 36-minute promotional tape, and Bob Shaye was the last man in Hollywood who might build a bridge to the dream waiting on the other side.

When the tape finished, Shaye's comment was, 'I don't get it. Why would you be wanting to do two *Lord of the Rings* films?'

At first Jackson did not know what Shaye could possibly be meaning. But when it became clear that he was proposing that *Rings* might work better as three movies rather than two, Jackson began to kick his agent under the table.

Just a few weeks later, on August 24, 1998, New Line Cinema sent out a press release announcing it was making three movies of *The Lord of the Rings*, to be filmed back to back, all of them to be released over a one-year period. It had also acquired the rights to *The Hobbit*. Miramax relaxed its formerly tight deadline, allowing all the legal legwork to be sorted. Considering the miracle that had just been achieved, it could hardly do otherwise. Round one had been won: Jackson had entered the dark forest that is the Hollywood deal, and thanks to luck, courage and expert aid, emerged clutching three Rings.

He flew back home to New Zealand. There was work to do.

JRR TOLKIEN

The man who created Middle-earth retired from his professorship at Oxford in 1959. Progress on his epic *The Silmarillion*, begun way back in 1917, was delayed by time spent replying to the many *Lord of the Rings* fans who continued to write from around the globe. Tolkien's last story, *Smith of Wootton Major,* reflected his grief at the approach of old age. Tolkien died in September 1973, two years after his wife. Son Christopher took over the task of amalgamating Tolkien's many versions of *The Silmarillion*, and the epic finally saw publication in 1977. Christopher Tolkien has had little to do with Peter Jackson's movie — and in a sad denouement, his barrister son Simon claimed in 2001 that Christopher now refused to talk to him, partly because Simon dared to suggest that Jackson's filmmaking plans might be worth encouraging. Simon's own novel *The Stepmother* is about a father who publicly disowns his teenage son.

JOHN BOORMAN

After his plans for *Rings* were rejected by United Artists, John Boorman made his name elsewhere with the thriller *Deliverance*. Many of the special-effects techniques and locations discovered during his encounter with Middle-earth were later applied to *Excalibur* (1981), his adaptation of Arthurian legends. A founding editor of the annual film journal *Projections*, Boorman continues to travel the world making movies. His filmography includes 1987's *Hope and Glory*, a memoir of a childhood in London during the Blitz and *The Tailor of Panama* (2002).

RALPH BAKSHI

Following the animated movie of *The Lord of the Rings*, Ralph Bakshi made one more fully-fledged fantasy — the beautifully-animated but underwritten *Fire and Ice* (1983), inspired largely by the warriors and bikini-clad women of fantasy artist Frank Frazetta, who helped make it. After a brief retirement, Bakshi returned to animation and began producing the innovative series *Mighty Mouse: The New*

Adventures; his job apparently involved calming worried television executives, while secretly encouraging the animators to be as outrageous as they desired. Despite its popularity, the series was cancelled after two seasons. Bakshi continued to animate in many mediums until the cancellation of the 1997 television series *Spicy City.* Reportedly tired of 'fighting and selling out as an artist', Bakshi has since turned his back on Hollywood to concentrate on painting.

CHAPTER THIRTEEN

ROLL CAMERA

'I just about dropped what I was holding. I thought they were insane.'
PHILIPPA BOYENS ON HEARING OF PLANS TO MAKE A *LORD OF THE RINGS* MOVIE

'We realised that the fantasy had to be underpinned with a severe reality. We set about designing a world that could exist.'
LORD OF THE RINGS CO-DESIGNER RICHARD TAYLOR

Filmmaking is an act of madness. The process of getting a film finished involves devoting thousands of hours — and a huge amount of cash — to something that could easily end up condemned to a life sentence at the back of the video library. In the case of *Rings*, such a fate was never likely. But when it came to putting Peter Jackson's vision of Middle-earth onscreen, the craziness that defines the filmmaking process was only multiplied. Leaving aside the lunacy of taking on one of literature's great unfilmable works, the complications of shooting three movies at once would drive many people insane.

To spend nine weeks filming one battle scene, all of it under cover of darkness, is just one example of this project's madness. So is the idea of making something that requires special effects not just for all the trolls and creatures, but almost every time the main cast appear together onscreen. Some would argue, though, that the craziest thing about *Rings* is New Zealand itself — the idea of completing the most ambitious film project in the history of fantasy in a place where 'movie epic' has traditionally been a contradiction in terms.

When *Rings* was still being developed as two movies under the wing of Miramax, the company sent a staff member down to New Zealand to check on progress. The situation could easily have become tense, but soon the American envoy and some of the heads of department at WingNut found common ground. The executive told them that many of those back at Miramax half-expected that Jackson's special-effects team would be operating from a tin shed behind his house. On top of that, the executive revealed, they expected that the computer-effects department would be working on a mezzanine floor in that tin shed.

Perhaps Miramax had taken the moviemaking myths of *Forgotten Silver* a little too much to heart. Yet the idea of New Zealand as the tin shed of world filmmaking is not such a bad metaphor. When you consider the quality of some of the movies the country has managed to produce on minuscule resources, it could even be taken as some kind of backhanded compliment.

New Zealand directors have been spotted pointing their cameras at debonair secret agents on the beaches of Spain; New Zealand cinematographers have coaxed eye-catching images from Turkish prisons and Irish slums; Kiwi actors have performed more than ably in dinosaur-ravaged jungles and strife-torn flats from Edinburgh to Dunedin. But what New Zealanders lack is a pedigree for epics made on their home soil — the kind of movies loaded with battle scenes and reams of effects which Hollywood pumps out every other year.

Rudall Hayward chronicled historical battles between Pakeha and Maori in a number of early movies, thanks partly to ingenuity and lots of volunteer labour. But fifty years had passed since Hayward's last epic *Rewi's Last Stand*, and since then New Zealand movies have mostly been decidedly small-scale. The ambitious 'Maori western' *Utu* did feature rows of colonial soldiers, and running gun battles across New Zealand hillsides, but for all its excitement, *Utu* was more ambitious than truly epic.

The 1988 fantasy *The Navigator* put the local movie scene in a nutshell. Vincent Ward's tale of fourteenth-century peasants trying to journey across a modern-day cityscape manages to seem grand when its most fantastic elements are a church, a cave, a swimming horse and a great deal of vision. Yet at $4.3 million it was one of New Zealand's costliest films to date, and Ward faced endless nightmares, downsizing his ambitions to the resources available.

In the same year that *The Navigator* crew were stealing their final shots from under the demolition men, a much larger crew arrived in the South Island to shoot footage around Queenstown for the George Lucas-produced fantasy epic *Willow*. More than 30 locals, from stunt people to cameramen, joined the month-long shoot. Even without expensive stars, the movie's generous budget left *The Navigator* for dead (though many critics would prefer the later fantasy). Six years later, two American producers, attracted by New Zealand's scenic variety and weak dollar, journeyed Down Under to make a series of low-budget *Hercules* telemovies. The telemovies would soon spawn a mini-industry of spin-off television shows, providing local crews with valuable experience in the basics of building mythical kingdoms and props, and throwing stuntmen through the air. Although much of the post-production work for the *Xena* and *Hercules* shows was handled back in Los Angeles, the monsters were partly created by New Zealanders, including the staff at Weta.

Jackson's *The Frighteners* marked another significant step upwards in scale for New Zealand filmmakers, especially in showing Hollywood that the country could take on the demands of digital effects. Yet despite the movie's epic-length shooting schedule, in terms of the scale of a Hollywood film, *The Frighteners* was really nothing unusual. No precedent had been set for a genuinely big local movie, the kind of spectacle-laden project that merits those annoying voice-overs about being 'epic beyond your imagination'. The Film Commission's total yearly budget was less than the average cost of a Hollywood movie. The chasm was one of persuading anyone with money that there was a point in coming here.

Yet Jackson was determined from the beginning that if he was going to make it, *Rings* would be made in his home country. He went to longtime associate Richard Taylor, whose special-effects expertise by now covered pretty much everything that didn't involve a computer, to ask what departments Taylor's Weta Workshop wanted to handle.

In Hollywood, big-budget movies are often farmed out to a score of special-effects companies, each rushing to handle a different scene or element in time for release date. The effects for *Contact*, for example, were handled by nine different companies; the first *X-Men* went to nine as well. The challenge then becomes one of making sure that the movie retains a cohesive look and feel. A small group of topline, one-stop companies like the George Lucas-owned Industrial Light and Magic also nab a share of blockbuster effects jobs for themselves.

Taylor and his Weta Workshop partner Tania Rodger were aware of the danger that much of the behind-the-scenes work on *Rings* could end up farmed out to more experienced companies overseas. The more they took on, the more work would stay at home. Taylor and Rodger decided that Weta Workshop would design and handle the trilogy's makeup effects and prosthetics, the physical creatures, armour, the weapons and the miniatures.

Despite the apparent madness of one company taking on so much — even the ever-positive Taylor admitted it was 'a bloody nightmare of a thought' — there was an element of practicality in the decision. By utilising a roster of staff, working cheaply over a long period, most of the design and effects work could be contained within the one building. That way Jackson could easily monitor progress, at least until he needed to be on location. This all-in one approach would help maintain a consistent vision, the 'singular Tolkienesque brushstroke' that helped unite every element seen onscreen. Judging by how often Taylor mentioned this brushstroke idea during interviews, it seems to have become a Weta Workshop mantra, as did the strong spirit of historical realism that Peter Jackson wanted to bring to the look of the production.

In the early stages of *Rings*'s development, Miramax campaigned for Jackson to hire experienced American designers, and it is likely that New Line did the same. But Taylor would have none of it. He felt the relative inexperience of his crew in one sense to be an advantage, even though it would require training many of his technicians on the run.

> The Lord of the Rings *required a youthful innocence. It required a level of sensitivity . . . something in the New Zealand psyche still. I even question whether this film could have been made in England today. Because of the union-based, slightly aggressive filmmaking mentality I don't believe that this youthful enthusiasm, this innocence, could have been brought to this project.*

THE LOOK OF MIDDLE-EARTH

Taylor hired six young designers to begin work on thousands of sketches, paintings and models to define the look of Middle-earth's inhabitants. Some, like *Braindead* storyboard artist Christian Rivers, had worked at Weta before, while others had no film experience. Long before any of the hobbit actors had been cast, the designers were sorting out the look of many of their foes — the cave troll who attempts to hammer the Fellowship to death in the Mines of Moria, the octopus-like Watcher which tries to stop them getting inside, the various races of orcs and the devilish Balrog (although the Balrog would also be inspired by the work of Tolkien artists who had conjured up the monster before). Each step of the way, Jackson offered his thoughts, and designs were refined accordingly. Most of the creatures were then built as three-dimensional sculptures, known as maquettes.

After gaining the final stamp of PJ approval, many of these designs were scanned into a computer for the team at Weta Digital to animate (the scanning process, whereby all the surface skin detail on a sculpture is transferred onto a computer, made use of equipment normally found in the meat-processing industry). Plans for the unearthly Black Riders to be created by CGI were later abandoned partly due to worries over expense. The Weta Workshop crew of 148 included only twenty-eight who had worked on a film before. Taylor employed blacksmiths, sculptors, jewellers, and leather-workers. Foam-latex ovens spewed out elf ears and oversize hobbit feet at all hours.

When costume designer Ngila Dickson (*Heavenly Creatures, Xena*) arrived on the scene, design work for the armour had already been started on. That still left plenty for her and a team of fifty to get on with: for example, creating hundreds of costumes for seven separate cultures. Many of them had to be replicated multiple times in both 'mini-me' and tall sizes, to create the illusion that the hobbits were around 120 centimetres high. Just one other example of the size of the workload: the rags on one Ringwraith alone required fifty metres of fabric.

There is an attic in Switzerland piled high with shields, spears and lances from all number of historical periods. Many of the weapons were made by their owner John Howe, a Canadian artist who has lived in Switzerland for the last twenty years, and who regularly dons sword and chainmail to take part in historical re-enactments. The practice with heavy weaponry helps add to the realism of his work as one of the world's most admired artists of Middle-earth. In early 1998 Howe was on a Singapore Airlines flight to New Zealand, and much of his armour collection lay in the plane's cargo-hold. On the same flight Howe met Alan Lee, the gentle, grey-bearded British artist acclaimed for his watercolour illustrations for *The Hobbit* and *The Lord of the Rings*. Howe had corresponded occasionally with Lee by fan letter and telephone, but the plane flight marked the first time they had met — two of Peter Jackson's favourite interpreters of Middle-earth, heading down to the Antipodes to reimagine Europe.

Jackson was lucky to have the two of them on board. Unknown to Howe, Jackson had been showing samples of Howe's artwork in Hollywood, while trying to sell movie executives on why they should put some money into Middle-earth. One Howe painting in particular pulled at the director's imagination: that portrait of the wizard Gandalf striding through a rain-lashed field with staff in hand, a look of determination on his face. Possibly its elemental nature rang in Jackson's head because it made it easy to imagine that the Middle-earth Gandalf walked in was the countryside of New Zealand. Finally Jackson contacted Howe and (after quite a search) English-based Lee, asking them if they would like to join *Rings* as conceptual designers. For Lee, the offer turned up at the first time in years he faced no imminent deadline. He took only a few hours to decide.

Once in New Zealand, the artists got busy drawing and redrawing the various environments of Middle-earth to Jackson's satisfaction. They came originally for four months, but the design team found their background in things both English and European invaluable; apart from a brief trip home in mid-1988, while the *Rings* project hung over the abyss, John Howe stayed for thirteen months, while Lee would still be in New Zealand four years later. By all accounts the work divided up quite easily. Howe handled the darker elements of the piece: the Dark Towers of Barad-dûr and Minas Morgul, along with lots of armour and, on a lighter note, the interior of Bilbo's house at Bag End. Lee's ornate, atmospheric drawings shone a light mostly on nicer places, filling in much of the village of Hobbiton, the great hall of the Rohan and the elven kingdom of Rivendell. In later months, Howe could occasionally be spotted jousting with a crew member in front of the Weta headquarters in Miramar, making sure that the swords were up to the combat readiness required. Lee, meanwhile, would be on set touching up a final detail of the ornate buildings of the elves, which was where he fell through a hole in Rivendell and broke his arm. He was back behind the drawing board within days.

For Lee and Howe, the mission promised some great travel perks. They often accompanied Jackson across the diverse landscapes of New Zealand when the director was scouting for locations, 'flying over mountains and down fiords'. Among other places, their travels took them to a low bunch of hills in the rolling farmlands of the Waikato. There, a few kilometres from the nearest road, Howe and Lee sat down on the grass with their sketchbooks and began transferring the village of Hobbiton stored for so long in their imaginations onto another canvas: the landscape in front of them.

Back in Wellington, still awaiting the final go-ahead to make *Rings*, Taylor had heard about a large empty property close to Jackson's Miramar production base that might serve as a movie studio. When Jackson and Taylor went to have a look inside, they discovered a battered copy of *The Lord of the Rings* on a table in the former cafeteria. When the former paint factory went up for sale, a housing developer offered more money than they could afford. But the owner, enthused by their plans, sold what would become Stone Street Studios to them anyway.

Once New Line took on the *Rings* project in August of 1998, and decided it would make three films, Taylor and Rodger sat down to budget exactly how much it would cost to produce thousands of weapons and suits of armour, hundreds of fake hobbit feet and thousands of hand-fletched arrows. They sat at a computer full-time for more than three months, setting up pictorial representations of every character appearing in the movies, enabling them to break down every item from helmet to buckle, and how much it would cost to make. Some argue that Taylor and Rodger, for all their leadership brilliance, cut their own profit margins much more tightly than they should have. 'On a film as big as this, if we were out by one percent, we would have collapsed Weta,' Taylor later said. 'We pulled it off with a tolerance that was so fine. Tania and I have no business training whatsoever. The whole trick with this sort of work is you cut the cloth to fit the suit.'

Perhaps Jackson felt some *déjà vu* at this point. Years before, during the making of *Meet the Feebles*, he had put himself in the position of rushing to write an entire script at the same time as the film sets were being built, and half his puppet characters were under construction. Now, a decade later, a similar process had been set in motion as scripting, casting, location hunting, and effects work on *Rings* all proceeded simultaneously. This time, though, the planning time was a great deal more generous, and so was the budget. The challenge with *Rings* was not about trying to turn limitations into greatness, but meeting the high expectations which another writer's greatness had already created. Clearly there were an infinite number of possible ways to go down in flames. One of them was getting the wrong actors.

NEW LINE CINEMA

When New Line Cinema began in 1967, it was not in the business of making movies, but distributing them to play on college campuses. Six years later, company founder and award-winning filmmaker Robert Shaye began distributing movies to cinemas. Detroit-born Shaye continued to carve his own niche by concentrating on edgier fare: from foreign, sexploitation and gay films to cult titles like *Pink Flamingos* and *The Texas Chainsaw Massacre*.

In the 1980s New Line began to dip its toes in film production, signing controversial horror director Wes Craven to make *A Nightmare on Elm Street* (1984). This tale of a razor-bladed psycho who invades the dreams of teenagers spawned a series that grew more successful with each episode. The company commissioned Peter Jackson and writing partner Danny Mulheron to write a script for the fifth *Elm Street* sequel. Unknown to them, New Line executive Michael De Luca had also been asked to write a script — *Freddy's Dead* — and Jackson and Mulheron's was never used.

The profits generated by the demonic Freddy Krueger were vastly overshadowed by the success of *Teenage Mutant Ninja Turtles* in 1990, one of the most successful independent films then made. That year, New Line created in-house division Fine Line Features, to handle arthouse films and more offbeat fare. The split allowed the company to release new movies with both Robert Altman and Jim Carrey in short order.

Today, New Line continues to straddle two worlds. In Bob Shaye, it remains the only film studio in the US still commanded by its founder. But, as with Miramax, its claims to independence are compromised by recent history. Since 1993, New Line has been owned by a succession of multimedia conglomerates, ending with AOL Time Warner, which took over after *Lord of the Rings* had been given the green light. Flushed with corporate ownership, Shaye began making the big-budget, star-driven vehicles he had long avoided, and found a franchise in *Austin Powers*. New Line's

relationship with its parent company has faced some tensions —
during cutbacks in 2001, AOL Time Warner made Shaye fire 100 of
his 600-plus staff, and publicly singled out New Line's big-budget
comedy *Little Nicky* for damaging AOL's earnings. Many in
the industry felt that *Lord of the Rings*'s fate would determine the
company's future. Now co-running New Line with Michael Lynne,
Shaye continues to leave the media spotlight to his senior
executives.

HUNTING SOME HOBBITS

The casting process for *Rings* must have felt at times as if it were being
conducted by megaphone, with half of the world's Tolkien fans standing
by on the Internet. Speculation over who will take on the screen mantle of
a famous story is hardly new, but in the case of *Rings*, the world wide web
took things to a new level of transparency. A titbit about casting heard in
New Zealand or London often spread across the globe within days,
sometimes hours. Though many of the rumours and pieces of 'inside'
information turned out to be wrong, a number proved eerily accurate. On
more than one occasion, Jackson could not hide his frustration at all the
speculation. 'At this point in time, NO RUMOURS ARE TRUE!' he told
fans via the Internet in mid-1998. 'If you hear rumours, then you can safely
assume they are 100 percent false!'

Yet the Internet also had positive spin-offs. On at least two occasions
Tolkien fans got the chance to stand at the director's shoulder via their
computer, as if watching the creation of their mega-movie at firsthand.
Twice in 1988 Jackson volunteered to go online at movie-site Ain't it Cool
News to answer questions posed by Tolkien fans. The questions had been
honed down to twenty each time, from a total of more than 10,000
submitted. Jackson proved remarkably open about the process of
transferring a beloved novel to cinema. Fans were treated to the kind of
minor trivia which film companies often guard fearfully until release date.
(Jackson on the armour: 'We have a foundry set up at Weta. Steel is heated
red-hot and beaten on anvils!' On perfecting the monstrous Balrog: 'Our
designs have wings at the moment.' On what accents the actors would
speak in: 'New Line are concerned that having no American accents will
alienate a US audience, so that debate has yet to be resolved.') The insight
shown by fans into the complexities of adapting Tolkien's text made it
sound as if both sides were gaining from the Internet experiment.

Once casting properly began in late 1998, New Line's Michael De Luca
did what few movie executives before him had dared: he treated fans like
humans, and actually replied to some of their emails. De Luca, a self-
confessed fan of movie websites, dropped a number of hints about casting

progress in emails and online interviews. In this fashion he confirmed the signing of British actor Sean Bean as Boromir days ahead of the official announcement. The breakdown of the normal walls between fan and movie made for some strange moments. During the first Q & A session with Jackson in August 1998, movie addict turned web guru Harry Knowles introduced the first question about casting by offhandedly mentioning the interest in the *Rings* project of his friend, actor Elijah Wood. The question concerned whether Jackson planned to concentrate on big-name actors or unknowns. Jackson's answer was: unknowns.

Moviemakers are often criticised for casting actors more for their looks, than for the talents they might bring to a part — encouraging stereotypes by always making black men the baddies, and giving all the female roles to teenagers with waists smaller than their wrist size. But with *Rings*, picking the right physical type became a vital component in creating a believable Middle-earth. The elves needed to be tall, thin, and sharp-featured. For the hobbits, Jackson wanted the opposite. 'They had to be between five foot five and five foot seven,' he says, 'because we just figured that somebody who was six foot tall wouldn't make a good hobbit once they were shrunk down. We were looking for hobbits with round cute faces — character faces.' The team who later hunted down the movie's hobbit extras would often refer to their desired type as 'roundies' — round cheeks, round eyes, round tummies.

Some actors slotted quickly into their roles. Scottish theatre actor Billy Boyd signed early to play Pippin, one of the hobbits who accompanies Frodo on his mission — in the actor's past vocation as a bookbinder, Tolkien's epic had been one of the few books to pass by him that he hadn't got around to reading. Says Jackson: 'We saw him as Pippin, and never saw a better Pippin.' Other actors took a more roundabout route. Orlando Bloom originally auditioned as a human named Faramir, not an elf named Legolas. Off set, the self-proclaimed adrenaline junkie helped introduce many of the *Rings* cast members to the delights of surfing — as a result, one of them had a close encounter with his surfboard and turned up on the Mines of Moria set with a massive bruise on one side of his face.

Horror legend and longtime *Lord of the Rings* fan Christopher Lee auditioned for Jackson in a church on London's Tottenham Court Road; Lee had long dreamed of playing Gandalf, although he would later be fond of saying that Saruman, the part he won, was the most powerful wizard of all. Meanwhile, despairing of ever finding the right actor to play the hobbit Merry, Jackson and the casting team found Dominic Monaghan's performance on a videotape of more than 200 actors who had auditioned to play Frodo. Monaghan learned he had the part in a car in France, while there for an acting role.

The search for the trilogy's four main hobbits concentrated mainly in England, but when it came to finding someone to play Sam, loyal friend and employee of Frodo, there were few likely contenders.

I thought Sam would be easy to find in England — a sort of slightly plump, good solid working-class lad. We didn't really find anyone. We met up with Sean Astin in Los Angeles, and really liked what Sean did. So we basically called his agent and said, 'Look, if he can put on thirty pounds we'll offer him the role.' His agent said, 'No problem, Sean will put on thirty pounds.' And he did, which was very decent of him. I used to make sure at the catering table each day that Sean's plate was a little higher.

Astin had recently run the Los Angeles marathon, but it would be a couple of years before he was able to try it again. By this point, around Easter 1999, the mechanics were running around madly greasing the wheels of that unwieldy machine known as a film shoot. After two cancelled dates to start filming, the decision was made to begin in October — but *Rings* still did not have a lead hobbit.

We literally started to panic. We auditioned in London, in Australia, in New Zealand. We'd met 200 English actors and hadn't really seen Frodo. Because you know the second someone comes into the room whether they are right. And this videotape turned up in the mail in the casting office in England. I had never seen an Elijah Wood film in my life. I had heard his name, but I didn't know what he looked like. What Elijah had done was got a friend of his to go up into the woods behind his house somewhere. He had rented a hobbit costume and got a dialect coach to teach him an English accent, because he knew we were looking for an English actor. It was a sort of Cockney accent. We put the tape in the machine and I was totally struck by Elijah. I just thought, 'Wow, this guy's amazing.'

Wood had been asked to audition in a Los Angeles casting office, but decided that the videotape route stood a better chance of communicating his passion for the role. Though keen to cast him, Jackson made sure to arrange a meeting first.

I thought that if I ended up with someone who was difficult, a bit of an egotist and was a problem, it would become a nightmare. The film was hard enough to make without having an actor issue to deal with every single day. I was determined that whoever we cast in any of these roles would have to be nice people.

Again the wizards of the web moved fast, revealing Wood's success a month before the official announcement. In July, a writer for The One Ring website unveiled more casting coups — rising Irish actor Stuart Townsend would play the trilogy's most important human role, the exiled warrior Aragorn, while model turned actor Liv Tyler had nabbed another key part. Fans began speculating who exactly the star of *Stealing Beauty* was going to play — the feisty Eowyn from the later books perhaps, or maybe elven Queen Galadriel? Tyler's relatively minor role as Arwen would fuel more coverage than almost any other *Rings* cast member apart from Orlando Bloom — less from speculation about Jackson's attempts to modernise the book's female element than from the media's obsession with using pictures of photogenic young women to help sell magazines.

Another name kept rising from the casting mist: Sean Connery. Jackson, who was a Bond fan, had dismissed the idea of Connery playing the wizard Gandalf over the Internet, but that did not help the rumour go away. Michael De Luca confirmed that Connery was considering a part (possibly that of Saruman, the role later taken by Christopher Lee). Connery later reportedly admitted turning the project down because he could not understand the script. Instead Jackson offered the part of Gandalf to Shakespearian actor Ian McKellen (*X-Men*, *Richard III*), whose chameleon-like abilities the director maintained had been in his head all along. Other actors who tried for roles in *Rings* include David Bowie, Ethan Hawke, Keanu Reeves (who had enough on already) and hobbit-sized Warwick Davis (the star of *Willow* hoped to play Gimli). Previous Jackson cast members John Astin, Ian Watkin and Melanie Lynskey auditioned but failed to win parts (Lynskey: 'They asked me to audition for Eowyn, this Nordic warrior princess. But it was a good excuse to see them.')

In many ways, the completed casting mirrored the successful 'no superstars' approach taken by the classic *Star Wars*, years before. In movie terms, *Rings*'s protagonists were relative unknowns, helping lend believability to a film set in another time. Legends of British acting took on the older roles in both trilogies: that of lead wizard (*Star Wars*'s Alec Guinness as Ben Kenobi, and Ian McKellen as Gandalf) and secondary villain (Hammer horror stalwarts Peter Cushing as *Star Wars*'s Grand Moff Tarkin, and Christopher Lee as Saruman).

On arrival in New Zealand, the cast went through an intensive five-week period of training — horseriding, canoeing, learning to speak in the right dialect, and to wield swords in a style appropriate to their particular characters. Some were also asked to get both fit and fat.

What was missing from the cast-list was New Zealanders. Jackson has long been a tireless promoter of New Zealand's filmmaking talent, but considering the sheer size of the ensemble cast, it is sad how few New Zealanders got important roles — *Price of Milk* star Karl Urban as Rohan warrior Eomer is arguably the only contender, while the talented Martin Csokas gets only a few lines as the Elf King Celeborn. When *Fellowship of the Ring* emerged, journalists struggling to find a New Zealand acting angle were sent to Lawrence Makoare (so good in *Crooked Earth*), who spends the entire film buried beneath even more makeup than John Rhys-Davies as the monstrous Lurtz.

Pressures from a worried American studio played a part here: at one point, New Zealand star Danielle Cormack (*The Price of Milk*) was a prime contender to play warrior woman Eowyn, but New Line felt that Australian talent Miranda Otto had more international box-office appeal. (Whether the studio or Peter Jackson swung the final decision, is unknown.)

The casting directors also faced the task of employing literally thousands of extras to play orcs, Urak-hai, horseriders and hobbits. There was no shortage of phone calls. In the early days, those with claustrophobia, allergies or tantrums were progressively sifted out. Many would have to endure uncomfortable prosthetics, and a number found a couple of fourteen-hour days filming in the rain of Helm's Deep enough to cure them of any Hollywood ambitions. By the end of the shoot, things were getting desperate. The casting office now had a sign on the wall: 'If you're breathing, you're hired.'

ROLL FILM

On October 11, 1998, almost three years after Jackson finished shooting *The Frighteners*, he went behind a camera again. The location was a patch of forest not far from Wellington hospital, as a group of hobbits cowered in fear by the side of a leaf-strewn track. Compared to the scale of *Rings*, the seven-month shoot of *The Frighteners* was a cakewalk. The next few months would see Jackson ranging from a lakeside in Queenstown, to the new Stone Street studio in Wellington, to the rolling hills of the Waikato.

The extensive location filming, much of it off the beaten track, kept people on their toes. 'It became a sort of dark expectation that whenever we turned up on a new location the weather would turn bad,' Jackson later wrote. One day might require liberal doses of sunscreen; the next day snow goggles. Some sets were washed away by floods. At one point landslides caused by heavy rain in the South Island forced Sean Bean and Orlando Bloom to abandon their journey, and stay with kind locals. The two actors were later ferried out by helicopter, precisely the thing that Bean had been using a car to avoid. He could sometimes be seen clambering up hillsides in his Boromir costume to make his morning call time without having to get in another one.

Some sets required months of preparation. Once the rural environs of

Hobbiton had been perfected, the set and its many gardens were allowed to grow for a year, before shooting commenced. The clifftop city of Edoras on the Canterbury Plains took eight months to build, much of it in sub-zero temperatures. A beautiful model of a ruined hobbit mill took three months, and is seen onscreen for a few seconds.

Some of the trilogy's most spectacular landscapes — including the valley of Rivendell and Gandalf's arrival at the circular fortress of Isengard — are testament to movie magic more than actual locations. The Weta wizards cut and pasted a number of photographic elements together to create such imaginary landscapes, and also made extensive use of miniatures. Production designer Grant Major argued that New Zealand viewers might recognise the Remarkables, 'but that'll be about it'.

The trilogy's use of local scenery would later be mined extensively to promote both the movies themselves and New Zealand as a prime location for tourists and filmmakers. Special maps showing where sections of the trilogy had been shot were much in demand, and a detailed pocketbook that helped fans pinpoint each location became a national bestseller. Yet for Jackson, the obsession with spot-the-location occasionally felt a little contrary to what the movies were about. He said that seeing *Fellowship of the Ring* with the film's real-life locations in mind 'defeats the purpose of a film like this'.

> *What I am trying to do as a filmmaker is transport you away to Middle-earth. I am wanting more than anything for people to forget the real world . . . and be transported away with a bit of escapist entertainment. In a way I hope the film overwhelms people in the sense that they actually forget that it's New Zealand after a while. That would be a good thing.*

And the place Jackson found most difficult to shoot in? The shrunken interior of Bilbo Baggins's house back at the studios in Wellington — where thirty-plus cast and crew spent a number of weeks knocking their heads on some very low ceilings.

THE SIZE OF IT ALL

The decision to make three films back to back was an extraordinary one, although not quite as unique as the hypesters kept claiming. A number of big movies with six-to-eight-hour running times had been shot back in the 1920s while a number of directors have made two features back to back. (The final two *Matrix* movies being recent examples.) But the project which bears most similarities to Jackson's epic is a four-part version of *War and Peace* from the 1960s.

Based on Tolstoy's epic novel about Napoleon's invasion of Russia, *War and Peace* was released in Russia in separate parts over a four-year period. Cinematographer Anatoli Petritsky recalls that the filming for all four parts was done over one extended schedule, and the only time shooting stopped was when director Sergei Bondarchuk fell ill. The Soviet government put phenomenal resources into the movie, including supplying 12,000 soldiers from the Soviet army for some of the epic battle scenes. Petritsky says that even at the time, few of those working on the film had any idea how much it actually cost (some estimates have put it as high as American $500 million in today's prices).

One thing is clear: shooting big-budget movies back to back is extremely rare, partly because of the logistical nightmares involved. European producers Alexander and Ilya Salkind and Pierre Spengler found this out when they made the first two *Superman* movies. Slowed by the special-effects demands of trying to make its superhero fly, and a perfectionist director, *Superman* quickly began to go over-budget and behind schedule. The Salkinds came close to firing director Richard Donner, accusing him of slowing production to the point of near-bankruptcy. Faced with such problems, many of the scenes for *Superman 2* were put aside in the race to get the first film finished. Warner Brothers, originally set only to distribute *Superman*, eventually agreed to save the production through a large cash injection against future royalties. The second film was later completed with another director.

LONG MOVIES

Once you start searching for the biggest, longest and most expensive movies — all superlatives that have been applied to Jackson's *The Lord of the Rings* — the line between art and self-indulgence can become muddled. Many of these epics were so long that they faced major cuts by studios, distributors or even the directors themselves, and many now exist in a confusing variety of lengths.

Cinema giant DW Griffith was one of the earliest to test the boundaries of big. The recreation of Babylon built for his 1916 epic *Intolerance* rose twenty-seven metres above Los Angeles. With a rough cut that ran to eight hours, Griffith considered releasing his multi-story movie in two parts. After exhibitors rejected the idea, *Intolerance* was edited closer to three hours. In the 1920s, French director Abel Gance took the idea of long movie, and ran with it. His script for *Napoleon* grew into at least six interlinked movies, but financial problems and occasional moments of sanity meant that only one episode finally emerged. Still, the unmangled cut of *Napoleon* ran an impressive eight hours.

The award for longest film in cinema history goes not to *Napoleon* or the infamous *Greed*, but to *The Longest Most Meaningless Movie in the World* (1970) which ran forty-eight hours straight. Like a number of the main contenders for longest, most self-indulgent film in history, *Longest Most* screened only once in its epic form, before being sliced back to a more conventional length.

Closer comparisons to the *Rings* trilogy are found in the classic *Die Nibelungen* (1924), which comes complete with dwarves, dragons, misty forests and warriors on horseback. *Metropolis* director Fritz Lang, an early king of mega-budget epics, shot it over one nine-month period in a studio outside Berlin. *Die Nibelungen*'s two parts ran to more than six hours, and were meant to be watched as one. At the time, the second film was rarely seen outside of Germany.

Though not the longest in running time, arguably the most expensive and longest-shooting film in history is Sergei Bondarchuk's four-part version of the Tolstoy classic *War and Peace*. With an original length of around seven hours (sources vary), the project had more than 300 speaking parts and one of the battle scenes is almost an hour long.

'I thought somewhere there would be some sort of a saving, where three would be as hard as doing two or something,' commented Jackson on the trilogy. 'But it was three times as difficult.' He was well aware that if the movies began falling significantly behind schedule, the 'snowball effect' that resulted over such a long shoot could be disastrous.

Jackson, whose love of controlling all elements of a film has rarely extended to working with second-unit directors, had another unit working on *Rings* from an early stage. (Second units are separate camera crews, often used to catch location footage that does not require the supervision of the actual director — *Braindead* made extensive use of such a crew, but in that case Jackson commanded both units simultaneously.) As the months rolled by for *Rings*, the sheer volume of footage needed meant that two more units were added, one commanded by veteran Geoff Murphy. At one especially mad point, the number of separate units reached as high as nine, with everyone from producer Barrie Osborne to Fran Walsh getting behind the camera (try to imagine the logistics, if Frodo was needed on set by only four of them). Often, Jackson was able to watch the work of other units on set through a satellite link and offer his opinions. On other days he would arrive at work just as second-unit director John Mahaffie had arrived back from a long night of battle scenes.

The spectre of the schedule derailing arose early on. In the weeks before he began filming his very first shots with the trilogy's hobbit characters,

Jackson grew worried that actor Stuart Townsend was not right for the part of Aragorn. 'I was there rehearsing and training for two months, then was fired the day before filming began,' Townsend later told *Entertainment Weekly*. 'After that I was told they wouldn't pay me because I was in breach of contract due to not having worked long enough.' The producers have never publicly responded to Townsend's complaints in the media. Jackson must at least be given credit for making the decision early — if he had delayed it, valuable days would have been lost having to reshoot footage with a different actor.

New Line's Mark Ordesky made calculations as to how much money would be lost by delaying Aragorn's first scenes, due to begin in a few days. The amount was worryingly high. He quickly rang Viggo Mortensen (*GI Jane*, *Portrait of a Lady*) and tried to persuade him that New Zealand was the best place he could spend the next fourteen months. Thankfully Mortensen's son agreed. Like many prospective *Rings* cast members before him (Wood, Astin, McKellen and Tyler included), Mortensen had yet to read Tolkien's epic. At first he said no. But then he got on the plane.

If, as Jackson has argued, *Rings* was a film that was meant to happen, then Mortensen may well have been fated to play Aragorn. His Scandinavian background meant that he had been raised on a number of the Nordic myths which had inspired Tolkien, and his ability to speak three languages aided his efforts to learn Elvish. Still, having to fight five Ringwraiths on one of your first days on set, when you hardly know your way around a sword, would be a challenge for any actor. Mortensen used his self-doubt as a way into the conflicts of Aragorn's character, and his identification with Aragorn's love of nature — occasionally sleeping in costume in the bush — has quickly become the stuff of *Rings* legend. For Mortensen, working on location helped him remain immersed in the story. 'The woods were nearby,' he said. 'A beautiful river was always nearby. No matter how urban a place was, it was never very far away from something that felt more or less primeval.'

In the last few months of filming, many of the promised break periods began to drop off the trilogy's schedule, and the cast increasingly found themselves having to act scenes from three different movies in short order. The increased workload came down especially hard on Wood and Mortensen. 'We motored for the last six months or so,' Mortensen told *Pavement*. 'It was six days, fourteen to sixteen hours a day, constant, just to get it done.'

In the case of *Rings*, some of the most priceless moments of performance would never be heard. Rerecording of dialogue occurs far more often in movies than we might think, partly thanks to noises from aircraft and electronic equipment. But in the case of the *Rings*, only two percent or so of the original dialogue proved to be usable, partly because the Wellington studios used sat right under the flight paths to Wellington airport. News that most of Gandalf's dialogue would have to be rerecorded emerged through Ian McKellen's website, along with a mention that the studios had not been soundproofed. As the story spread, a WingNut publicist told media that the same was true of most New Zealand film studios, arguably not the most obvious way to promote movie making Down Under.

VIGGO MORTENSEN — THE TRAVELLING ACTOR

Journeys seem to run in Viggo Mortensen's blood. By the age of twenty-five, he had already lived in Venezuela, Argentina, Denmark and the US. Often portrayed in interviews as serious and intro-verted, Mortensen also has a lighter side: he is a fan of the movie parodies found in *Mad* magazine — not least when they are poking fun at his own acting roles.

Michael Douglas once described Mortensen as 'a method actor in a leading man's body'. Mortensen's physicality and quiet intensity have largely been showcased through darker roles in thrillers and action movies, with only rare chances to show a more sensitive side onscreen, as in the romance *A Walk on the Moon*.

Mortensen's father was Danish, his mother American. He grew up mostly in South America, but when his parents split, he and two brothers ended up with their mother in New York. After acclaim onstage, he had his screen debut in the television mini-series *George Washington* (1984). His first two movie roles — as an actor in *The Purple Rose of Cairo* and a flirting sailor in Goldie Hawn's *Swing Shift* — ended up on the cutting-room floor.

This slow-burning career path was cemented by Mortensen's next two films: a small role as one of the Amish in *Witness*, and a much bigger one in the offbeat, little-seen religious satire *Salvation!* It was while making the latter that he met his future wife, punk rocker Exene Cervenka (they have one child, but are now amicably divorced). Around this time, Mortensen decided he would have to lower his standards and find acting roles that would support his family, even if they failed to satisfy him artistically. Hence *Texas Chainsaw Massacre 3*.

In the early 1990s, Mortensen began to win Hollywood's eye with brief but memorable roles as an ex-con in *Carlito's Way*, an arrogant sports magnate in Stallone's *Daylight*, and Lucifer in *The Prophecy*. In 1997, he won attention as the poetry-quoting military instructor who puts Demi Moore through hell in *GI Jane*. By this point, he had twice worked with New Zealand directors — Geoff Murphy on *Young Guns 2* and Jane Campion on *Portrait of a Lady*. Campion jokingly called him 'kiddie' in an effort to overcome his shyness.

Two years later, Mortensen showed another side to his character in the Michael Douglas thriller *The Perfect Murder*, and finally won major attention from the American media. The paintings executed by his character in the film are Mortensen's own, but scandal mags expressed more interest in the romance they wanted him to be having with co-star Gwyneth Paltrow. Already a published poet, Mortensen had his first photography exhibition in July 2000.

FLASHBACK

When New Line gave the go-ahead to make *Rings* as three movies rather than two, the film suddenly sprouted an extra head. By then the scriptwriting team had sprouted an extra head of its own. The first Philippa Boyens heard of the project was when a phone call came for a close friend, *Braindead* writer Stephen Sinclair. Said Boyens:

> *It was in my kitchen actually. I remember it distinctly. He got off the phone and said, 'You won't believe what they're doing.' I thought he was being really smart and said, 'Yeah, they're doing* Kong.' *He went, 'No, they're not, they're doing* The Lord of the Rings.' *And I just about dropped what I was holding. I went, 'You're shitting me.' I thought they were insane [peals of laughter]. I still think they're insane.*

Sinclair's involvement in the writing of the *Rings* trilogy would finally stretch to around eighteen months; Boyens would be walking in Middle-earth for at least another five years. Though she had written, produced and edited plays in Auckland, and headed an organisation for writers, Boyens came to the movies as a first-time screenwriter. But she was not exactly new to Tolkien's world, having read the trilogy seven times. Initially Jackson and Walsh asked her for some feedback on their ninety-page treatment, a document that summarised the main events of *The Lord of the Rings* books.

> *It pretty much still stands up today . . . The key landmarks of that event story are still as they pulled them out in that treatment. I think Peter had an initial instinct on how to tell these stories — and Fran as well. They knew what to leave out, almost immediately. It wasn't as traumatic as some people would consider. The decisions to leave Tom Bombadil out, not to film the episodic nature of the ending of book three, they were relatively clean, clear decisions, made at a very early stage, which were never revisited, never rethought of. That was driven by the demands of film. It was pretty simple.*

Simple, but not completely simple. For Jackson, Walsh and Boyens, the writing process would continue all the way through the trilogy's fifteen-month main shoot and beyond, as they laboured on perfecting the story for the screen. 'We started with twenty-seven copies of the paperback, and none of them are intact,' laughs Boyens. 'Some of them are probably in caravans left on the side of Mount Ruapehu. There's probably some left in little tiny hotel rooms in Te Anau.'

The writing process normally involved Boyens manning the laptop while an 'absolutely exhausted' Jackson reclined on the couch after a filming day that had often started as early as 5am. Walsh would be spread out on the hotel-room floor with various copies of the script and the book scattered around her.

Once filming began, Boyens says she and Walsh were 'pretty much driving the revisions, with Peter overseeing'. But for Boyens, the key word to apply to the *Rings*'s writing process is 'collaboration': 'Every single line was filtered through all three of us.' During filming, this collaborative writing process never really ended, with constant fine-tuning and occasional reshooting of scenes. The dropping of one sequence would require going back and filming new dialogue for one that had already been shot, in order to make mention of a plot point that might otherwise have been lost.

The same concept of a script in constant evolution which had caused consternation to some of the Universal executives during the making of *The Frighteners* was now being applied to one of the biggest and most complex productions in the history of cinema. For the *Rings* cast such a method made for some testing moments. Often they would arrive on set to find the lines they had learned the night before had been changed. Said Australian actor Hugo Weaving, who played the elf Elrond:

They were continually honing the script, chucking out less important storylines, focusing on other ones, and then changing their minds. The script was always changing. You've already had four versions of the one scene, and then you'd have another one the night before, and then you'd get in there on the day and there would be another one. Sometimes we'd shoot half the scene, and they'd be working on the second half of it. Now that sounds all very chaotic, and in one way it was. But everyone realised it was because we wanted to try and clarify the main storyline. With the wealth of material there, that was one of the major difficulties they faced.

Such comments help give the impression that for the scriptwriters, the shooting of the *Rings* epics was a constant race to catch up with a schedule they were never quite able to meet. The classic model of a studio movie is of a script that is completely locked in place before filming starts. The idea that major changes might be required, or scenes reshot, is often seen as a warning sign that something has gone wrong with the process. However, the evolution of a movie is rarely so simple. Scripts ideally develop and change in the shooting and editing, and it is not until a film has first been seen in rough form on an editing bench that it is possible to get some idea of how it plays. Yet film remains one of the only artistic mediums where the very process of improvement is often viewed as a weakness, even before the finishing line is in sight. The idea of going back and shooting extra footage has often been regarded by the media as a sign that a movie is in trouble. Innovators like Woody Allen and George Lucas are among the few moviemakers who regularly build reshoots into their schedules.

Whether the *Rings* scriptwriting process was a case of continuing chaos, or ongoing refinement, would ultimately be decided only after the movies were released and people were able to look at the results. Certainly the expanding budget and multiple deadlines of *Rings* allowed Jackson's team to do things differently, in terms of reworking the movies as they went along. As the Christmas 2000 deadline to finish shooting began to loom, the staggered deadline for the three movies became useful in other ways — allowing the filmmakers the possibility of following *Superman*'s example, and quietly dropping scenes from the later episodes off the shooting schedule. The hope was that there would be an opportunity to go back and film them later, if the first movie proved successful.

For many in the cast, the unconventional nature of the trilogy's making — an epic-length shoot, much of it on location, and scriptwriters who actually wanted to talk to actors about their parts — only increased their enthusiasm for the project, and the strength of the actors' on- and off-screen bond. Elijah Wood talks about 'the organic feeling' he found in the filmmaking process, a process fuelled by a collective passion for the material of all involved.

> There wasn't anything Hollywood about the experience: nothing sterile, we weren't going to a soundstage every day. We were in an old factory that was turned into a studio. It felt like a massive independent film. And I think that the atmosphere really allowed us to be more free with what we were doing. Had it been done in the States, it would have been going to somewhere like Warner Brothers every day, in the Valley. I don't think that we'd have been able to contribute as much passion, or feed it with as much of the journey that we were taking as people, because it wouldn't have been the same. This is a very special kind of project.

Peter Jackson clearly has similar feelings. Asked at the press launch for *Fellowship* if the film felt like more of a heart-on-his-sleeve project than his previous productions, he couched his agreement by talking immediately about the people he had worked with.

It is not just a solitary single exercise. It must be similar to what it's like fighting a war, with a platoon of guys around you. We worked together for this long period of time, and we all got through it because we loved what we were making. We all knew that we were never going to do this again in our lives, make three movies back to back. Obviously I was doing it because I wanted to do this book. Everyone else was doing it on the basis that they had to make a lifestyle decision. When the actors decided to come to New Zealand to work on the movie, it wasn't just deciding to do a job, which is usually for three or four months. Once they were committed, there was a real feeling of, 'I'm not spending fifteen months working on a film that I'm not proud of.' There was certainly a lot of passion involved.

MICHAEL DE LUCA

The longtime golden boy of New Line finally left the company in 2001, missing the glory of helping see the riskiest production in the company's history through to completion. Joining New Line as an intern aged nineteen, fresh out of New York film school, he had spent the last seven years at the company as president of production, written a number of his own scripts and was named as one of the producers of the *Rings* trilogy. De Luca's tastes typified New Line's ability to satisfy a wide audience — a fan of popcorn fare like *Rush Hour* and *The Mask*, he also green-lit movies from offbeat talents like *Magnolia* director Paul Thomas Anderson. De Luca now heads production at Steven Spielberg's Dreamworks.

THE WIZARD GANDALF

The painting of Gandalf striding through rain and grass that so inspired Peter Jackson was stolen from an exhibition in northern France one night in March 1997. Of the eleven stolen Tolkien paintings by John Howe, eight were returned damaged, thanks to a call from a man claiming to be the father of the burglar. The Gandalf painting was not among them.

CHAPTER FOURTEEN

SPIES IN MIDDLE-EARTH

'Quiet, and action.'
LORD OF THE RINGS CREW MEMBER, DECEMBER 2000

'People love secrets.'
AMERICAN MOVIE GEEK TURNED INTERNET GURU HARRY KNOWLES

With the beginning of filming of *Rings* in October 1999, an elaborate game of cat and mouse moved into high gear — a game in which representatives of Peter Jackson and American studio New Line attempted to tie a magical cloak around their production, controlling exactly what information emerged, while everyone else kept pulling up the edges to peek inside. To make matters worse, many of the cloaklifters were effectively employed by New Line themselves. A number of extras and crew working on the films wrote in to *Rings*-related websites to report details of what they had seen: many adopted pen names inspired by Tolkien's universe. But it was a complicated game — some of the exclusive information fed to the websites actually came from New Line executives; secrecy has long been a great way to get people talking. Nonetheless, New Line's strong desire to control publicity on such a risky project seems to have stirred some feelings of defiance: thousands of New Zealanders agreed to sign a confidentiality agreement for the biggest film in their country's history. But by the end of filming, *Rings* had become one of the most spied-upon, talked-about movies yet made.

While extras talked in pubs about the rigours of filming the battle of Helm's Deep, a small number of crew and extras were fired for stealing movie props and property. A police operation involving negotiations by email to buy *Rings* footage led to the arrest of a crew member who had taken a number of videotapes. A criminal case was taken against an extra turned security guard, who had made off with at least sixty costume items and models: he had tattooed himself with *Rings*-related symbols and planned to use many of the stolen props in a shrine devoted to *The Lord of the Rings*.

Outside the various film sets, fans and newspaper photographers stood on public land with their cameras, and occasionally had altercations with security guards. Musician and One Ring website writer Erica Challis (webname Tehanu) was presented with a trespass order after writing that she planned to sneak onto some of the *Rings* sets. The trespass news spread quickly around the international network of Tolkien-related fan-sites, spinning New Line into damage control. Soon afterwards, Challis was invited unexpectedly onto the Hobbiton set in the Waikato during filming, where she wrote a long report. Designs for the pivotal character of Gollum appeared mysteriously one day on a website, then disappeared as quickly after a request from the company.

Yet the Internet was a vital element in New Line's campaign to build up awareness for the movies. Unofficially and officially, New Line staff began feeding information and casting news to selected Tolkien-related fan-sites. In April 2000, the broadcast of a few short minutes of *Rings* footage over the web was downloaded by 1.7 million people in twenty-four hours, far outstripping a *Star Wars: The Phantom Menace* promotion the previous year. New Line executives were keen to recognise that the success of the promotion owed much to the cooperation of at least twenty-five key *Rings* sites. In the last week of the shoot, Jackson and the studio allowed American web guru Harry Knowles wide access to the *Rings* set, joining an *E! Online* reporter who had been filing monthly reports.

Early in August, Tehanu reported seeing some strange 'wheel-like' props amid the flotsam of a *Rings* set in Lower Hutt. Three days later, an *Evening Post* photographer, desperate for an image to put on the front page, scored an international scoop with a shot of what appeared to be a wizard spiked on a wooden wheel going before the cameras. The moment did not chime with anything from Tolkien's original book, and some fans speculated that shooting such a vital moment in public view was part of an elaborate plan to lead spies off the scent. When the *Evening Post* sent a photographer up on a hillside to photograph one of the grandest sets in the trilogy, on a quarry near Wellington, the moviemakers had had enough. The newspaper was put in the sinbin, and left off the list of one of the movie's rare press conferences.

Filming of the *Rings* trilogy rolled swiftly towards the finish date, scheduled for a few days before Christmas 2000. By now, my own options were running out. A year of enquiries about the chances of going on the *Rings* set had been met by answers like 'No reply yet' and 'Peter won't be able to decide if you can go on set until the end of filming'. In spite of the temptation to join the hundreds of New Zealanders who had already got in the castle door by playing orcs and Uruk-hai in battle scenes, I knew that such a sneaky path would only prove counterproductive. By

December, the realisation had finally dawned on me: if I was going to find any hobbits, I would have to get out from behind my desk, and join the rabble of fans spying in the hills.

MONDAY

Twenty minutes' drive from the centre of Wellington, the green dome of an ancient chapel-like building juts out above the road. Just beyond the rocky outcrop, a stone's throw from the motorway, a large hole has been cut into the hillside. The target of the day's spying: Dry Creek Quarry, home to one of the biggest sets in the whole *Rings* trilogy. As I park my car opposite the quarry entrance, some bulldozers and a cherry picker exit the quarry, followed by long clouds of dust. The quarry signs out front mix enticements for ready-mixed concrete, with dire warnings to any intending trespassers.

Unfortunately the fortress city of Minas Tirith, which has recently taken over half of the quarry site, faces in precisely the wrong direction for roadside spectators. The effect is a little like having front-row seats, only on the far left of the theatre. Apart from some figures milling about on top of a long section of castle wall, the only other sights of interest are the white banners flying above them in the breeze. In front of the castle, a tiny guardhouse marks the edge of the film set. Occasionally the security staff drag their guard dogs out of the hut, to lie down on the dirt; that way observers can see what they are up against.

Drive on further up Haywards Hill Road, and the hills and greenery quickly take over again, blocking further views into the quarry. But a kilometre further on, a road-cum-pathway disappears off into the bush. I edge by the low barrier gate. Enormous power-pylons march across the hills against a blanket of clouds, and the drone of electricity hangs in the air, merging with the fading traffic. I continue walking southwards, hoping that the winding path through the scrub is leading me closer to the edge of the quarry. After a quarter of an hour of gentle hill track, the road begins a long, slow curve up to the right. Here the bush abruptly drops away, to reveal a much better angle on Middle-earth.

Suddenly exposed, I begin to crawl forward on all fours, feeling like one of the monkeys from *Planet of the Apes*. An old sign pokes up from the edge of the bank, warning people not to trespass on quarry land. But just in front of it, still safely on public land, a handy tree and a bush-camouflaged foxhole offer two of the best spying spots for miles around.

These days we are often being reminded about the magic which computers have brought to movie fantasy. But the wonders of pixellated creatures should never be allowed to dull our awe at an older magic — a magic whose roots lie closer to film pioneers like DW Griffith than the age of Bill Gates. Under the elm tree on the edge of the quarry, I catch sight of a little of this magic now — a city from someone's imagination, seemingly carved in three dimensions from the surrounding rocks, awaiting only the arrival of movie cameras.

The city of Minas Tirith is something to behold. The angular, imposing castle rises at least five storeys from the quarry floor, up to the domes atop its ramparts. The giant arched door at the front of the castle opens into an internal courtyard, on the other side of which is the main exterior castle wall, seen earlier from the road. From there, Minas Tirith's main street leads down past various Romanesque-style buildings — all big arches, long columns of rock, and rows of narrow windows. Still closer is another oversized courtyard, complete with statues, greenery and an elaborate carved fountain. And all of it, bar the wood of the giant main entrance gate, is clad in a whitish rock which looks as though it has been aging here in the sun for the last hundred years.

High on the furthest hill of the quarry sits the grand chapel-like building that could be seen from the motorway. Steps lead most of the way down from the chapel to Minas Tirith, seemingly cut into the quarry earth itself.

For an actor, there is surely much to be said for being able to wander the streets of Minas Tirith — certainly better than having to stand around for days in a studio in front of a blue screen; imagining an environment that won't actually exist until the computer wizards have added their magic. And there is another advantage to being in Minas Tirith — you're not standing so high up on the hill that the illusion is compromised when you see that many of the buildings don't have any roofs.

Above and behind the city, a road cuts in long zig-zags up the back quarry wall. The road leads up to a wide lip of land, which overlooks the whole valley. A security guard sits on a moped on the edge of the bank, talking to a man in a construction helmet. Hundreds of metres away, standing behind a tree, I watch them through binoculars. Within a minute of my arrival, both turn around, fixing their gaze in my direction. I try to slide back behind the tree, then crawl off to the foxhole.

When I lift my head slowly above the bushline again, the security guard has driven along the ridge a little, and is scanning the valley through his binoculars. Fans have occasionally tried to sneak onto the set from the parkland directly behind him, and motorcycles can periodically be heard patrolling in the area. But the route around to my side of the valley is such a long one that any noise should provide me with ample warning.

It starts to rain. Hardly anything moves on the set. A good time for a quick nap. Not long after, after hours of hearing only birdsong, a ute roars by from out of nowhere, passing just metres from my foxhole.

By four o'clock the weather has improved, and activity steps up a gear. Staff sweep the nearest courtyard and make final adjustments to the set, while others adjust lighting. For some reason, other crew are taking large sections of the front castle wall to pieces. Then things go quiet again. If I spend any longer out here freezing, I will be spending the rest of the week nursing a hot water bottle. On the far side of the valley, the security guard stretches back across the seat of his moped. For a moment he looks once more in the direction of the bush where I sit, then pulls his sunglasses further down his nose.

TUESDAY

Work commitments make it impossible for me to return to the Hutt Valley, to stand in the rain. An article appears in the *Evening Post*, arguing about the legality of taking photographs or videos of the *Rings* sets. A sign has recently been erected at the entrance to Peterkin Street in Lower Hutt, one of Wellington's main sets. The sign includes the statement that 'Three Foot Six may expose any unauthorised photographic film and erase any unauthorised videotape footage with images of the set and/or costumes/props.'

None of the five lawyers questioned about the legality of taking photographs is prepared to state much categorically. But the impression given is that although props and costumes might be a problem, a person is unlikely to be breaching the Copyright Act when taking photographs of the set alone, from a public space.

Lawyer John Terry argues that even if photographs were taken of costumes and props, no one has to hand over film or videotape. 'They can't just walk up and take your camera away from you. That's basically theft. What they would have to do in that situation is bring a [legal] action against you for copyright infringement and get a court order that you deliver up your camera.'

My impression is that Three Foot Six and/or New Line, after months of dealing with unwanted photographers operating on and off set, has grown increasingly worried as the main shoot rushes to a close, and is resorting to more heavy-handed scare tactics.

WEDNESDAY

When I park across the road from Dry Creek Quarry, a Television New Zealand cameraman is shooting some video footage of the Minas Tirith set under cloudless blue skies. The young cameraman is talking to a man dressed in black. Walking towards them, I realise too late that the man in black is one of the *Rings* security guards.

I smile, attempting to play the innocent onlooker. 'Do you know if they're filming today?'

The guard fixes me with a suspicious squint, but is otherwise unresponsive. After he wanders back over the road to his hut, the cameraman tells me that he is filming material for a news item on the possible future for the *Rings* crew once the main shoot finishes. He doesn't think any filming will be going on at the quarry today. Apparently someone was served with court orders on Tuesday after taking photographs of the set from the top of the hill. There are even rumours that the security company have cameras pointed up in that direction to monitor any visitors. That way, it is said, they can have staff waiting at the bottom when the intruders come back down the track to Haywards Hill Road.

On the other side of the Hutt River, behind the suburb of Taita, a mini-industrial zone of scrapdealers and panelbeaters sits beneath low hills. Turn off the main Eastern Hutt Road into the relative quiet of Peterkin Street, and a large blue sign sits on the roof of the local wood supplier: 'Wellywood'. The Peterkin Street property, also known as Wingate, has been one of the main *Rings* bases for much of the year. People who work in Peterkin Street tell of arriving for work in the morning just as the film crew are finishing off for the night — of catching glimpses through the fence of Gandalf on a raft on an artificial lake, of half-destroyed castles, of pitched battles with bows and arrows.

Through the green mesh of the perimeter fence, I spy a wide, ornately-decorated building or palace — or more precisely, the building's bottom storey (the Weta computer wizards will presumably add the rest later). In front of the palace is a large, withered, leafless tree. Could this be the famed White Tree from the cover of so many Tolkien novels, symbol of the royalty of Gondor?

On the grassy area in front of the building, two figures stand dressed in long white robes, protected by umbrellas from the afternoon sun. One of them is Ian McKellen. Crew members mill around, but it is hard to get a sense of much going on. On the edge of the grassy courtyard, two low fake stone walls stretch all the way down towards my position, running parallel with the fenceline.

A bearded figure can be made out standing among all those on the grass. Then he begins striding forward from the scene, a little rounder, a little faster than any of those that begin to follow. His dark head of hair blows in the breeze, and in one hand he carries the script. His eyes remain focused on the ground. The director I have spent all year trying to get permission to meet comes to a stop just metres from my position at the fence. When the crew catch up with him, Jackson starts talking about the scene, and the best place to set up the camera. His arm shoots out briefly in my direction, though his head does not follow. 'So Ian tells a story . . . he'll be up on the box. We could do it two ways . . .'

Within minutes the cameraman has jumped onto the low wall, squinting through a lens to frame the shot, and soon after that others are securing the camera into position. Around them, the crew grows quickly from eight people to more than thirty. A number busy themselves setting up the video village, a small, open-sided tent that serves as Jackson's command post. Much of his working day is spent here. Built with canvas walls which can be raised or lowered, the village is home to a great variety of electronic equipment — most important is a bank of television monitors that allow Jackson to see what every camera is capturing, including some of those on other sets.

'We might do a little rise,' he tells the cameraman. 'There's a lot of dialogue before Gandalf starts moving.'

McKellen soon wanders up, clad in the long white robes, long white beard and long white staff of Gandalf, Mark Two. The shot involves a long speech from McKellen, during which a line of soldiers is seen emerging from a set of underground steps back by the courtyard. Another character, also clad in white robes, will appear in the frame as the shot comes to an end.

Though the crew rarely look towards the nearby footpath, a man in black jeans and T-shirt keeps turning to glance back at me as I stand watching by the fence. Eventually the gate swings open and he wanders nonchalantly towards me. He walks on and lies down nearby, on the grass next to the footpath. We commence a game of pretending not to notice one another as he plays lazy sentry, occasionally talking into his walkie-talkie. Maybe he can order us up some pizzas. The first of a number of passers-by wanders up to join me at the fence and quickly spots the star of the proceedings. 'He's a scruffy-looking kind of a fellow,' the man tells me wisely. 'That's Peter Jackson there in the red shirt, holding the bit of paper.'

The man in the red shirt stands close to the actors as they quietly go through the dialogue for the scene. Ten minutes after they first began running through their lines, he says a quick, 'Okay, let's go', and wanders back to his tent. An assistant director takes up Jackson's command. 'Okay, we're going to run a rehearsal. Please, everyone keep still.' The atmosphere seems calm and efficient, rather than especially tense.

The call goes out for 'Quiet, and action.' Moments later a train begins to trundle noisily along the back of the property. Then everything starts to go downhill. A woman materialises in front of me on the other side of the electrified fence. She smiles broadly, then asks if I might be able to move just a little to the left as I am directly in McKellen's eyeline, making it hard for him to concentrate. In all the film sets I have visited, this is the first time I have been told I am in someone's eyeline — and today I am not even standing on the set. But the woman is so friendly and polite about it that I reluctantly move off a couple of metres to the left.

It seems that my move does not go quite far enough. When I express surprise that McKellen's eyeline extends twenty metres off to the left, beyond even some crew members who are larking around on the edge of the film set, the public relations woman informs me that in this scene, 'he moves his head all around'. But this is not a move your head around kind of scene. Another passerby, stomach threatening to come loose from his singlet, is sent off to join me in the sinbin, muttering expletives about film people who think they are God.

THURSDAY

At Dry Creek Quarry, a large contingent of horses and extras congregate on one edge of Minas Tirith. Most of the morning has been spent filming a sequence in which Gandalf, Frodo and others rush on horses at breakneck speed towards the outer gate of the city. In the scene, the gate opens just in time to let the group inside. For this scene, none of the main actors are present: stand-ins or dummies do their work for them. At least five separate cameras film the flurry of horses, a number shooting from the top of the city wall. An endless supply of lollipops and soft-freeze ice-creams helps keep spirits up.

The horses on set divide into two categories: the group ridden regularly by the main *Rings* cast and a larger group, around eighty, which have been assembled in Wellington especially for the scene. Some of the horses have been driven from as far as Matamata (at least six hours' drive) and the South Island.

After lunch, horsemen, horsewomen and villagers start to fill the courtyard, next to a large statue of an old King of Gondor. The warrior Faramir (Australian actor David Wenham) and his rangers will dismount from their horses and greet the villagers, who now crowd the courtyard.

'You're tired, you're exhausted. You've come home from battle,' the assembled extras are told before the scene begins shooting. 'You're greeting your family. Just say something that would suit the situation. But don't use any modern words.'

The scene is shot a great number of times. On some takes, the extras playing the villagers improvise their lines as instructed. Then they act the scene in silence. Before each take, the horse-wranglers help actors and extras up onto the cumbersome saddles. Those getting on and off horses require little extra tuition in acting tired. After a couple of hours of this, almost everyone is exhausted.

As one take nears its end, a group of extras standing on the far edge of the courtyard suddenly surprise me when their heads turn in unison to face the hilltop on which I am standing. I quickly duck down. When they repeat the motion again at the end of the next take, the sheer distance between us makes it difficult to be sure where the scene stops and getting caught standing on a hill begins. Time to slink home perhaps.

I learn later from contacts working on set that an onlooker was spotted that day. Twice the film crew were heard saying into their walkie-talkies: 'They've called security. They've seen someone up on the hill.' My spies were somewhat torn, wanting to yell out 'Get off the hill, you stupid idiot' while aware that such a comment might not be the best idea. The film crew sounded weary of all the spying.

'The set's awesome to wander around on,' says one of my contacts. 'It looks very realistic from far away . . . but even from a couple of centimetres away, all the rock looks like rock. And then you realise it's only half a centimetre thick, because it's all painted polystyrene and fibreglass. There's so much intricate detail on all the buildings.'

FRIDAY

I set off first for Jackson's twin command posts in Miramar. Stone Street Studios, once the home of a paint factory, is a sprawling collection of large, nondescript buildings, surrounded by other nondescript buildings. Plus more security guards, and a long metal fence. Without bionic vision, there is very little to see. At the other end of Miramar's main street is Jackson's mission control at Camperdown Studios, housed in an unpretentious building which appears to have been dropped directly from an aeroplane, to land in the middle of cosy suburbia. Directly next door is the nerve centre of Jackson's digital-effects empire; inside, computer boffins from around the globe are busy creating visions. I spot some bored people out in the sun, having coffee. Time to head out to the quarry.

Much of the morning has been devoted to a scene where a group march through Minas Tirith just before leaving for battle. In the scene, endlessly reshot, peasants lined one of the city's steepest streets, throwing flowers as the heroes pass. Gandalf walks alongside Faramir, begging him not to go. But the rainy weather, which necessitated putting rubber shoes on the horses, also forced the abandonment of plans to capture a grander shot as part of the same sequence — one involving the full contingent of horses cantering down the street behind the actors. There was talk of completing the rest of the scene at a later date.

When I arrive at the foxhole that afternoon, little at first appears to be happening. In the enclosed courtyard below the main castle building, knights in armour lean against the polystyrene walls, taking a break from massacres unseen. After a few minutes they disappear back through the giant arched doors of the castle, to join the action. From high on the hill, the angle of the castle buildings is so bad that all I can make out are the people not currently required for the scene.

Off to the left, near the steps running down from the chapel building, some workers have paused from dismantling a line of teepee-like tents and begun attacking each other violently with prop swords. The battle rages on across the hillside. It is probably the most exciting thing I have witnessed all week.

Within a quarter of an hour, another scene is being readied. Crowds of extras now mill about the courtyard in front of the castle door. Most are sent forward to the raised area near the edge of the ramparts. Above them, armoured figures begin to appear at the topmost ramparts of the castle. As the crew rush to ready cameras and actors beside him, Jackson edges away to the very furthest end of the castle wall, trying to talk into a cellphone. Finally he turns around, leaning back to look up at the soldiers high above. The sky is growing misty with cloud.

Just twenty minutes after the last scene stopped filming. 'Action.' A crowd of distant figures, mostly in armour, jostle near the castle edge. The lights throw a rim of gold onto each actor. From nowhere, the figure of Gandalf appears amid the horde, stepping forward towards the camera stationed at the edge of the rampart. But the lighting helps transform McKellen into a spine-tingling sight: silent, staff in hand, golden robes spread wide, he is a figure from one's imagination.

Then Gandalf is suddenly gone again — leaving only the crowd and the mist which has drifted further into the valley. For a moment, you wonder if you had the vision at all. But then Gandalf appears from nowhere again and the magic is repeated, until slowly it begins to fade, like a trick that has been performed too many times. There is a burst of applause, Gandalf raises his staff, and then proceeds to serve drinks. The knights start wandering down the hill towards the car park, and the crew load up camera gear. As the numbers dwindle around them, McKellen and Jackson remain on the ramparts talking. The director looks like a tourist; the actor more like a monk.

Now, as day turns to night, the crew continue to douse fire pots and carry camera equipment down from the castle. The biggest movie project many of them will ever know is within days of moving to a different phase. For most of them, that means both a decent sleep and a good chance of unemployment. For the first time in hours, yells and laughter echo across the quarry. But others seem reluctant to leave, and stand talking quietly in groups outside the walls of the city.

I have been lucky: witnessing Gandalf materialise from the crowd, I have at last had my little epiphany. But on the drive back to Wellington from Dry Creek Quarry, I can't resist detouring across to the other side of the Hutt Valley, to take one last look at the palace set on Peterkin Street.

Night-time in Wellywood, with a glow rising from behind the chain-mail fence. Banks of lights shine down on the palace from the top of cherry-pickers, bouncing giant shadows directly onto the nearby hills. Crew members yell instructions up to the lighting man, holed up on a tiny platform atop one of the pickers. But that is about all you can see: overnight, long sheets of black plastic have appeared all the way along the fence-line, blocking the roadside view into the set.

I begin walking towards the railway tracks at the back of the site. Normally one can stand there by the fence unseen, close to the timber framing that holds up the arches of the palace. But before getting to the railway I stop myself going any further. I have realised that the most exciting thing to see here on Peterkin Street is not to see anything at all — to know only   that there are mysterious goings-on, hidden behind walls of black plastic.

What I'm trying to say is this: sometimes there can be more magic in waiting.

CHAPTER FIFTEEN

UNVEILING THE RING

'There are people who are waiting for this film with
an anticipation which could prove fatal.'
ACTOR IAN MCKELLEN, TALKING ABOUT LORD OF THE RINGS
AT THE CANNES FILM FESTIVAL IN MAY 2001

'Rings is made by a genius masquerading as a normal human being.'
FINANCIAL TIMES CRITIC NIGEL ANDREWS, REVIEWING
THE FELLOWSHIP OF THE RING IN DECEMBER 2001

Like sitting in a darkened cinema, reading a book is partly about imagining yourself in someone else's place. So imagine this.

Your name is Peter, and you are very tired. For the past fortnight you have been crisscrossing oceans and nations in an aeroplane — never one of your favourite places to be, and, after the recent tragic events of September 11, even less so. The rest of the time has been spent shaking hands and trying to appear calm, as the first results of four years of your labours are unveiled to audiences wearing expensive clothes and famous smiles. Behind the gladhanding, there is a keen awareness that if people do not applaud loudly enough after each of these premiere screenings, the Ring may be trying to tell you something: namely that your movie loses much of its sheen upon first exposure to an audience. The possible consequences of such a situation really do not bear thinking about.

Now it is the last Wednesday before Christmas, and you and your partner have just touched down on an airport runway from a cloudy sky. Outside the window the wind is cold, and there is talk of rain. On an ordinary day this would signify only good news: that you are back home in Wellington. But today is not an ordinary day. In fact, the fervour associated with this particular Wednesday is such that the cityscape itself has been altered in tangible ways.

Judging by the signs adorning Wellington International Airport, the city has shifted sideways into one of those time-travel stories beloved of science-fiction writers, stories in which one tiny mistake has permanently mangled the fundamentals of the universe. In central Wellington, similar reality shifts are in evidence, especially in the buildings surrounding the Civic Square, the most impressive mixture of architecture and public space in the city. The public art gallery, City Council building and the glasshouse of the central library have each been plastered over with new signs proclaiming that Wellington is now Middle-earth.

In the nearby tourist information centre, visitors are guided towards their hotels by wizards in pointy hats and young women in medieval dresses. The *Evening Post* has also gone through some kind of time warp. For the first time in 137 years of publication, its normal title has been ditched. For the duration of premiere week, street vendors sell the *Middle Earth Post* instead.

As Wednesday morning passed into the afternoon, the epicentre of the *Rings* project had finally begun to move outwards from the trilogy's headquarters in Miramar. The new epicentre was a grand old picture palace overlooking one end of Courtenay Place, the street where many of Wellington's bars, theatres and restaurants are found.

Over the weekend, an eight-metre-high cave troll had been spotted travelling along the edge of Wellington harbour. The troll was on the back of a truck heading from Miramar towards town. Now it stood frozen in polyurethane above Peter Jackson's favourite cinema, wielding a large club. As a child, Peter Jackson had created models of such monsters in his bedroom in Pukerua Bay. Now his special-effects staff had installed a monster overlooking one of Wellington's main streets.

By midday the suburban buses that normally stopped to pick up passengers opposite the Embassy Theatre had disappeared, as workers began laying out lengths of red carpet from the bus stops to the theatre entrance. Close by, the Wellington City Council was casting a rare shadow over the day by towing away people's cars in order to create a detour route for buses. A number of Wellingtonians only discovered this upon going outside, when they found that their vehicles had disappeared.

Meanwhile Jackson and *Rings* producer Barrie Osborne had a date with the Prime Minister. The previous month, Helen Clark announced that the Labour government would be investing more than $4 million in promoting New Zealand at various *Rings*-related events. The least Jackson could do was come to Parliament and get his photo taken.

When Jackson emerged from his car onto the red carpet that evening, more than 10,000 people had gathered along Courtenay Place. People lined nearby verandahs and rooftops. *Fellowship*'s instant heart-throbs — its three hobbit co-stars and elfin archer Orlando Bloom — were greeted with spirited yells from some of the younger members of the crowd. But it was Jackson's arrival that got the loudest and most enthusiastic reaction. In one moment, the director had finally overturned that long-standing mantra of cinema which demands that actors must excite more public adulation than the person who actually calls the shots. There were so many autographs to sign that a half-hour passed before minders managed to get Jackson up towards the front of the theatre for speeches. Quoting a line from a story published in the *Middle Earth Post*, someone near the front of the crowd had readied a sign for him: 'Take a bow Mr Jackson'. So he took two.

Wellington's notoriously changeable weather adds to the drama of making movies, but on some days the added excitement is not required. The organisers of the premiere were very lucky: though the rain occasionally began to whisper, it never grew any louder. Meanwhile Black Riders strode around on the tarseal, refusing to discuss their roles with the crowd of international journalists in the media pen. The VIP guests trapped inside the theatre craned their necks to watch events from the windows.

Jackson had already donned his regulation purple shirt and black trousers for *Fellowship*'s world premiere in London nine days before, along with its first official screenings in New York and Los Angeles. But it was as if today the film had come home, along with the man who directed it. 'This is the real premiere,' Jackson told the enthusiastic audience. 'We can forget all the others.' Minutes before, he had told a reporter that after the 'VIP-type occasions' overseas, Wellington was the home crowd. 'They're all slightly biased out there.'

That night, the enthusiasm of Jackson's multinational cast helped fuel a hallucinatory notion that Wellington might indeed be the new creative centre of the universe. Asked what made *Rings* unique for him, Orlando Bloom's answer pretty much summed up the evening. 'New Zealand,' he replied. 'Wellington — we're home. This turnout says it all. We've been in London, Los Angeles, New York — and this kicks it, man.' Bloom was talking about raising his children there. Elijah Wood had fallen in love with it. Each time one of the hobbit cast members opened their mouths, the eyes of New Zealand's tourism chiefs grew a little wider.

To see Courtenay Place overflowing with so many people, it was clear that *Fellowship* had become a symbol of local, if not national, pride. But there was irony that now a New Zealand film had finally arrived with the scale and trappings of Hollywood, many of those who had long shunned local cinema could suddenly afford to stand on the streets and be patriotic. Hard though it can be to climb the mountain of public acceptance, there is a point in New Zealand culture where personal taste has nothing to do with it. *The Piano* is another good example: once its international profile had reached a certain level, New Zealanders embraced the film's achievements before they even knew what it was actually like.

By Thursday afternoon, when 6000-plus prints of *Fellowship* began unspooling from cinema projection booths around the globe, premiere razzmatazz would be replaced by financial reality. The true test of *Fellowship* had little to do with New Zealand cinemas — where the movie was already a virtual slam-dunk — but everywhere else.

Jackson knew from past experience that great word of mouth and masses of publicity are no guarantee of financial success. *Heavenly Creatures* had managed to achieve both, yet in the US at least, it had never broken out of the arthouse. His first Hollywood-funded movie *The Frighteners* had opened in 1600 theatres stateside and won some positive reviews, yet barely made a profit. With *Rings,* the stakes were far higher. If the first film failed to become a major blockbuster, there was a more than reasonable chance that the next two episodes would get kneecapped before completion — not necessarily assassinated, but starved of the post-production funding needed to make them shine.

As the premiere train hit Wellington, Jackson spoke of his relief that the walls of hype had finally lifted a little so that people could finally see the film that lay inside. But his relief was tempered with the tension of having to wait to find out how they would react.

AFTER THE PARTY

Almost a year before the premiere of *Fellowship of the Ring,* the cast and crew of the trilogy congregated in a warehouse on Wellington's waterfront. After a final rush of filming that Jackson compared to jet lag combined with the worst kind of hangover, the main shoot had come to an official end, just in time for Christmas. The party was nicknamed '*Escape from Middle-earth*', and it offered the opportunity to let everything out. One newcomer later wrote of walking into 'an enormous feeling of empathy and togetherness'. Amid the music, the drunkenness and the gift-giving, screens hanging from the rafters showed images of spectacular landscapes, of creatures in battle, of actors fluffing their lines.

As 2001 began, the studio bosses who had set the *Rings* odyssey in motion faced problems of their own. New parent company Time Warner forced Robert Shaye and Michael Lynne to slash their staff as part of company-wide cutbacks. Meanwhile two expensive projects — the Adam Sandler comedy *Little Nicky* and Cuban missile-crisis movie *Thirteen Days* — were falling short at the box office. During the next few months, Shaye said goodbye to Michael De Luca, and a number of other executives were replaced. In months to come, the rush to finish *Fellowship* would inevitably see tensions between its perfectionist director and the company whose well-being partly depended on what he pulled out of the hat.

In Wellington, the pressure now moved from the soundstages to the editing rooms, and the offices of Weta Digital, which was having some staffing issues of its own. In the last few weeks of the main shoot, the special-effects team saw the departure of three key figures — the trilogy's effects supervisor Mark Stetson (to be replaced by Jim Rygiel), and number one and number three in the Weta Digital hierarchy, Charlie McClellan and John Sheils. McClellan and Sheils had played a vital part in the company's expansion during the heady days of *The Frighteners*: neither was able to comment on their departure because of legal conditions imposed by their Weta contracts.

Early in 2000, *Rings* co-producer Tim Sanders had also left the building after working nearly three years on the trilogy. Media speculation, dismissed by Sanders in one of his few public comments, talked of clashes between him and New Line over budgeting and scheduling. (Later, there would be more speculation over New Line 'accidentally' leaving Sanders out of their lists of potential nominees when Academy Award promotions began.)

In the months before *Rings* started filming in October 1999, the company had searched the globe for someone willing to take on the job of being the trilogy's overall effects supervisor. At this point Weta Digital's international profile was not high. Finding a high-calibre candidate willing to relocate to New Zealand for a madly ambitious three-film project proved challenging. Stetson, whose effects work spanned more than sixty films from *Blade Runner* to *The Fifth Element*, got the job. When he left New Zealand just over a year later, the website E! Online cited 'creative differences' with Jackson as the reason.

SOMETHING BORROWED, SOMETHING NEW

While some filmmakers can become over-reliant on new technology as the magic answer to all their problems, Jackson knew that *Rings* would fly higher if it made use of old tricks as well as new. The trilogy's showpiece creatures — film one's trio of Cave Troll, octopus-like Watcher and fire-breathing Balrog, film two's Gollum, and film three's spider Shelob and airborne Nazgul — owed their existence to computer-generated effects. But the monsters were all born of more old-fashioned skills: close computer copies were made of monster designs which had been painstakingly sculpted in clay by members of Richard Taylor's Weta Workshop team. As for the walking, talking Treebeard, he is a combination of a four-metre high animatronic puppet and computer-generated imagery.

Though computer wizardry was often used to massage different images together in one shot, the majority of the film's buildings and structures were built for real, as large-scale miniatures: one model of the treetop kingdom of Lothlorien required 30,000 leaves to be applied by hand. Miniatures expert Alex Funke has spoken of the realism gained from shooting models which are so detailed that the camera can be brought as close in as two centimetres. 'It was actually easier and better to do it with miniatures,' he told *Cinefex* magazine. 'That was Peter's thinking. But it was a daring use of miniatures . . . we were talking about hundreds and thousands of miniature shots for the three films, and that was a huge commitment of personnel, time and equipment.' To add to the challenge, many of those working in the miniatures department were newcomers to this very specialised field.

Weta Workshop began filming the miniatures alongside the main shoot in October 1999, and would continue to point cameras at models for at least another three years. Not that miniature is necessarily the appropriate word: many of the models were bigger than houses. An outdoor model of Saruman's circular fortress at Isengard was eighteen metres in diameter, and survived four months out in the elements. The model included 1000 smaller miniatures, from crushing equipment to water sluices. In showing such models onscreen, Jackson challenged conventional views of how one goes about filming miniatures, by showing his keenness for sweeping, technically-demanding camera shots.

To convince the audience that 120-centimetre tall hobbits were real, the production made use of two golden rules of special effects: mix together every technique you can, and don't show anything onscreen for too long. Scenes in which hobbits and full-size humans interacted made use of every effects trick in the book, from blue-screen and short actors wearing sophisticated masks, to old-fashioned perspective tricks and double-sized sets.

Weta Workshop cranked out thousands of oversized hobbit feet which were laboriously glued on to the actors most mornings, and more than 10,000 foam-latex facial body parts, most of them for the orcs. Gelatine ears were applied to the elf characters, and nose extensions added to the actors playing Gandalf and Saruman. Excess noses were often gratefully gobbled up by honorary Weta staff member Gemma the dog.

Stuntmen in wigs did much of the work of Gandalf and Saruman during the wizard battle that leaves Gandalf exiled to the top of Orthanc's tower. Elsewhere, computers came in handy. Digitally-created humans filled in for members of the Fellowship during some of the more dangerous moments of their fight with the Cave Troll, and also the scene where the

Fellowship run over the narrow underground bridge of Khazad-dûm. Computer wizardry also allowed Elijah Wood's face to be digitally glued onto a shot of his smaller double. Elsewhere, digital doubles were used simply because Wood was needed in a number of sets at the same time.

DISCOVERING A NEW WAY TO FIGHT

Battle scenes involving thousands of warriors have always been difficult to pull off onscreen, partly because large regiments of soldiers can be difficult to find. Back when *Rings* was going to be *The Hobbit*, Jackson approached Weta digital-effects man Stephen Regelous and asked him to try to find a way that computers could make him some crowds. Rejecting the particle-based approaches favoured by other computer experts, Regelous began work on an ambitious program called Plod. This gave thousands of digital warriors primitive intelligence and the ability to react to those around them. The program allowed the development of epic battles that followed the collective whims of individual warriors, although aggressiveness and other features could be switched on and off by the programmers at will. The warriors generated a humming sound which helped them avoid crashing into one other, and the sound changed pitch depending on whether they were orcs or elves. In early tests of the program, later renamed Massive, Jackson and Regelous watched as hundreds of warriors attacked one another. Far off in the background, some soldiers could be seen leaving the field, looking for the enemy in entirely the wrong direction.

Twenty thousand computer-animated Massive warriors are seen in the prologue of *Fellowship*, while the climactic battle of *Return of the King* promises shots with close to 100,000 participants. In fact, Massive can be so realistic that even its creator cannot always pick which shots are using it. Regelous is now marketing his breakthrough program internationally.

Digital technology also proved useful in giving the film a distinctively soft look, in keeping with the work of Tolkien artists Alan Lee and John Howe. A whopping eighty percent of the first *Rings* movie underwent a digital grading process, which allows colours to be heightened at the touch of a computer wand, and a sunny day made to look overcast. The digital grade helped soften New Zealand's bright light, but rumours that it was used to make Elijah Wood's eyes even more blue than usual are not to be trusted. The opportunities opened up by computer technology meant that the look of entire sequences could be altered by Jackson right up until the last minute, which had negatives as well as positives — one effects technician referred to it dryly as 'an infinite tweakability problem'.

As *Fellowship* drew closer to completion, the number of special-effects shots had grown to almost 600, and it became obvious that Weta was not going to be able to make its October 2001 deadline without outside aid. Wellington company Oktobor were enlisted to take on some of the overflow, along with two companies in Australia. In America Digital Domain (*Titanic*) took on an ambitious scene where a river takes on the appearance of a torrent of horses, allowing Arwen and Frodo to escape the Black Riders. Back in Wellington, *Rings* paranoia had now spread beyond even Miramar and New York — at Oktobor, even staff who had no involvement in the *Rings* effects work were asked to sign contracts promising they would not talk about the project. (The involvement of non-Weta companies was later revealed in *Fellowship*'s closing credits.)

By early October, a number of Weta workers could be seen walking around Wellington in a state of bliss: after more than a month of working eighty-hour weeks, people began to imagine a new kind of future: one where they could actually go home at a reasonable hour. That Friday, many of the crew gathered as they often had before, to watch a selection of completed digital-effects work. Though a number of shots remained to be finished, the screening was also a signal that they would meet their schedule. The shots, taken from scenes scattered throughout the first film, added up to ten minutes or so in length. The theme to TV's *The Love Boat* played over some of the images, along with other cheesy tunes.

THE TENSIONS OF DREAMING BIG

When New Line boss Robert Shaye announced the company's plans to make three *Lord of the Rings* movies in one hit, he was gambling on Jackson's ability and good faith. 'There's no question that Peter didn't have the experience for a project this big, and to be honest, I hadn't liked all his movies,' Shaye told the *LA Times*. But he liked Jackson, was a fan of *Heavenly Creatures* and in *Rings* saw the potential for a massive built-in audience. 'It doesn't sound very rational, but sometimes trusting your instincts isn't a very rational thing to do.'

As the shooting date saw delay after delay, and the original plan to release all three movies over one twelve-month period began to look increasingly unwieldy, Shaye's decision to go with his gut must have given him some sleepless nights. Jackson's agent Ken Kamins has spoken of Shaye having 'moments of complete panic and stress, caused in part by his AOL parents'. New Line had handed the reins for three ambitious, effects-heavy movies to a person with only one film on a low-end Hollywood budget behind him, a film that had taken more than six months to shoot.

Italian director Bernardo Bertolucci (whose movie *1900* runs for over four hours) has talked of a feeling of omnipotence that often afflicts directors over especially long shooting schedules, when life and film start to become intertwined. Watching the seasons change while making *1900*, and accumulating more and more celluloid, Bertolucci found that he didn't want his movie to come to an end. In Jackson's case, with ample resources available, the worst-case scenario was that the director might do a Michael Cimino, and get so trapped in the filmmaking process that the sheer expense threatened to cripple the studio — as happened to MGM after the epic cost overruns of Cimino's western *Heaven's Gate*.

When New Line first announced *Rings* in August 1998, the proposed budget was 'more than $130 million', a figure that in reality sat closer to $US180 million. By the time the shoot began in October 1999, and Barrie Osborne (*The Matrix*) had signed on as producer, the figure stood at a more realistic $US270 million. The total is now thought to be closer to $US320 million, a figure in line with three medium / large Hollywood effects movies.

Around $US160 million of this budget was covered by a series of pre-sales deals which New Line had arranged with distribution companies around the globe — with the companies agreeing to exhibit all three films, sight unseen. *Harry Potter* was released in most countries by Warner Brothers, which helps explain why it might have been a little more devoted to its success than to *Rings*. *Variety* compared the distribution of *Fellowship* to a 'guerilla campaign fought by a loose network of local tribes with an unrivalled knowledge of the terrain'. Some of these local companies were in danger of going out of business if their gamble on the *Rings* failed.

New Line had shown its marketing nous in the 1980s with a number of tie-ins based on the *Nightmare on Elm Street* franchise. For *Rings*, it sold merchandising rights for more than forty products. When these rights were added to major sponsorship deals with companies like Burger King and JVC, more than $US70 million was shaved off New Line's costs for the trilogy. It was later revealed that a German investment company had also put money into *Rings*. New Line announced that its risk was no more than $US20 million a picture.

While New Line co-chairmen Robert Shaye and Michael Lynne both signed four-year contracts in the months before the release of the first *Rings* movie, their new corporate boss Richard Parsons admitted that he had 'looked real hard' at merging New Line and Warner Brothers. Lynne later said cryptically of *Fellowship*'s release that everything was at stake, 'and everyone knows it'.

With those kinds of pressures, conflicts between New Line and Jackson were probably inevitable. There were tensions about the rising budget, and disagreements about what scenes to chop out, Weta's capacity to handle the special effects, and how to promote the trilogy. Jackson had strong opinions on how the films should be marketed. Some say that friction between Jackson and New Line marketing head Joe Nimziki played a part in Nimziki's departure from the company in June 2001.

That month, Shaye, Lynne and six of their top executives flew to New Zealand by private plane for their first chance to watch a complete, though unpolished version of *Fellowship*. Just a few weeks before, at the Cannes Film Festival, twenty-five minutes of advance footage had met with an enthusiastic reaction from the press. Watching the three-and-a-half-hour rough cut, the New Line executives were relieved. The film was good.

In the final stages of finishing *Fellowship*, more heated discussions occured. Shortly before Jackson got on a plane for London to supervise the recording of the soundtrack, New Line staff told him that *Fellowship* needed a prologue, to help explain the complex history of the Ring. According to Jackson, they were not asking: they also demanded that it be only two minutes long. The scriptwriters had wrestled with the prologue idea before. After writing various versions narrated variously by Frodo, Gandalf and Isildur, they had decided to cut the idea entirely and put the information into other scenes of the film. In the end, you could argue that both sides won the day, and the film gains as a result — the spectacular final prologue, narrated by Cate Blanchett, runs six minutes. Composer Howard Shore had to write the music for it while recording the final soundtrack for the rest of the film.

UNLEASHING EPISODE ONE

Peter Jackson's dabblings in film have been winning international press for more than a decade, but the *Lord of the Rings* phenomenon took things to a different level. Among all the coverage, *Time, Newsweek,* the *Wall Street Journal* and *Entertainment Weekly* devoted long articles to Jackson, the usually little-quoted Fran Walsh and the *Rings* movies. A number of magazines (the normally trusty *Empire* among them) encouraged fans to indulge their collector's bent by shelling out for multiple copies of the same magazine, each with a different *Rings*-related cover. In the process, New Zealand's scenery got a great deal of free publicity. A writer from *Newsweek* swooped across craggy limestone plateaus and fern-touched beaches, so moved by the scenery that he started throwing up in the back of the helicopter. The man who had put the green vomit in *Bad Taste* would have loved it.

The media's desperation to be the first to the story reached some ridiculous heights. Even the normally movie-hype resistant *Listener* was drawn into the fold, wasting hundreds of words speculating exactly which films *Fellowship* would be going up against, in an article published a good eleven months before the premiere. In England, *Arena* published a map of New Zealand showing the breadth of *Rings*-related activity, but gremlins in the works meant that most of the action appeared to be happening in the ocean, south of a severely deformed South Island.

In the days before the world premiere in London on December 10, Tolkien fans awaited the first reviews of *Fellowship* in a state of mingled hope and fear. Again, the Internet was the place where the first news broke. Sometime in the early hours of November 28, twelve days before the official world premiere in London, an American home-theatre website posted the first review. Writer Ronald Epstein called *Fellowship* 'one of the most visually entertaining films ever made', and a great many other things as well. Meanwhile, an interesting fax was passing across the desk of OneRing.net co-founder Michael Regina in Montreal — a fax that contained the top-ten list of *Rolling Stone* critic Peter Travers, a week before it was due to hit the newsstands. *Fellowship of the Ring* was his number-one film of 2001.

The movie that is universally loved by all viewers simply does not exist, as anyone who has worked in a video store will tell you. But those first few days, where the early reviews grew from a trickle to a deluge, pretty much summed up the path to follow: the vast majority of viewers, whether film critics, Tolkien fans, or lucky moviegoers, were reaching for the accolades.

Newsweek's David Ansen, facing the unenviable job of being first critic into hard copy, praised 'Jackson's fierce, headlong movie' for its passion, emotion, terror and tactile sense of evil. The film, he wrote, 'takes high-flying risks: it wears its earnestness, and its heart, on its muddy, blood-streaked sleeve'.

Lisa Schwarzbaum at *Entertainment Weekly* spoke of intelligence, artistry and enchantment. *USA Today*'s Susan Wloszczyna found the film restored her faith in the epic blockbuster. CNN reviewer Paul Clinton wrote that the movie was the most successful adaptation of a book since *Gone With the Wind*. Some reviewers felt that the film did not provide enough gaps for viewers to breathe. Others called it flawless, thrilling, and extraordinary, and compared it to the work of David Lean and Akira Kurosawa.

At the Ain't it Cool News website, a reviewer known as Vertigo was reminded of the time long long ago when, as a seven-year-old, he had come out of a cinema with his heart beating at double speed, after watching the original *Star Wars*. Watching *Fellowship*, 'I feel like a child again because a film has won me over so completely, transported me so effectively, that I didn't want it to end.' One fan wondered if they could last the distance until the release date. 'How can I make it through the next thirteen days!'

On December 19, *Fellowship* opened simultaneously in eighteen countries. These days, the first fortnight of a big 'event' movie increasingly determines its overall returns. It does not matter if the film took eight years or one to make — death can be swift, especially at the American box office. In its crucial first weekend on nearly 3400 American screens, *Fellowship* made $66 million, more than double Jackson's entire American box office for the previous twelve years. A few weeks later, *Variety* published a list of the biggest-grossing movies of 2001 internationally. *Fellowship* had jumped up the list to eighth most successful movie of the year, twelve days after first hitting cinemas. By the end of the following year, it was the seventh most successful film of all time.

The movie industry is generally too fixated with dollar signs to bother much with judging movies by the number of people who actually paid to go see them. If they did, *Fellowship* would be somewhat lower on the chart. Either way, its success was difficult to deny.

Inevitably some Tolkien fans had problems with Jackson's changes. Yet by and large, Jackson seemed to have achieved irreconcilable aims — making a film that pleased an audience unfamiliar with Tolkien's world, while satisfying the majority of the fans for whom the text meant so much.

With *Fellowship* following *Harry Potter and the Philosopher's Stone* into cinemas, comparisons were inevitable. There is little doubt that *Harry Potter* won more criticism than it deserved as a result. Director Chris Columbus lamented that his film had been attacked for being a corporate machine, when *Rings* was the one whose characters could be seen as plastic figures at fast-food outlets. If Columbus had committed a crime, it was the forgivable one of following his source material too slavishly. A number of critics put their admiration for *Rings* in terms of criticism of *Harry Potter*, but clearly not all viewers agreed: the latter went on to become the second most successful film in the history of cinema (again, not adjusted for inflation).

TOUCHING A NERVE

Tolkien scholar Tom Shippey has argued that Tolkien's *The Lord of the Rings* offers a highly contemporary portrait of the nature of evil, and places Tolkien among a group of writers who fought in the two World Wars and were profoundly affected by it. For Shippey, the final chapters of the book, in which Sam and Frodo return to the shire, echo also the sense of disillusion and injustice felt in England directly after the Second World War.

After September 11, it was probably inevitable that the movie adaptation of Tolkien's work would be read through the prism of a new generation's headlines. *Fellowship* follows a group of disparate races who band together and journey to overcome a powerful evil. As they once had with Tolkien's book, some reviewers criticised Jackson's movies for showing us a world where good and evil are always easy to tell apart. But such a viewpoint missed sight of the way the well-meaning Boromir begins to fall under the spell of the Ring, let alone Frodo's own journey towards darkness.

A number of American journalists wrote features arguing that the cinematic success of *Rings* and *Harry Potter* signalled a shift in popular culture towards a distrust of technology. But while some saw in fantasy a welcome return to a simpler world, others found in Tolkien's work a place to express their anger. The launch of an online petition arguing that the movie of *The Two Towers* was intentionally capitalising on the tragic events at the World Trade Center proved counterproductive. The main result was a wave of joke-filled emails, expressing amazement that so many signatories were unaware that Tolkien's title had been in existence for four decades before the tragedy.

However, it was a strange quirk of fate that two of the twentieth century's most successful fantasy books arrived on cinema screens at the moment they did. *Harry Potter* and *Fellowship* offered a chance for a few hours' escape from a world living under threat of terrorist attack. Their success may yet spark a renaissance in putting fantasy onscreen: at the time of writing, movies or mini-series were in development for at least five major fantasy epics, including Eion Colfer's *Artemis Fowl* series and CS Lewis's *Chronicles of Narnia*.

The American studios increasingly rely for their financial well-being on an endless series of effects-heavy cinematic thrill-rides. But with *Fellowship*, New Line soon found itself in possession of that rarest of things: a film that reeled in millions while retaining artistic credibility and a coterie of adoring film critics. When awards season rolled around in the months following *Fellowship*'s release, Jackson's film vied for a number of major awards.

At London's Bafta awards in February 2002, 100,000 members of the public voted for their favourite film of the previous year. It had been a strong one for crowd-pleasers — what with *Shrek, Harry Potter* and *Bridget Jones's Diary*. When *Fellowship* won the public vote, Jackson's first words of thanks were for those back in Hollywood: New Line executives Shaye, Lynne and Ordesky, followed by his American lawyer and agent. But the award was also for 'everybody that really worked their guts out for fifteen months'. Later in the evening, Jackson ran directly up the stairs into the arms of Kate Winslet, who presented him with the award for best director. This time he gave thanks to his mother and father, his partner Fran and their two children, 'who know nothing in their lives other than Dad being on this film'. That evening, *Fellowship* took away the Bafta for best picture.

The Academy Awards remained. Fantasy and science-fiction movies can often be found on Academy Award nomination lists, though usually in technical categories like sound and special effects. When it comes to the all-important awards — especially best film and best director — many argue that fantasy is unfairly marginalised. In the quarter-century since *Star Wars* suddenly made fantasy viable in 1977, fantasy and science-fiction films have featured in best picture nominations on nine occasions. But in all those years, not one of those nominees went on to take the best picture award (unless, that is, you widen the fantasy genre to include the horror thriller *Silence of the Lambs*, which scored a clean sweep of the five major awards in 1991).

When the Oscar nominees for 2001 were announced, *Fellowship* had scored thirteen — a number shared with just six other films before it, and beaten only by the fourteen nominations managed by *All About Eve* and *Titanic*.

In *Fellowship*'s favour, the trend throughout the history of the Academy Awards has been for the most-nominated film that year to go on to take the best picture award. *Fellowship* also fitted snugly into the niche of epic movie, with an epic running time, that had ensnared Oscar voters in recent years. The question was whether the film's themes of good versus undeniable evil would count for or against it in a country sent into trauma by the events of September 11. In that sense, *Gosford Park* and the visually-opulent Australian contender *Moulin Rouge* were likely marginalised for being too lightweight.

The year 2002 saw something of an Australasian Oscar invasion. Aside from the Australian-made *Moulin Rouge* and the *Rings* crew (including the trilogy's unflappable Australian director of photography Andrew Lesnie), the nominees that year also included New Zealanders Russell Crowe (for *A Beautiful Mind*) and *Shrek* director Andrew Adamson.

The best picture Oscar was taken by Ron Howard's *A Beautiful Mind*. Jackson had to be content with *Fellowship*'s four Oscars for special effects, cinematography, makeup and original score. That night, Weta Workshop commander Richard Taylor became the first New Zealander to win two Academy Awards in an evening, and then hold one to each ear.

THE LORD OF THE RINGS ON FILM — A TIMELINE

1995 November: Peter Jackson mentions idea of filming Tolkien's work to Miramax boss Harvey Weinstein.

1997 April: Miramax wins rights to turn *The Lord of the Rings* into a film. Scriptwriting and research and development continues.

1998 June/July: Weinstein decides *Rings* should be made as one movie. The films are put into turnaround. Weinstein gives Jackson four weeks to find a company willing to make two *Rings* movies, after which the rights will return to Miramax.

1998 August: New Line Cinema announces three *Rings* movies to be made concurrently, beginning in May 1999, and released at six-month interludes over the space of one year. Pre-production and redrafting the screenplay goes into high gear.

1999 July 10: New Line announces Elijah Wood will star as Frodo Baggins.

1999 October 11: The trilogy begins filming on a hill overlooking Wellington city, for a scene where the hobbits first hide from a Black Rider.

2000 September 26: New Zealand Film Commission certifies to New Zealand tax authorities that the first film, *The Fellowship of the Ring* is complete to 'doublehead fine-cut' stage.

2000 December 22: Main shoot finishes around Wellington, followed by a party on the waterfront.

2001 May: Twenty-five minutes of *Rings* footage plays to media at Cannes Film Festival.

2001 October: Weta Digital completes its work on *The Fellowship of the Ring*.

2001 December 10: World premiere of *Fellowship* in London.

2002 February/March: *Fellowship* nominated for thirteen Academy Awards, and wins four. Its host of other awards includes five Baftas, one of them for best picture.

2002 August: *Fellowship* is released on video and DVD, followed in November by an extended version containing thirty minutes of new footage. The two-tiered release pattern will be repeated for the next two *Rings* movies.

2002 December: World premiere of *The Two Towers* in New York.

2003 December: World premiere of *The Return of the King* in Wellington.

CREATING GOLLUM

The Two Towers presented Jackson and Weta with some of their toughest challenges yet. Computer-animated, hyena-like wargs would fight off humans on horseback. Walking, talking tree creatures carried hobbits around the forest. Thousands of Uruk-hai warriors fought to conquer

Helm's Deep. But most terrifying of all was the creature Gollum, who crawls down a sheer cliff in Tolkien's book, muttering about the moon, and makes a permanent place for himself in the history of fantasy. If any one character had the potential to test Weta's new standing in the world of special effects, it was him. Seen in only six brief, shadowy shots in *Fellowship*, Gollum would need to be onscreen in *The Two Towers* for long periods, fighting, arguing and interrelating with Frodo and Sam as they journeyed towards Mount Doom.

Jackson had rejected the idea of creating Gollum with an actor in makeup, worried that his emaciated look and cliff-climbing abilities would be too difficult for a human to recreate. Sometime early in 2000, a team laboured to prepare a digital screen test to show Robert Shaye that Weta was up to the job. Gollum won the audition. English actor Andy Serkis, cast partly for the amazing voice he had offered at his first audition, found himself playing Gollum on-set as well, partly to give the human cast someone to act against. By January 2002, after the successful release of *Fellowship*, Jackson decided that Gollum needed a redesign from the neck up. The idea was to bring him closer in look to Serkis, whose performance Jackson now realised was key to bringing Gollum to life.

The complications of Gollum were enormous — even the twenty-five hairs on his head were a nightmare to animate. Computer-effects staff worked closely with design and makeup staff from Taylor's team to come up with a convincing look for the character, and 'paint' believable skin onto the computer model. Much time was spent trying to place Gollum convincingly into original footage of Serkis interacting with the rest of the cast, and extra muscles were added to Gollum's body to make his flexibility more convincing.

By coincidence, staff at Industrial Light and Magic in America were also in the final stages of breathing life into two other distinctive digitally-created characters at this time — the warrior Yoda in the second *Star Wars* prequel, and Dobby the nervous elf who steals an early scene in *Harry Potter and the Chamber of Secrets*. Though all were impressive creations, Gollum spent a lot more time onscreen, and the character's emotional complexity would win him praise as a major advance in the art of effects. A relative of one partially deaf person wrote in to TheOneRing.net to say that Gollum was the first CGI character he had seen whose lips made shapes that could be understood.

In the course of making *Rings*, Weta Digital has expanded from thirty staff to more than 250, three-quarters of them drawn from around the globe. In the midst of twenty-four-hour-a-day production demands, the company has tripled its disk storage, and spread across a number of buildings. The next problem will be updating half that equipment at the end of the trilogy.

ALL IN THE EDIT

By the time the main shoot of the *Rings* trilogy came to an end, over five million feet of film had been shot. Of this, around 3.5 million feet — or roughly 650 hours — was printed. To give a comparison, Terrence Malick's three-hour *Thin Red Line,* which used perhaps the most film of any fictional movie production, shot 1.5 million feet of celluloid, and 1.3 million feet were printed for the infamous *Heaven's Gate.* With months of reshoots still to come, there was a lot of film.

Unsurprisingly, one of the major challenges in the editing room lay in deciding exactly how long each *Rings* movie should be allowed to stretch. Anyone who has tried their hand at making a movie — even a short film done on an old camcorder — will know the temptation of stretching their little tale into two or three different ones: from the tight six-minute cut to the lazy version that contains all the pointless yet lovely shots one can't bear to lose. When your story has a main cast of more than twenty, all caught from multiple takes and angles, and a storyline that has always leaned on the epic side, the task of editing becomes entirely scarier.

In the case of *Fellowship,* one of the pressures on Jackson and editor John Gilbert was to make a film that did not harm its own potential box-office appeal by outstretching the attention span of the audience. They came up with various versions — one that ran to three and a half hours in length, another at three hours and eighteen minutes, and a 'short' cut which clocked in at a little under three hours. Apart from the promise that Jackson would supply New Line with a PG-13 rating for *Fellowship,* his contract stipulated that he deliver a two-hour movie. When he handed in an edit that was close to three hours, New Line would have been perfectly within its rights to ask him to take an hour of footage right out again and, if Jackson refused, to hire their own editor to complete the job.

When it came to how many minutes *Fellowship* would run, one question appears to have been uppermost in Jackson and Gilbert's minds: the precise point at which a bum on a cinema seat starts to become sore. As Jackson told *Onfilm*: 'We were finding out that, if the film was simply too long, people's emotions were somewhat numbed by the fact that they had been sitting down for so long. We found as we made the film shorter that people's tears would start to flow a bit more freely at certain times.' The decision to make the film Frodo-centric — and to cut away material that did not follow Frodo's journey — made the task of editing a little easier, but it also meant losing some strong scenes between other characters.

Filmmaker Krzysztof Kieslowski once suggested editing multiple versions of the same movie, each one slightly different from the last. That way, depending on which particular cinema you went to, you could experience a different movie. These days, his concept of a movie which exists simultaneously in multiple forms has come a step closer to reality. The arrival of another home-viewing format — DVD — has opened moneymen and audiences to the possibility that a film can be different things, depending on which particular copy you take home.

Until recent years, this possibility rarely raised its head in public apart from the bootleg cuts of certain films, like the butchered Goldie Hawn movie *Swingshift*, which circulated in certain parts of Hollywood and fandom. Then in 1980 Steven Spielberg reworked *Close Encounters of the Third Kind*, complete with a climactic glimpse inside the mothership. The success of the Kevin Costner epic *Dances with Wolves* in 1988 saw the release of a substantially longer cut. George Lucas later lavished phenomenal amounts of care on relatively minor editing changes and improvements to the first three *Star Wars* movies, which spoke volumes at the box office (on video, you can now pick which particular cut of *Star Wars* you want to rent). But these re-edits have been very much the exception, and on home video, fascinating, dramatically-extended 'director's cuts' of *Aliens* and *The Abyss* have often proved difficult to locate on rental shelves.

Sometimes the forces of commerce can bring unexpected benefits. With the increasing popularity of DVD, any potential extras that might make a movie's release seem more special than its competitors have been eagerly embraced. Partly as a result, the unusual nature of making three films in one go allowed Jackson to indulge his completist streak to the nth degree, and satisfy many *Rings* fans in the process.

At least as far back as the big-budget *Star Trek: The Motion Picture* in 1979, effects-heavy movies have often found themselves rushed through post-production, facing creative compromise in order to meet cast-iron release dates. But instead of rushing through editing, the extended schedule and staggered release dates of the *Rings* trilogy allowed constant rewriting and reappraisal, and the addition of newly filmed scenes. And the overwhelming success of *Fellowship* put Jackson in a position where he was given the resources to come up with a significantly longer cut of the film for video and DVD release. This knowledge must surely have had a beneficial effect on the editing process of *The Two Towers* and *Return of the King*. 'Darlings' which Jackson didn't want to murder, could be put safely into a coma, in the knowledge that the scenes could be resurrected later on the longer cut.

The DVD release of the trilogy has allowed Jackson to indulge the film-geek side of his personality. He has often dreamed of creating documentaries about the making of his movies. Despite the existence of extensive behind-the-scenes footage, such plans have so far been delayed by lack of time, and also by the desire that someone else pay for the result. With the *Rings* trilogy, New Line's resources and the extended space of the DVD format combined to allow the creation of one of the most exhaustive documentations of moviemaking yet seen onscreen.

The success of *Fellowship* meant that New Line was willing to put up extra money to shoot additional scenes for *The Two Towers*. An interview with Shaye before the film's release indicates that the relationship between director and studio boss might have had its rocky moments. Shaye described his and Lynne's concerns over a lack of clarity in early cuts of *The Two Towers* to *Entertainment Weekly* writer Gillian Flynn: 'It wasn't like, go ahead, and let's see your vision! It was, we can't stand this, we don't understand what's going on the first twenty minutes, and the film is four hours long! . . . It was his vision and he'd worked hard on it, but it was our $300 million. If you want a patron, go to Medici Films down the block.' (During one early cut, Gollum did not appear until over thirty minutes into the movie — perhaps this was the version Shaye referred to.)

However, we should bear in mind that Shaye has a reputation for straight talking, a quality so rare in Hollywood that it is easily misunderstood. New Line executive turned director Rachel Talalay recalls that Shaye appreciates honesty: 'If he was unhappy there was no mistaking it, but at least you could say what you thought.' It wasn't till after Talalay left New Line that she realised many in Hollywood smile and nod, and then put knives in your back: 'At least I always knew where I stood with Bob.'

Shaye spoke of the strong-mindedness of Pacific Rim people. 'They don't express the strong-mindedness in your face, so it's a little passive-aggressive thing, which isn't impossible to deal with.'

The promise that Jackson would be able to release the films at a greater length on DVD might well have been the glue which stopped such discussions from spinning out of control. That, and the presence of executive producer Mark Ordesky, who has spent much of the last few years on aeroplanes between Wellington and New York, performing a vital role as both door-to-door movie courier and diplomatic middleman. Ordesky had been a Tolkien fan and Dungeons and Dragons player from an early age. Later, when he ended up in the acquisitions department at New Line, he tried in vain to persuade his bosses to take a gamble on *Bad Taste* and *Meet the Feebles*. Then, he had helped get Jackson and Danny Mulheron the commission to write a screenplay for *A Nightmare on Elm Street*. Ordesky was a valued member of the *Rings* team. By the end of filming, when nine of the cast decided to band together to get a special tattoo with 'nine' printed in elvish, some of them suggested that Ordesky should get a tattoo as well. His tattoo is number ten.

THE TAXMAN

The most controversial aspect of *Rings* funding in New Zealand was the generous tax breaks afforded to the trilogy by the government. In 1999 the National government closed the loophole that made the *Rings* deal possible, yet reluctantly put a retrospective exemption in the law allowing the trilogy to escape the change. Incoming Labour finance minister Michael Cullen later said, 'No one wanted to look like they were out to destroy hobbits in election year.'

Under the scheme that is most commonly used, a subsidiary company is created in New Zealand, which qualifies it for tax deduction. The company is then sold back to an overseas film producer, say New Line, once the film has made a profit. (A similar scheme was used by an anonymous New Zealand investor for *The Frighteners*.) Essentially the scheme allows a local investor to get a large tax write-off, the bank (in the *Rings*' case, the Australian-owned Bank of New Zealand) to get a tax deduction, and the film producer not to have to pay for a film until later.

In July 2001, Michael Lynne said that the *Rings* tax incentive had saved around $US10–12 million for each film. The final figure looks to have been somewhat higher — estimates later put the cost to the New Zealand taxpayer at anywhere between $NZ200 and $NZ400 million. Michael Cullen thinks it unlikely that many of the *Rings* profits will return to New Zealand as taxable income. Others argue that the $200 million-plus tax 'loss' fails to take account of the trilogy's economic benefits, including hundreds of jobs.

Jackson has commented often about the positives of tax incentives, saying that local filmmakers are 'being penalised' by living in a country that does not have them, as opposed to say Canada, Ireland, Australia or England. The argument goes that Hollywood producers will not come here without them, although the arrival in New Plymouth of the Tom Cruise epic *The Last Samurai* in 2002 provided promising signs this is not always the case. In an interview just before the release of the first *Rings* movie, Jackson argued that if it had not been for the tax break, 'there was some talk' that the trilogy would shift into a Canadian-based production, 'and I would have been going up there with it'. In 2003, the Labour government, which had been resistant to tax breaks, introduced legislation that aimed to avoid the revenue-draining potential of previous tax loopholes while still encouraging foreign investment in film.

On the plus side, the trilogy provided hundreds of jobs, and gave New Zealand unprecedented exposure both as a possible filming location and as a place where expensive, technically complicated movies can be taken through to completion. And a number of crew members have survived the most concentrated upskilling of their lives. When *Fellowship of the Ring* had its Australasian premiere, journalists from Asia and America were invited inside Weta Workshop, to be wowed by models of Middle-earth. But many were fairly impressed by New Zealand's scenery as well.

COMING AT YA

When the *The Two Towers* arrived in cinemas in December 2002, it broke opening records in Australia, Argentina, Germany, Holland, Scandinavia, Switzerland and New Zealand. In the US, it made more money in its first week than either its predecessor, or the two *Harry Potter* films that Jackson's epics kept getting compared with. In two weeks *The Two Towers* had scored $US200 million in the US alone, and the same again around the rest of the world. At the time of writing, *The Two Towers* sat at number five on the list of top international blockbusters, $US40 million and two places ahead of *Fellowship of the Ring,* three places behind *Harry Potter and the Philosopher's Stone.*

Many critics of *The Two Towers* found the film sharper and faster than its predecessor; others felt that the epic nature of the movie came at the cost of characterisation. Almost everybody praised Gollum (apart perhaps from one disgruntled Tolkien scholar, aghast at Jackson's 'debased' changes to the text, who found even Gollum 'too evidently computer-generated'). Even those rare critics who were less than enamoured of the movie tended to agree that Tolkien's second book was a challenging task for anyone to adapt. *New York Times* reviewer Elvis Mitchell called *Towers* 'one of the most accomplished holding actions ever', a film whose engrossing action and grandeur would keep viewers gripped until the major plot developments of *Return of the King.* The *Guardian* described *Towers* as 'a majestic second installment; a saga of pace and weight that runs on a kind of demented, wing-and-a-prayer ambition'. Meanwhile Roger Ebert was one of many critics who sounded simultaneously awestruck and yet not completely won over. He found the movie visionary, rousing, and 'one of the most spectacular swashbucklers ever made', but in steering the film towards the action mainstream, he felt that Jackson had lost touch a little with the hobbits at its core.

As the Oscar campaign went into overdrive, New Line began putting ads in *Variety,* asking that the Academy consider six of the *The Two Towers* cast for supporting actor nods, including Elijah Wood, Viggo Mortensen and Andy Serkis. In the end, the film won six nominations, most of them in technical categories.

The Oscar season for 2003 came at a strange time. Over in the Middle East, captured American soldiers were being paraded on television screens, and the American military machine's plans for a lightning fast 'liberation' of Iraq were not moving as hoped. In the days leading up to the ceremony on March 24, the Oscar organisers struggled to decide how to play things in the face of real-life war.

Interviewed in the week before the Oscars, Jackson questioned the timing of the prizegiving and wondered whether there would be much of a mood of celebration on the night. 'I don't think it's a particularly great thing for people to be in tuxedos congratulating themselves when people are dying in another country.' In the end, the Oscar organisers decided to let the show go on, but minimised the razzle-dazzle aspects of the festivity, cut back on the red-carpet arrivals, and asked award-winners to keep speeches short and non-political.

Jackson decided to stay home, joining many of his crew to watch the Oscars from a bar in Wellington. The decision was not just his own: New Line had expressed worries that a terrorist incident might close airports, trapping him in the US, just weeks before reshoots for *Return of the King* were due to begin.

The Academy did not seem to know what to make of *The Two Towers*. There were rumours that it had been shut out of the nominations for best makeup, because it was considered the same film as *Fellowship*. *Towers* also came close to being disqualified for best score for the same reason, until the Academy's music committee decided to delay a stricter re-interpretation of the rules for another year.

In Wellington, just down the road from the *Rings* get-together, the Embassy Theatre made arrangements once more to beam the awards live onto the cinema screen. Four hundred people turned up to celebrate. The afternoon's compères set up a special voting board — any Oscar for *Towers* would earn it two bonus points, while each joke about Renée Zellweger needing a good meal meant that *Chicago* had lost a point. In the end, the deeply partisan scoring offered *The Two Towers* its only chance at victory. Twenty minutes in, *The Two Towers* effects team beat out *Star Wars Episode 2: The Attack of the Clones* and *Spiderman* to win the visual-effects Oscar, but the Wellington audience had to be content with just one more technical award from its original six nominations.

Though *The Two Towers* had been nominated for best picture — one of the only sequels ever to have done so, which for a fantasy film was an achievement in itself — the movie failed to score any Oscar nominations in acting, writing or direction. Instead, the evening became a tussle between *The Pianist*, which took major awards in all three categories, and the Miramax musical *Chicago*, nominated for thirteen awards and eventual winner of six, including best picture.

The *Rings* trilogy has become much more than just a collection of movies. It is also a museum exhibit, a collection of New Zealand-made sculptures, a bus tour of film locations, a questionable government report and a miniature book industry all on its own. The films have inspired comedy from MTV, the *South Park* show, Tolkien fans and British comedians French and Saunders. There have been reports of *Rings*-related piracy in Shanghai, Serbia and cyberspace. In Moscow, a man has made a mint redubbing the first two movies with the orcs as Russian gangsters, and Gandalf prone to showing off how much Karl Marx he knows.

New Zealand has embraced the trilogy, and not just because almost everyone knows someone who was involved in making it. *Fellowship* is now the most successful film in the country's history, having managed to dislodge the behemoth that is *Titanic*; *The Two Towers* ranks at number three. Whether the films will lead to a surge in visitors to New Zealand remains unclear. Statistics to date show no major rise, but given the impact of September 11 on air travel, it may be too early to tell. Certainly, New Zealand's profile overseas has risen massively as a result.

A DIFFERENT WAY

The compound stresses of making the *Rings* trilogy are difficult for anyone to imagine. On top of bringing Tolkien's mammoth work to the screen, Peter Jackson has lost both his parents. His father died at the age of 78, just weeks before Miramax put the films into turnaround. Joan Jackson passed away three years later, a few weeks before *Fellowship* began conquering the globe.

The man who began his career editing, shooting and creating his own movie monsters now has an empire encompassing almost every aspect of filmmaking. It started, of course, with the special-effects company Weta, which Jackson established with a small group of his filmmaking collaborators. In December 1998 he purchased New Zealand's largest film laboratory, the former National Film Unit, and began modernising its editing and sound suites. Three years later, work began on relocating the Film Unit to a custom-built facility in Miramar, saving many other filmmakers the half-hour drive to Lower Hutt. There are hopes that the facilities will attract international filmmakers not only to shoot in New Zealand, but also to complete their films here as well. Altogether, Jackson has a stake in at least eight film-related companies.

'I'm pouring a lot of my own dough into it,' he told *Onfilm*.

> *I'm taking a gamble because I'm building a post-production facility that I know is not viable in New Zealand . . . What I'm trying to do is make overseas productions the bread and butter of the facility, so New Zealand films can benefit from the fact that there's one of the best mixing facilities in the world here . . . I'm ultimately doing it for myself because I'm in a situation now*

where I want to stay in New Zealand, and be able to continue to make the sort
of films I'm doing. I just want to make sure that I've got facilities for me to use
that are as good as what George Lucas has got to use up at his place. I want to
be on an even playing field with these guys. So I'm going for it, and keeping
my fingers crossed that I'm not making a huge mistake.

For Jackson, planning and improvisation go hand in hand. In one sense the preparations for *Rings* were more thorough than one might expect: before the first day of shooting, the entire trilogy already existed as a primitive animated movie made up of hundreds of production drawings, complete with voices and music. But when it came to the actual shoot, actors were encouraged to bring their own ideas about characters, and the script was in a constant state of change. Miranda Otto describes Jackson as 'very much a guerilla filmmaker, working everything out on the day'.

Jackson is a director who adapts quickly to problems. When one set in the South Island was rendered unusable by heavy rain, he simply got in a helicopter, and spotted another location they could use instead.

The director is known for shooting a lot of coverage of his scenes — allowing more latitude in the editing room — and for closely monitoring the development of special-effects shots. These days, expensive effects-heavy movies are sometimes rushed through post-production in as little as six months. But not *Rings*. Through a combination of factors — notably Robert Shaye, a courageous, gutsy studio head willing to bankroll a three-film project, and the cushioning provided by phenomenal success — Jackson has been permitted to complete the last two *Rings* movies at a more relaxed pace, and to indulge his urge for perfectionism. As he told *Onfilm*:

You always try for the very best and never stop trying. You always push until
you can push no more. It's a philosophy I feel very strongly about . . . I never
like to settle for anything and then just say, 'Okay, this is as good as it can be.'
Because I think everything can always be improved, everything can be better.
It just comes down to a question of . . . you run out of time to make things
better, so you buy what you've got.

Moviemaking is ultimately a battle between the quest for perfection, and the time you have to try to catch it in. There are always compromises. *Rings* producer Barrie Osborne wrote a memo to staff before the completion of the first film on this very subject. The so-called 'elephant memo' was inspired by Osborne's time as a production manager on *Apocalypse Now*, a film that famously went months over schedule. He arrived in the Philippines and found that director Francis Ford Coppola was obsessed with filming a scene that required an elephant. Osborne, who spent time in Korea as a US Army engineer, spent days trying to work out the logistics of getting an elephant to the set, a job that would require rebuilding eight bridges. Then Coppola reappeared, and told Osborne to forget the elephant.

'But that sequence was so important to you — why have you changed your mind?' asked Osborne.

'Because I've been trying to make a perfect movie,' replied Coppola, 'and I've finally realised that it's impossible.'

When it came to *Rings*, Osborne remembered the incident. He wrote a memo to key personnel, reminding them of the elephant and what it signified. 'All of the key creatives have been striving to make a perfect movie — there's always a bit more that can be improved on,' Osborne later said at a film conference. 'But finally it was down to me to say, "Peter, we've got to deliver the movie."'

Jackson's next film is called *The Return of the King*. It has been cooking for at least three years. One does not have to put one's neck out very far to say that expectations are high.

ORLANDO BLOOM

Of all the actors who got tattoos to commemorate working on *Rings*, Orlando Bloom has been the quickest to make his mark on other projects. On Tolkien fan-sites, posters of him as the long-haired elf Legolas outsold every other *Rings*-related image after the release of *Fellowship* (New Line even took his popularity among teenage girls into account in their marketing plan for *The Two Towers*). Bloom went on to appear in *Black Hawk Down* and *Ned Kelly*, and a run of magazine covers, before cementing his stardom opposite Johnny Depp in *Pirates of the Caribbean*. His first starring role is as a boxing milkman in *The Calcium Kid*.

PHILIPPA BOYENS

The woman whose first experience of movie scriptwriting became one of the largest projects in cinema history is now working once more with Peter Jackson and Fran Walsh, rewriting the Beauty and the Beast epic *King Kong*. Signed with major American agency ICM, Boyens also wrote the script for a mini-series of the Ursula Le Guin classic *A Wizard of Earthsea*.

CHAPTER SIXTEEN

PAST AND FUTURE

'Holy mackerel — what a show!'
MOVIEMAKER CARL DENHAM, WHILE SEARCHING A REMOTE ISLAND
FOR AN APE CALLED KING KONG

'Crikey!'
WOMAN IN MONTY PYTHON TELEVISION SKETCH, ON DISCOVERING
A TENNIS RACQUET EMBEDDED IN HER STOMACH

*'The movie is what it is. I don't analyse it. I watch it, and I'm happy,
and I'm more interested in what to do next.'*
PETER JACKSON

Of necessity this biography comes to a close in September 2003, with its subject caught in freeze-frame, halfway across a pedestrian crossing. Behind him lies a series of movies encompassing bloodshed, comedy and multiple Academy Awards. Just ahead, the view is blocked by the last episode of a trilogy, and an ape called King Kong.

Only time will tell whether Jackson's career continues to be defined through the prism of one movie project — a project whose sheer scale threatens to blot out the range he displayed in earlier films. That would be a shame, because Jackson's shadow had already gone to some extraordinary places before arriving in Middle-earth.

Two childhood inspirations are key to exploring the creative path taken by New Zealand's most commercially successful director: an increasingly dark, relentless fantasy about a gigantic ape, and an eighty-second television sketch in which some upper-class toffs keep losing their limbs. *King Kong* and Monty Python illustrate some of the dangers of trying to marshal Peter Jackson's first seven movies into a neat pattern, and make any sense of his career.

The Monty Python sketch 'Salad Days', which Jackson claims as a key influence on his early work, begins with some people grouped around a piano in the sun, and ends for no intelligent reason, with serious health problems for most of those present. A lot of blood flows onto the lawn, though the man who loses his hands in the piano looks only mildly annoyed. If we were to take this short sketch as a template for his career, the picture that emerges is of Jackson as an absurdist of carnage, finding his voice with a trio of films (*Bad Taste, Meet the Feebles* and *Braindead*) which turn bodily dismemberment into the stuff of comedy. From this perspective, many of Jackson's splatter fans see *Rings* less as progression than as transgression, for daring to abandon the outrageous humour that first made his name.

The alternative is to begin with the 1933 classic *King Kong* — which Jackson says first turned him into a filmmaker — and argue for Jackson as a fantasist for whom splatter movies have been part of a learning curve, as he reaches for the resources and skills to unleash his urges towards epic fantasy. But either of these approaches leaves the most fascinating movies from his second, more experimental cycle — *Heavenly Creatures* and *Forgotten Silver* — out of the picture.

In fact, there is only one major element common to every feature film Jackson has made to date, and that element is special effects. In three of Jackson's movies — *Meet the Feebles, The Frighteners*, and *Lord of the Rings* — many of the cast rely on the presence of special effects for their very existence (for the sake of thematic ease, this chapter will count the *Rings* trilogy as one movie, though discussing only the two films released at the date of writing.) Spectacular special effects effectively hijack the final reels of *Bad Taste* and *Braindead*, and provide a key function in creating the alternative worlds of *Heavenly Creatures*. Although the fake television documentary *Forgotten Silver*, co-directed with Costa Botes, uses special effects sparingly, it does so again in important scenes. *Forgotten Silver* may take a different route, but it works from a similar urge to con the audience, and shares with many of Jackson's films a joy in creating ridiculous visions.

Like many of Jackson's early influences, both *King Kong* and 'Salad Days' depend on special effects for much of their impact. Jackson quickly made the jump from enjoying such scenes of cinematic illusion, to finding out exactly how they were created. His own childhood dream of becoming a special-effects man provided a path into directing short films, but even into his twenties, he appears to have still felt conflicted over whether his future lay in making illusions or making movies.

An over-reliance on stunts and special effects is often blamed for the wrongs of modern cinema. The big Hollywood studios have been accused, with some reason, of flooding the marketplace with movies that are more interested in easy spectacle than storytelling or character. Yet the power to excite and deceive viewers has long been part of what makes cinema distinct from other media. The visions created by special effects encourage the kinds of responses that are forgotten by adult viewers at the price of the worst kind of maturity: the ability to laugh for no intelligent reason, and make strange noises like 'wow' and 'yuck'. The 'wow', the 'yuck' and the giggle of laughter are as vital to Jackson's films as anything he might have to say about the world, and that is no bad thing.

Like Steven Spielberg, another master of special effects, Jackson in his films displays a childlike sensibility, the instincts of a popular entertainer, and a desire for periodic reinvention. Both immersed themselves in film technique as children, thanks to supportive parents and an 8mm camera. They both like to *wow* an audience. But the child found in Jackson's films is closer to Roald Dahl than to the Walt Disney found in early Spielberg. There is something childlike in Jackson's idea that a puppet massacre is funny, that chainsawing your way through the inside of an alien is the stuff of entertainment.

Jackson's first cycle of movies — the splatter cycle of *Bad Taste, Meet the Feebles* and *Braindead* — are packed with special effects, yet their urge is essentially comedic. Watching *Bad Taste*, you get a sense of a bunch of young New Zealand males returning to adolescence and indulging in some of the most basic joys of childhood for the camera — chases, acting like idiots, dangling off cliffs. The film benefits from the unglamorous, untutored nature of its cast. In some of its best moments, special-effects technique is put to the service of comedy — the priceless scene where Ozzy drop-kicks an alien head out the window, the yell of 'Mummy!' which accompanies one character's long fall to a sticky end. Jackson spent hours working on the special effects used for such scenes, and pulling off such illusions provided him with a film school where he could learn from his own mistakes.

LIKING OURSELVES

A pragmatic, no-nonsense spirit has long been celebrated as a vital part of the New Zealand character. This knack for finding a way through in the face of low budgets and bad weather helped ambitious movies like *Bad Taste* and *Goodbye Pork Pie* reach the screen. But that same 'talk less, get on with it' attitude can also prove a cultural liability. Creativity is about ideas and images that grab us for reasons which are not always easy to explain. We can be pulled towards the ridiculous, the beautiful and the revolting. Talking openly about your reaction to a particular movie or book therefore requires putting more of yourself on the line than just saying that the scrums were good.

Scared to sound pretentious, or stretch their heads above the crowd by showing admiration for a book or film that the rest of the world has yet to see, New Zealanders will often fall back on the safety of old mindsets: the idea that New Zealand films must automatically be crap, that New Zealand comedy is an oxymoron, that sports are all we do well. But we live in an age where the cultural cringe is being asphyxiated by cultural riches — in music, the cringe is already thankfully dead. In the medium of cinema, the release of *Rings* will be seen as a key moment in making New Zealanders face up to the fact that their filmmaking talent is equal to any on the planet.

Peter Jackson grew up in a culture that was fiercely proud, yet which frowned upon show-offs and people in fancy cars. The Kiwi cliché of hero has long been that of the rugby player who says little, but just puts his head down and gets on with it. Jackson's childhood idols put their heads down in other ways — they were possessed skeletons, and annoyed apes, alongside the special-effects men who laboured to bring such creatures to the screen. Jackson's own way of getting on with it was to labour for hours in his bedroom, creating his own monster movies.

That Kiwi distrust of showing off for the sake of it has fed into Jackson's distinctive handling of screen illusion. There is something quintessentially Kiwi about creating an eye-opening image, and then feeling compelled each time you show it to make a joke. Right from the bloodsoaked opening of *Bad Taste*, Jackson has shown a compulsion to mix outrageous imagery with humour. His early movies are caught up in a battle to be both tasteless and likeable at the same time. *Braindead* is anchored by a romance with the naivety and charm of a Chaplin movie: but the poor hero has to undergo one of the bloodiest climaxes in cinema history. *Meet the Feebles* stars a cute hedgehog who looks and acts like something from Walt Disney. Almost everyone else in the *Feebles* cast has a dark secret, an addiction, or is doomed to be massacred in the finale.

Comedy, horror and splatter ultimately spring from the same well. Putting each on the screen is about combining an effective lead-up with an effective punch-line — whether it be the comic payoff, a monster jumping into frame or an eruption of violence. But splicing horror or splatter together with comedy is a delicate balancing act, requiring precise command of timing and mood. Jackson's first film *Bad Taste* sometimes lacks both, but its best moments are a comic delight. By the time Jackson finished making his superlative third movie, *Braindead*, he had joined the small group of international filmmakers to have mastered the difficult genre of splatter-comedy.

Braindead (whose opening location, Skull Island, nods to *King Kong*) is a rare case where an overload of special effects works to the movie's advantage. Yet the danger with fantasy and splatter is how easily spectacle can overwhelm the storyline. In *Meet the Feebles*, the wharfside battle scene feels more like a special-effects showreel than part of the plot, and the puppet massacre that follows makes clear the film's major limitation: it is more interested in bad-taste humour than in our sympathies for the characters. Some of those characters are wonderful comic creations, and the Vietnam take-off is a marvel. But after about an hour, the gags begin to pall.

Braindead seems to have got the spirit of special-effects excess out of Jackson's system. The finale is a twenty-five-minute orgy of sight gags, moving from possessed intestine to zombie with pot on his head with such wit and pace that there are only a couple of chances to gag.

Part of what makes Jackson's work distinctive is the balance he strikes between showing off, and avoiding the pits of movieland cliché. Though his films are loaded with special effects, there are precious few scenes in which the plot comes to a standstill, and the music swells up to showcase a grand special-effects moment. He is the best kind of stylist — one with a gift for turning technique to suit the needs and pace of the scene, and for grounding fantastic images in reality. His wizards are mudsplattered; his monsters don't stop to pose. In *Rings*, the sequences where the demon-like Balrog battles Gandalf are state-of-the-art, yet their magic lies partly in Jackson's knowledge that illusion is about not giving the audience too much. He manages the difficult task of keeping the firebreathing Balrog as shadowy and elemental on first appearance as Tolkien's original description on the page. The aerial battle between Balrog and Gandalf which kicks off *The Two Towers* is a surrealistic thrill-ride of motion and fire.

Such moments connect directly to the 'wow' felt by Jackson as a child watching *King Kong* and the stop-motion monsters of Ray Harryhausen. The scene in *Fellowship*, where the heroes battle an angry cave troll in Balin's tomb, plays as if a documentary camera crew has jumped inside a *Sinbad* movie, and run off with all the most exciting shots.

The years of honing his skills on silent home movies can be seen in Jackson's work. The movement of the camera, and the magic of the edit, are key elements in his cinematic vocabulary. His camera is often impossible to tie down, and he has a knack for intensifying drama by cutting back and forth between different time periods in the middle of a scene (most obviously in the hospital climax of *The Frighteners*, and Aragorn tracking Merry and Pippin into Fangorn forest in *The Two Towers*). Perhaps the biggest technical achievement in *Rings* is the one that is least showy: an effortless use of editing and special effects to create a world where tall and short believably co-exist.

OTHER WORLDS

Jackson's love affair with special effects plugs directly into his interest in taking audiences beyond the everyday, an interest fuelled by the dinosaur-infested world of *King Kong*. 'I like movies that will take you places that you would never normally go in your life,' he said in 1991. 'They're fairground rides where you jump on board and go for a ride, hop off again and you're back in the real world.'

Sometimes Jackson's worlds plug directly into the traditions of the fantasy and horror genres — whether it be warriors and little people, or bloodthirsty zombies. Yet even when his movies are set in a carefully defined historical period, imaginary kingdoms normally provide a key element in the story.

Jackson often achieves a satisfying tension by indulging in a brand of naivety and gormlessness, while simultaneously celebrating the idea of cinema as a gateway to a stranger, more exciting world. Poor Lionel in *Braindead* is still probably the best example of this, but there is an essay to be written on all those Jackson movies in which something outlandish crashes into a defiantly humdrum Kiwi universe — whether it be the aliens in small-town Kaihoro in *Bad Taste* or *Heavenly Creatures*'s visions of paradise in 1950s Christchurch. But we should be wary in trying to find too much meaning in seeing conservative New Zealand so often under attack. Jackson has never been the kind of man to have much time for peace and harmony, especially with a potential massacre in the offing. Working on low budgets, it is natural that he would use the country outside his front door as the main location for his bloodshed.

After five movies, *The Frighteners* marks Jackson's first attempt to play a different kind of trick, by convincing his audience that New Zealand is really the US. The result is an unpredictable fun ride that ricochets back and forth between comedy and thrills before its *tour-de-force* finale. Ghosts, grim reapers, serial murderers and plain emotional wrecks populate the film. The premise of a man using friendly ghosts to scare up work as a paranormal housecleaner is an ingenious one, but the universe established by the movie finally fails the test that separates great fantasy from rollercoaster ride: it does not always obey its own rules. The thrill-a-minute opening sequence sadly turns a key plot revelation from brilliant twist into a betrayal of the audience, and a couple of important plot-points — including the reason why the villain dresses as the Grim Reaper — appear to have been neglected in the rush to meet the film's tight deadline.

In their first movie with American actors, Jackson and Walsh demonstrate yet again their near-total mastery of casting, and nowhere more so than in the person of *Re-Animator* star Jeffrey Combs. His portrait of an FBI man who finds strong women more stressful than psychokillers is a dark comic delight. The movie's ghost characters are the only ones to come off badly: the guntoting judge aside, their gags are tired.

The central characters in Jackson's movies tend to be underwritten, but Frank Bannister is a special case. The storyline demands a character who, in the eyes of the audience, may not be entirely trustable — for the movie's first hour, it is as if the scriptwriters are trying to increase Bannister's likeability by making everybody around him more annoying, or more annoyed. But in the second half, Michael J Fox is permitted to bring an understated vulnerability to the role: the humanity of he and co-star Trini Alvarado helps knit the many collisions of *The Frighteners* together.

Fantasy has taken Peter Jackson from cult fame to Hollywood force. His handling of Tolkien's best-known tale has put Frodo Baggins alongside James Bond and Luke Skywalker as one of the most successful ongoing stories in movie history, and with good reason. *The Fellowship of the Ring* is the pot of gold that fans of the fantasy genre have long hoped for: a thing of vision and magic, and respect.

Key to Jackson's achievement is his awareness that realism is as important to Tolkien as to John Grisham. Obviously that realism is a heightened one, but in a world as complex as Tolkien's, keeping the storyline both accessible and believable takes consummate skill. Jackson achieves the difficult task of setting up a race of undersized characters with a love of the good things in life that could easily have drifted into kitschiness. And once Frodo leaves Hobbiton carrying the Ring, Jackson creates a palpable sense of the danger of his mission and of the terrifying forces that follow.

The movie does not lack for high-tech thrills, but there is something old-fashioned and down-to-earth about it. *Fellowship* puts storytelling ahead of the urge to constantly wow the audience. It dares to embrace goodness and good fellowship above winks to camera. As Frodo, Elijah Wood's effortless performance and childlike features personify sensitivity and innocence under threat. The character may have lost some hobbit years and rough edges on the way to the screen, but he makes you believe.

Beside Frodo, Ian McKellen's Gandalf and Viggo Mortensen's Aragorn are lessons in how to bring iconic characters to life, reinvigorating the roles of likeable wizard and reluctant hero with authority and understatement. As for the rest of the Fellowship, Jackson's decision to make the theatrical cut of the film Frodo-centric leaves them few chances to make their mark, which is probably inevitable in a movie with so many characters. The extended DVD cut of *Fellowship* reveals that Jackson was probably never all that interested in the rest of the Fellowship anyway — only Sean Bean's Boromir, already one of the stronger characters, benefits from the increased running time.

When it comes to Tolkien's elven characters, *Fellowship* stalls when it should soar. Hugo Weaving's grand, declamatory Elrond derives not from another race but the wrong drama entirely. The film's quasi-mystical low point is found in the forests of Lothlorien, with the appearance of flowing-haired Galadriel (Cate Blanchett) and a jug of water. For a rare moment, you sense a director who has lost his way in Middle-earth, reduced to putting a great actor through the motions. However, the scene's 'wow' moment, when Galadriel transforms briefly into something darker, has a certain over-the-top magic despite the incomprehensibility of Galadriel's dialogue.

The elves were never going to be easy to pull off, and their uninspired, overly abbreviated treatment is the price we pay for a director more in his element when the elves are on horseback or firing arrows. Jackson's strengths are not the ethereal moments but the darker, more immediate qualities of caves overrun with orcs and monsters, and the unearthly cries of approaching Black Riders.

For all his mastery of screen excitement, it is finally our connection to the characters that makes this movie work. The most powerful moment in *Fellowship* is not Gandalf's battle with the demonic Balrog, spectacular though that is. It is the one following straight after where time seems to stand still, and Aragorn watches helplessly as arrows continue to fly past him. He is looking back to where Gandalf has fallen. In years to come, after another deluge of heartless Hollywood spectacles, we will turn on our DVD players and be reminded anew that *Fellowship* is more than just a thing of bluster and hype: it is a landmark in fantasy film.

THE TWO TOWERS

The book published as *The Two Towers* lacks the narrative drive that carried Frodo through the majority of *The Fellowship of the Ring*. Jackson's movie adaptation minimises the weaknesses, saves the spider till later, and makes the most of the positives. The result is a movie of great confidence and sweep, which nonetheless occasionally feels less certain of its tone. The danger in measuring the 'difficult' middle episode against the brilliance of *Fellowship*, is of unfairly finding one of the most energetic movies of 2002 wanting. But with Frodo falling increasingly under the power of the Ring, and Gandalf reborn in a new and more clichéd form, it is probably inevitable that *The Two Towers* loses something of the heart of the first movie. One senses too a director relaxing a little in the editing suite, allowing himself some regrettable moments of silliness that would not have made it into the final cut of *Fellowship*, simply because back then too much was riding on the movie's success.

The most memorable characters in *The Two Towers* owe as much to special-effects wizards as actors. After the emaciated Gollum crawls down a cliff to try to steal the Ring from Frodo, the creature quickly becomes unforgettable in the way only great fantasy characters can. He is a thing both elemental and out of this world. Gollum helps to dramatise the Ring's increasing power over Frodo: the scene where the creature sits down close to the camera and we watch as a psychological battle wages between his good side and his bad is like watching that scene in *2001*, when the bone transforms into a spaceship. In a moment of movie time, the art of special effects has jumped exponentially forward — by taking us at last inside someone's mind, special effects have given us a new and more special kind of *wow*.

While Sam and Frodo try to decide whether Gollum can be trusted, Merry and Pippin are escaping from capture into the darkness of Fangorn forest. There they meet an ancient creature known as Treebeard. Witnessing the first scene where the tree opens its eyes, and begins to carry Merry and Pippin through the forest, all my critical facilities were lost. Great fantasy is ultimately about such moments, individual though they are for each viewer — moments where the familiar has become alien.

At its best, the first two *Rings* movies show us a director in absolute command of sound and vision: a man who can spin unbearable suspense from four hobbits hiding terrified in a tree-hollow, and who makes us feel and hear every flap of the wings of the creature that hunts Frodo in the dead marshes.

The battle of Helm's Deep provides the second film with a spectacular, though slightly wearying climax. In this narratively complex middle episode, Frodo's path into darkness does not entirely work, though the task is not an easy one. As Eowyn, Miranda Otto is left to add some doses of much-needed humanity, Viggo Mortensen shines in almost every scene and Liv Tyler's Arwen cries a little.

 In the film's final few minutes, we are left with that extraordinary speech by Sam about hope, shortly after Frodo offers himself up to a winged Nazgul. In this scene, added late in the movie's development, Sam compares his and Frodo's situation to the stories 'that really mattered', stories in which the characters kept fighting for the idea 'that there's some good in this world'. Some of Sam's lines sound embarrassingly biblical, but that does not stop it being a courageous moment for Jackson. It is difficult to read this scene as anything other than an argument for the worth of fantasy in a complicated world. One of Jackson's only obvious statements of theme to date comes in the form of a defence of storytelling as a force linked to courage and good.

A COMMUNITY OF TALENT

It would be taking the auteur theory to its illogical extreme to argue that Peter Jackson is the only force involved in making his films what they are. Indeed, it could be argued that Jackson is at his best when the starting point is another person's story. His best films support this theory — *Braindead*, from an idea by Stephen Sinclair; *Heavenly Creatures*, adapted from a real-life tragedy, and instigated by his partner Fran Walsh; *Forgotten Silver*, instigated by co-director Costa Botes; and *Rings*, adapted from Tolkien. Thankfully Jackson does not suffer from the delusion of many directors that he can write great scripts on his own — the scripts to his movies have all been collaborations.

The most obvious people to mention here are Sinclair, who had a hand in writing three of Jackson's seven films to date; and Walsh, who co-wrote five. Walsh also played a vital part in the music and production of the *Rings* trilogy, the casting of *Braindead*, and was pivotal in the development of *Heavenly Creatures* and *The Frighteners*. Actor Brad Dourif has famously commented that the most difficult person to please on the *Rings* set was not Peter Jackson, but Fran Walsh.

In the world of movies, close-knit creative collaborations between romantic partners are rare, unless one or both of them appears onscreen. A number of male directors make a habit of giving starring roles to their partners, but behind-the-camera examples are much harder to find. Alfred Hitchcock's wife Alma Reville helped write a number of his movies, and continued to offer valued advice on scripts and editing for four decades. Acclaimed documentary filmmakers DA Pennebaker and Chris Hegedus (*Down from the Mountain*) have directed more than fifteen films together, and Bernardo Bertolucci and Clare Peploe collaborate occasionally on each other's scripts.

Clearly Walsh and Jackson form a tight creative unit, but Walsh, seldom seen at public events, has chosen to leave the job of celebrity to the one who has been at it the longest. In a rare early interview, she once joked to a journalist about how she and Sinclair tried occasionally to outvote Jackson on certain story points during scriptwriting sessions — both forgetting that once he got on the film set, he would be making the final decisions regardless. Though there is some crossover between them, Walsh's professed strengths are in dialogue and character, while Jackson's lie in visualising how to bring scenes to life.

Beyond its four scriptwriters, *Rings* has benefited from the creative and emotional contributions of a large team. Over the years, Jackson's films have benefited from the talents of some key creative partners: writers Stephen Sinclair and Philippa Boyens; special-effects talents, Richard Taylor and Tania Rodger; cinematographers like Murray Milne, Allun Bollinger, and Andrew Lesnie; editor/producer Jamie Selkirk, production designer Grant Major, and producers Barrie Osborne and Jim Booth. But especially in the case of *Rings*, everything would have fallen apart without a strong leader. *Rings* production designer Grant Major has described Jackson as a control freak, and the trilogy as 'a totalitarian system' with Jackson at the top: 'He was the last word.' Second-unit directors were sometimes kept waiting for hours so that he could signal his approval of their shot, and at times the trilogy's design system came to a standstill as people anxiously awaited the stamp allowing work to go to the next stage: *P.J. Approved.* The degree to which that PJ stamp of approval can be taken these days to mean a combined Jackson/Walsh stamp as well, can only be speculated at.

THE HEROIC LONER

New Zealand filmmakers have often refused to tailor their work to the demands of the marketplace. That defiance has resulted in a run of films — *The Navigator, Scarfies* and *Topless Women Talk about their Lives* among them — that straddle multiple genres at once. From *Bad Taste* to *The Frighteners*, the same is true for Peter Jackson. *Rings* is the only film Jackson has yet made which doesn't spill out beyond one genre, even though 'fantasy' is a word which its director appears to want to avoid.

This desire to make movies for himself, rather than the narrow dictates of genre, may have gained Jackson his following at the expense of wide commercial success in the US. But the results have been worth it.

Jackson (or is that Jackson/Walsh?) has always preferred making movies that entertain to those that preach, and his films are never especially critical of the mores of their period. *Heavenly Creatures* sidesteps close examination of the conservative attitudes shown towards Parker and Hulme's relationship, partly by ending before the actual murder trial. *Forgotten Silver* has all the makings of an attack on New Zealand's treatment of its artistic talent, except that a surprising number of the hero's setbacks are partly his own fault. Perhaps this reluctance is because Jackson is ultimately something of a nostalgist, attracted to the trappings of the past. If you count *King Kong*, four of his eight movies are set there — five if, like Jackson, you argue that Middle-earth is ancient history.

Many of the characters in Jackson's films are loners, living in ways that separate them from the rest of society. Lionel spends most of his time trapped in the house with his mother. Frank Bannister prefers the company of the dead to the emotional complications of the living. The Parker and Hulme seen in *Heavenly Creatures* form a society of two and shut everyone else out of their lives. Even Derek in *Bad Taste*, who clearly has a few screws loose, gets on better with birds than with humans.

The alienated, emotionally cut-off protagonist is common to many movies, certainly in New Zealand anyway, but it seems to hold a special appeal for Jackson. *Braindead, Forgotten Silver* and *The Frighteners* and, to a lesser degree, *Heavenly Creatures* all centre around a shy or alienated character who discovers the courage to overcome difficult odds, finding love in the process. In *Heavenly Creatures* and *Forgotten Silver*, the protagonists discover happiness partly in exploring their own creativity, but creativity is not enough: their obsessions ultimately lead to tragedy.

The tensions in Jackson's work between naturalism and movie as thrill-ride come through in his characters. While many of his protagonists lean towards quietness and shyness, the secondary characters are often overheated and over-the-top, as befits a directorial CV which leans towards melodrama and farce. Even in *Heavenly Creatures*, based upon a true story, a number of secondary characters (Pauline's doctor, inspired by a real-life figure, the girls' teachers) are treated in a comical, exaggerated fashion.

Like many talented directors of fantasy, Jackson is at his weakest when it comes to dealing with the complications of human relationships. The romance in *Braindead* is loaded with exuberant close-ups of the stars gazing lovingly into camera, and the winning performances of Tim Balme and Diana Peñalver are enough to pull it through. *The Frighteners* tries to go a little deeper, with a character who has closed himself off from his emotions, seemingly guilt-ridden after the death of his wife. As Bannister's new love interest, Trini Alvarado does a more than capable job, but the script gives her little to work with, and even less reason to fall so quickly for him.

Jackson is yet to go further than the kind of romance which is written in the stars, whether through tarot cards, the myths of Tolkien or the laws of movie convention, which state that the lead character must have a love interest. (In the case of Aragorn and Arwen, the *Rings* films are less interested in their relationship, than in the act of saying goodbye.)

But if Jackson is so bad at human relationships, how does one explain *Heavenly Creatures*, the tale of teenage friendship and murder that won him and Walsh their first Academy Award nomination for scriptwriting? *Heavenly Creatures* is an extraordinary film, partly for its courage, partly for its achievement, and partly its presumption. The movie sweeps us into the world of its teenage protagonists, thanks to dizzying camerawork and the spirited performances of Kate Winslet and Melanie Lynskey. *Heavenly Creatures* is like watching events through a telescope — while capturing the euphoria of their friendship, Jackson manages to hold the characters at arm's length, neither judging them nor pretending they are perfect.

At the same time there is a sense that for all their attention to detail, Jackson is in the grip of the very forces he should be investigating. To make a Steven Spielberg comparison, *Close Encounters of the Third Kind* follows one man's obsessive, irrational search for the truth about UFOs. That obsession is ultimately shown to be justified, because it helps the protagonist towards a close encounter with beings from another universe (while simultaneously giving Spielberg a chance to indulge in the light shows he loves so much). *Heavenly Creatures* follows and celebrates a friendship which led to murder; on another level it represents Jackson and Walsh's obsessive search for the truth behind what really happened. In my opinion the film has little interest in the idea that the girls' private world of fantasy might have played a part in alienating them from others, because indulging in that fantasy world was key to what attracted Jackson and Walsh to the story in the first place.

Heavenly Creatures is at once operatic, original and off-kilter, and its portrait of puberty has touched something in a wide audience. Some of the scenes between Pauline and her mother have a raw emotion in them quite unlike anything else in Jackson's work. Whatever its intentions, the movie leaves questions of the girls' sexuality and sanity open for the audience, which is either a sensitive decision or a dangerous one, depending on how one looks at it. Key moments — the film's handling of Pauline losing her virginity, the *tour-de-force* scene where Orson Welles chases them home — bear little resemblance to the corresponding entries from Pauline's diary, to which the opening titles of the film claim to pay close fidelity. For all Jackson and Walsh's concerns with capturing factual accuracy, as shown at other points in the film, many of *Heavenly Creatures'* best moments occur when it drifts closest to invention and speculation — notably in the places where the girls' real and imaginative worlds start to intermingle.

*Heavenly Creatures'*s final sequence recreates and reinterprets the murder of Honora Parker in June 1954. Even if the first hour of this movie were forgettable (which it clearly is not), this would remain one of the most powerful and humane murder scenes yet put on film. Watching Juliet and Pauline walking through Victoria Park, carrying the brick which will be used to smash Honora's skull, the audience is given long moments in which to contemplate the enormity of taking another person's life. At the point of the murder Jackson manages something extraordinary, in making us feel for both victim and perpetrators: sadness for Honora's death, and sadness for Parker and Hulme's belief that killing her could ever have helped keep them together.

Some have pointed to *Heavenly Creatures* as the logical end point of an obsession in Jackson's films with themes of matricide. They point to the bloodsplattered death of an abrasive solo mother, witnessed by her baby child, during the final massacre of *Meet the Feebles,* and the murder of Old Lady Bradley in *The Frighteners.* The plotline of *Braindead* centres on a henpecked young man still living at home, who cares for and ultimately kills his dominating, increasingly monstrous mother. But splatter is a genre that digs gleefully into social taboos — death being the obvious one — and in *Braindead*, matricide is just one of them. The film also spends time making fun of Nazis, priests, paedophiles and the idea of baby as monster.

Forgotten Silver, made with Wellington director Costa Botes following *Heavenly Creatures*, is another film in which truth and the imagination intertwine, though to more light-hearted effect. Its subject is a filmmaker whose visions are difficult to contain. *Forgotten Silver*'s tone is respectful and above board, but the narrator periodically finds elements of the ludicrous wandering into the narrative. Despite the film's brilliance at wearing the coat of documentary, *Forgotten Silver* shines with a wonderment at how easily life can segue between heroism and absurdity, between courage and failure.

Perhaps it is the closest that Jackson has yet got to putting his heart on his sleeve. Part comedy, part spectacle, *Forgotten Silver* is ultimately a love letter to the madness of attempting to create cinematic visions.

PRESENT AND FUTURE

Wherever you looked in September 2003, from museum exhibitions in London, to video stores across the globe, it was easy to trace a line back to Peter Jackson. On DVD *The Two Towers* was setting records for Internet sales, while the finale of *Lord of the Rings* inched towards completion under that rarest of states for the third episode of a corporate franchise: near universal goodwill. In the US, show-business magazines reported that the pay packet for his next film *King Kong* lay higher than $US20 million. Some Hollywood sources said that the deal gave him total creative control, up to a $US150 million budget. Earlier in 2003, *Premiere* magazine rated Jackson as one of the most powerful directors in the US, with only studio boss Steven Spielberg, and *Star Wars* creator George Lucas higher on the list.

Clearly Peter Jackson is a workaholic, and some say you have to be a workaholic to make movies with him. Actor Jake Busey recalls that the only time he saw Jackson get frustrated on set, was when he was forced to take a break. The period from 1993 to mid-1996 saw so many films in development — including *Heavenly Creatures*, *Forgotten Silver*, *The Frighteners*, *The Black Max*, *King Kong* and *Jack Brown Genius* — that Jackson and Fran Walsh appear to have been working more or less continuously for the entire period. The following year, Jackson began serious work on *Rings*, a project whose sheer workload would have driven many to nervous breakdown.

Peter Jackson's tale is about the confluence of talent, positivity and willpower. He has made films happen by turning on a camera and willing them into being, sometimes in the absence of a script, or even any kind of sponsorship apart from parental support and his own meagre wages. His gift is that of being blind to the kinds of barriers that would normally give pause — like the fact that four other directors might be working on the same project as he is, or that doing a trilogy in one go could be a recipe for disaster.

Jackson's belief in the fun of making movies is communicated to those around him; and he seems to find a calmness amid the chaos of the film set. Despite the director's oft-repeated belief in the importance of the script, part of him does not seem to be happy unless he is making it up on the day, and finalising dialogue on the run. Jackson has had his share of luck, but much of it is the kind of luck that sparks when talent is already in motion. A number of key people in positions of power have been impressed enough by that talent to gamble on Jackson's potential: people like his late producer, Jim Booth, Hollywood director Robert Zemeckis, the brothers Weinstein at Miramax, and New Line boss Robert Shaye.

The complications of *The Frighteners* and *The Lord of the Rings* have seen the flowering of Jackson into a shrewd and hard-nosed dealmaker. Having earlier refused to cut *Rings* back to one movie, he has now managed to persuade New Line that a successful franchise will only grow more profitable if more is pumped into it. What has resulted is one of the most director-friendly schedules in recent cinema history, to the point where Jackson seems reluctant to let go of his final episode: a series of movies in an extended state of fine-tuning and reinterpretation, whose total time before the cameras has gone far beyond the oft-quoted 274 days of shooting.

Although he may not have a cupboard full of clones waiting at home, Peter Jackson exists as many people at the same time. Even when dealing in slaughter, pornography and matricide, his movies plug into something childlike and wide-eyed. The *Rings* cast talk about the director's relaxed, good-humoured nature and his openness to ideas, yet Jackson and Walsh's dealings with the media and the Film Commission have been those of people increasingly unwilling to accept that there might be another side to any story. Perhaps such contradictions lead us back to what makes Jackson so good as a director: his desire to control each element of his work.

In an insightful interview by Phil Edwards around the release of *Braindead* in 1993, Jackson described himself as a 'control freak', who preferred to have 'total control of every aspect' of his films. At that point he felt that venturing to Hollywood might be important for his career — partly because studio executives refused to take directors seriously until they had worked in Los Angeles. Yet Jackson felt 'an enormous incentive' to stay in New Zealand, where he could continue to make movies without interference.

Since that interview, Jackson has become a major Hollywood player, yet his preferred relationship with the US remains that of the man who rides into town, negotiates a loan, then heads home to spend it. After seven movies, the only time he has turned on a movie camera in the US to date, has been to shoot a series of mock interviews for *Forgotten Silver*, itself a tale about creating grand cinematic spectacles with other people's cash. Like Stanley Kubrick before him, Jackson prefers using major-league Hollywood resources to make movies in the country where he lives, partly for his own comfort. Kubrick, who recreated Vietnam for *Full Metal Jacket* without leaving England, remains one of the only directors who pulled this off on a regular basis. Time will tell if Jackson can do it again after *King Kong*, or whether he will even want to. For now, Hollywood players have been known to fly down to Wellington in order to get the chance to speak to him.

Jackson's desire to work on his own terms has seen him investing in his own moviemaking empire, and dealing with the attentions of a country that has raised him to the status of national hero. Everyone wants a piece of him, and his staff sometimes wait hours to get to the front of the queue. Every now and then, Jackson is quoted talking wistfully about going back to the old days, and making a little film on weekends.

The temptation to milk opportunity after *King Kong*, by jumping into another Hollywood mega movie, will be large. The grab-bag of other filmic possibilities ranges from splatter to true-life history. Judging by the director's eclectic CV to date, there is every chance his next movie will fit comfortably inside Kong's hand — a little beauty that screams out in some strange new way, loses him millions of newfound fans, and wins him a whole new audience in the process. By then, it should be clearer whether the health of the Weta special-effects operation is bound by umbilical cord to Jackson's own career.

One writer has described American filmmaker John Ford as an intelligent man who spent a great deal of energy cultivating a persona as someone with no artistic pretensions, or vulnerabilities. If Peter Jackson has been cultivating a persona, then it only helps make him seem less powerful and ambitious than he is. Jackson is a shrewd, highly motivated man for whom moviemaking is life, and whose relationships are defined almost entirely by family and work. His success has brought with it wealth beyond imagination, an increasing insensitivity to criticism, and the pressure of knowing that the fate of movie empires can hang upon his decisions.

Even if we choose to ignore the footprints made by passing hobbits, Peter Jackson has left a series of indelible marks on New Zealand cinema. These days his images are reflected back in hamburger advertisements, on fan websites, and in posters on American children's walls. And when some of those children grow up, *The Lord of the Rings* will be one of the cinematic experiences that stays with them, the way a movie called *King Kong* once lodged itself in the mind of a young boy from Pukerua Bay.

IN A HOUSE BY THE SEA

Back in the house above the sea, the troupe of Peter clones continued to watch horror videos and take their sleeping pills. For Peter had sent all his clones out to the coast after he had no more use for them, to live the rest of their days in peace and quiet.

Actor Peter had already left for the morning, for his weekly session telling stories at the local kindergarten. The teachers hung back anxiously by the door, hoping there would be no more mentions of that All Black who practised drop kicks by moonlight, using the decapitated head of his old captain. Back at the house, Stuntman Peter had emerged from his hobbit hole in the garden to dangle from the back verandah by a length of bungy cord. His knees ached much more these days than they used to, but he found that hanging by his feet in the sea air did wonders for his circulation. Chainsaw Peter sat in a radio studio nearby, opposite a nervous politician. Peter smiled, and asked innocently why the politician could not see that the only way to make decent decisions about movies was to ask moviemakers. Meanwhile, Sensitive Peter beavered away each night on his new script, an epic about all the ages of man. But the only people taking his calls these days were youngsters wanting to ask him about that damned *Lord of the Rings*. It was as if the other sixteen films had only been in his imagination.

And what of the original Peter, the Peter who had long ago discovered a magical machine that allowed him to use all the very best parts of himself, and one or two of the worst? His tale is linked to that of another storyteller, a bright-eyed woman named Fran. The two often sat together and laughed while labouring over tales of monsters, magic and meat patties. And then one day, as Fran finished typing out a sentence she especially liked the look of, Peter had a wonderful idea for the final scene. He reached without thinking for the L key — but instead, found her hand on the key already.

A few years later, Peter and Fran were the proud parents of two wide-eyed children. For the sake of our story, we shall call the younger one

Rosie. Rosie loved dandelions and reading about thermodynamics. When Rosie grew tall, she rushed home one day to tell Peter of a clever idea that had just arrived in her head, an idea involving an orchestra of electric guitars, powered by the energy from a line of volcanoes. She was sure it had the makings of something.

Peter turned from his spot by the window and raised his greying eyebrows. The flicker of a grin began to spread across his face. Looking at him, Rosie suddenly imagined the smile as it might have been without the messy beard, back in the days when the cliffs of Pukerua Bay had marked the entire horizons of her father's world.

'A steam-driven guitar?' Peter said with a giggle. 'Down to the workshop, before someone beats us to it.'

I first saw Peter Jackson's low-budget debut *Bad Taste* on a television set in Wellington in 1988, shortly before it premiered at the Cannes Film Festival. The movie was great fun: amiable yet ambitious, gory and idiotic. At the time I saw it, I was about to cross the line between impartial journalist and participant. When Jackson followed *Bad Taste* with a short puppet film called *Meet the Feebles*, I volunteered to take photographs on the set of drug-snorting anteaters and depressed elephants, and later used a couple to illustrate an interview with Jackson I wrote for the university newspaper. More interviews with Jackson followed. When I wrote a negative review of the feature-length version of *Meet the Feebles*, he handled it with good grace.

After I had begun writing features and film reviews for Wellington's *Evening Post* newspaper, I proposed to some of those at Jackson's company WingNut the idea of writing a book about him and his movies. On Jackson's next film, *Heavenly Creatures*, I was one of the only journalists allowed on set. I still have a copy of the letter signed by Jackson's producer Jim Booth, allowing me to visit the *Heavenly Creatures* set specifically for a book about Jackson.

Jackson later expressed annoyance over an article I had written about the Venice Film Festival, which mentioned *Heavenly Creatures*. The piece said that reaction to an early screening of *Heavenly Creatures* had been mixed, but had been somewhat mangled by subeditors. If you tied a group of journalists who write about cinema for the mainstream media to a tree, I'm sure that in the end many would crack, by admitting their job is as much about hyping movies and maintaining relationships as it is about honest journalism. My strong feeling is that the main sin of my article, unfortunately amplified by questionable editing, was that it failed to hype at a vital moment in Jackson's career.

By the time Jackson got around to *Lord of the Rings*, a great many creatures had passed out of the Weta special-effects factory. The idea of the book had now been with me for more than six years, and Jackson's increasing fame had created publisher interest, providing the deadline I needed to write it. I now knew of at least two other writers who desired to write books about him. I made a number of requests to his assistant, asking if I could visit the set of *Lord of the Rings*. Finally I was told that Jackson would not be able to cooperate with me, as he planned a book of his own.

After some to-ing and fro-ing, I decided to go ahead with my book. My feeling was that an unauthorised book on Jackson was inevitable, and that my background in writing about Jackson and New Zealand film made me as qualified as anyone to write it. Months later, having conducted many more interviews, I learned that one of Jackson's assistants had begun asking some people not to talk to me. A number of interviews were suddenly cancelled, after calls from Jackson's assistants.

Jackson's power in the film industry provided a powerful disincentive to go on the record. Clearly looking to the future, a major-league Hollywood executive known for straight talking made sure that his short refusal was also a tribute to the director's talents. A writer for a leading US entertainment magazine felt obliged to check with Jackson before speaking to me, helping me to realise that the relationship between filmmaker and journalist becomes even more complicated when the first movie in a trilogy is a box-office smash. Though the writer had the courage to meet me against Jackson's wishes, on arriving for the interview he said that our discussion could go ahead only on condition that any quotes I wanted to publish were approved by him.

The writing of this book has also seen a case go before the Ombudsman. Jackson requested that the New Zealand Film Commission, which helped finance five of his films, not release to me relevant movie stills or sales information for his movies. The Commission's stated functions include encouraging the appreciation of New Zealand films and filmmaking — but I can understand how they might have felt caught in the headlights of two cars speeding towards them from opposite directions, one with much more powerful lights than the other. Some box-office data was eventually supplied, and the Commission's staff have proven helpful in tracking down a number of those people spoken to in the course of my research.

I decided to include a reasonable amount of material on Jackson's own upbringing and his parents, both of them now passed away. Jackson has spoken freely about his childhood in many published interviews, and I felt that this background was relevant to a biography.

I conducted more than 120 interviews, some of them short, some of them anonymous, the majority neither. Most of the interviews concerning *Lord of the Rings* were conducted at press launches of Jackson's trilogy in Wellington, during which time I was writing articles for another publication (this was arguably sneaky, and the following year I was not allowed in at all). Because of this, none of the interview comments given by any of the *Lord of the Rings* cast or crew imply that they knew about this book. None of the quotations from Peter Jackson or Fran Walsh given to me or other interviewers imply that they approve of this biography in its present form. Also, I should make it clear that most of those quoted in the text spoke to me before Jackson's lack of approval of the book became clear.

ACKNOWLEDGEMENTS

I would like to thank all those who have done interviews for this book, who have universally been generous with their time and their memories: Jonathon Acorn, Gilbert Adler, John Barnett, the late Jim Booth, Jake Busey, Gordon Campbell, Suzanne Carty, Cameron Chittock, Caterina De Nave, Roger Donaldson, Gina Draklich, Lin Ferguson, Janice Finn, Glenis Foster, Michelanne Forster, David Gapes, John Girdlestone, Lee Gottsegen, Ken Hammon, Joyce and Charlie Herbert, Tony Hiles, Hanno Huth, Bridget Ikin, the late Bill and Joan Jackson, Richard Jordan, Diana Kent, Mike Kane, Grant Lahood, Dean Lawrie, Melanie Lynskey, Beryl Mackay, Wayne McDaniel, Grahame McLean, Clive Merrison, Murray Milne, Mike Minett, Elizabeth Moody, Ian Mune, Danny Mulheron, Andrew Neal, Louis Nowra, Diana Peñalver, Anatoli Petritsky, Sam Pillsbury, Tom Pollock, George Port, John D Porter, John Reid, Don Reynolds, Michelle Scullion, Lindsay Shelton, Craig Smith, Alan Sorrell, Tim Swain, Wes Takahashi, Rachel Talalay, Nelly Taylor, Jimmy Wachtel, Ian Watkin, Mike Wheeler, Kate Winslet, Justine Wright, Jane Wrightson, and Brian Yuzna.

THIS BOOK ALSO INCLUDES EXCERPTS FROM PAST INTERVIEWS BY THE AUTHOR WITH:

Tim Balme, Philippa Boyens, Jed Brophy, Bill Gosden, Peter Jackson, Mike Hopkins, Kevin Leonard-Jones, Grant Major, Liz Mullane (back when she was acting in *Braindead*), Sarah Pierse, Jamie Selkirk, Richard Taylor and Fran Walsh. Their presence on these pages should not be taken to imply their knowledge or approval of the current text.

PUKERUA BAY AND KAPITI COLLEGE SECTIONS:

Thanks to Julie Armstrong, Joanne Bishop, Ashley Blair, Lois Bullock, Meg Campbell, Roger Childs, Shona Davidson, Leone Downes, Mark Hudson, Liz and Barry Johnson, Ian Middleton, Anne Morris, Gary Mosen, Ian Reid, Catherine Saville, Trevor Shoesmith, Jan Spencer, Prue Ursell, Steven Valentine, Jean Watson, Jack Wadilove, Jillian and Lesley Willcocks and all those others who helped me and/or were kind enough to do interviews.

I doubt I would have survived writing this book without the kindness of the following people in particular: my close friend Tracey Lewis who kept it secret for far too many years, and remained full of positivity and good advice. Tracey, I owe you bigtime. My friend Karen Hester, for kindness beyond all rational belief. Beverly Martens, for reading my mind, and Judith and Keith Marshall, for saving my bacon in the final leg. And Carole O'Connor for transcribing interviews and listening to me blather on.

Valuable feedback on sections of the text was provided by Karen Hester,

Glenn Donovan, Phil Wakefield, Jason Gush, and the incomparable Georgie Ames and Arthur Jack. Brian Johnson coined the book's title.

I am bound to have missed someone in following list of thank yous — please hassle me later. Helen Gaeta, Roger Peach and Annaleise Gaeta for their kindness and generosity in New York, Brian Johnson for putting up with the stress, and Amanda Mason, for her kindness and support. Thanks also to Andrew Armitage, Ian Apperley, James Brown (who cannot sing), Erica Challis, Lorena Garrido, the encouragement of Michael Gifkins, the patience of Jason Gush, Simon Haxton (photographer extraordinare), Nicky Hager, Catherine Hill, Donna Huggard, Bobby Jackson (not related), Annabelle Leyden, Bill Manhire, Sean Molloy, Mike, Mum and Dad, Paul on a cycle, Helen Rickerby, Greta Riley, Daniel Riordan, Bernie Steeds, Jane Tolerton, Phil Wakefield, and all of the old *Evening Post* features crew from 1989 to 1993. Jane Thomson at the New Zealand Film Commission provided valuable contact information, and thanks also to all the various agents here and overseas. I would also like to thank Lynley Hood for sound advice, and her example of courage. Thanks to everyone at Random House NZ, and all at Marjacq, especially Philip Paterson and Mark Hayward.

ARCHIVES AND LIBRARIES

The New Zealand Film Archive are an indispensable resource for anyone researching Kiwi film. Their staff extended only kindness to me before, during, and after a move to new locations. Thanks especially to archive staff Lissa Mitchell, Erica Andersen, Miranda Kaye and Diane Pivac. I should also mention the help of Sandra Archer and Kristine Krueger of the Margaret Herrick Library at the Center for Motion Picture Study in Los Angeles, Karen Johnson at the National Library of Australia, and Deborah Gordon and Philippa Guthrey at the New Zealand Office of Film and Literature Classification. Also Wellington Public Library, Playmarket, the Alexander Turnbull Library, and the quite miraculous Internet Movie Database.

In America: Lee Gottsegen at Punch Productions, Julie Corman at New Concorde, Anthony D'Alessandro at *Variety*, Parker and Hulme expert John D Porter, Karen Wright at the MPAA, Charles Taylor and Ty Ruben. Special thanks to Tony Timpone and Michael Gingold at *Fangoria* who were generous in helping me check out their back issues, as were Margie Duncan and Don Shay at *Cinefex*.

Elsewhere: in the United Kingdom, Kerrie Melville and Steph Anderson, Sophie Barr and Liz Cloud. In Germany, Roland Seim of Telos, and in Australia, Tanya Simpson and Peter Jackson expert Michael Helms. In Russia: Vlad Derkatch (at Ruscico), Gaine Ambartsumian (at Mosfilm), and the New Zealand Embassy of Russia.

So much help; but all errors of fact and judgement remain my own.

Early 1950s: Joan Ruck and Bill Jackson immigrate separately to Wellington, from the United Kingdom

1953, November 9: Joan and Bill marry and later move to the coastal town of Pukerua Bay, north of Wellington

1961, October 31: Peter Jackson born in Wellington Hospital

1969 (approx): First picks up the family's 8mm camera

1971: Has begun his first fictional short film

1978: Enters *Spot On* television contest with the eighteen-minute short *The Valley*. The film wins a cash prize through the *Kapiti Observer*

1979: Begins working as photo-engraver at Wellington Newspapers Ltd

1981: Starts the feature-length vampire movie *Curse of the Gravewalker*, which is later abandoned

1983, October 27: After buying a secondhand 16mm camera, begins making a short movie that will eventually become his feature-film debut *Bad Taste*

1985/6: Begins the first of many scriptwriting collaborations with Fran Walsh and Stephen Sinclair. Also shows *Bad Taste* to New Zealand Film Commission executive director Jim Booth

1987, December: *Bad Taste* finally completed with funding from the Film Commission. Development of zombie movie *Braindead* continues, plus the writing of *Meet the Feebles*, a short puppet film for television

April: The short version of *Meet the Feebles* is filmed in a house near Parliament

May: *Bad Taste* has its first market screening at the Cannes Film Festival in France, and goes into profit within days. World premiere of *Bad Taste* at a festival of fantasy and science-fiction in Paris follows in June

July 8: New Zealand premiere of *Bad Taste*, Wellington

1988, September: Jim Booth leaves New Zealand Film Commission to produce Jackson's next three movies

1989, January: *Braindead* postponed after withdrawal of funding by private investor

April 23–mid-July: Filming of feature-length version of *Meet the Feebles* in a Wellington railway shed

October: Flies to Italy for the first market screenings of *Meet the Feebles*

1989/90: Jackson and Danny Mulheron are commissioned to write a script for *A Nightmare on Elm Street* for New Line Cinema, which is never used. They continue work on their own fantasy script *Blubberhead*

1990, April: World premiere of second feature film, *Meet the Feebles*, at a fantasy film festival in Hamburg

September 28: New Zealand premiere of *Meet the Feebles*, Auckland

1991, Sept 3–mid-November: Filming of *Braindead* at Avalon Studios, and around Wellington. The film is unveiled at the Cannes Film Festival the following May

1992, August 13: New Zealand premiere of Jackson's third feature film, *Braindead*, Wellington

1993, February 12: US release of *Braindead* (as *Dead Alive*)

March–early June: Filming of *Heavenly Creatures* in and around Christchurch

August: Formation of special-effects company Weta Limited, of which Jackson is a partner, and purchase of Camperdown Studios building in Wellington

1994, January 4: Death from cancer of Jackson's producer Jim Booth

July 8: World premiere of Jackson's fourth feature film, *Heavenly Creatures*, Wellington

July: Miramax signs Jackson to a first-look deal, and buys majority of international rights to *Heavenly Creatures*

July 31: The *Sunday News* tracks down the real-life Juliet Hulme, and discovers she is now a successful murder-mystery writer living in Scotland

September: *Heavenly Creatures* wins the Silver Lion, one of the major prizes at the Venice Film Festival. Jackson executive-produces the Tony Hiles movie *Jack Brown Genius*

1995: Weta Digital relocates from cramped quarters in central Wellington to Camperdown Studios in Miramar

February: After the American success of *Heavenly Creatures*, Jackson's first two films *Bad Taste* and *Meet the Feebles* finally begin a small-scale American release

February 15: Jackson and Fran Walsh are nominated for an Academy Award for the writing of *Heavenly Creatures*

Late April: End of filming of mock-documentary *Forgotten Silver*, directed by Jackson and Costa Botes

May 15–early November: Filming of Jackson's first American-funded movie, *The Frighteners*, in Wellington and Lyttelton. Development work begins on *King Kong*

September 3: World premiere of *Salome*, Wellington

October 29: Television premiere of *Forgotten Silver*. Many viewers believe the film is real

Late 1995: Jackson asks Miramax co-chief Harvey Weinstein to check who owns the rights to Tolkien's books *The Hobbit* and *Lord of the Rings*

1996, April: Universal Pictures announces Jackson is to remake *King Kong*. Jackson signs a two-picture deal with Miramax and Universal

July: World premiere of Jackson's sixth feature film, *The Frighteners*, LA

December 9: New Zealand premiere of *The Frighteners*, which opens nationwide on December 26

1997: Development of *Lord of the Rings* continues throughout the year with Miramax funding, after news that rights to *The Hobbit* are problematic

January: Universal Pictures announces postponement of Jackson's remake of *King Kong*

1998, July: Miramax gives Jackson four weeks to find new backers for *Lord of the Rings*, after making it clear it wants to reduce the project from two movies to one

August 24: New Line Cinema announces the funding of three *Lord of the Rings* movies

December: Jackson purchases film laboratory The Film Unit

1999, October 11: Filming starts for *Lord of the Rings*. The extended three-movie shoot takes place around New Zealand, finishing in December 2000

2001, December 10: World premiere of Jackson's seventh feature film, *The Fellowship of the Ring*, London

December 19: *The Fellowship of the Ring* opens in eighteen countries

2002, February: *The Fellowship of the Ring* is nominated for thirteen Academy Awards, putting it among the nine most-nominated films in Oscar history

March: *The Fellowship of the Ring* wins four Academy Awards

November: *The Fellowship of the Ring* released on video and DVD in substantially extended form, after video release of the original film in August. This two-tiered release pattern will be repeated for the next two episodes of *Lord of the Rings*

December 5: World premiere of Jackson's eighth feature film, *The Two Towers*, New York

2003, February: *The Two Towers* is nominated for six Academy Awards, and later wins two

March: Universal announces Jackson is to direct *King Kong* after the completion of the last *Rings* movie

December: World premiere of Jackson's ninth feature film, *The Return of the King*, Wellington

APPENDIX 2: FILMOGRAPHY

AMATEUR FILMS (PARTIAL LIST)

Peter Jackson has been quoted as saying he made anything between twelve and twenty films before beginning work on the short film that became *Bad Taste*. Many were never completed; others were more about trying out visual ideas than rounded narratives. The following list is necessarily incomplete, and some of the films mentioned may be part of a larger narrative. All films were shot on 8mm. Short excerpts from a number of the following films can be found on the documentary *Good Taste Made Bad Taste*.

1970?: The disappearing cat film. One of Jackson's first explorations of special effects.

1970/71?: *The Dwarf Patrol*. World War II boy's own adventure, filmed in trenches dug into the Jackson family's backyard. With Peter Jackson, Peter O'Herne and Ian Middleton.

Date unknown: Time-lapse film. In this short, the use of time-lapse techniques gives the illusion of people moving around streets and pathways, seemingly without moving their limbs.

Date unknown: Time-lapse car trip. By switching on the camera only intermittently, Jackson captured a long car trip to the Central Plateau in a matter of minutes of screen time.

Date unknown: The cycle film. The camera captures the bicycle ride down to the beaches of Pukerua Bay.

1971/73?: The ape movie. After watching *King Kong*, Jackson used an old fur stole of his mother's to make a miniature gorilla. 'Then I made a cardboard cut-out of the Empire State Building for him to stand on, and I painted a backdrop of Manhattan.' The Kong movie was never made, although there is a possibility that Jackson's dabblings with ape masks were utilised in other films: photographs exist of Jackson's filmmaking friend Peter O'Herne dressed in a gorilla suit.

1973?: First stop-motion animation film. Jackson made a number of films during this period in which he created his own spaceships and stop-motion monsters. In some accounts, Jackson says that his first stop-motion film involved a hunchback rat made from papier-mâché.

1973: *World War II*. With Jackson in uniform, wandering the hills above Pukerua Bay.

1974: 'Monty Python' movie. See Chapter Two. Film made with classmates at Pukerua Bay School, to raise funds for a school trip. It included direct imitations of Python sketches, and also attempted to recreate the cut-out animation of Python member Terry Gilliam. Teacher Trevor Shoesmith agreed to be blown up on film, thanks to the magic of special effects. Jackson recalled that the final result was screened at the school assembly hall.

1978: *The Valley* (20 minutes). See Chapter Two. Fantasy adventure about a small group of gold prospectors who find themselves in a lost valley, battling for their lives against strange creatures. Winner of *Kapiti Observer* scholarship.
Directors: Peter Jackson, Ken Hammon, Andrew Neal. *Cast:* the directors, and Ian Middleton.

1979?: *The Bond Thing* aka '*Coldfinger*'. Jackson's homage to James Bond, with Jackson playing a man in a tuxedo fighting off Hammon.
Cast: Peter Jackson, Ken Hammon, Peter O'Herne.

Date unknown: The intruder film. Possibly inspired by *Halloween* and Stanley Kubrick's *A Clockwork Orange*, this all-in-one-take movie has the camera taking the point of view of an intruder entering a house, and discovering a terrified man inside.
Cast: Peter O'Herne.

1982–3: *Curse of the Gravewalker*. See Chapter Three. Vampire epic inspired partly by Hammer horror movies, and set in eastern Europe. Around an hour of footage was shot before the project was abandoned.
Cast: Peter Jackson, Ken Hammon, Peter O'Herne, Andrew Neal.

FILMS DIRECTED BY PETER JACKSON

Due to restrictions of space, the following list is limited to key crew and cast members. All films listed in this section are directed by Peter Jackson, except for *Forgotten Silver*. Running times are based where possible upon the New Zealand censor's certificate for original cinema release.

1987: *Bad Taste* (93 minutes, R16 certificate). First official screening, Cannes Film Festival, May 1988. Working titles: *Roast of the Day, Giles' Day Out*. *Screenplay, Producer, Photography, Makeup Effects and Special Effects:* Peter Jackson. *Additional Script Material:* Tony Hiles and Ken Hammon. *Consultant*

Producer: Tony Hiles. *Editors:* Peter Jackson and Jamie Selkirk. *Post-production Supervisor:* Jamie Selkirk. *Music:* Michelle Scullion. *Sound Mix:* Brent Burge. *Film Crew:* Ken Hammon, Peter O'Herne, Terry Potter, Mike Minett, Craig Smith, Dean Lawrie, Philip Lamey. *Makeup Effects Assistant:* Cameron Chittock. *Songs:* 'Bad Taste' (closing credits song) composed by Mike Minett and Dave Hamilton; performed by The Remnants. 'Rock Lies' (first appearance of 'the boys' in their Ford Capri) composed and performed by Madlight.

Cast: Ozzy, Terry Potter; *Barry,* Peter O'Herne; *Giles,* Craig Smith; *Frank,* Mike Minett; *Derek/Robert,* Peter Jackson; *Lord Crumb,* Doug Wren; *voice of Lord Crumb,* Peter Vere-Jones; *Lord Crumb (after transformation),* Dean Lawrie; *various aliens,* Ken Hammon.

Filmed around the Kapiti Coast, Makara and Porirua (WingNut Films).

1988: *Meet the Feebles* (episode for television — abandoned before completion).

Screenplay: Peter Jackson, Frances Walsh, Stephen Sinclair. *Director of Photography:* Steve Latty. *Puppet Designer:* Cameron Chittock. *Supervising Puppeteer:* Jonathon Acorn. *Heidi performed by:* Danny Mulheron.

Filmed in a house in Wellington.

1989: *Meet the Feebles* (98 minutes, R16 certificate). First screening, MIFED film market, Italy, October 1989.

Screenplay: Frances Walsh, Stephen Sinclair, Danny Mulheron and Peter Jackson. *Producers:* Jim Booth and Peter Jackson. *Director of Photography/ Stills Photography:* Murray Milne. *Camera Operator:* Peter Jackson. *Music:* Peter Dasent. *Editor:* Jamie Selkirk. *Production Designer:* Mike Kane. *Puppet Designer:* Cameron Chittock. *Supervising Puppeteers:* Jonathon Acorn and Ramon Aguilar. *Puppetmakers:* Cameron Chittock, Richard Taylor, Tania Rodger, Peter Jackson. *Camera Operator:* Peter Jackson. *Special Effects:* Steve Ingram.

Songs: composed by Peter Dasent, with Fane Flaws and Danny Mulheron; lyrics by Fane Flaws, Arthur Baysting, Peter Dasent, Garth Frost, Danny Mulheron and Frances Walsh. Performed by Mark Hadlow, Stuart Devenie and Fane Flaws.

Puppeteers: Eleanor Aitken, Carl Buckey, Sarah Glensor, Danny Mulheron, George Port, Ian Williamson, Justine Wright, Terri Anderton, Sean Ashton-Peach. *Heidi performed by:* Danny Mulheron. *Voices:* Donna Akersten, Stuart Devenie, Mark Hadlow, Ross Jolly, Brian Sergent, Peter Vere-Jones and Mark Wright.

Filmed in a Wellington railway shed, and around the city of Wellington (WingNut Films).

1992: *Braindead* (105 minutes, R16 Certificate). First screening, Cannes Film Festival, May 1992. Working title: *Housebound*. North American title: *Dead Alive* (cut to 97 minutes).

Screenplay: Stephen Sinclair, Frances Walsh, Peter Jackson. *From an original story idea by:* Stephen Sinclair. *Producer:* Jim Booth. *Director of Photography:* Murray Milne. *Editor:* Jamie Selkirk. *Creature and Gore Effects:* Richard Taylor. *Prosthetics Makeup Designer:* Bob McCarron. *Prosthetics/Makeup Supervisor:* Marjory Hamlin. *Stop-motion Animation:* Peter Jackson and Richard Taylor (Jackson is also listed among the miniatures crew). *Production Designer:* Kevin Leonard-Jones. *Casting:* Frances Walsh. *Sound Design:* Mike Hopkins and Sam Negri. *Associate Producer:* Jamie Selkirk. *Music composed, performed and produced by:* Peter Dasent. *Songs:* 'The Stars and Moon' (closing credits song) composed by Peter Dasent and Jane Lindsay; sung by Kate Swadling.

Cast: Lionel, Tim Balme; *Paquita,* Diana Peñalver; *Mum (Vera Cosgrove),* Elizabeth Moody; *Uncle Les,* Ian Watkin; *Father McGruder,* Stuart Devenie; *Nurse McTavish,* Brenda Kendall; *Void,* Jed Brophy; *Zombified Vera Cosgrove,* Brenda Kendall; *Zombified Father McGruder,* Stephen Papps; *Nazi Vet,* Brian Sergent; *Undertaker's Assistant,* Peter Jackson.

Filmed at Avalon Studios in Lower Hutt, and around Wellington City and the Wairarapa (WingNut Films, in association with the New Zealand Film Commission and Avalon/NFU Studios).

1994: *Heavenly Creatures* (110 minutes, GA certificate). World premiere, Wellington Film Festival, July 8, 1994. *Note:* Overseas versions are usually shorter in length.

Screenplay: Frances Walsh and Peter Jackson. *Producer:* Jim Booth. *Co-producer:* Peter Jackson. *Cinematographer:* Alun Bollinger. *Editor/Post-production Supervisor:* Jamie Selkirk. *Music:* Peter Dasent. *Production Designer:* Grant Major. *Art Director:* Jill Cormack. *Costume Designer:* Ngila Dickson. *Casting:* (UK) John and Ros Hubbard, (NZ) Liz Mullane. *Executive Producer:* Hanno Huth.

Visual Effects: WETA Ltd. Digital Effects; George Port. *Prosthetic Effects Designer/Miniatures Designer:* Richard Taylor. *Borovnian Prosthetics and Suit Effects Co-ordinator/Foam Technician:* Tania Rodger.

Source Music includes: 'The Humming Chorus' (murder sequence) from *Madame Butterfly,* composed by Giacomo Puccini, performed by the Hungarian State Opera. 'You'll never walk alone' (closing credits song) composed by Richard Rodgers and Oscar Hammerstein, sung by Mario Lanza.

Cast: Pauline Parker, Melanie Lynskey; *Juliet Hulme,* Kate Winslet; *Honora Parker,* Sarah Peirse; *Hilda Hulme,* Diana Kent; *Henry Hulme,* Clive Merrison;

Herbert, Simon O'Connor; *John/Nicholas,* Jed Brophy; *Bill Perry,* Peter Elliott; *Orson Welles,* Jean Guerin; *Mario Lanza,* Stephen Reilly; *tramp outside cinema (uncredited),* Peter Jackson.
Filmed in Christchurch and Lyttelton (WingNut Films, co-produced with Fontana Film Production GmbH, in association with the New Zealand Film Commission).

1995: *Forgotten Silver* (53 minutes). First television screening, October 29, 1995. Working title *Forgotten Silver: The Extraordinary Life and Death of Colin McKenzie.*
Note: In keeping with the nature of the film itself, the original credits for *Forgotten Silver* are not entirely reliable. The following list is an attempt at accuracy. In the case of fictitious credits, the more accurate credit is listed afterwards in brackets.
Written and directed by: Peter Jackson and Costa Botes. *Script Consultant:* Frances Walsh. *Producer:* Sue Rogers. *Cinematography:* Alun Bollinger and Gerry Vasbenter. *Archive Stills Restoration (Archive Stills Recreation):* Chris Coad. *Editors:* Eric De Beus and Michael Horton. *Music:* Dave Donaldson, Steve Roche, Janet Roddick. *Production Designer:* John Girdlestone. *Genealogical Research (Casting):* Liz Mullane. *Executive Producers:* Peter Jackson and Jamie Selkirk. *Archive Film Restoration (Artificial Film Degradation):* Brian Scadden and Geoff Rogers. *Post-production Supervisors:* Ross Chambers and Charlie McClellan. *Antique Film Equipment & Memorabilia (Props and Set Construction):* Richard Taylor and Tania Rodger. *Digital Enhancement (Digital Effects):* Matt Aitken and Frank Wegerhoff. *Military Advisor (Physical Effects):* Steve Ingram.
Cast: Narrator, Jeffrey Thomas; *As themselves,* Peter Jackson and Costa Botes; *Colin McKenzie,* Thomas Robins; *Hannah McKenzie,* Beatrice Ashton; *Maybelle,* Sarah McLeod; *Stan the Man,* Peter Corrigan; *Brooke McKenzie,* Richard Shirtcliffe; *As themselves,* Jonathon Morris, Leonard Maltin, Sam Neill, Harvey Weinstein, John O'Shea and Lindsay Shelton.
Filmed around Greater Wellington (WingNut Films in association with The New Zealand Film Commission and New Zealand on Air).

1996: *The Frighteners* (112 minutes). World Premiere, Universal Studios Los Angeles, July 1996. (Laserdisc version approx 124 minutes.)
(Robert Zemeckis presents) Screenplay: Fran Walsh and Peter Jackson. *Producers:* Jamie Selkirk and Peter Jackson. *Directors of Photography:* Alun Bollinger and John Blick. *Editor:* Jamie Selkirk. *Associate Editor:* John Gilbert. *Music:* Danny Elfman. *Production Designer:* Grant Major. *Art Director:* Dan Hannah. *Costume Designer:* Barbara Darragh. *Second Unit Director:* John Blick. *Casting:* (US) Victoria Burrows, (NZ) Liz Mullane. *Co-producer:* Tim

Sanders. *Executive Producer*: Robert Zemeckis. *Associate Producer:* Fran Walsh. *Digital and Creature Effects:* Weta Ltd. *Digital Effects Producer:* Charlie McClellan. *Visual Effects Supervisor:* Wes Ford Takahashi. *Creature, Makeup and Miniature Effects Designer:* Richard Taylor. *Judge Makeup Design:* Rick Baker. *Songs:* 'Don't Fear the Reaper' (closing credits song) written by Donald Roeser of Blue Oyster Cult; performed by The Muttonbirds.

Main Cast: Frank Bannister, Michael J Fox; *Lucy Lynskey,* Trini Alvarado; *Milton Dammers,* Jeffrey Combs; *The Judge,* John Astin; *Ray Lynskey,* Peter Dobson; *Patricia Bradley,* Dee Wallace Stone; *Johnny Bartlett,* Jake Busey; *Cyrus,* Chi McBride; *Stuart,* Jim Fyfe; *Old Lady Bradley,* Julianna McCarthy; *Man on street with Grim Reaper shirt (uncredited),* Peter Jackson.

Filmed at Camperdown Studios, Wellington, and in Wellington, Lyttelton and the Wairarapa (WingNut Films for Universal Pictures).

2001: *The Lord of the Rings: The Fellowship of the Ring* (178 minutes, PG certificate). World premiere, London, December 10, 2001. Extended version released November 12, 2002 (219 minutes, M certificate).

Screenplay: Fran Walsh, Philippa Boyens and Peter Jackson. *Based on the book by:* JRR Tolkien. *Producers:* Barrie M Osbourne, Peter Jackson, Fran Walsh, Tim Sanders. *Director of Photography:* Andrew Lesnie. *Editor:* John Gilbert. *Music composed, orchestrated and conducted by:* Howard Shore. *Production Designer:* Grant Major. *Art Director:* Dan Hennah. *Makeup and Hair Design:* Peter Owen and Peter King. *Costume Design:* Ngila Dickson and Richard Taylor. *Casting:* (UK) John Hubbard and Amy Maclean, (US) Victoria Burrows, (NZ) Liz Mullane, (Australia) Ann Robinson. *Conceptual Designers:* Alan Lee and John Howe. *Second Unit Directors:* John Mahaffie and Geoff Murphy. *Executive Producers:* Mark Ordesky, Robert Shaye, Michael Lynne, Bob and Harvey Weinstein. *Co-producers:* Rick Porras and Jamie Selkirk. *Associate Producer:* Ellen M Somers. *Special Effects*: *Special Makeup, Creatures, Armour and Miniatures:* Weta Workshop, led by Richard Taylor. *Digital Effects:* Weta Digital Ltd. *Visual Effects Supervisor:* Jim Rygiel. *Animation designed and supervised by:* Randall William Cook. *Visual Effects Producer:* Eileen Moran. *Visual Effects Supervisor (Research and Development/ Pre)*: Charlie McClellan. *Digital Effects Supervisor (Research and Development/ Pre)*: John Sheils. *Additional Visual Effects:* Digital Domain, Animal Logic Film, Oktobor Films and Rhythm & Hues GMD.

Song: 'May It Be' (closing credits song) composed and performed by Enya, lyrics by Roma Ryan.

Main Cast: Frodo Baggins, Elijah Wood; *Gandalf,* Ian McKellen; *Aragorn,* Viggo Mortensen; *Sam Gamgee,* Sean Astin; *Peregrin Took,* Billy Boyd; *Merry Brandybuck,* Dominic Monaghan; *Boromir,* Sean Bean; *Gimli,* John Rhys-Davies; *Legolas,* Orlando Bloom; *Arwen,* Liv Tyler; *Bilbo Baggins,* Ian Holm;

Saruman, Christopher Lee; *Elrond,* Hugo Weaving; *Galadriel,* Cate Blanchett; *Lurtz,* Lawrence Makoare; *Albert Dreary* (uncredited cameo), Peter Jackson. Filmed at Camperdown and Stone Street Studios, Wellington, and at locations around New Zealand (Wingnut Films / New Line Cinema).

2002: *The Lord of the Rings: The Two Towers* (172 minutes, M certificate). World Premiere, New York, December 5, 2002. Extended version released November 18, 2003 (222 minutes).
Main credits as listed for *The Fellowship of the Ring,* except: *Screenplay:* Fran Walsh, Philippa Boyens, Stephen Sinclair and Peter Jackson. *Producers:* Barrie M Osbourne, Fran Walsh, Peter Jackson. *Editor:* Michael Horton with Jabez Olssen. *Digital effects:* Weta Digital. *Visual Effects Supervisor:* Joe Letteri. *Additional visual effects by:* Sony Pictures Imageworks and Oktobor Films.
Songs: 'Gollum's Song' (closing credits song), music by Howard Shore, lyrics by Fran Walsh, performed by Emiliana Torrini.
Main Cast: All as listed in *Fellowship of the Ring,* with the addition of: *Gollum* (seen only briefly in *Fellowship*), Andy Serkis; *Theoden,* Bernard Hill; *Eowyn,* Miranda Otto; *Faramir,* David Wenham; *Wormtongue,* Brad Dourif; *Eomer,* Karl Urban; *Soldier at Helm's Deep* (uncredited cameo), Peter Jackson. (WingNut Films for New Line Cinema)

2003: *The Lord of the Rings: The Return of the King* World premiere, Wellington, December 2003. Extended version released November 2004.
Main credits as listed for *The Two Towers,* except: *Screenplay:* Fran Walsh, Philippa Boyens and Peter Jackson. *Editor:* Jamie Selkirk.
Main Cast: All as listed in *The Two Towers,* with the addition of: *Denethor,* John Noble. (WingNut Films for New Line Cinema)

OTHER FILMS INVOLVING JACKSON

FEATURE FILMS

1995: *Jack Brown Genius* (90 minutes), WingNut Films. Tony Hiles's fantasy / romance starring Tim Balme as a man possessed by the spirit of a flight-obsessed monk. See end of Chapter Nine.
Director: Tony Hiles. *Screenplay:* Tony Hiles, Frances Walsh and Peter Jackson. *Executive Producer, Second Unit Director:* Peter Jackson.

1997: *Contact* (143 minutes). Weta was among the seven companies contracted to provide special effects for this adaptation of Carl Sagan's novel about alien contact. Jackson is listed in an untitled role among the twenty-one Weta special-effects staff. See Chapter Ten.
Director and Co-producer: Robert Zemeckis. *Script:* James V Hart and Michael Goldenberg. *Additonal Special Effects:* Weta Ltd (including Peter Jackson).

SHORT FILMS AND TELEVISION

1987: *Stalin's Sickle* (29 minutes). Award-winning short about a young Catholic boy who imagines that Stalin lives close by.
Director/Co-producer: Costa Botes. *Script:* Costa Botes and Anne Kennedy. *Special Effects* (uncredited): Peter Jackson.

1988: *The Lounge Bar* (12 minutes). Quirky, highly regarded shaggy-dog story created by multimedia group *The Front Lawn* found on the short film compilations *Short Takes: Dark Tales* and *Kiwi Shorts Volume 1.*
Direction, Screenplay, Music, Main Cast: Harry Sinclair and Don McGlashan. *Special Effects:* Peter Jackson.

1988: *The Quick Window* (15 minutes). Experimental film about memory, shot in Australia and New Zealand.
Director: Kate Jason-Smith. *Script:* Pauli Kaakaineu, Kate Jason-Smith, Kostas Matsoukas. *Second Unit Camera:* Peter Jackson.

1992: *Valley of the Stereos* (15 minutes). WingNut Films. Off-screen, this short involved many of the loose-knit WingNut family. Originally shown as the opening feature during the New Zealand release of *Braindead.* A culture-clash comedy between hippie and hoon, with the hippie played by Danny Mulheron. The film, which features elaborate special effects, is found on the short film compilations *Short Takes: Comedy* and *Kiwi Shorts Volume 2.*
Director: George Port. *Script:* George Port and Costa Botes. *Story:* George Port, Costa Botes, Peter Jackson, Danny Mulheron. *Executive Producer:* Peter Jackson.

1994–97: Various *Hercules* telemovies. Jackson is listed among the special effects for a number of these productions, for which Weta supplied a menagerie of monsters.

1995: *Dirty Creature* (12 minutes). WingNut Films / Top Shelf Productions. Comical adventure directed by Grant Campbell about an imaginative girl and her exploits. Campbell's association with Jackson goes back to helping provide the special effects that destroyed the car in *Bad Taste.*
Director: Grant Campbell. *Script:* Frances Walsh and Grant Campbell. *Executive Producers:* Peter Jackson and Vincent Burke.

ONSCREEN APPEARANCES

1987: Jaffas™ television commercial (30 seconds). Jackson's mainstream acting debut. The commercial features a number of movie icons invading a suburban living room, including Frankenstein and a Marilyn Monroe lookalike. Jackson, wearing his own homemade gorilla suit, crashes through a wall, and is onscreen for less than two seconds.

198?: *Worzel Gummidge Down Under* (television series). Jackson had a brief part in an episode of this television series about a talking scarecrow. *Acting cameo/special effects:* Peter Jackson.

1988: *Good Taste Made Bad Taste* (documentary, 23 minutes). Interviews include Peter Jackson, his parents, and the cast of *Bad Taste*. The only place to date in which Jackson has unveiled some of his early cinematic dabblings, including a short sequence from one of his earliest films as a child, *Dwarf Patrol*, and the Cyclops battle from *The Valley* (1978). The documentary is included on some DVD releases of *Bad Taste*.
Director, Producer: Tony Hiles.

1989: *Sex, Drugs and Soft Toys* (documentary, 27 minutes). This documentary on the making of *Meet the Feebles* was produced for Television New Zealand, and appears to have been used in some countries (possibly illegally) to help promote the movie. *Feebles* puppeteer George Port filmed material for another documentary on the film, which to date exists only in rough cut form. Interviews include Peter Jackson.

1998: *Lord of the Rings* **sales pitch** (promotional film, 36 minutes). A film made quickly in mid-1998 by Peter Jackson, in an effort to demonstrate to potential funders in Hollywood that he and Weta had the design and effects capability to make *Lord of the Rings*. Copies of this one-off film at one point found their way into the hands of website TheOneRing.net, but it is unclear whether the full version will ever be shown publicly.

2000: *Behind the Bull: Forgotten Silver* (documentary, 22 minutes). Documentary about *Forgotten Silver*, featuring interview material with a tired-looking Peter Jackson. Made for *Silver*'s DVD release, the DVD also includes an audio commentary by *Silver* co-director Botes, and eight minutes of material cut from the original mockumentary.
Director, Producer: Costa Botes.

2001–3: Various *Lord of the Rings* **documentaries.** The full list of *Rings*-related documentaries for which Jackson has been interviewed is far too long to include here, although many of them can be found on the extended DVD editions of the trilogy.

2002: *The Long and Short of It* (6 minutes). Wordless tale about working together, directed by *Rings* actor and sometime filmmaker Sean Astin during reshoots for *The Two Towers*. *Rings* cinematographer Andrew Lesnie plays the main role; Jackson's cameo is all of 20 seconds long. Included on the DVD of *The Two Towers*, alongside a light-hearted eight-minute documentary chronicling the making of the short.

Director, Writer, Producer: Sean Astin. *Story:* Sean Astin and Dominic Monaghan. *Appearing as Bus Driver/Executive Producer:* Peter Jackson.

Unfinished: *Eighth Wonder.* Jackson is one of many film figures interviewed in this exhaustive portrait of events said to have inspired the original *King Kong.*

Director: James Mansfield.

APPENDIX 3: INSPIRATIONS AND INFLUENCES

KING KONG (MOVIE, 1933)

After *The Lord of the Rings*, the next chapter in Peter Jackson's career was a return to what he has called 'the first movie: the first movie I ever saw that put me on the path to where I am today'. First released in Depression-era 1933 (and on many occasions since), *King Kong* follows a mission to an uncharted island, where the natives are said to worship a creature known as Kong. An explorer/filmmaker hopes to capture the creature on film, and has brought along the photogenic Ann Darrow (Fay Wray) to make the result more marketable. The ape takes Ann, battles snakes, dinosaurs and humans, and ends up in New York, battling for his life. *King Kong* used virtually every special-effects technique then known, and in creating Kong, animator Willis O'Brien took the art of stop-motion beyond anything previously achieved. Many critics have commented on the film's primal, nightmare quality; some argue that these qualities conceal questionable attitudes towards race and gender. *King Kong*'s continuing popularity has withstood such attacks. As directed by former documentarians Merian C Cooper and Ernest B Schoedsack, *Kong* is widely seen as one of the classic movies of the twentieth century.

'The day after I saw it,' Jackson has said, 'I got out my parents' Super 8 camera and started taking pictures of the Plasticine dinosaurs. I can't tell you what an effect it had on me.' Kong helped steer Jackson towards his lifelong interest in special effects, and showed him firsthand how a film can take viewers to an imaginary cinematic world. The movie's overall darkness of mood is at odds with much of Jackson's own work as a director — its clearest link is found in the narratively complex *Lord of the Rings*, which shares *Kong*'s theme of exploiting nature for questionable ends.

Filmography: *King Kong* (1933), *The Son of Kong* (Sequel, 1933), *King Kong* (Remake, 1976)

RAY HARRYHAUSEN (SPECIAL-EFFECTS EXPERT, 1920–)

American Ray Harryhausen was only thirteen when he first saw the original *King Kong* in Los Angeles. It was a life-changing experience. After reading up on how stop-frame animation worked, Harryhausen began animating his own figurines frame by frame, in a garage studio built by his father. Sixteen years after first seeing *Kong*, Harryhausen worked alongside *Kong* effects wizard Willis O'Brien on *Mighty Joe Young* (1949), this time handling much of the ape animation himself. After gaining wide experience on a succession of low-budget monster movies, Harryhausen and his longtime producer Charles Schneer found success with a series of fantasies inspired by Greek myths and the *Arabian Nights*, movies in which special effects were the stars. The films generally followed an adventurer on a quest, who encounters a series of mythical creatures. The best film of this cycle is generally seen as *Jason and the Argonauts* (1963), for which Harryhausen spent four and a half months animating a now classic sequence where seven skeletons battle live-action actors. As a teenager Jackson idolised Harryhausen, reading everything he could about him, and the eighteen-minute film *The Valley* includes monsters partly inspired by his work. Later Jackson would arrive at Tolkien's *Lord of the Rings* partly out of a desire to re-explore some of the 'fantastical' Harryhausen movies he had seen as a child.

Despite major advances in the art of stop-motion in the 1980s, the technique has now been largely superseded by the possibilities of computer-generated effects, as demonstrated by the CGI dinosaurs of *Jurassic Park* (1993). Peter Jackson has flown Harryhausen to New Zealand on at least one occasion, and planned to use stop-motion effects for his as yet unmade fantasy *Blubberhead* (stop-motion effects were also utilised for the rat monkey in Jackson's *Braindead).* It remains unclear whether Jackson will return to stop-motion in future. Noted stop-motion animator Jim Danforth (*When Dinosaurs Ruled the Earth*) offered his services to Jackson when the director was first set to remake *Kong* in 1996, but despite Jackson's reported keenness on working with Danforth, he supposedly never received a reply.

Select Harryhausen filmography: *The Beast from 20,000 Fathoms* (1953), *The Seventh Voyage of Sinbad* (1958), *Jason and the Argonauts* (1963).

MONTY PYTHON

Comic collective of mixed parentage and absurdist tendencies, whose four television series and feature films have inspired a generation of comedians. Monty Python consisted of four Englishmen (the late Graham Chapman, John Cleese, Eric Idle, and Michael Palin), a transplanted Welshman (Terry Jones) and a transplanted American (animator Terry Gilliam). Debuting on British television one Sunday night in 1969, the Python team soon established a loyal audience, though they originally rated at a fraction of traditional comic shows like *Morecambe and Wise.* The team of writers-cum-actors made mockery of authority figures, housewives and the norms of television presentation; their sketches either stopped without a punch-line or continued without logic.

Peter Jackson began watching Monty Python around the age of twelve, and recreated some of their sketches in his early 8mm films. He later claimed Python as a key influence on his first 'bad taste' cycle of movies. 'I like the way Monty Python took intellectual concepts and applied them to silly things,' he told *Stamp* magazine in 1992. 'It's an intellectual humour rather than the crass idiocy of someone like Mel Brooks.' The link between intellectual humour and Jackson's own work has not always been as obvious as the inspiration Jackson has taken from Python's crasser images. It was a Python sketch that first helped Jackson realise over-the-top bloodshed could be the stuff of comedy: the bloodspurting 'Salad Days' sketch from 1972, which parodied *Wild Bunch* director Sam Peckinpah. Other Monty Python sketches that speak the same language as Peter Jackson include the belching Mr Creosote, whose refusal to stop dining has unfortunate consequences, and the knight who continues to taunt his attacker after losing most of his limbs in *Holy Grail* (a moment surely referenced in the chainsaw sequence of *Bad Taste*). Possibly Jackson's most Pythonesque work to date remains the unseen *Blubberhead*. Python's influence can also be seen in Jackson and Costa Botes's *Forgotten Silver*, which like many Python sketches embraces the absurd from a position of complete seriousness.

Select Filmography: 'Salad Days' massacre seen in episode seven of the third Python television series (first broadcast in England, November 27, 1972), The Black Knight fights in the movie *Monty Python and the Holy Grail* (1975), Mr Creosote eats in *Monty Python's Meaning of Life* (1983).

THUNDERBIRDS (TELEVISION SERIES, 1964–1966)

Puppet series about the adventures of International Rescue, a secret organisation based on an island in the Pacific Ocean. When disaster strikes, the Tracy family retreat into the bowels of the island to launch a fleet of specialised rescue vehicles. Each hour-long *Thunderbirds* episode plays like a motion picture in miniature, complete with square-jawed heroics, pyrotechnics and cliffhanger rescues, lifted by a full orchestra and ambitious special effects. *Thunderbirds* is the brainchild and greatest success to date of former dubbing editor Gerry Anderson, whose run of mainly puppet-based television shows spans four decades.

Anderson's shows have been repeated often on New Zealand television: Jackson has spoken of watching *Thunderbirds* avidly from the age of five or six, which would put it among his earliest visual influences. The show's appeal to children drew partly from its puppet adventures and gadgetry becoming part of their imaginative play. As late as 1993, a British children's show offering instructions on how viewers could construct their own Tracy Island drew more than 70,000 responses. Jackson's fascination with the show's spaceships and special effects would be reflected in some of his early dabblings in 8mm film.

Select Gerry Anderson filmography: *Stingray* (1963–64), *Captain Scarlet and the Mysterons* (1967), *Space 1999* (1973–76), *Terrahawks* (1983–84), *Lavender Castle* (1997–98).

BUSTER KEATON (COMEDIAN / DIRECTOR 1895–1966)

Buster Keaton grew up on the road, as a performer in a vaudeville family. At the age of twenty-one he appeared in the first of many shorts with comic star Roscoe 'Fatty' Arbuckle, and was instantly fascinated by the mechanics of cameras and filmmaking. After Arbuckle's departure for another studio, Keaton got the chance to direct and appear in his own shorts, which quickly attracted a sizeable audience. By 1927 Keaton had starred in nine feature films, and directed or co-directed all but one of them. Keaton often played the perplexed, stony-faced pragmatist, and his films are remembered for their eye-opening stunts, pratfalls and camera tricks. Keaton's Civil War chase movie *The General* (one of Jackson's favourites) cost a fortune, and was met with reviews that labelled it 'long and tedious'. The film, which is neither, is now regarded as one of the crowning achievements of the silent era.

The press releases for Peter Jackson's early films claim Keaton as a major influence. 'I've always loved Keaton as a performer and a director, and Keaton over Chaplin, because Keaton's was intellectual slapstick,' Jackson has said. Keaton's keenness for doing his own stunts and his love of improvisation have obvious echoes in *Bad Taste*, and some of the physicality of Keaton's humour is present in Jackson's third movie *Braindead*.

Select filmography: *The General* (1926), *Steamboat Bill, Jr* (1928), *The Navigator* (1924), *The Playhouse* (Short, 1921).

OTHER INFLUENCES

For a long period, Jackson was fond of mentioning a trio of classic horror movies in his press interviews: *Re-Animator* (1985), *The Evil Dead* (1983), and George Romero's zombie epic *Dawn of the Dead* (1978). Though each ranks among Jackson's favourites, it would be unwise to draw strong comparisons between the trio and the director's own 'bad taste' cycle of *Bad Taste, Meet the Feebles* and *Braindead*. Each film is its own beast, the only thing common to all are scenes that appear designed to outdo all competitors in terms of gore or bad taste.

Subconsciously or not, filmmakers at the beginnings of their careers often imitate the work of others. Up until he began *Bad Taste*, many of Jackson's cinematic dabblings copied or parodied particular films and filmmakers — among them Monty Python, James Bond, Harryhausen-style fantasy, and Hammer horror. But in his professional career, Jackson's work has rarely been directly imitative, despite individual scenes that include homages to some of his favourite movies.

Jackson is also a big fan of a number of directors who often work outside the fantasy genre, among them Martin Scorsese and Stanley Kubrick.

For every movie that a director gets onto a cinema screen, there are usually at least as many again that he or she turns down, abandons, or fails to get financing for. The compendium of unmade movies that Jackson has been involved in is long, as befits a man who constantly has projects in development. The following list is necessarily incomplete. The date in brackets marks the last time that the film was mentioned in the press, or confirmed as still being in development

OFFERS FROM HOLLYWOOD

In Hollywood, scripts often pass through the hands of a number of potential directors before making it to the screen. Claims that a certain director has been 'offered' a film can signal anything from a studio making preliminary enquiries, to a concrete job offer. Going by comments he has made in interviews, the list of American films that Jackson has been 'offered' in recent years includes episodes of the *Friday the 13th* and *Nightmare on Elm Street* horror series, the little-seen comedy *My Boyfriend's Back,* and *Alien Four*. After making *Heavenly Creatures,* the director found himself being sent many scripts with a strong female theme. From time to time Jackson has also spoken of one of his earliest movie offers, involving a sequel to the classic splatter movie *Re-Animator.* The claim appears to have originated from a conversation with a French producer following the 1988 release of *Bad Taste*. Longtime keeper of the *Re-Animator* flame, American producer/ director Brian Yuzna is a major fan of Jackson's work, but the job offer is news to him. He thinks it may have come from a French distributor who had little to do with the *Re-Animator* films.

As Nature Made Him (2000)

In late 2000, the *Hollywood Reporter* announced that Jackson was developing a movie based on the non-fiction book *As Nature Made Him: The boy who was raised as a girl*. Author John Colapinto expanded his own award-winning *Rolling Stone* article about a landmark case in medical history: that of David Reimer, whose childhood in Winnipeg was spent living as a girl after a botched circumcision as a baby effectively resulted in castration. Born as an identical twin, Reimer's case became a cornerstone of arguments regarding gender reassignment, and the importance of biological factors over environmental ones in determining gender. The story's New Zealand connection is that of renowned sex researcher John Money, who encouraged David's parents to reassign his sexual identity, and followed the case closely until David/Brenda refused to see him anymore.

Bad Taste 2 (1988–92)

The idea of a sequel to Jackson's debut feature film began appearing in interviews with the director in 1988, the year *Bad Taste* was released. At that point, Jackson hoped to start work on *Bad Taste 2* directly after finishing *Braindead*. A multitude of potential plotlines existed, one involving mutant monsters rampaging through Wellington, one involving the return to Earth of Derek. Some say there were even plans for a series of sequels. Four years later, Jackson won funding from the New Zealand Film Commission to write a script, and spoke of making a movie that was even more gory than *Braindead*. In later years, as Jackson's movies have begun to grow increasingly expensive, he has talked from time to time about the appeal of returning to simpler times — of making a film on weekends, and having 'a bit of fun with it'. 'I definitely want to do *Bad Taste 2*,' Jackson told *Empire* before the release of *Fellowship of the Ring*. 'I'm still that person.'

The Black Max (1994)

A comic strip about a villainous German fighter pilot, which appeared in the weekly British comic *Thunder* in the early 1970s. Baron Maximilien Von Klorr discovers an ancient potion that turns bats into giants, and uses two of these Kingbats to attack allied forces during World War I. Von Klorr's main enemy is a British lieutenant. In late 1994, the same year Jackson signed a two-year deal with Miramax, *Variety* announced that Jackson was developing a script called *The Black Max* to show *Heavenly Creatures* producer Hanno Huth. Little else is known about this project.

Blubberhead (1990–95)

Arguably the most fascinating lost movie in the Jackson canon is the fantasy epic *Blubberhead*. The film appears to be the missing link between Jackson's early bad-taste cycle and *Lord of the Rings*, bringing together many of his major interests: the humour of Monty Python, and his interest in stop-motion animation and fantasy. Set 'in a world like *Lord of the Rings*', complete with castles, giants, an upside-down city and talk of mass buggery, Jackson compared *Blubberhead* at one point with Terry Gilliam's *Time Bandits*. 'It appeals to children, but it also has another edge to it that goes over children's heads a bit. It's action packed and a real rollercoaster ride.'

'We wanted to marry fantasy and comedy,' adds co-writer Danny Mulheron. He says that the script that resulted was 'kind of excessive, but there were some amazing things in it.' Jackson hoped to make use of New Zealand landscapes, but failed to find the necessary budget. As late as 1995, he was still hopeful of bringing the film to life.

The Creature from the Black Lagoon (1995)

Universal were developing a remake of their classic '50s horror movie for many years. In 1995, Universal Studios had preliminary talks with Jackson about taking on the remake. He passed, so they offered him *King Kong* instead.

Invasion of Privacy (1992, released 1996)

After German producer Hanno Huth was won over by *Braindead*, he met Peter Jackson and offered him this Larry Cohen script for a drama/thriller, about a woman whose ex-boyfriend holds her hostage in an isolated house, in order to force her to go through with a pregnancy. Jackson turned the script down, and instead won Huth's interest in his own script *Heavenly Creatures* (by coincidence, both films feature strong female characters, themes of motherhood, and deal in controversial material).

Jamboree (1994)

Proposed title of a film being developed by Jackson in 1994, soon after he signed a deal with Miramax in America. *Variety* speculated that the film might be in two parts. Some accounts of the development of *The Hobbit* and *Lord of the Rings* have pegged Jackson's interest in filming Tolkien back to this same period. If true, it is entirely possible that *Jamboree* was the early code-name for Jackson's Tolkien project.

Jamboree was also the title used on film schedules and call sheets for the *Lord of the Rings* trilogy during shooting in New Zealand. The choice of the word *Jamboree* is a movie in-joke — it was the title used during the filming of *The Son of Kong*, sequel to the original *King Kong* back in 1933, in an effort to keep fans off the set.

Jean Batten

Jackson has often spoken of his desire to return to making a true story, set in New Zealand, a la *Heavenly Creatures*. The story of Jean Batten at least partially fits the bill. Jackson at one point took an option on screen rights to *Jean Batten: Garbo of the Skies*, the acclaimed biography of the famous aviatrix. The book, by writer/documentarian Ian Mackersey, follows Batten's story from her birth in Rotorua in 1909, through a series of record-breaking flights and international fame, to Mackersey's 1987 discovery of her unmarked grave in Palma.

Johnny Zombie (1992, released in 1993 under the title *My Boyfriend's Back*)

The script for this little-seen zombie comedy was offered to Jackson by Walt Disney subsidiary Touchstone in 1992, soon after the director had finished work on *Braindead*. Largely devoid of bloodshed, *Johnny Zombie* revolves around a lovestruck teenager who refuses to let his own accidental death get in the way of his major mission: persuading the girl of his dreams to come to the prom with him. As directed by actor / director Bob Balaban, the finished movie mines most of its comedy from making zombieness part of the everyday. Johnny's parents take the news calmly, and are soon helping him with his meals, while students use it as an excuse to socially ostracize him. Jackson turned the project down, as he had other teenagers on his mind: Pauline Parker and Juliet Hulme.

A Nightmare on Elm Street (1990–91)

Jackson's first Hollywood paycheck involves the complex family tree of Freddy Krueger, the bastard son of a thousand maniacs. The success of the carnivalesque, at times surrealistic *Elm Street* series played a major part in the rise of independent film company New Line Cinema. Jackson's first films *Bad Taste* and *Meet the Feebles* caught the attention of a number of New Line staff, including scriptreader Mark Ordesky. Though Ordesky failed to persuade his bosses to distribute either film, Jackson and *Feebles* scriptwriter Danny Mulheron were instead offered the chance to write a script for *Elm Street*. 'Mark really went out on a limb for him then,' recalls Mulheron, 'and fought for New Line to give Peter a shot at the script, if not the movie itself. We always knew we were the outside chance, but I think Mark was in for the long haul. It was him more than anyone else there that recognised Peter had the patience and determination to make bigger things.'

Jackson and Mulheron's script begins with Freddy initially having lost much of his power to terrify. Teenagers in Springfield take sleeping pills so that they can go into the dream world and take turns attacking him. The film's hero is a policeman in a coma, who finds himself in the dream world, where he discovers Krueger. 'The climax of it was the deconstruction of Freddy Krueger,' says Mulheron. 'By confronting him with his impotence, he lost his ability to scare.' Jackson and Mulheron's script was paid for but never used, partly because *Elm Street* production veteran Rachel Talalay had drafted a treatment for her own film *Freddy's Dead: The Final Nightmare*. New Line commissioned a script based upon this treatment, which failed to satisfy, after which Talalay asked New Line executive Michael De Luca to write the script himself. *Freddy's Dead* was filmed in early 1991. New Line staff, enthused by the Jackson / Mulheron script, later asked Jackson if he might want to work on their long-in-development *Freddy versus Jason*, but Jackson turned them down.

The Planet of the Apes Movie (1993)

Little is known about this project, except that Jackson had an idea for his own Apes movie (apparently not a remake). He flew to America and met executives from 20th Century Fox, having won the interest of *Planet of the Apes* star Roddy McDowall, who hoped to appear in a supporting role. Jackson's name joined a long line of directors and apes-related proposals stretching back to at least 1988. In 1995, 20th Century Fox announced that Oliver Stone would be at the helm of a *Planet of the Apes* movie. The project finally saw the light in 2001 under director Tim Burton (*Batman*).

Small Change (1989)

Romantic comedy written by Fran Walsh for director Costa Botes. The original press material for *Meet the Feebles* mentioned that the script had been completed, although the film has not yet seen the light of day.

The War Movie (1992)

Jackson has long had an interest in war, and some of his earliest dabblings in film as a child were war movies. On one trip overseas, he attended a memorial service at Gallipoli, site of the ANZAC defeat during World War I. Plans to make a war movie based on Gallipoli appear to have been in his head from at least as early as 1988. Four years later, a writer for British magazine *Monstroid* asked Jackson if he planned a war movie influenced by the Vietnam war segment of *Meet the Feebles*. 'I do want to do a war movie actually,' Jackson replied, 'but about New Zealanders in the 1915 Gallipoli campaign.' Some of those who have worked with Jackson say that when he saw Steven Spielberg's *Saving Private Ryan*, the director's plans for a 'big, definitive' account of Gallipoli went on the backburner.

The Warrior Season (1992)

A Western-style action adventure set in Central Otago in the 1800s, centering around a Chinese immigrant. Jackson and future *Forgotten Silver* collaborator Costa Botes worked on the script on and off over a number of years, which Botes at one point planned to direct. *Forgotten Silver* references the proposed movie in the title given to cinema's first-ever sound film, shot in Chinese.

The World War Zombie Film

Jackson has spoken often of returning to splatter, armed with the manifold possibilities unleashed by computer-generated effects. Speculation exists over possible plans for him to make a movie combining his interest in both war and splatter — a zombie film in which dead soldiers rise from the trenches, as mentioned to some of his colleagues from *Bad Taste* at least a decade ago.

BIBLIOGRAPHY

The following publications have all followed Peter Jackson's career closely, and have been referred to a great deal in the writing of this book: Wellington newspapers the *Evening Post* and the *Dominion* (now amalgamated as the *Dominion Post*); film industry magazine *Onfilm*; the *Listener*; and American horror magazine *Fangoria* (www.fangoria.com). Philip Wakefield and Russell Baillie have written often and ably on Jackson's career, as has Australian Michael Helms (the latter usually in *Fangoria*).

Aside from my own interviews, and the press-kits for each of Jackson's films, especially useful sources in writing this biography include Costa Botes's 'Made in New Zealand: The Cinema of Peter Jackson', on the New Zealand Edge internet site (http://www.nzedge.com/hot/ar-jackson.html), and the wide-ranging interview with Jackson conducted by *The Bastards Have Landed* website before the announcement of *Lord of the Rings*. The most thorough coverage of the special effects in Jackson's Hollywood-funded movies is that in *Cinefex* magazine. For *Bad Taste*, try Ken Hammon's article on the making of the film on the Ultimate Bad Taste website (http://tbhl.theonering.netbadtaste cast_hammon_makingof.htm). The single most comprehensive information source on both the Parker–Hulme murder and the film *Heavenly Creatures* is found in version two of the database compiled by John D Porter, viewable among other places on http://www.geocities.com/Hollywood/Studio/2194/index.html. Also important in the writing of the *Heavenly Creatures* chapters were the book *Parker & Hulme: A Lesbian View* by Julie Glamuzina and Alison J Laurie, and Tod Lippy's exhaustive 1995 interview with Peter Jackson and Fran Walsh for *Scenario* magazine.

The most persuasive account of the deal-making behind *Lord of the Rings* is found in Chris Petrikin's 'The war of the wizards' on the Salon.com website (http://dir.salon.com/ent/movies/feature/2001/11/15/lotr/index.html.) Also highly useful among the mountain of writings consulted for the *Rings* chapters were two *Hollywood Reporter* features by Martin A Grove and Stephen Galloway, and the website TheOneRing.net.

The reference books referred to most often about New Zealand cinema were *New Zealand Film 1912–1996*, by Helen Martin and Sam Edwards (Oxford University Press, Auckland, 1997), and *Film in Aotearoa New Zealand*, edited by Jonathan Dennis and Jan Bieringa, (Victoria University Press, Wellington, 1996).

Full details are included on the first mention only. The quotations at the start of each chapter are taken from interviews and/or set visits by the author, unless otherwise noted.

CHAPTER ONE: THE LUNATICS ARE TAKING OVER THE FIELD

Anonymous. Review of *The Fellowship of the Ring*. On website *UK Hotmovies.com*
http://www.ukhotmovies.com/reviews/lordoftherings1/

Andrews, Nigel. 'Spellbound by Jackson and Gandalf'. *Financial Times*,
December 13, 2001.

Groves, Don. 'Strained relations for NZFC'. *Variety*, October 13–19, 1997.

Weldon, Michael J. *The Psychotronic Video Guide*. Titan Books, London, 1996.

CHAPTER TWO: BEGINNINGS

Boswell, Joyce. *The Book of Shenley*. Barracuda Books, Buckingham, 1984.

Cairnes, Barbara, and Martin, Helen. *Shadows on the Wall: A Study of Seven
New Zealand Feature Films*. Longman Paul, Auckland, 1994.

Campbell, Gordon. 'Homegrown Hollywood'. *Listener*, February 18, 1995.

Fordyce, Linda. *Seaside Towns* (booklet). Porirua Museum, Wellington, 1989.

Hiles, Tony. *Good Taste Made Bad Taste* (documentary film). New Zealand, 1988.

Piper, Alan. *A History of Brixton*. The Brixton Society, London, 1996.

Warren, Patricia. *British Film Studios: An Illustrated History*. BT Batsford Ltd,
London, 2001 (2nd edition).

CHAPTER THREE: THE MOVIE THAT GREW

Anonymous. 'Bad Taste makes classy splash'. *Dominion Sunday Times*, August
7, 1988.

Anonymous. *NZ Film 34: Cannes Special Edition* (promotional booklet). New
Zealand Film Commission, May 1988.

Ballantyne, Stephen. 'Jackson's home movie'. *Dominion Sunday Times*, July 24,
1988.

Cairnes, Barbara, and Martin, Helen. *Shadows on the Wall*.

Davenport, Hugo. Review of *Bad Taste*. *Daily Telegraph*, September 1989.

Davies, Steven Paul. *A-Z of Cult Films and Film-makers*. BT Batsford, London,
2001.

Fitzgerald, Michael. 'Wizard with a Camera'. *Time*, December 31–January 7,
2002.

Hammon, Ken. 'This has buggered your plans for conquering the Universe:
The making of Bad Taste' (website article). *The Ultimate Bad Taste Fan Site*
http://tbhl.theonering.net/badtaste/cast_hammon_makingof.htm.

Newman, Kim. Review of *Bad Taste*. *Monthly Film Bulletin* Vol 56, No 668,
September 1989.

Nic (Nicolaidi, Mike) Review of *Bad Taste*. *Variety*, June 1, 1988.

Norman, Neil. 'Wired for the sound of venom'. *Evening Standard*, September 14,
1989.

Parker, John. Review of *Bad Taste*. *Metro*, September, 1988.

Roberts, Greg. 'Qld dumps film censorship board' *Sydney Morning Herald*, July 2, 1990.

Towgood, Hamish. Cast and Crew Interviews. *The Ultimate Bad Taste Website*. http://tbhl.theonering.net/badtaste/mainpage_castcrew.htm

Warren, Bill. *The Evil Dead Companion*. St Martin's Press, New York, 2000.

CHAPTER FOUR: NOT YOUR EVERYDAY AVERAGE CREATURES

Anonymous. *Meet the Feebles* press-kit. 1989.

Anonymous. 'Feebles, filth, and fun'. *Melbourne Herald*, March 24, 1991.

Botes, Costa. 'Feebles a subversive success'. *Dominion*, October 22, 1990.

Botes, Costa. 'Made in New Zealand. The Cinema of Peter Jackson' (website article). http://www.nzedge.com/hot/ar-jackson.html, May 2002.

Bowron, Jane. 'Filmmaker introduces puppets to adult world'. *Dominion*, August 9, 1989.

Butcher, Margot. 'The Weird World of Peter Jackson'. *North and South*, April 1992.

Cartwright, Garth. 'No Ordinary Joker'. *Metro*, December 2001.

Galloway, Stephen. 'Write of Passage'. *Hollywood Reporter*, March 2003.

Haddock, Frank. 'The Secret of My Excess'. *3D*, March 25, 1991.

Hannaham, James. Review of *Meet the Feebles*. *Village Voice*, February 28, 1995.

Hannan, Deborah. 'Lack of money puts Brain Dead on the ice'. *Evening Post*, January 28, 1989.

Hegan, Chris. 'Gross-out genius'. *Listener*, October 15, 1990.

Jackson, Peter. 'Jim Booth 1945–1994'. *Onfilm*, February 1994.

Maslin, Janet. 'Playful Puppetry, for Adults Only'. *New York Times*, February 22, 1995.

Menzies, Steve. 'Cute puppets' image takes a nose dive'. *Dominion*, October 13, 1990.

Vine, Bettina. 'The J Files'. *Feature*, December 1996/January 1997.

CHAPTERS FIVE AND SIX: *BRAINDEAD*

The opening 'day in the life' section of Chapter Six originally appeared in slightly different form as the November 16, 1991, feature 'Welcome to my Nightmare', written by the author for the *Evening Post*.

Anonymous. 'Head lost in cemetery'. *Nelson Evening Mail*, September 25, 1991.

Anonymous. 'Graveyard film "insulted" family'. *Dominion*, July 29, 1992.

Anonymous. 'Cemetery scenes land film in court'. *Evening Post,* July 30, 1992.

Anonymous. 'Producer defends use of tombstone in horror film'. *Evening Post*, July 31, 1992.

Anonymous (NZPA Reporter) '"Best film" choice infuriates judge'. *New Zealand Herald*, March 23, 1993.

Anonymous. 'Awards night dissent not on — chief'. *New Zealand Herald*, March 24, 1993.

Baillie, Russell. 'Splatter with a laugh — new use for the good old kiwi lawnmower'. *Sunday Star*, August 9, 1992.

Bunbury, Stephanie. 'Not for Aunt Mabel'. *Melbourne Age*, February 26, 1993.

Cortini, Mario, and Nutman, Philip. 'Peter Jackson, Master of Bad Taste'. *Gorezone* No 5, January 1989.

Craig, Duncan. Interview with Peter Jackson. *Salient*, September 7, 1992.

Crow, Tom. 'Staying Alive. Gorefest proves entertainingly fast on its feet'. *Los Angeles Village View*, July 23–29, 1993.

Eden, Sue. 'Living in Never-Never Land'. *Daily Post*, April 20, 1991.

Edwards, Phil. 'Peter Jackson'. *Movie Trader* Vol 12, No 10, March 1993.

Hannaham, James. Review of *Dead Alive*. *The Village Voice*, February 9, 1993.

Helms, Michael. 'Down Under and Braindead'. *Fangoria* 115, August 1992.

Helms, Michael. 'Action Jackson'. *Fangoria* 121, April 1993.

Jillett, Neil. Review of *Braindead*. *Melbourne Age*, March 2, 1993.

Mann, Natasha. Review of *The Ballad of Jimmy Costello*. *The Scotsman*, August 18, 1997.

McCarthy, John. *Splatter Movies*. Columbus Books, Bromley, 1984.

McLennan, Patrick. 'Laughing through the Splatter'. *Dominion*, March 14, 1992.

Menell, Jeff. Review of *Dead Alive*. *Hollywood Reporter*, January 21, 1993.

Peñalver, Diana. 'Mi Amigo Peter'. *El Mundo*, May 20, 1995.

Seim, Roland. *Zwischen Medienfreiheit und Zensureingriffen* (Between Freedom of the Media and Intrusions of Censorship). www.telos-verlag.de. Germany, 3rd edition, 2003.

Shannon, Paul. 'Ich Bin Eine Zombie'. *Scope* No 8 March/April 1992.

Williams, David E. 'The Dead from Down Under (And to the left)'. *Film Threat* Vol 2, No 7, December 1992.

CHAPTERS SEVEN AND EIGHT: *HEAVENLY CREATURES*

Opening quotations (for full details see below): Chapter Seven, Gurr and Cox, *Famous Australasian Crimes*; Walsh, from Tod Lippy's interview in *Scenario*. Chapter Eight, Jackson from author's interview at Venice Film Festival; Pierse from James Graham's interview in *Woman's Day*.

Anonymous. Compilation of highest rated films. 'Nilohamiticnine'. *Cinema Papers*, March 1995.

Anonymous. 'Heavenly Creatures a "global" creation'. *Onfilm*, February 1993.

Anonymous (NZPA reporter). 'Jackson woken at 3am with news of Oscar nomination'. *Ashburton Guardian*, February 15, 1995.

Anonymous (NZPA reporter). 'Jackson set to defend making of movie'. *Northern Advocate*, February 1, 1997.

Baillie, Russell. 'Creature Comforts'. *Sunday Star-Times*, October 9, 1994.

Baillie, Russell. 'Stars shining bright in movie made in heaven'. *Sunday Star-Times*, October 9, 1994.

Ballantyne, Stephen. 'Jackson's home movie'.

Barr, Jim and Mary. 'The Films of Peter Jackson and Fran Walsh'. *Film in Aotearoa New Zealand*. Victoria University Press, Wellington, 1996 (2nd edition).

Bignardi, Irene. 'Se la mamma finisce nel mirino'. *La Republica*, September 9, 1994.

Calder, Peter. 'Heaven Sent'. *New Zealand Herald*, October 14, 1994.

Campbell, Gordon. 'Homegrown Hollywood'.

Carter, Angela. *The Curious Room. Plays, Film Scripts and an Opera*. Chatto and Windus, London, 1996.

Conway, Matt. 'Snubbed film tipped as our next big hit'. *Sunday Star-Times*, May 8, 1994.

Conway, Matt. 'Film stirs school's shame on murder', *Sunday Star-Times*, June 19, 1994.

Cookson, John, and Dunstall, Graeme (editors). *Southern Capital: Christchurch. Towards a City Biography 1850–2000*. Canterbury University Press, Christchurch, 2000.

Corliss, Richard. 'It's All In The Family'. *Time*, September 26, 1994

Corliss, Richard. 'A Heavenly Trip Toward Hell'. *Time*, December 5, 1994

Cropp, Amanda. 'A deadly scandal that rocked Christchurch society'. *Dominion Sunday Times*, October 20, 1991.

Darnton, John. 'Author Faces Up to a Long, Dark Secret'. *New York Times*, Feburary 14, 1995.

Davies, Lewis (compiler). Peter Jackson FAQ, The Bastards Have Landed website, December 1997. http://tbhl.theonering.net/peter/faq.html.

Evans, Greg. 'Miramax snags Jackson'. *Variety*, July 8, 1994.

Ferguson, Lin. 'Murder She Wrote! Best-selling British author's grisly Kiwi past revealed'. *Sunday News*, July 31, 1994.

Furneaux, Rupert. *Famous Criminal Cases*. Roy Publishers, New York, 1955.

Graham, James. 'Heavenly horror'. *Woman's Day*, October 25, 1994.

Gristwood, Sarah. 'When murder catches up with you'. *Daily Telegraph*, August 5, 1994.

Gurr, Tom, and Cox, HH. 'Death in a Cathedral City', *Famous Australasian Crimes*. Frederick Muller Ltd, London, 1957.

Gurr, Tom, and Cox, HH. *Obsession*. Frederick Muller Ltd, London, 1958.

Hruska, Bronwen. 'New Controversy Over '50s Murder — Crossfire in the press over "Heavenly Creatures". *Newsday*, February 20, 1995.

Jackson, Peter. 'Jim Booth 1945–1994'.

Laurie, Alison, and Glamuzina, Julie. *Parker & Hulme: A Lesbian View*. New Women's Press, Auckland, 1991.

Lippy, Tod. 'Writing and Directing Heavenly Creatures — A talk with Frances Walsh and Peter Jackson'. *Scenario* Fall 1995, Vol 1, No 4.

McDonald, Bernard D. 'Celluloid Sisters'. *Pavement*, December 1993/January 1994.

McDonald, Bernard D. Review of *Heavenly Creatures*. *Pavement*, October 1994.

McNabb, Denise. 'A good school for scandal'. *Dominion,* October 10, 1994.

Medlicott, RW. 'Some Reflections on the Parker–Hulme, Leopold–Loeb Cases with Special Reference to the Concept of Omnipotence'. *New Zealand Law Journal* 37, 1961.

Murray, Scott. 'Peter Jackson Heavenly Creatures'. *Cinema Papers New Zealand Supplement*, No 97/98, 1994.

Neill, Sam and Rymer, Judy (writer/directors). *Cinema of Unease: A Personal Journey by Sam Neill* (documentary film). New Zealand, 1995.

O'Brien, Geraldine. 'Murder made in a girls' own heaven'. *Sydney Morning Herald*, January 21, 1995.

Oomen, Monique. 'Cancer quells Booth's inferno'. *Onfilm*, February 1994.

Philp, Matt. 'Deadly Delusions'. *Evening Post*, October 13, 1994.

Porter, John D, and various contributors, Heavenly Creatures FAQ/database version 2.0. http://www.geocities.com/Hollywood/Studio/2194/index.html. August 1995, updated by Adam Abrams.

Ranoja, Ingrid. Interview with Peter Jackson. *Now,* January 19–25, 1995.

Romney, Jonathan. Review of *Heavenly Creatures*. *New Statesman and Society*, Vol 8, No 339, February 10, 1995.

Rooney, David. Review of *Heavenly Creatures*. *Variety*, September 12–18, 1994.

Vine, Bettina. 'The J Files'.

Webster, Andy. 'The Frightener'. *Premiere* Vol 9, No 12, August 1996.

CHAPTER NINE: EMPIRE-BUILDING

Opening quotations: letter to the editor from *TV Guide*, November 10, 1995; Costa Botes from letter to the editor, *Evening Post*, (see below).

Anonymous. 'Film Documentary An Elaborate Hoax — TVNZ'. *West Coast Times*, October 30, 1995.

Anonymous (NZPA Reporter). 'Yes Folks, it was a hoax!' *Marlborough Express*, October 30, 1995.

Anonymous. 'Authority rejects hoax complaints'. *Evening Post*, February 17, 1996.

Barr, Jim and Mary. 'The Films of Peter Jackson and Fran Walsh'.

Botes, Costa (letter to the editor). 'Forgotten Silver's media message revealed'. *Evening Post*, November 16, 1995.

Botes, Costa. 'Laughter and chaos in Venice'. *Onfilm* Vol 13, No 10, November 1997.

Campbell, Gordon. 'Homegrown Hollywood'.

Chapple, Geoff. 'Gone, not forgotten'. *Listener*, November 25, 1995.

Cubey, Mark. 'Heavenly images'. *City Voice*, October 13, 1994.

Davies, Lewis (compiler). Peter Jackson FAQ.

Dixon, Greg. 'Pioneer of film was mythical'. *New Zealand Herald*, October 31, 1995.

Jenkin, Douglas. 'Hunting for Stalin'. *Listener*, October 17, 1987.

McNeill, Joanne. 'Forgotten Silver found to be fool's gold'. *Northern Advocate*, November 4, 1995.

Murray, Scott. 'Peter Jackson Heavenly Creatures'.

Rickitt, Richard. *Special Effects: the history and technique*. Virgin Books, London, 2000.

Sharp, Keith. 'Actor fooled by TV hoax'. *TV Guide*, November 24, 1995.

Smith, Val. 'Gullible viewers caught up in act'. *Taupo Times*, November 30, 1995.

Swain, Pauline. 'Out of the wilderness'. *Dominion*, October 26, 1995.

Vaz, Mark Cotta. 'The Frighteners: The Thrill of the Haunt'. *Cinefex* No 67, September 1996.

Welch, Denis. 'Heavenly features'. *Listener*, October 28, 1995.

CHAPTER TEN: FINDING HOLLYWOOD WITHOUT REALLY LOOKING

Opening quotations (for full details see below): John Boorman, *Money into Light*; Lenny Kornberg from 'A vote of confidence' by Gordon Campbell.

Anonymous (Reuters reporter). 'Films last in Olympic race'. *Evening Post*, August 10, 1996.

Arnold, Gary.' "Frighteners" proves frightfully good scare'. *Washington Times*, July 19, 1996.

Baillie, Russell. 'Sticking to his roots'. *Auckland Star*, December 1988.

Boorman, John. *Money into Light — The Emerald Forest: A Diary*. Faber & Faber Ltd, London, 1985.

Botes, Costa. 'Made in New Zealand: The Cinema of Peter Jackson'.

Brunas, Michael, Brunas, John, and Weaver, Tom. *Universal Horrors: The Studio's Classic Films, 1931–1946*. McFarland & Company Inc, Jefferson, 1990.

Byrge, Duane. Review of *The Frighteners*. *Hollywood Reporter*, July 14, 1996.

Campbell, Gordon. 'A vote of confidence'. *Listener*, December 2, 1995.

Floyd, Nigel. 'Spooky Business'. *SFX* No 22, February 1997.

Helms, Michael. 'Who's scared of The Frighteners?' *Fangoria* 154, July 1996.

Helms, Michael. 'Fox in the Ghosthouse'. *Fangoria* 154.

Helms, Michael, with Gingold, Michael. 'Giving form to the Frighteners'. *Fangoria* 155, August 1996.

Kagan, Norman. *The Cinema of Robert Zemeckis*. Taylor Trade Publishing, Lanham, 2003.

Mabbett, Charles. 'Frighteners' team feels the pressure'. *Daily Post*, May 4, 1996.

McBride, Joseph. *Steven Spielberg: A Biography*. Simon & Schuster, New York, 1997.

McCarthy, Todd. Review of *The Frighteners*. *Variety*, July 15, 1996.

Mordden, Ethan. *The Hollywood Studios*. Alfred A Knopf, New York, 1988.

Vaz, Mark Cotta. 'The Frighteners — The Thrill of the Haunt'.

Wakefield, Philip. 'Scary rollercoaster ride'. *Onfilm*, Vol 12, No 11, December 1996.

Webster, Andy. 'The Frightener'. *Premiere.*

Williams, David E. 'Scared Silly'. *American Cinematographer* Vol 77, No 8, August 1996.

Wilmington, Michael. 'Fright of fancy'. *Chicago Tribune*, July 19, 1996.

Wilson, Calvin. 'Oh, the horror . . . the horror . . . oh, the humor . . . the humor . . .' *Kansas City Star*, July 19, 1996.

CHAPTER ELEVEN: THE POLITICAL ANIMAL

Opening quotations: Michael Powell from *The Man in Lincoln's Nose* (Corey and Ochoa); Peter Jackson from 'Horror story', *Metro*.

Anonymous. Joint press release from the Film Unit and the New Zealand Film Commission, March 20, 2003.

Anonymous. 'Note to our readers'. *Listener*, March 23, 2002.

Various authors. New Zealand Film Commission 20th Anniversary Supplement, *Onfilm* Vol 13, No 10, November 1997.

Campbell, Gordon. 'Scare tactics'. *Listener*, November 30, 1996.

Campbell, Gordon. 'Monkey business'. *Listener*, February 1, 1997.

Campbell, Gordon. 'Hats off to Larry'. *Listener*, February 8, 2003.

Cleave, Louisa. 'Scriptwriter to continue fight.' *New Zealand Herald*, March 16, 2002.

Corey, Melinda, and Ochoa, George (compiled by). *The Man in Lincoln's Nose*. Simon & Schuster, New York, 1990.

Espiner, Guyon. 'Upton out of touch — Jackson'. *Evening Post*, December 10, 1997.

Gapes, David. 'Filmmakers Aim Broadsides at "Passionate" Commission'. *Onfilm* Vol 13, No 10, November 1997.

Heal, Andrew. 'Horror story'. *Metro* 198, December 1997.

Jackson, Peter. Press release concerning 'self-serving' actions of New Zealand Film Commission. December 17, 2002.

Matthews, Philip. 'Spectral Steel'. *Listener*, December 14, 1996.

Rendle, Steve. 'Post Pipped at Party Gate'. *The Evening Post*, November 13, 2000.

Walsh, Frances (journalist). ' "Lord" . . . what next?' *Listener*, March 9, 2001.

Walsh, Frances R. (scriptwriter). '*Listener* article triggers defamation action' (press release), March 7, 2002.

Wood, Bret. 'Lolita Syndrome'. *Sight and Sound* Vol 4, No 6, June 1994.

CHAPTERS TWELVE AND THIRTEEN: *THE LORD OF THE RINGS*

Opening quotations: Anthony Mann from *The Man in Lincoln's Nose* (Corey and Ochoa, see above); Peter Jackson from an interview with Melissa J Perenson 'Director Peter Jackson proves to be the lord of *The Fellowship of the Rings*', 2001, http://www.scifi.com/sfw/issue244/interview.html.

Anonymous. Press announcement of *Lord of the Rings* movie trilogy. New Line Cinema, Los Angeles, August 24, 1998.

Baillie, Russell. 'A long expected party'. *New Zealand Herald*, December 8–9, 2001.

Bonin, Liane. 'Interview with the Vampire'. *Entertainment Weekly*, August 2002.

Boorman, John. *Money into Light — The Emerald Forest.*

Carpenter, Humphrey. *JRR Tolkien: A Biography*. George Allen & Unwin, London, 1977.

Carpenter, Humphrey (assisted by Tolkien, Christopher). *The Letters of JRR Tolkien.* George Allen & Unwin, London, 1981.

Ciment, Michel (translated by Gilbert Adair). *John Boorman*. Faber & Faber Ltd, London, 1986.

Grant, John. *Masters of Animation*. Watson-Guptill Publications, New York, 2001.

Grove, Martin A. 'How Peter takes *Lord of the Rings* to the screen'. *Hollywood Reporter*, February 15, 2002.

Helms, Michael. 'Who's scared of *The Frighteners*?'

Hoffman, Katja. 'An Epic in the Making'. *Financial Times*, March 18, 2002.

Howe, John. *Myth & Magic: The Art of John Howe*. HarperCollinsPublishers, London, 2001.

Jackson, Peter. Announcement concerning his latest film. On defunct *Peter Jackson Forum* website, January 30, 1998.

Jackson, Peter, and Knowles, Harry Jay. 'Peter Jackson answers THE GEEKS!!! 20 Questions About Lord of the Rings!!!' Two sets of 20 Questions on Ain't it cool News website, August 30, 1998.
  http://www.aint-it-cool-news.com/lordoftherings.html and http://www.aint-it-cool-news.com/lordoftherings2.html

Jackson, Peter. 'Filming Three Tales at Once? A Little Madness Helps'. Article on *TheOneRing.net* website, December 16, 2001. http://www.theonering.net/perl/newsview/8/1008522263

Levy, Emanuel. *Oscar Fever: The History and Politics of the Academy Awards*. Continuum, New York, 2001.

Mantel, Kathleen. 'The human: Viggo Mortensen'. *Pavement* No 50, December 2001/January 2002.

McDonald, Bernard D. 'The Director: Peter Jackson'. *Pavement* No 50, December 2001/January 2002.

Norman, Philip. *Shout! The True Story of the Beatles*. Corgi Books, London, 1982 (updated edition).

Oliver, Greg. 'Man behind original "Lord of Rings" speaks out'. Jam! Showbiz website, June 21, 2001. http://www.canoe.ca/JamLordOfTheRings/jun21_bakshi-can.html.

Oliver, Greg. 'The man with the key to "The Rings" '. Jam! Showbiz website May 9 2001. http://www.canoe.ca/JamLordOfTheRings/may9_zaentz-can.html.

Petrikin, Chris. 'The war of the wizards'. Salon.com website, November 15, 2001. http://dir.salon.com/ent/movies/feature/2001/11/15/lotr/index.html.

Petrou, David Michael. *The Making of Superman the Movie*. WH Allen & Co. Ltd, London, 1978.

Robinson, Tasha. 'Ralph Bakshi'. *The Onion* Vol 36, No 44, December 6, 2000.

Shotton, Peter, and Schaffner, Nicholas. *John Lennon: In My Life*. Hodder & Stoughton Ltd, London, 1983.

Wyatt, Justin. 'The formation of the "major independent": Miramax, New Line and the New Hollywood.' From *Contemporary Hollywood Cinema*. Routledge, London, 1998.

Zwigoff, Terry (director). *Crumb* (documentary). United States, 1994.

CHAPTER 14: SPIES IN MIDDLE-EARTH

Opening quotations: Harry Adam Knowles from 'Wild about Harry', Raindance website, April 2002, http://www.raindance.co.uk/reelscene/2002/april/wildaboutharry.html.

Anonymous. 'Millions of Downloads'. New Line press release, August 2000.

Cardy, Tom. 'Copyright law and snaps of Lord of the Rings'. *Evening Post*, December 12, 2000.

Challis, Erica. 'Tehanu's Set Visit: Hobbiton'. TheOneRing.net website, January 27, 2000. http://www.theonering.net/feature/exclusives/firstvisit.html.

Van Beynen, Martin. 'Filmmaker tries to suppress images'. *Press*, August 31, 2000.

CHAPTER 15: UNVEILING THE RING

Opening quotation: review of *Fellowship of the Ring*, 'Spellbound by Jackson and Gandalf', in the *Financial Times*.

Unknown. 'Best Risk Oscar?' *Daily Variety*, March 26, 2002.

Anonymous. 'Fantasy Island'. *Arena* 100.

Ansen, David. 'A "Ring" to Rule the Screen'. *Newsweek*, December 10, 2001.

Alley, Oskar. 'They made us famous but Rings films "no benefit"'. *Sunday Star-Times*, August 24, 2003.

Cagle, Jess. 'Lure of the Rings'. *Time*, December 2, 2002.

Campbell, Gordon. 'Planet Middle Earth'. *Listener*, December 15, 2001.

Clinton, Paul. 'Dazzling, flawless "Rings" a classic'. CNN.com, December 18, 2001.

Duncan, Jody. 'Ring Masters'. *Cinefex* No 89, April 2002.

Ebert, Roger. Review of *The Two Towers*. *Chicago Sun-Times*, December 18, 2002.

Epstein, Ronald. Review of *The Fellowship of the Ring*. Home theater forum website, November 28, 2001. http://www.hometheaterforum.com/sneak/lord/lord.html.

Finarfin (Alias). 'Report from the Wrap Party!' TheOneRing.net website, January 9, 2001. http://www.theonering.net/perl/newsview/2/979058712.

Flynn, Gillian. 'The Power of Towers'. *Entertainment Weekly* No 682, November 15, 2002.

Forde, John. 'And Now the Work Really Begins . . .' E! Online website, February 1, 2001. http://www.eonline.com/Features/Specials/Lordrings/Word/010201.html.

Fordham, Joe. 'Middle-earth Strikes Back'. *Cinefex* No 92, January 2003.

Galloway, Stephen. 'Changes, "LOTR" shape the new face of New Line cinema'. *Hollywood Reporter*, July 17, 2001.

Giles, Jeff. 'Lure of the Rings'. *Newsweek*, December 10, 2001.

Goldstein, Patrick. 'The Big Picture — A Studio Executive Tries His Hand at Wizardry'. *LA Times*, December 11, 2001.

Grant, Nick. 'Interview with the Ring Master'. *Onfilm* Vol 20, No 3, March 2003.

Harris, Dana and Dawtrey, Adam. 'Can B.O. Postman "ring" Twice? New Line hopes to emulate "Harry" hoopla'. *Variety*, November 26–December 2, 2001.

Kieslowski, Krzysztof and Stok, Danusia (editor). *Kieslowski on Kieslowski*. Faber & Faber, London, 1993.

Mitchell, Elvis. 'Soldiering on In Epic Pursuit of Purity'. *New York Times*, December 18, 2002.

Nathan, Ian. 'Battlefield Middle Earth' (*Lord of the Rings* special issue). *Empire*, January 2002.

Nazzaro, Joe. 'Dark Secrets'. *Fantasy Worlds* No 2, 2002.

Pfefferman, Naomi. 'Lord of the Oscars'. *Jewish Journal of Greater Los Angeles*, March 1, 2002.

Schwarzbaum, Lisa. Review of *Fellowship of the Ring*. *Entertainment Weekly*, December 5, 2001.

Shippey, Tom. *JRR Tolkien: Author of the Century*. HarperCollins Publishers, London, 2000.

Sibley, Brian. *The Lord of the Rings: The Making of the Movie Trilogy*. HarperCollins Publishers, London, 2002.

Ungari, Enzo, with Ranvaud, Donald. *Bertolucci by Bertolucci*. Plexus, London,1987.

Wakefield, Philip. 'Directing the three Ring circus'. *Onfilm* Vol 19, No 1,

December 2001/January 2002.

Vertigo (alias). Review of *Fellowship of the Ring*. Ain't It Cool News website. http://www.aintitcool.com/display.cgi?id=10965.

CHAPTER 16: PAST AND FUTURE

Eden, Sue. 'Living in Never-Never Land'. *Daily Post*, April 20, 1991.

Edwards, Phil. 'Peter Jackson'. *Movie Trader*.

Unknown (*Premiere* staff). 'The Power List — Class of '03'. *Premiere* Vol 16, No 9, May 2003.

Walker, Angela. 'The Production: Grant Major'. *Pavement* No 50.

APPENDIX MATERIAL

Archer, Simon, and Hearn, Marcus. *What Made Thunderbirds Go! The Authorized Biography of Gerry Anderson*. BBC Worldwide Limited, London, 2002.

Cohen, David. 'The nature of the beast'. *Sunday Times*, January 19, 1997.

Colapinto, John. *As Nature Made Him: The Boy Who Was Raised as a Girl*. HarperCollins Publishers, New York, 2000.

Craig, Duncan. Interview with Peter Jackson. *Salient*, 1992.

Dunkley, Cathy. 'D'Works pens "Author" deal'. *Hollywood Reporter*, December 1, 2000.

McGlashan, Stephen. 'Bring out yer Dead', *Stamp* No 32, June 1992.

Meade, Marion, and Dragga, Jack (filmography). *Buster Keaton: Cut to the Chase*. HarperCollins Publishers, New York, 1995.

Nathan, Ian. 'Battlefield Middle Earth'. *Empire*.

Ross, Richard. *Monty Python Encyclopedia*. BT Batsford Ltd, London, 1997.